✳

Debating Democracy

A Reader in American Politics

Debating Democracy

A Reader in American Politics

SEVENTH EDITION

BRUCE MIROFF
State University of New York – Albany

RAYMOND SEIDELMAN
Sarah Lawrence College

TODD SWANSTROM
University of Missouri – St. Louis

Australia • Brazil • Japan • Korea • Mexico • Singapore • Spain • United Kingdom • United States

WADSWORTH
CENGAGE Learning

Debating Democracy: A Reader in American Politics, Seventh Edition
Bruce Miroff, Raymond Seidelman and Todd Swanstrom

Publisher/Executive Editor: Suzanne Jeans

Executive Editor: Carolyn Merrill

Acquisitions Editor: Edwin Hill

Development Editor: Lauren Athmer

Assistant Editor: Kate MacLean

Media Editor: Laura Hildebrand

Marketing Manager: Amy Whitaker

Marketing Coordinator: Josh Hendrick

Marketing Communications Manager: Heather Baxley

Content Project Management: PreMediaGlobal

Art Director: Linda Helcher

Print Buyer: Fola Orekoya

Rights Acquisitions Specialist: Katie Huha

Production Service: PreMediaGlobal

Compositor: PreMediaGlobal

Cover Designer: Harold Burch

Cover Image: © Lee Lorenz

Library of Congress Control Number: 2010928459

ISBN-13: 978-0-495-91347-4

ISBN-10: 0-495-91347-2

Wadsworth
20 Channel Center Street
Boston, MA 02210
USA

Cengage Learning is a leading provider of customized learning solutions with office locations around the globe, including Singapore, the United Kingdom, Australia, Mexico, Brazil and Japan. Locate your local office at **international.cengage.com/region**

Cengage Learning products are represented in Canada by Nelson Education, Ltd.

For your course and learning solutions, visit **www.cengage.com**.

Purchase any of our products at your local college store or at our preferred online store **www.cengagebrain.com**.

Printed in the United States of America
2 3 4 5 6 7 14 13 12 11

In Memory

On October 30, 2007, Ray Seidelman, our coeditor and friend, died after a four-year battle with colon cancer. An incisive political thinker and inspiring teacher, Ray was also a model of the democratic intellectual who refuses to retreat into theory or succumb to cynicism.

A graduate of the University of California–Santa Cruz, Ray earned his M.A. and Ph.D. degrees from Cornell University. For twenty-five years he taught at Sarah Lawrence College, where he held the Sarah Yates Exley Chair in Teaching Excellence. Devoted to his students, in 2002 Ray won the college's Lipkin Prize for Inspirational Teaching. His 1985 book, Disenchanted Realists, *critically examines the efforts of professional political scientists to marry the scientific study of politics to political reform.*

In the summer of 1988 we joined Ray on a camping trip in the Catskills that ended up in a rundown motel room. Accompanied by the steady patter of rain on the roof, that night we came up with the idea for an introductory textbook in American politics that would draw its inspiration from the homegrown traditions of participatory democracy. The Democratic Debate *is now in its fifth edition. Conceived as a companion to our textbook,* Debating Democracy *has taken on a life of its own, and this is its seventh edition.*

Ray loved political debate. Over the years the three of us argued long and loudly about what to include in the textbook and the reader. Ray always pushed us to go deeper in our analysis and to challenge students to think more critically. His sharp wit could penetrate the thickest skin and make you squirm. But he never came across as morally superior. You always had the feeling that Ray's views were tentative, open to constant interrogation and change. Maybe that is why he was such a great teacher.

Listening to Ray criticize the distortions and elite manipulations of American democracy, you might have concluded that he was a cynic. You would have been wrong. Cynics don't argue about global warming with strangers at a gas station. Cynics don't accompany carloads of students to demonstrations against the war in Iraq. His views were not those of a cynic but of a lover of American democracy. Ray is greatly missed—not only by his family, friends, and students—but by supporters of democracy everywhere.

Bruce Miroff
Todd Swanstrom

However unwillingly a person who has strong opinion may admit the possibility that his opinion may be false, he ought to be moved by the consideration that, however true it may be, if it is not fully, frequently, and fearlessly discussed, it will be held as a dead dogma, not as a living truth.

John Stuart Mill, *On Liberty* (1859)

Contents

Preface

We have been very pleased by readers' and reviewers' enthusiastic reactions to the previous editions of *Debating Democracy*. They warmly endorsed our belief in the need for a reader for courses in American politics that makes democracy its unifying theme. Of course, Americans agree in the abstract about democracy, but in practice we often disagree about democracy's meaning and implications. To explore these crucial disagreements, the seventh edition is constructed around a series of debates about democracy in America.

Special Features of *Debating Democracy*

Debating Democracy is different from other readers in American politics. The selections in our reader are organized around a common theme—the meaning and improvement of American democracy. Thus, reading through the selections has a cumulative effect, helping students to think more clearly and deeply about democracy.

Our experience as the teachers of introductory courses in American politics suggests that debate-type readers can leave students confused, wondering how to respond to a bewildering array of different arguments. Many students conclude that political debates are just a matter of opinion, that there is no cumulative knowledge generated by debating the issues. To prevent such confusion, we provide an introduction, praised by reviewers, that gives students a framework for evaluating democratic debates. This framework is designed to help students develop their own political philosophies and critical abilities for analyzing political issues. In the end, we believe, engaging students in these democratic debates will help them to understand that democracy is a complex and contested idea and that although there is no One Truth, the search for democratic truths is well worth the effort.

In order to engage students in the search for democratic truths, we have included lively and clearly written selections from political leaders, journalists, and scholars. In each case we have chosen two contrasting views on a controversial topic. To help students in evaluating the selections, we introduce each debate with a short essay that places the issue in a meaningful context and alerts the reader to be on the lookout for contrasting values and hidden assumptions.

Debating Democracy seeks to generate further debate. After each set of selections we include questions that can be used by readers to analyze the issues or by teachers to spark class discussions. We end with suggested readings and websites that students can use to pursue the topic further.

Each chapter in the book can be used as the basis for a structured in-class debate. Our own introductory lecture courses have included discussion sections of ten to twenty students led by teaching assistants. The TA divides the class in two and assigns each group one side in the debate. The students are asked to meet outside of class and prepare their arguments based on the readings. A session of the discussion section is then devoted to a formal debate. We do several of these structured debates in the course of a semester. Students enjoy these debates and often report that this is the high point of the course for them.

Following the formal debates, each student is required to write a short paper setting out the arguments of her or his side and rebutting the arguments of the other side. We are convinced that this exercise helps students to achieve what is often an important goal in introductory American politics courses: improving writing skills. Requiring students to take a stand on a political issue and develop a coherent argument for their position in a thematic essay is an effective way, we believe, to teach writing.

Structure of *Debating Democracy*

Debating Democracy has been structured to fit with almost all introductory texts in American politics. We cover topics usually covered in an introductory text, but we have also included debates on political economy, immigration, and religion because we believe these are important subjects for understanding contemporary American democracy.

The editors of this book make no claim to being impartial observers of democratic debates. We support the extension of democratic decision making into broader spheres of the economy and society with greater emphasis on equality and community. Our participatory democratic inclinations are evident in our textbook, *The Democratic Debate: American Politics in an Age of Change,* Fifth Edition (Cengage Learning 2010).

Although we make no claim to impartiality, we have made every effort in the chapters that follow to select the strongest arguments on both sides of the issues. The reader can be used with any textbook in American government, no matter what the political inclinations of the professor. The reader can also stand by itself as an introduction to the critical issues facing American democracy at the beginning of the twenty-first century.

New to the Seventh Edition

The seventh edition contains twelve new selections, comprising nearly 35 percent of the book. Several of the new chapters address profound issues currently facing American democracy, including the debates over corporate spending in elections, same-sex marriage, and negative campaigning.

There are four new chapters:

Chapter 6   Civil Liberties and Elections: Is Corporate Spending on Elections the Equivalent of Free Speech?

Chapter 7   Civil Rights: Debating Same-Sex Marriage

Chapter 11   Campaigns and Elections: Do Negative Ads Damage Democracy?

Chapter 12   The Federal Budget: Is the Deficit a Threat to the Nation?

In addition, we have one or two new selections in three chapters continued from the previous edition:

Chapter 9   Digital Media: Do They Expand or Shrink Democracy?

Chapter 13   Congress: Can Our Representatives Serve the Public Good?

Chapter 17   Foreign Policy: Has the United States Become an Imperial Power?

Many of the essays in the book have been written by leading figures in political science, law, journalism, and politics. We are grateful to two leading scholars of the presidency, Fred Greenstein and Stephen Skowronek, for updating their essays in Chapter 14 specially for this edition in order to incorporate the presidency of Barack Obama.

Acknowledgments

We are grateful to all of those who helped us to carry forward our original hopes for *Debating Democracy*. At SUNY, Albany, skillful research assistance was supplied by Molly Flynn, Paul Goggi, Timothy Gordinier, Christopher Latimer, Liu Runyu, Jordan Wishy, Christopher Witko, and Fred Wood. At Saint Louis University, Allan Lamberg, Ann Robertson, and Scott Krummenacher provided invaluable help. Jennifer Edwards and Bruce Hanebrink at the University of Missouri, St. Louis skillfully helped with the seventh edition. We would like to thank the outside reviewers who have reviewed *Debating Democracy* in all its forms over the years. Their incisive suggestions led us to change some selections, add new subjects, and improve our pedagogical framework.

Scott Adler, University of Colorado at Boulder

John L. Anderson, University of Nebraska at Kearney

Juan Arroyo, Ithaca College

Stephen C. Baker, Jacksonville University

Alan Beck, Santa Fe College

Matthew H. Bosworth, Winona State University

Max Brown, Willamette University

Jerry Calvert, Montana State University

Stefanie Chambers, Trinity College

Edmond Costantini, University of California at Davis

Jennifer Disney, John Jay College of Criminal Justice

Thomas P. Dolan, Columbus State University

Keith Rollin Eakins, University of Central Oklahoma

Dana K. Glencross, Oklahoma City Community College

Eric Grulke, Wright State University

James R. Harrigan, State University of New York – Oswego

Joseph P. Heim, University of Wisconsin – LaCrosse

Thomas Hensley, Kent State University

William J. Hughes, Southern Oregon University

Ronald King, San Diego State University

Fredrick Paul Lee, Winona State University

William R. Lund, University of Idaho

Suzanne Marilley, Capital University

Christopher McDonald, Lincoln Land Community College

Philip Meeks, Creighton University

Noelle Norton, University of San Diego

Paula L. O'Loughlin, University of Minnesota at Morris

David J. Olson, University of Washington

Marvin L. Overby, University of Mississippi

Travis N. Ridout, Washington State University

Delbert J. Ringquist, Central Michigan University

Gregory G. Rocha, University of Texas at El Paso

Stuart W. Schulman, Drake University

Larry Schwab, John Carroll University

Dennis Shea, State University of New York College at Oneonta

James R. Simmons, University of Wisconsin–Oshkosh

Kevin Smith, University of Nebraska, Lincoln

Donna J. Swarthout, Montana State University

Robert C. Turner, Skidmore College

Linda O. Valenty, San Jose State University

Bruce Wallin, Northeastern University

Kenneth F. Warren, Saint Louis University

Stephen Wiener, University of California at Santa Barbara

Finally, we continue to depend on the love, the support, and especially the patience of our families: Melinda, Nick, and Anna; Fay, Eva, and Rosa; Katie, Jessica, Madeleine, and Eleanore.

B. M.

R. S.

T. S.

Introduction

✳

How to Read This Book

When we think of democratic debates, we often think of the presidential debates that take place every four years. Beginning with the 1960 Kennedy–Nixon debate, these nationally televised events have been a crucial part of presidential campaigns. Presidential debates, however, are very different from the debates about the key issues facing American democracy that we have gathered together in this volume. A good way to understand this difference is to examine one of the most widely publicized exchanges between Barack Obama and Hillary Clinton in their closely contested battle for the Democratic presidential nomination in 2008.

The debate in question took place in Myrtle Beach, South Carolina, five days before the crucial South Carolina primary. Nasty exchanges between the candidates at this debate caused it to be quickly dubbed the "brawl on the beach." Early in the debate the moderator, CNN's Wolf Blitzer, asked Obama about one of Clinton's criticisms of his programs. "What she said wasn't true," Obama said, going on to knock down other Clinton statements he thought were untrue. On whether he had said that Republicans had better economic policies in the 1980s, Obama said, "This simply is not true."

"This is not the case," Clinton retorted. "When it comes to a lot of the issues that are important in this race, it is sometimes difficult to understand what Senator Obama has said, because as soon as he is confronted on it, he says that's not what he meant."

When he got the microphone back, Obama counterattacked: "Hillary, we just had the tape. You just said that I complimented Republican ideas.... What I said was that Ronald Reagan was a transformative political figure because he was able to get Democrats to vote against their economic interests to form a majority to push through their agenda, an agenda that I objected to. Because while I was on those streets watching those folks see their jobs shift overseas, you were a corporate lawyer sitting on the board at Wal-Mart."

A little later Clinton came back to the issue, saying that it certainly sounded as though Obama was praising Republican ideas. "Bad for America," Clinton declared. "And I was fighting against those ideas when you were practicing law and representing your contributor, Rezko, in his slum landlord business in inner-city Chicago."

All Obama could say was, "No, no, no."

In presidential debates the candidates often ignore the issues and attack their opponents. The average voter is primarily interested not in who is the better debater but in who has the best character, temperament, and leadership qualities to be president. In an issues debate, like the ones in this book, attacking one's opponent is considered a logical fallacy (called the *ad hominem* fallacy, literally, addressing the man instead of the issue). Because the issue in presidential debates is choosing a president, attacking your opponent's judgment or character is relevant. Clinton was trying to convince the voters that Obama was corrupt and not to be trusted, while Obama was trying to persuade them that Clinton was out of touch with ordinary Americans.

Instead of trying to persuade voters to change their positions on the issues, presidential candidates generally try to convince the voters that they are closest to the positions most voters already hold. Thoroughly briefed by pollsters about what the voters want to hear, each candidate, without appearing unprincipled, tries to mold his or her views to please the undecided voters.

Above all, skilled politicians try to use language to frame the issues in ways that favor their side. If you succeed in having your framing of the issue accepted, your opponent is at a distinct disadvantage. If Clinton can succeed in having the debate revolve around whether Obama praised Republican ideas, then no matter how hard Obama protests, Democratic primary voters will be reminded of this unflattering connection. No wonder Obama tried to shift the debate by charging that Clinton was cozy with Wal-Mart. Professor George Lakoff begins his class in linguistics by telling his students, "Don't think of an elephant!" He has never found a student able to do this—illustrating his point that when we criticize a frame, we end up reinforcing it.[1] It is for this reason that politicians often end up speaking past each other, ignoring what their opponents have said and repeating again and again their own framing of the issue.

The preceding analysis of presidential debates could easily lead one to the cynical conclusion that political debates are nothing but rhetoric and manipulation. In the real world, however, debates range from manipulative to principled and everything in between. In the real world no debate is perfectly free and fair, if only because one side has more resources to make itself heard. The debates we have gathered together in *Debating Democracy* approximate the conditions of a free and fair debate. Each chapter addresses a central issue in American democracy. The debaters are experts and focus exclusively on the issue; the personality or background of the debaters is irrelevant. Each gets equal time. For the most part, they avoid begging (ignoring) the question, mudslinging, or manipulating stereotypes. They still try to frame the issue their way, but these frames are usually easier to see and analyze than is the case with the vague rhetoric of a political campaign. The contest is decided not by who has the most money or who projects the best image; you, the readers, decide who has the best argument using logical reasoning and facts.

Political debates are not just methods for acquiring information in elections; they are the heart of a democratic system. In a true democracy, debates do not just concern who will be elected to office every few years; they address the issues of everyday life, and they occur every day, extending from television studios to dinner tables, from shop floors to classrooms. Even though political debates can become heated because they involve our most deeply held beliefs, democracies do not deny anyone the right to disagree. In a democracy we recognize that no one has a monopoly on the truth. Debates are not tangential to democracy; they are central to its meaning. "Agreeing to disagree" is the essence of democracy.

Debate as the Lifeblood of Democracy

Debate as dialogue, not demagoguery, is the lifeblood of democracy. Democracy is the one form of government that requires leaders to give reasons for their decisions and defend them in public. Some theorists argue that free and fair deliberation, or debate, is not only a good method for arriving at democratic decisions but the essence of democracy itself.[2]

Debate is essential in a democracy not just because it leads to better decisions but also because it helps to create better citizens. Democratic debate requires that we be open-minded, that we listen to both sides. This process of listening attentively to different sides and examining their assumptions helps us to clarify and critically examine our own political beliefs. As the nineteenth-century British political philosopher John Stuart Mill wrote:

> So essential is this discipline [attending equally and impartially to both sides] to a real understanding of moral and human subjects that, if opponents of all-important truths do not exist, it is indispensable to imagine them and supply them with the strongest arguments which the most skillful devil's advocate can conjure up.[3]

According to Mill, if we are not challenged in our beliefs, they become dead dogmas instead of living truths. (Consider what happened to communist ideologies in Eastern Europe, where they were never tested in public debate.) Once we have honed our skills analyzing political debates, we are less vulnerable to being manipulated by demagogues. By hearing the rhetoric and manipulation in others' speech, we are better able to purge it from our own.[4] Instead of basing our beliefs on unconscious prejudices or ethnocentric values, we consciously and freely choose our political beliefs.

In order for a debate to be truly democratic, it must be free and fair. In a free and fair debate, the only power exerted is the power of reason. We are moved to adopt a position not by threats or force but by the persuasiveness of the argument. In a democratic debate, proponents argue for their positions not by appealing to this or that private interest but by appealing to the *public* interest, the values and aspirations we share as a democratic people. Democracy is not simply a process for adding up the individual preferences that citizens bring with them to the issues to see which side wins. In a democratic debate people are required to frame their arguments in terms of the public interest.[5] And as citizens deliberate about the public interest through debates, they are changed.[6]

In this book we have gathered two contrasting arguments on a range of the most pressing issues facing American democracy. The reader's task is to compare the two arguments and decide which is more persuasive. After reading the selections, readers may feel frustrated seeing that opponents can adopt diametrically opposed stands on the same issue depending on their point of view. It may seem as if political positions on the issues are based only on personal values, as if political judgments are simply a matter of opinion. Being able to understand viewpoints divergent from our own, however, is the beginning of political toleration and insight. There is no One Truth on political issues that can be handed to us on a platter by experts. Nevertheless, public choices are *not* simply based on opinion. Americans subscribe to fundamental political values and struggle to realize them in our political decisions. Political stands are not just a matter of opinion, because some decisions will promote the democratic public interest better than others.

The purpose of this introduction is to give you, the reader, tools for evaluating democratic debates. The agreements and disagreements in American politics are not random; they exhibit patterns, and understanding these patterns can help orient you in the debates. In the pages that follow we draw a preliminary map of the territory of democratic debates in the United States to guide you in negotiating this difficult terrain. Your goal should be not just to take a stand on this or that issue but to clarify your own values and chart your own path in pursuit of the public interest of American democracy.

Democratic Debates: Conflict within Consensus

In order for a true debate to occur, there must be both consensus and conflict. If there were no consensus, or agreement, on basic values or standards of evaluation, the debaters would talk past each other, like two people speaking in foreign tongues. Without some common standard of evaluation, there would be no way to settle the debate. However, if there were no fundamental disagreements, no conflict, the debate would be trivial and boring. Factual disagreements are not enough. Consider a debate between two political scientists about this question: How many people voted in the last election? The debate might be informative, but few people would care about the outcome because it does not engage deeply held values or beliefs. Factual disputes are important, but they rarely decide important political debates. Democratic debates are interesting and important when they engage us in struggles over the meaning and application of our basic values.

Judging a political debate is tricky. Political reasoning is different from economic reasoning or individual rational decision making. Political debates are rarely settled by toting up the costs and benefits of alternative courses of action and choosing the one that maximizes benefits over costs. It is not that costs and benefits do not matter; rather, what we see as benefits or costs depends on how we frame the issue. In political debates each side tries to get the audience to see the issue its way, to frame the issue in language that reinforces its position. On the issue of abortion, for example, is your position best described as pro-choice or pro-life? Should programs to help minorities be characterized as affirmative action or reverse discrimination? Clearly, the terms we use to describe a political position make a difference. Each term casts light on the issue in a different way, highlighting different values that are at stake in the controversy. The terms used to describe the abortion position, for example, emphasize either the right of an unborn fetus or the right of a woman to control her body.

As these examples illustrate, in political debates the outcome frequently hinges on the standard of evaluation itself, on what values and principles will be applied to the decision at hand. In political debates the issue is always what is good for the community as a whole, the public interest, not just some segment of the community. The selections that follow are all examples of debates over the meaning of the public interest in American democracy. In the United States, political debates, with the notable exception of debates over slavery, have been characterized by consensus on basic democratic principles *combined with* conflicts over how best to realize those principles in practice.

As conflicts within a consensus, democratic debates in this country go back more than 200 years to the nation's founding and the original debate over the U.S. Constitution. Americans worship the Constitution as an almost divinely inspired document that embodies the highest ideals of democracy. Yet throughout history Americans have disagreed vehemently on what the Constitution means. This is not surprising. The Constitution was born as much in conflict and compromise as it was in consensus. In the words of former Supreme Court Justice William J. Brennan, Jr., the framers "hid their differences in cloaks of generality."[7] The general language of the Constitution left many conflicts over specifics to later generations. For example, the Constitution gave the federal government the power to provide for the "general welfare," but we have been debating ever since about what this should include. Thus, the Constitution is both a source of consensus, by embodying our ideals, and a source of conflict, by failing to specify exactly how those ideals should be applied in practice.[8]

Three Sources of Conflict

Behind the words of the Constitution lie three ideals that supposedly animate our system of government: democracy, freedom, and equality. Americans agree that we should have a government of, by, and for the people (as President Lincoln so eloquently put it), a government that treats everybody equally, and a government that achieves the maximum level of freedom consistent with an ordered society. These ideals seem simple, but they are not. While Americans are united in their aspirations, they are divided in their visions of how to achieve those aspirations.[9] Democracy, freedom, and equality are what political theorists call "essentially contested concepts."[10]

I. Democracy

Democracy comes from the Greek words *demos*, meaning "the people," and *kratein*, meaning "to rule." Hence, democracy means, simply, "rule by the people." Americans agree that democracy is the best form of government. They disagree, however, on what this means.

Elite (Limited) Democracy   For some, democracy is basically a method for making decisions. According to this minimalist definition of democracy, a decision is democratic if it is made according to the criterion of majority rule. Of course, there are other requirements of democratic decision making, such as open nominations for office and free speech, but once the basic conditions have been met, the resulting decision is by definition democratic.

Following this limited definition, the most important characteristic of a democracy is free and fair elections for choosing government officials. Democracy basically means the ability of citizens to choose their leaders.[11] Elites compete for the votes to win office, but once in office, they have substantial autonomy to rule as they see fit. According to this view, ultimate power rests in the hands of the people at election time, but between elections they cede decision-making authority to elites who have the expertise and experience to make the right decisions in a technologically complex and dangerous world. We call this school of democracy *elite democracy*.[12]

Elite democrats favor a minimal definition of democracy not because it is ideal but because it is the only type of democracy that is achievable in large modern nation-states. Thus, as you will see in the selection by John Mueller in Chapter 2, elite democrats question the validity of many of the precepts of participatory democracy. In contrast, Paul Rogat Loeb maintains that active citizens who sacrifice for the common good are possible, even in our flawed democratic system.

Popular (Expansive) Democracy   Opponents of elite democrats adopt a more demanding definition of democracy. They argue that we cannot call a decision democratic just because it came out of a democratic process. Democratic decisions must also respect certain values such as tolerance, a respect for individual freedom, and the attainment of a basic level of social and economic equality. If the majority rules in a way that violates people's rights or enacts policies that result in extreme inequalities of wealth, the system cannot be called democratic. For this group, democracy means more than a political system with free and fair elections; it means an economy and society that reflect a democratic desire for equality and respect for differences.

For adherents of an expansive definition of democracy, democracy means more than going to the polls every few years; it means citizens participating in the institutions of civil society, including corporations, unions, and neighborhood associations. In Chapter 5, Samuel Bowles, Frank Roosevelt, and Richard Edwards represent this position, calling for expanding democratic decision making into the economy. Countering the view of elite democrats that people are not interested in or capable of governing effectively, those who advocate a more participatory system argue that in an atmosphere of toleration, respect, and rough equality, citizens are capable of governing themselves fairly and effectively. We call those who advocate a more participatory conception of democracy *popular democrats.*[13]

II. Freedom

Most of us have a basic intuitive idea of freedom: To be free means being able to do what we want, without someone telling us what to do. Any time we are forced to do something against our will by somebody else, our freedom is reduced. Freedom seems like an exceedingly simple idea. Once again, however, we find that there is plenty of room for disagreement.

Negative (Freedom From)   The central issue for freedom is deciding where to draw the line between the power of the group and the freedom of the individual. In other words, how far should government power extend? Any time the government imposes a tax or passes a law, it limits someone's freedom. In a justly famous essay, *On Liberty*, John Stuart Mill argues that the only justification for government power over individuals is self-protection: "[T]he only purpose for which power can be rightfully exercised over any member of a civilized community, against his will, is to prevent harm to others."[14] In other words, your freedom to swing your arm ends where my nose begins.

In Mill's view, the purpose of government is to maximize individual freedom. Freedom is understood negatively, as freedom from external constraints. Because government actions always reduce individual freedom, their only justification is to counter other restrictions on our freedom, as when the government passes laws against robbery or assault. Clearly, this view places severe limits on what democracies can legitimately do, even under the principle of majority rule. If the majority passes laws that restrict someone's freedom, without those laws being justified by the principle of self-protection, then it is no longer a true democracy because the laws violate a basic democratic value.

Positive (Freedom To)   In contrast to the negative conception of freedom—freedom *from*—there is an equally compelling positive definition of freedom—freedom *to.*[15] The positive idea of freedom recognizes that in order to be free, to exercise meaningful choice, we need to possess certain resources and have certain capacities. Education, for example, increases our freedom because it increases our ability to imagine alternatives and find solutions to problems. Freedom, therefore, is not simply the absence of external coercion but freedom to get an education, travel to foreign countries, or receive expert medical care.

A positive conception of freedom justifies an expanded role for government and for citizens acting together in other ways. When government taxes us, it reduces negative freedom, but when it uses the money to build a highway or a public library, it gives us a greater freedom to do things we previously were unable to do. Under the positive conception of freedom, the scope of freedom is increased when the capacity of individuals to act is enhanced by government action, such as protecting the right of workers to join a union (thus giving workers the ability to bargain collectively over wages and working conditions) or requiring buildings to be handicapped accessible (thus giving the handicapped access to places they were previously excluded from).[16]

Whether one subscribes to a positive or a negative conception of freedom will make a big difference in one's political philosophy. The negative conception of freedom is conducive to limited government and highlights the more acquisitive and competitive side of human nature. Under this view, the expansion of power in one part of society necessarily leads to a reduction of freedom in some other part of society. The selection by Milton Friedman on political economy in Chapter 5 is based on a negative conception of freedom. Friedman warns that too much government leads to coercion and a reduction in individual freedom, which is maximized by free competition in the marketplace. The positive conception of freedom emphasizes the more cooperative side of human beings. According to this conception, government as a form of social cooperation can actually expand the realm of freedom by bringing more and more matters of social importance under human control.

III. Equality

Like democracy and freedom, equality seems an exceedingly simple idea. Equality marches forward under banners that read "Treat everybody equally" or "Treat like cases alike." These are not working definitions, however, but political rhetoric that hides serious ambiguities in the concept of equality. In truth, how we apply the idea of equality depends on how we envision it in a broader context.

Process Orientation   For some people, equality is basically generated by a fair process. So long as the competition is fair—everybody has an equal opportunity to succeed—then the results are fair, even if the resulting distribution is highly unequal. Inequalities that reflect differences among people in intelligence, talent, ambition, or strength are viewed as legitimate. Inequalities that result from biases in the rules of competition are unjustified and should be eliminated.

The process orientation toward equality is best reflected in free-market theory. According to market theory, the distribution of income and wealth is fair if it is the result of a process of voluntary contracting among responsible adults. As long as the requirements for a free market are met (perfect competition, free flow of information, the absence of coercion or manipulation, and so on), no one exerts power over the market and market outcomes are just and fair. Market theorists such as Milton Friedman stress equal opportunity, not equal results. The role of government, in this view, is to serve as a neutral umpire, enforcing the rules and treating everyone alike.[17]

Results Orientation   Opponents argue that if the government treats everybody equally, the results will still be highly unequal because people start the race from very different positions. Some have a head start in the race, while others enter with serious handicaps. To ignore these differences is to perpetuate inequalities. Treating unequals equally is, in effect, unequal. The French writer Anatole France mocked what he called "the majestic egalitarianism of the law, which forbids rich and poor alike to sleep under bridges, to beg in the streets, and to steal bread."[18] Even though the law formally treats everyone alike, it is clear that only certain people will suffer the consequences.

Those who take a results orientation toward equality do not deny the importance of equal opportunity but argue that equal opportunity means the ability of everyone to participate equally in the decisions that affect their lives. These democrats charge that their opponents elevate the individual over the community and privileged elites over ordinary citizens, as if the wagon train could make it to the promised land only if some of the weak and frail were left behind alongside the trail. Those who support a results orientation argue that it is possible for everyone to make it together.

Those who support a results orientation do not believe in a strict leveling of society but argue that certain resources are necessary for people to participate fully in society and realize their potential. In other words, government cannot just stand aside and watch people compete; it must establish the conditions for equal participation. At a minimum, many would argue, adequate nutrition, good education, safety, and decent health care are necessary for a fulfilling life.

American Ideologies: Patterns in Political Stands

With two contrasting positions on each of the three issues just discussed—democracy, equality, and freedom—there are eight possible combinations of issue positions. Stands on the three issues are not random, however; they correlate in ways that generate distinct patterns characteristic of American political ideologies.

One of the clearest ideological distinctions in American politics is between those who favor markets and those who favor government. As Charles Lindblom has noted, "Aside from the difference between despotic and libertarian governments, the greatest distinction between one government and another is in the degree to which market replaces government or government replaces market."[19] A central issue in American politics is where to draw the line between the public and private sectors. If you believe that the market is basically free and fair, then you will support only a limited role for government. Generally, those who favor the market subscribe to a negative conception of freedom and a process orientation toward equality. This position corresponds to what we call *free-market conservatism.* If, however, you believe that markets are penetrated by relations of power and are prone to discrimination, then you will support an expanded role for political participation and democratic government. Those who advocate an increased role for government generally subscribe to a positive conception of freedom and favor a results orientation toward equality. These views correspond to what is commonly called *liberalism.*

Usually, we think of social conservatives as adhering to a more elite view of democracy and social liberals as being more inclined toward popular democracy. In the 1960s, for example, *left-wing populists* supported maximum feasible participation by poor people to solve poverty and advocated democratic control of corporations. In recent years, however, because they support a large role for the federal government in Washington, D.C., liberals have been accused by conservatives of being, in effect, elitist. A *right-wing populist* movement has arisen that combines popular democratic appeals with a negative conception of individual freedom and a process approach to equality, opposing the redistribution of wealth through government. To add to the complexity, however, right-wing populists do not always favor limiting the role of government. The *religious right* generally wants the government to interfere less in the economy but more in society—exerting more government control over moral issues, such as abortion and pornography.

Although distinct patterns appear in American politics on the issues of democracy, freedom, and equality, they are not set in stone. It is possible to mix and match various positions in putting together your own political philosophy. In developing your own political philosophy, you will need to address a fundamental question: What are human beings capable of; that is, what is your conception of human nature?

Human Nature: The Big Debate

Throughout history, political philosophers have debated various conceptions of human nature. Human nature is the clay out of which all political systems must be molded. The nature of this clay, its elasticity or hardness, its ability to assume different shapes and hold them, largely determines what we can and cannot do in politics. Since the original debate over the U.S. Constitution, Americans have disagreed about human nature and therefore about politics.

The Private View   Many argue that Americans are quintessentially individualistic, well suited to the marketplace and private pursuits but not well suited to democratic citizenship. The framers of the Constitution, the Federalists, argued that the common people were self-interested and passionate creatures who should not be entrusted with all of the reins of government. Thus, as you will see in Chapter 1, James Madison argues in "Federalist No. 10" that the greatest danger in a democracy is the tyranny of the majority, especially the majority of common people taking away the property of wealthy elites. Madison recommended various checks on majority rule that would guarantee the rights of minorities and give elites substantial autonomy to rule in the public interest.

This view of human nature is reflected in contemporary debates. In the United States the debate shifts from human nature to the nature of Americans as a people and whether we are different from other people. According to the theory of exceptionalism, Americans are more individualistic and self-interested than other people.[20] As a nation of immigrants, we fled feudal systems and traditional cultures in search of greater freedom and assimilated into an American value system that stressed upward mobility through individual effort. The pursuit of fortune in the marketplace is the special genius of Americans. Whether this is good or bad depends on your view of markets and governments.

The Social View During the debate over the Constitution in the 1780s, a group of dissenters, the Anti-Federalists, argued that the Constitution placed too many limits on citizen participation. (We have included a selection by the Anti-Federalist Brutus in Chapter 1.) The Anti-Federalists argued that the common people could overcome or check their selfish inclinations through democratic participation and education in civic virtue. As much power as possible, therefore, should be placed in the hands of the people at the grassroots level. The main threat to democracy, Anti-Federalists believed, came not from the tyranny of the majority but from power-hungry elites. The best way to protect against elite tyranny was to have the people participate directly in deciding important issues. The Anti-Federalists founded the tradition of popular (expansive) democracy that is still alive in the United States.

Even today, when Americans seem caught up in acquisitive pursuits and politics seems so mean-spirited, some observers argue that there are important sources of social commitment in American culture. An influential book by Robert Bellah and colleagues, *Habits of the Heart*, argues that Americans are attached to powerful civic traditions that pull us out of our individualistic orientations. These civic traditions are rooted in religion and republicanism, both of which emphasize commitments to public service. Indeed, Americans exhibit lively commitments to grassroots participation and public service.

Conclusion: A Guide to Critical Thinking

Everyone has a political philosophy. Whether we recognize it or not, we bring certain assumptions about democracy, freedom, equality, and human nature to political debates. The goal is not to give up these assumptions but to convert them from unconscious prejudices into carefully chosen elements of a political philosophy. A good way to develop a thoughtful political philosophy is to analyze political debates like those included here. Clever debaters, for example, will appear as if they are supporting equality in general, but in order to make their argument work they must adopt one conception of equality over another. Readers must delve beneath the rhetoric and evaluate these assumptions, as well as the logic and evidence of the argument itself.

As a guide to critical thinking, we suggest that readers keep in mind the following five questions and evaluate the evidence that supports their answers. (Some questions may not apply to some selections.)

1. What is the author's concept of democracy—elite (limited) or popular (expansive)?
2. What is the author's concept of freedom—negative (freedom from) or positive (freedom to)?

3. What is the author's concept of equality—process or results?

4. How would you classify the author's ideology?

5. What concept of human nature, individualist or social, lies behind the author's argument?

This book is going to press during a time when the nation is deeply divided along partisan lines. Bitter conflicts over the financial bailout of Wall Street, the ballooning deficit, Obama's health care reform, the wars in Iraq and Afghanistan, global warming, and cultural issues such as abortion and gay marriage tear at the political fabric of our democracy. Especially during times like these, we need to keep in mind that there is one thing that finally does unite us: the belief that open and public debate is the best, in fact the only, democratic way to settle our differences.

Notes

1. See Lakoff's *Don't Think of an Elephant: Know Your Values and Frame the Debate* (White River Junction, Vt.: Chelsea Green, 2004). The Frameworks Institute has developed a set of tools for strategic framing of issues in policy advocacy; see www.frameworksinstitute.org.

2. See Jon Elster, ed., *Deliberative Democracy* (New York: Cambridge University Press, 1998). The German political theorist Jürgen Habermas has spent many years developing a theory of the ideal speech situation as the foundation of democracy. See especially his *The Theory of Communicative Action*, 2 vols. (Boston: Beacon Press, 1984–87).

3. John Stuart Mill, *On Liberty*, ed. and with an introduction by Currin V. Shields (Indianapolis, Ind.: Bobbs-Merrill, 1956), p. 46.

4. See Stephen L. Esquith, *Intimacy and Spectacle: Liberal Theory as Political Education* (Ithaca, N.Y.: Cornell University Press, 1994).

5. Amy Gutmann and Dennis Thompson call this the principle of reciprocity—that in a democratic debate citizens appeal to reasons that can be mutually acceptable to other citizens. See *Democracy and Disagreement* (Cambridge, Mass.: Harvard University Press, 1996).

6. Joshua Cohen, "Deliberation and Democratic Legitimacy," in *The Good Polity: Normative Analysis of the State* (Oxford: Basil Blackwell, 1989), p. 29.

7. Justice William J. Brennan Jr., "Federal Judges Properly and Inevitably Make Law Through 'Loose' Constitutional Construction," in *Debating American Government*, ed. Peter Woll (2nd ed.; Glenview, Ill.: Scott, Foresman, 1988), p. 338.

8. It is neither possible nor desirable for a constitution to specify every application. If it did, it would be a rigid constitution that would be incapable of adapting to changing conditions.

9. The following discussion of the sources of democratic disagreements in the United States draws heavily on Deborah A. Stone, *Political Paradox: The Art of Political Decision Making* (New York: W. W. Norton, 1997), and Frances Moore Lappé, *Rediscovering America's Values* (New York: Ballantine Books, 1989).

10. For an insightful discussion of essentially contested concepts, see William E. Connolly, *The Terms of Political Discourse* (2nd ed.; Princeton, N.J.: Princeton University Press, 1983). For an excellent overview of core political debates in the U.S., see Howard Fineman, *The Thirteen American Arguments that Define and Inspire Our Country* (New York: Random House, 2008).

11. For the most influential definition of democracy along these lines, see Joseph A. Schumpeter, *Capitalism, Socialism, and Democracy* (3rd ed.; New York: Harper, 1950), p. 269.

12. For elaboration on the concepts of elite and popular democracy, see Bruce Miroff, Raymond Seidelman, and Todd Swanstrom, *The Democratic Debate: An Introduction to American Politics* (5th ed.; Boston: Wadsworth, Cengage Learning, 2010).

13. Robert A. Dahl is the most influential contemporary political scientist who has written on the ideas of elite and popular democracy. Dahl began his career by defending a version of elite democratic theory in *A Preface to Democratic Theory* (Chicago: University of Chicago Press, 1956), and *Who Governs? Democracy and Power in an American City* (New Haven, Conn.: Yale University Press, 1961). In later works, Dahl shifted dramatically to a more popular democratic position. See *A Preface to Economic Democracy* (Berkeley and Los Angeles: University of California Press, 1985); *Democracy and Its Critics* (New Haven, Conn.: Yale University Press, 1989); and *How Democratic Is the American Constitution?* (New Haven, Conn.: Yale University Press, 2001).

14. Mill, *On Liberty*, p. 13.

15. The classic statement on positive and negative freedom is Isaiah Berlin's "Two Concepts of Liberty," in *Four Essays on Liberty* (New York: Oxford University Press, 1969), pp. 118–72.

16. For an eloquent defense of a positive conception of freedom, see President Franklin D. Roosevelt's speech to Congress on "An Economic Bill of Rights," in *Documents of American History*, ed. Henry Steele Commager (New York: Appleton-Century-Crofts, 1963), vol. 2, pp. 483–85.

17. One of the best statements of a process orientation toward equality is Robert Nozick, *Anarchy, State, and Utopia* (New York: Basic Books, 1974).

18. *The Oxford Dictionary of Quotations* (3rd ed.; Oxford: Oxford University Press, 1979), p. 217.

19. Charles Lindblom, *Politics and Markets: The World's Political-Economic Systems* (New York: Basic Books, 1977), p. ix.

20. For an influential statement on American exceptionalism, see Louis Hartz, *The Liberal Tradition in American Thought* (New York: Harcourt, Brace, 1955).

Chapter 1

✳

The Founding: Debating the Constitution

Although Americans relish political controversy in the present, we project onto the distant past of our nation's origins a more dignified political consensus. The founders of our republic—Washington, Adams, Jefferson, Hamilton, Madison—are cast in stone monuments and treated as political saints. Their ideas are invoked as hallowed truths that should inspire us. Seldom are these ideas treated as arguments that we should ponder and debate.

In fact, consensus was hardly the hallmark of the era in which the American republic was founded. Passionate political controversies raged during the American Revolution and its aftermath. These controversies ranged over the most basic issues of political life. The most profound was the debate over the ratification of the Constitution. The supporters of the Constitution, known as Federalists, and its opponents, known as Anti-Federalists, disagreed over what kind of a republic Americans should have. Although the debate took place more than 200 years ago, it still illuminates the core dilemmas of our democratic society.

The readings that follow highlight some of the fundamental issues debated by Federalists and Anti-Federalists. They pit the greatest thinker among the Federalists, James Madison, against a New York Anti-Federalist, who used the pseudonym Brutus, in an argument over the appropriate scale of democratic political life. (Scholars are not absolutely certain who Brutus was; the most likely candidate is Robert Yates, a New York judge. The pseudonym, by recalling the Roman republican who killed the tyrant Julius Caesar, evokes the threat allegedly posed by the Constitution to republican liberty.)

In his classic essay "Federalist No. 10," Madison favors the large, national republic established by the Constitution over small republics (state governments). In small republics, Madison warns, selfish factions can attain majority status and will use their power over the government to oppress minorities (such as the wealthy or those who hold unorthodox religious beliefs). Small republics thus allow the worst qualities in human nature to prevail: They allow irrational passion to overwhelm reasoned deliberation and injustice to supplant the public good.

The large republic created by the new Constitution, Madison prophesies, will be more rational and more just. Elected in large districts, representatives will likely be the most distinguished and patriotic citizens, and they will "refine and enlarge the public views" by filtering out the most selfish and shortsighted popular impulses. There will also be a greater diversity of factions in the large republic, making it unlikely that a majority can come together except on the basis of the common good. In Madison's essay, the chief threat to republican liberty comes, ironically, from the people themselves. His solution is to create a large republic in which the people will be divided into so many different interest groups that they can do little harm, while a small number of decision makers at the top take care of the common needs.

Brutus's essay (the first in a series that he wrote) takes issue with Madison on every count. He predicts that the large republic established by the Constitution will be run by aristocratic rulers who will eagerly expand their powers and oppress the common people. The greater distance from voters that Madison thinks will promote deliberation and public spirit in representatives will instead, Brutus argues, foster corruption and self-seeking in them. The diversity of the large republic is also, for Brutus, an unwelcome development because it will increase selfish factionalism, conflict, and stalemate.

Whereas Madison sees small republics as scenes of turbulence and misery, Brutus portrays them in a favorable light. In the smaller political scale of a state, the people will share common economic and social characteristics. Electoral districts will be smaller, therefore voters will personally know and trust their representatives and these representatives in turn will mirror their constituents' values and sentiments. Rather than breeding tyrannical majorities, small republics, as Brutus depicts them, educate law-abiding and virtuous citizens. In sum, Brutus rests his political hopes on the mass of ordinary people in the small republic, whose political impulses Madison fears, while directing his criticisms against a national elite, to whom Madison looks for wise political rule.

Anti-Federalist fears that the Constitution would create an oppressive government, fatal to republican liberty, strike us today as grossly exaggerated. Yet in at least one respect these fears were fortunate—they helped produce the Bill of Rights. Initially, Federalists such as Madison and his collaborator on *The Federalist Papers*, Alexander Hamilton, claimed that a national bill of rights was both unnecessary and undesirable. By establishing a national government that possessed only enumerated, limited powers, they insisted, the Constitution had not granted any authority to invade the liberties and rights of the people; but if a list of particular rights was nonetheless appended to the Constitution, it might imply that the government *could* invade rights that had not been listed. These arguments were brushed aside by the Anti-Federalists, who continued to argue that without specific guarantees the liberties for which Americans had fought in the Revolution might be usurped by a government of their own creation. To conciliate the Anti-Federalists and win greater public support for the new Constitution, Madison dropped his objections and took the lead in pushing for the Bill of Rights in the first Congress.

Although Federalists and Anti-Federalists could ultimately find common ground in the Bill of Rights, the philosophical and political differences between them remained profound. Their disagreements began the American debate between elite democracy and popular democracy. Nowhere is this more evident than in the contrast between Madison's reliance on a deliberative elite and Brutus's regard for the capacities of ordinary citizens. However, it can also be seen in the difference between Madison's belief that liberty will inevitably produce inequality of property and Brutus's belief that in a small republic large-scale inequalities can be avoided.

The Federalists and Anti-Federalists debated basic questions about democracy, and their disagreements still echo in our politics today. Thinking about the issues in their debate can help to clarify your own perspective toward democracy in the United States. Do you believe, with Madison, that it is only at the national level that selfish majorities can be blocked and government policies can be framed by deliberative and public-spirited representatives? Do you believe, with Brutus, that we should prefer state and local governments in order to promote greater civic participation and to enhance the trust between representatives and their constituents? Even more fundamentally, do you agree with Madison that ordinary citizens are too uninformed and self-seeking to be trusted with great political influence and that decisions are best left to elected representatives who can "refine and enlarge" what the people think? Or do you agree with Brutus that elites pose the greater danger to democracy and that democracy flourishes only when conditions are established that encourage ordinary citizens to involve themselves in the search for the public good?

Federalist No. 10

JAMES MADISON

Among the numerous advantages promised by a well-constructed Union, none deserves to be more accurately developed than its tendency to break and control the violence of faction.[1] The friend of popular governments never finds himself so much alarmed for their character and fate as when he

---

1. In modern terms, both interest groups and political parties are examples of Madison's factions. Note that by the definition Madison offers later, no faction can legitimately claim to represent the public interest.

contemplates their propensity to this dangerous vice. He will not fail, therefore, to set a due value on any plan which, without violating the principles to which he is attached, provides a proper cure for it. The instability, injustice, and confusion introduced into the public councils have, in truth, been the mortal diseases under which popular governments have everywhere perished, as they continue to be the favorite and fruitful topics from which the adversaries to liberty derive their most specious declamations. The valuable improvements made by the American constitutions on the popular models, both ancient and modern, cannot certainly be too much admired; but it would be an unwarrantable partiality to contend that they have as effectually obviated the danger on this side, as was wished and expected. Complaints are everywhere heard from our most considerate and virtuous citizens, equally the friends of public and private faith and of public and personal liberty, that our governments are too unstable, that the public good is disregarded in the conflicts of rival parties, and that measures are too often decided, not according to the rules of justice and the rights of the minor party, but by the superior force of an interested and overbearing majority. However anxiously we may wish that these complaints had no foundation, the evidence of known facts will not permit us to deny that they are in some degree true. It will be found, indeed, on a candid review of our situation, that some of the distresses under which we labor have been erroneously charged on the operation of our governments; but it will be found, at the same time, that other causes will not alone account for many of our heaviest misfortunes; and, particularly, for that prevailing and increasing distrust of public engagements and alarm for private rights which are echoed from one end of the continent to the other. These must be chiefly, if not wholly, effects of the unsteadiness and injustice with which a factious spirit has tainted our public administration.

By a faction I understand a number of citizens, whether amounting to a majority or minority of the whole, who are united and actuated by some common impulse of passion, or of interest, adverse to the rights of other citizens, or to the permanent and aggregate interests of the community.

There are two methods of curing the mischiefs of faction: the one, by removing its causes; the other, by controlling its effects.

There are again two methods of removing the causes of faction: the one, by destroying the liberty which is essential to its existence; the other, by giving to every citizen the same opinions, the same passions, and the same interests.

It could never be more truly said than of the first remedy that it was worse than the disease. Liberty is to faction what air is to fire, an aliment without which it instantly expires. But it could not be a less folly to abolish liberty, which is essential to political life, because it nourishes faction than it would be to wish the annihilation of air, which is essential to animal life, because it imparts to fire its destructive agency.

The second expedient is as impracticable as the first would be unwise. As long as the reason of man continues fallible, and he is at liberty to exercise it, different opinions will be formed. As long as the connection subsists between his reason and his self-love, his opinions and his passions will have a reciprocal influence on each other; and the former will be objects to which the latter will attach themselves. The diversity in the faculties of men, from which the rights of property originate, is not less an insuperable obstacle to a uniformity of interests. The protection of these faculties is the first object of government. From the protection of different and unequal faculties of acquiring property, the possession of different degrees and kinds of property immediately results; and from the influence of these on the sentiments and views of the respective proprietors ensues a division of the society into different interests and parties.

The latent causes of faction are thus sown in the nature of man; and we see them everywhere brought into different degrees of activity, according to the different circumstances of civil society. A zeal for different opinions concerning religion, concerning government, and many other points, as well of speculation as of practice; an attachment to different leaders ambitiously contending for pre-eminence and power; or to persons of other descriptions whose fortunes have been interesting to the human passions, have, in turn, divided mankind into parties, inflamed them with mutual animosity, and rendered them much more disposed to vex and oppress each other than to co-operate for their common good. So strong is this propensity of mankind to fall into mutual animosities that where no substantial occasion presents itself the most frivolous and fanciful distinctions have been sufficient to kindle their unfriendly passions and excite their most violent conflicts. But the most common and durable source of factions has been the various and unequal distribution of property. Those who hold and those who are without property have ever formed distinct interests in society. Those who are creditors, and those who are debtors, fall under a like discrimination. A landed interest, a manufacturing interest, a mercantile interest, a moneyed interest, with many lesser interests, grow up of necessity in civilized nations, and divide them into different classes, actuated by different sentiments and views. The regulation of these various and interfering interests forms the principal task of modern legislation and involves the spirit of party and faction in the necessary and ordinary operations of government.

No man is allowed to be a judge in his own cause, because his interest would certainly bias his judgment, and, not improbably, corrupt his integrity. With equal, nay with greater reason, a body of men are unfit to be both judges and parties at the same time; yet what are many of the most important acts of legislation but so many judicial determinations, not indeed concerning the rights of single persons, but concerning the rights of large bodies of citizens? And what are the different classes of legislators but advocates and parties to the causes which they determine? Is a law proposed concerning private debts? It is a question to which the creditors are parties on one side and the debtors on the other. Justice ought to hold the balance between them. Yet the parties are, and must be, themselves the judges; and the most numerous party, or in other words, the most powerful faction must be expected to prevail. Shall domestic manufacturers be encouraged, and in what degree, by restrictions on foreign manufacturers? are questions which would be differently decided by the landed and the manufacturing classes, and probably by neither with a sole regard to justice and the public good. The apportionment of taxes on the various descriptions of property is an act which seems to require the most exact impartiality; yet there is, perhaps, no legislative act in which greater opportunity and temptation are given to a pre-dominant party to trample on the rules of justice. Every shilling with which they overburden the inferior number is a shilling saved to their own pockets.

It is in vain to say that enlightened statesmen will be able to adjust these clashing interests and render them all subservient to the public good. Enlightened statesmen will not always be at the helm. Nor, in many cases, can such an adjust-ment be made at all without taking into view indirect and remote considerations, which will rarely prevail over the immediate interest which one party may find in disregarding the rights of another or the good of the whole.

The inference to which we are brought is that the *causes* of faction cannot be removed and that relief is only to be sought in the means of controlling its *effects*.

If a faction consists of less than a majority, relief is supplied by the republican principle, which enables the majority to defeat its sinister views by regular vote. It may clog the administration, it may convulse the society; but it will be unable to execute and mask its violence under the forms of the Constitution. When a majority is included in a faction, the form of popular government, on the other hand, enables it to sacrifice to its ruling passion or interest both the public good and the rights of other citizens. To secure the public good and private rights against the danger of such a faction, and at the same time to preserve the spirit and the form of popular government, is then the great object to which our in-quiries are directed. Let me add that it is the great desideratum by which alone this form of government can be rescued from the opprobrium under which it has so long labored and be recommended to the esteem and adoption of mankind.

By what means is this object attainable? Evidently by one of two only. Either the existence of the same passion or interest in a majority at the same time must be prevented, or the majority, having such coexistent passion of interest, must be ren-dered, by their number and local situation, unable to concert and carry into effect schemes of oppression. If the impulse and the opportunity be suffered to coincide, we well know that neither moral nor religious motives can be relied on as an adequate control. They are not found to be such on the injustice and violence of individuals, and lose their efficacy in proportion to the number combined to-gether, that is, in proportion as their efficacy becomes needful.

From this view of the subject it may be concluded that a pure democracy, by which I mean a society consisting of a small number of citizens, who assemble and administer the government in person, can admit of no cure for the mischiefs of faction. A common passion or interest will, in almost every case, be felt by a majority of the whole; a communication and concert results from the form of government itself; and there is nothing to check the inducements to sacrifice the weaker party or an obnoxious individual. Hence it is that such democracies have ever been spectacles of turbulence and contention; have ever been found incompatible with personal security or the rights of property; and have in general been as short in their lives as they have been violent in their deaths. Theoretic politicians, who have patronized this species of government, have erroneously supposed that by reducing mankind to a perfect equality in their political rights, they would at the same time be perfectly equalized and assimilated in their pos-sessions, their opinions, and their passions.

A republic, by which I mean a government in which the scheme of representation takes place, opens a different prospect and promises the cure for which we are seeking. Let us examine the points in which it varies from pure democracy, and we shall comprehend both the nature of the cure and the efficacy which it must derive from the Union.

The two great points of difference between a democracy and a republic are: first, the delegation of the government, in the latter, to a small number of citizens elected by the rest; secondly, the greater number of citizens and greater sphere of country over which the latter may be extended.

The effect of the first difference is, on the one hand, to refine and enlarge the public views by passing them through the medium of a chosen body of citizens, whose wisdom may best discern the true interest of their country and whose patriotism and love of justice will be least likely to sacrifice it to temporary or partial considerations. Under such a regulation it may well happen that the public voice, pronounced by the representatives of the people, will be more consonant to the public good than if pronounced by the people themselves, convened for the purpose. On the other hand, the effect may be inverted. Men of factious tempers, of local prejudices, or of sinister designs, may, by intrigue, by corruption, or by other means, first obtain the suffrages, and then betray the interests of the people. The question resulting is, whether small or extensive republics are most favorable to the election of proper guardians of the public weal; and it is clearly decided in favor of the latter by two obvious considerations.

In the first place it is to be remarked that however small the republic may be the representatives must be raised to a certain number in order to guard against the cabals of a few; and that however large it may be they must be limited to a certain number in order to guard against the confusion of a multitude. Hence, the number of representatives in the two cases not being in proportion to that of the constituents, and being proportionally greatest in the small republic, it follows that if the proportion of fit characters be not less in the large than in the small republic, the former will present a greater option, and consequently a greater probability of a fit choice.

In the next place, as each representative will be chosen by a greater number of citizens in the large than in the small republic, it will be more difficult for unworthy candidates to practise with success the vicious arts by which elections are too often carried; and the suffrages of the people being more free, will be more likely to center on men who possess the most attractive merit and the most diffusive and established characters.

It must be confessed that in this, as in most other cases, there is a mean, on both sides of which inconveniences will be found to lie. By enlarging too much the number of electors, you render the representative too little acquainted with all their local circumstances and lesser interests; as by reducing it too much, you render him unduly attached to these, and too little fit to comprehend and pursue great and national objects. The federal Constitution forms a happy combination in this respect; the great and aggregate interests being referred to the national, the local and particular to the State legislatures.

The other point of difference is the greater number of citizens and extent of territory which may be brought within the compass of republican than of democratic government; and it is this circumstance principally which renders factious combinations less to be dreaded in the former than in the latter. The smaller the society, the fewer probably will be the distinct parties and interests composing it; the fewer the distinct parties and interests, the more frequently will a majority be found of the same party; and the smaller the number of individuals composing a majority, and the smaller the compass within which they are placed, the more easily will they concert and execute their plans of oppression. Extend the sphere and you take in a greater variety of parties and interests; you make it less probable that a majority of the whole will have a common motive to invade the rights of other citizens; or if such a common motive exists, it will be more difficult for all who feel it to discover their own strength and to act in unison with each other. Besides other impediments, it may be remarked that, where there is a consciousness of unjust or dishonorable purposes, communication is always checked by distrust in proportion to the number whose concurrence is necessary.

Hence, it clearly appears that the same advantage which a republic has over a democracy in controlling the effects of faction is enjoyed by a large over a small republic—is enjoyed by the Union over the States composing it. Does this advantage consist in the substitution of representatives whose enlightened views and virtuous sentiments render them superior to local prejudices and to schemes of injustice? It will not be denied that the representation of the Union will be most likely to possess these requisite endowments. Does it consist in the greater security afforded by a greater variety of parties, against the event of any one party being able to outnumber and oppress the rest? In an equal degree does the increased variety of parties comprised within the Union increase this security. Does it, in fine, consist in the greater obstacles opposed to the concert and accomplishment of the secret wishes of an unjust and interested majority? Here again the extent of the Union gives it the most palpable advantage.

The influence of factious leaders may kindle a flame within their particular States but will be unable to spread a general conflagration through the other States. A religious sect may degenerate into a political faction in a part of the Confederacy; but the variety of sects dispersed over the entire face of it must secure the national councils against any danger from that source. A rage for paper money, for an abolition of debts, for an equal division of property, or for any other improper or wicked project, will be less apt to pervade the whole body of the Union than a particular member of it, in the same proportion as such a malady is more likely to taint a particular county or district than an entire State.[2]

In the extent and proper structure of the Union, therefore, we behold a republican remedy for the diseases most incident to republican government. And according to the degree of pleasure and pride we feel in being republicans ought to be our zeal in cherishing the spirit and supporting the character of federalists.

PUBLIUS

---

2. The examples of factional objectives (for example, paper money's benefiting debtors at the expense of creditors) that Madison cites are drawn from the economic conflicts that pervaded the states in the 1780s. The movement for a new national constitution aimed to put an end to the possibility that radical factional goals might be achieved in the states.

Anti-Federalist Paper, 18 October 1787

BRUTUS

To the Citizens of the State of New-York

Perhaps this country never saw so critical a period in their political concerns. We have felt the feebleness of the ties by which these United-States are held together, and the want of sufficient energy in our present confederation, to manage, in some instances, our general concerns. Various expedients have been proposed to remedy these evils, but none have succeeded. At length a Convention of the states has been assembled, they have formed a constitution which will now, probably, be submitted to the people to ratify or reject, who are the fountain of all power, to whom alone it of right belongs to make or unmake constitutions, or forms of government, at their pleasure. The most important question that was ever proposed to your decision, or to the decision of any people under heaven, is before you, and you are to decide upon it by men of your own election, chosen specially for this purpose. If the constitution, offered to your acceptance, be a wise one, calculated to preserve the invaluable blessings of liberty, to secure the inestimable rights of mankind, and promote human happiness, then, if you accept it, you will lay a lasting foundation of happiness for millions yet unborn; generations to come will rise up and call you blessed.... But if, on the other hand, this form of government contains principles that will lead to the subversion of liberty—if it tends to establish a despotism, or, what is worse, a tyrannic aristocracy; then, if you adopt it, this only remaining asylum for liberty will be shut up, and posterity will execrate your memory....

With these few introductory remarks, I shall proceed to a consideration of this constitution:

The first question that presents itself on the subject is, whether a confederated government be the best for the United States or not. Or in other words, whether the thirteen United States should be reduced to one great republic, governed by one legislature, and under the direction of one executive and judicial; or whether they should continue thirteen confederated republics, under the direction and control of a supreme federal head for certain defined national purposes only?

This enquiry is important, because, although the government reported by the convention does not go to a perfect and entire consolidation,[1] yet it approaches so near to it, that it must, if executed, certainly and infallibly terminate in it.

This government is to possess absolute and uncontrollable power, legislative, executive and judicial, with respect to every object to which it extends, for by the last clause of section 8th, article 1st, it is declared "that the Congress shall have power to make all laws which shall be necessary and proper for carrying into execution the foregoing powers, and all other powers vested by this constitution, in the government of the United States; or in any department or office thereof." And by the 6th article, it is declared "that this constitution, and the laws of the United States, which shall be made in pursuance thereof, and the treaties made, or which shall be made, under the authority of the United States, shall be the supreme law of the land; and the judges in every state shall be bound thereby, any thing in the constitution, or law of any state to the contrary notwithstanding." It appears from these articles that there is no need of any intervention of the state governments, between the Congress and the people, to execute any one power vested in the general government, and that the constitution and laws of every state are nullified and declared void, so far as they are or shall be inconsistent with this constitution, or the laws made in pursuance of it, or with treaties made under the authority of the United States.—The government then, so far as it extends, is a complete one, and not a confederation. It is as much one complete government as that of New-York or Massachusetts, has as absolute and perfect powers to make and execute all laws, to appoint officers, institute courts, declare offences, and annex penalties, with respect to every object to which it extends, as any other in the world. So far therefore as its powers reach, all ideas of confederation are given up and lost. It is true this government is limited to certain objects, or to speak more properly, some small degree of power is still left to the states, but a little attention to the powers vested in the general government, will convince every candid man, that if it is capable of being executed, all that is reserved for the individual states must very soon be annihilated, except so far as they are barely necessary to the organization of the general government. The powers of the general legislature extend to every case that is of the least importance—there is nothing valuable to human nature, nothing dear to freemen, but what is within its power. It has authority to make laws which will affect the lives, the liberty, and property of every man in the United States; nor can the constitution or laws of any state, in any way prevent or impede the full and complete execution of every power given. The legislative power is competent to lay taxes, duties, imposts, and excises—there is no limitation to this power, unless it be said that the clause which directs the use to which those taxes, and duties shall be applied, may be said to be a limitation: but this is no restriction of the power at all, for by this clause they are to be applied to pay the debts and provide for the common defence and general welfare of the

---

1. The Anti-Federalists charged that the proposed Constitution aimed not at federalism (a division of powers between the national government and the state governments) but at consolidation (the centralization of all powers in the national government).

United States; but the legislature have authority to contract debts at their discretion; they are the sole judges of what is necessary to provide for the common defence, and they only are to determine what is for the general welfare; this power therefore is neither more nor less, than a power to lay and collect taxes, imposts, and excises, at their pleasure; not only [is] the power to lay taxes unlimited, as to the amount they may require, but it is perfect and absolute to raise them in any mode they please. No state legislature, or any power in the state governments, have any more to do in carrying this into effect, than the authority of one state has to do with that of another. In the business therefore of laying and collecting taxes, the idea of confederation is totally lost, and that of one entire republic is embraced....

Let us now proceed to enquire, as I at first proposed, whether it be best the thirteen United States should be reduced to one great republic, or not? It is here taken for granted, that all agree in this, that whatever government we adopt, it ought to be a free one; that it should be so framed as to secure the liberty of the citizens of America, and such a one as to admit of a full, fair, and equal representation of the people. The question then will be, whether a government thus constituted, and founded on such principles, is practicable, and can be exercised over the whole United States, reduced into one state?

If respect is to be paid to the opinion of the greatest and wisest men who have ever thought or wrote on the science of government, we shall be constrained to conclude, that a free republic cannot succeed over a country of such immense extent, containing such a number of inhabitants, and these encreasing in such rapid progression as that of the whole United States. Among the many illustrious authorities which might be produced to this point, I shall content myself with quoting only two. The one is the baron de Montesquieu, spirit of laws, chap. xvi. vol. I [book VIII].[2] "It is natural to a republic to have only a small territory, otherwise it cannot long subsist. In a large republic there are men of large fortunes, and consequently of less moderation; there are trusts too great to be placed in any single subject; he has interest of his own; he soon begins to think that he may be happy, great and glorious, by oppressing his fellow citizens; and that he may raise himself to grandeur on the ruins of his country. In a large republic, the public good is sacrificed to a thousand views; it is subordinate to exceptions, and depends on accidents. In a small one, the interest of the public is easier perceived, better understood, and more within the reach of every citizen; abuses are of less extent, and of course are less protected." Of the same opinion is the marquis Beccaria.[3]

History furnishes no example of a free republic, any thing like the extent of the United States. The Grecian republics were of small extent; so also was that of the Romans. Both of these, it is true, in process of time, extended their conquests over large territories of country; and the consequence was, that their

---

2. Baron Charles de Montesquieu was an eighteenth-century French political theorist whose ideas were highly influential in the era of the American Revolution and the Constitution.

3. Cesare Beccaria was an eighteenth-century Italian legal philosopher.

governments were changed from that of free governments to those of the most tyrannical that ever existed in the world.

Not only the opinion of the greatest men, and the experience of mankind, are against the idea of an extensive republic, but a variety of reasons may be drawn from the reason and nature of things, against it. In every government, the will of the sovereign is the law. In despotic governments, the supreme authority being lodged in one, his will is law, and can be as easily expressed to a large extensive territory as to a small one. In a pure democracy the people are the sovereign, and their will is declared by themselves; for this purpose they must all come together to deliberate, and decide. This kind of government cannot be exercised, therefore, over a country of any considerable extent; it must be confined to a single city, or at least limited to such bounds as that the people can conveniently assemble, be able to debate, understand the subject submitted to them, and declare their opinion concerning it.

In a free republic, although all laws are derived from the consent of the people, yet the people do not declare their consent by themselves in person, but by representatives, chosen by them, who are supposed to know the minds of their constituents, and to be possessed of integrity to declare this mind.

In every free government, the people must give their assent to the laws by which they are governed. This is the true criterion between a free government and an arbitrary one. The former are ruled by the will of the whole, expressed in any manner they may agree upon; the latter by the will of one, or a few. If the people are to give their assent to the laws, by persons chosen and appointed by them, the manner of the choice and the number chosen, must be such, as to possess, be disposed, and consequently qualified to declare the sentiments of the people; for if they do not know, or are not disposed to speak the sentiments of the people, the people do not govern, but the sovereignty is in a few. Now, in a large extended country, it is impossible to have a representation, possessing the sentiments, and of integrity, to declare the minds of the people, without having it so numerous and unwieldy, as to be subject in great measure to the inconveniency of a democratic government.

The territory of the United States is of vast extent; it now contains near three millions of souls, and is capable of containing much more than ten times that number. Is it practicable for a country, so large and so numerous as they will soon become, to elect a representation, that will speak their sentiments, without their becoming so numerous as to be incapable of transacting public business? It certainly is not.

In a republic, the manners, sentiments, and interests of the people should be similar. If this be not the case, there will be a constant clashing of opinions; and the representatives of one part will be continually striving against those of the other. This will retard the operations of government, and prevent such conclusions as will promote the public good. If we apply this remark to the condition of the United States, we shall be convinced that it forbids that we should be one government. The United States includes a variety of climates. The productions of the different parts of the union are very variant, and their interests, of consequence, diverse. Their manners and habits differ as much as their climates and productions; and their sentiments are by no means coincident. The laws and customs of the several states are, in many respects, very diverse, and in some opposite; each would be in favor of its own interests and customs, and, of consequence, a legislature, formed of representatives from the respective parts, would not only be too numerous to act with any care or decision, but would be composed of such heterogenous and discordant principles, as would constantly be contending with each other.

The laws cannot be executed in a republic, of an extent equal to that of the United States, with promptitude.

The magistrates in every government must be supported in the execution of the laws, either by an armed force, maintained at the public expence for that purpose; or by the people turning out to aid the magistrate upon his command, in case of resistance.

In despotic governments, as well as in all the monarchies of Europe, standing armies are kept up to execute the commands of the prince or the magistrate, and are employed for this purpose when occasion requires: But they have always proved the destruction of liberty, and [are] abhorrent to the spirit of a free republic. In England, where they depend upon the parliament for their annual support, they have always been complained of as oppressive and unconstitutional, and are seldom employed in executing of the laws; never except on extraordinary occasions, and then under the direction of a civil magistrate.

A free republic will never keep a standing army to execute its laws. It must depend upon the support of its citizens. But when a government is to receive its support from the aid of the citizens, it must be so constructed as to have the confidence, respect, and affection of the people. Men who, upon the call of the magistrate, offer themselves to execute the laws, are influenced to do it either by affection to the government, or from fear; where a standing army is at hand to punish offenders, every man is actuated by the latter principle, and therefore, when the magistrate calls, will obey: but, where this is not the case, the government must rest for its support upon the confidence and respect which the people have for their government and laws. The body of the people being attached, the government will always be sufficient to support and execute its laws, and to operate upon the fears of any faction which may be opposed to it, not only to prevent an opposition to the execution of the laws themselves, but also to compel the most of them to aid the magistrate; but the people will not be likely to have such confidence in their rulers, in a republic so extensive as the United States, as necessary for these purposes. The confidence which the people have in their rulers, in a free republic, arises from their knowing them, from their being responsible to them for their conduct, and from the power they have of displacing them when they misbehave: but in a republic of the extent of this continent, the people in general would be acquainted with very few of their rulers: the people at large would know little of their proceedings, and it would be extremely difficult to change them.... The consequence will be, they will have no confidence in their legislature, suspect them of ambitious views, be jealous of every measure they adopt, and will not support the laws they pass. Hence the government will be nerveless and inefficient, and no way will be left to render it otherwise, but by establishing an armed force to execute the laws at the point of the bayonet—a government of all others the most to be dreaded.

In a republic of such vast extent as the United-States, the legislature cannot attend to the various concerns and wants of its different parts. It cannot be sufficiently numerous to be acquainted with the local condition and wants of the different districts, and if it could, it is impossible it should have sufficient time to attend to and provide for all the variety of cases of this nature, that would be continually arising.

In so extensive a republic, the great officers of government would soon become above the control of the people, and abuse their power to the purpose of aggrandizing themselves, and oppressing them. The trust committed to the executive offices, in a country of the extent of the United-States, must be various and of magnitude. The command of all the troops and navy of the republic, the appointment of officers, the power of pardoning offences, the collecting of all the public revenues, and the power of expending them, with a number of other powers, must be lodged and exercised in every state, in the hands of a few. When these are attended with great honor and emolument, as they always will be in large states, so as greatly to interest men to pursue them, and to be proper objects for ambitious and designing men, such men will be ever restless in their pursuit after them. They will use the power, when they have acquired it, to the purposes of gratifying their own interest and ambition, and it is scarcely possible, in a very large republic, to call them to account for their misconduct, or to prevent their abuse of power.

These are some of the reasons by which it appears, that a free republic cannot long subsist over a country of the great extent of these states. If then this new constitution is calculated to consolidate the thirteen states into one, as it evidently is, it ought not to be adopted....

Discussion Questions

1. How do the Federalists and the Anti-Federalists view human nature? Why does Madison think individuals are "much more disposed to vex and oppress each other than to co-operate for their common good"? Why is Brutus more hopeful that, under the proper political circumstances, citizens will cooperate for their common good? Whose perspective on human nature do you find more persuasive?

2. How do the Federalists and the Anti-Federalists view participation by ordinary citizens at the local level? Why does Madison feel that "pure democracy" leads to disaster? Why does Brutus have a more positive view of politics within local communities? Do you think a "face-to-face" politics of ordinary citizens fosters individual growth and public spirit, or does it produce ignorant decisions and unfairness to minorities?

3. How do the Federalists and the Anti-Federalists view the role of elected representatives? Why does Madison want representatives to deliberate at

a distance from the demands of their constituents? Why does Brutus want representatives to be closely tied to their constituents' ideas and interests? Do you think, like Madison, that representatives should be trustees who do what they think is best for the country, or do you believe, like Brutus, that representatives should be delegates who follow the expressed wishes of their constituents?

4. In what ways is the debate between Madison and Brutus reflected in today's political debates? In what ways have the arguments changed? Do contemporary defenders of a large policy role for the federal government share Madison's fundamental assumptions? Do contemporary critics of the federal government share Brutus's fundamental assumptions?

Suggested Readings and Internet Resources

The best source on the debate between the Federalists and the Anti-Federalists is the original texts themselves. For inexpensive editions, see Clinton Rossiter, ed., *The Federalist Papers* (New York: Mentor Books, 1999), and Ralph Ketcham, ed., *The Anti-Federalist Papers* (New York: Signet, 2003). On the political ideas of the founding era, see Gordon S. Wood, *The Creation of the American Republic, 1776–1787* (Chapel Hill: University of North Carolina Press, 1998), and Jack N. Rakove, *Original Meanings: Politics and Ideas in the Making of the Constitution* (New York: Alfred A. Knopf, 1996). In *If Men Were Angels: James Madison and the Heartless Empire of Reason* (Lawrence: University Press of Kansas, 1995), Richard K. Matthews provides a provocative interpretation of the great Federalist's political theory. Instructive commentaries on the political philosophy of the Anti-Federalists are Herbert J. Storing, *What the Anti-Federalists Were For* (Chicago: University of Chicago Press, 1981), and Saul Cornell, *The Other Founders: Anti-Federalism and the Dissenting Tradition in America, 1788–1828* (Chapel Hill: University of North Carolina Press, 1999).

Emory Law School
www.law.emory.edu/index.php
This searchable index of information on the Constitution and *The Federalist Papers* requires a forms-capable browser.

FoundingFathers.info
www.foundingfathers.info/federalistpapers
This site provides all of *The Federalist Papers* for downloading.

Chapter 2

✳

Democracy: Overrated or Undervalued?

Almost everybody in America believes in democracy. When interviewers ask Americans basic questions of majority rule, equality of opportunity, or individual freedom, more than 95 percent profess a belief in democratic values. As our introduction to this book suggests, however, once we probe a bit deeper into what Americans think democracy means, we find that they are not at all of one mind about how far democracy should extend into political, social, and economic life. Elite democrats believe that democracy is a valuable method for selecting those who will govern us, but they are skeptical about the political capacities and interests of ordinary citizens and want important decisions left to those with experience and expertise. Popular democrats distrust elites as potentially self-serving and believe that under the right circumstances ordinary citizens are both capable of and entitled to a significant share in deciding public matters.

The debate over democracy began at the time of the nation's founding and has continued to this day. In the previous chapter, we saw Federalists and Anti-Federalists arguing about whether the American experiment in self-government should rest on elite democracy or popular democracy. To James Madison, only a national republic manned by a deliberative elite, who could filter out the irrational passions of the public, could sustain the American experiment. In the eyes of Brutus, this national republic would breed an oppressive aristocracy, who would crush popular democracy, which must be rooted in law-abiding and virtuous citizens and flourish at the local and state levels.

Although the Federalists prevailed in the original American debate over democracy, securing the ratification of the Constitution, nineteenth-century America looked more like the Anti-Federalists' (and Thomas Jefferson's) vision of democracy than the Federalists' vision. For most of the century, political and economic life was small-scale and decentralized, with the federal government in Washington, D.C., exercising only limited powers. Nineteenth-century America witnessed the establishment of the most democratic society the world had contained since the Golden Age of democracy in ancient Athens. Levels of political involvement and rates of voting among ordinary citizens were remarkably high—much higher, in fact, than they would be a century later. To be sure, this was a white man's democracy; Native Americans, African Americans, and women paid a high price for white men's freedoms, and the latter two groups had to launch long and painful struggles for democratic inclusion that would not achieve much success until the twentieth century.

Between the Civil War and World War I, the United States evolved from being a largely agrarian and decentralized society into an urbanized and industrialized nation. This transformation called into question the popular democratic assumptions held by the heirs of the Anti-Federalists and Jefferson. Could ordinary citizens obtain, understand, and act on the increasingly complex information that characterized modern American society? America's premier journalist, Walter Lippmann, argued in the 1920s that ordinary citizens viewed the world through stereotypes, simplistic pictures that distorted reality, and that effective government for the industrial age required a greater emphasis on trained, dispassionate experts. Agreeing with Lippmann that the American public had been eclipsed by forces that seemed beyond its control, America's premier philosopher, John Dewey, warned of the elitist tendencies of Lippmann's experts. Dewey sought to revive popular democracy in face-to-face communities where ordinary citizens, informed by the latest findings of social science, would participate in public affairs.

In the 1950s (like the 1920s, a decade of apparent public apathy), Lippmann's argument received reinforcement from the empirical surveys conducted by political scientists. Most Americans, these surveys suggested, were not very interested in political life, did not know much about public affairs, and did not participate at very high levels in politics. Prevailing American conceptions about democracy would have to be modified, many political scientists then argued, to reflect what Robert Dahl called "citizenship without politics." However, in the 1960s a minority of political scientists began to object, on both theoretical and empirical grounds, to this redefinition of democracy, claiming that the new perspective was less democratic realism than it was democratic elitism. These critics found support among the emerging political movements that would mark the 1960s as a decade of popular democratic upsurge. Students for a Democratic Society (SDS), the most important organization of the '60s New Left, gave the period its political watchword: *participatory democracy*.

Our selections in this chapter are two of the more recent versions of the persisting debate over democracy. John Mueller, a political scientist, attacks what he considers to be the romantic and unrealistic conception of democracy put forward by popular democrats. All that is required for democracy, Mueller contends, is a political system that eschews violence and that allows citizens to criticize, pressure, and remove those in power. Democracy, he suggests, will always consist of a messy, unequal conflict for advantage among special interests. What it will never achieve, he argues, are the misty ideals of popular democrats: political equality, participation, and an enlightened citizenry. Holding democracy to these standards only fosters cynicism. Mueller's analysis updates the classic elite democratic perspective of Madison, Lippmann, and Dahl.

Paul Rogat Loeb, a political activist, represents the popular democratic perspective of the Anti-Federalists, Jefferson, Dewey, and the SDS. He ascribes the widespread cynicism about politics not to the romantic ideals of popular democrats but to the skeptical views of public involvement broadcast by the dominant forces in American society. "We've all but forgotten," he writes, "that public participation is the very soul of democratic citizenship, and how much it can enrich our lives." In our selection, Loeb tells the story of Pete Knutson (one of many stories in his book), a commercial fisherman who organized his fellow fishermen, environmentalists, and Native Americans to defeat an initiative by large industries that would have destroyed salmon spawning grounds. Loeb argues that active citizenship is required both to fulfill our responsibility to take care of the common good and to grow as individuals in psychological and spiritual depth.

Evaluating the debate between Mueller and Loeb should help to clarify your own conception of democracy. Do you believe, with Mueller, that Americans have many more interesting things to do than spend their time on political pursuits? Or do you believe, with Loeb, that political involvement is necessary for a sense of freedom and personal dignity? Do you believe, with Mueller, that self-interest and inequality will always characterize democracy and that attempts to reduce their influence through political and economic reforms will inevitably fail? Or do you believe, with Loeb, that politics can also reflect our more social impulses and can redress political and economic injustices? Above all, do you agree with Mueller that acceptance of elite democracy is the only realistic perspective, or do you agree with Loeb that the abandonment of popular democracy is a surrender to cynicism?

Democracy's Romantic Myths

JOHN MUELLER

There is a famous Norman Rockwell painting that purports to portray democracy in action. It depicts a New England town meeting in which a working-man has risen in a contentious situation to present his point of view. His rustic commonsense, it appears, has cut through the indecisiveness and bickering to provide a consensual solution to the problem at hand, and the others in the picture are looking up at him admiringly.

As it happens, that misty-eyed, idealized snapshot has almost nothing to do with democracy in actual practice. Democracy is not a process in which one shining idea conquers all as erstwhile contenders fall into blissful consensus. Rather, it is an extremely disorderly muddle in which clashing ideas and interests (all of them "special") do unkempt and unequal, if peaceful, battle and in which ideas are often reduced to slogans, data to distorted fragments, evidence to gestures, and arguments to poses. Speculation is rampant, caricature is routine, and posturing is de rigueur. If one idea wins out, it is likely to be severely compromised in the process, and no one goes away entirely reconciled or happy. And there is rarely a sense of completion or finality or permanence: in a democracy, as Tod Lindberg points out, "the fat lady never sings." It's a mess, and the only saving grace is that other methods for reaching decisions are even worse.

... I develop an approach to democracy that contrasts substantially with the romantic Rockwell ideal. It stresses petition and lobbying—the chaotic and distinctly nonconsensual combat of "special interests"—as the dominant and central characteristic of democracy and it suggests that while elections are useful and often valuable in a democracy, they may not be absolutely necessary. I also argue that democracy in practice is not about equality, but rather about the freedom to become politically unequal, and that it functions not so much by rule by the majority as by minority rule with majority acquiescence....

... I also contrast democracy with other governmental forms. Although the advantage is only comparative, democracy seems to do better at generating effective governments, choosing leaders, addressing minority concerns, creating a livable society, and functioning effectively with real, flawed human beings....

In defining democracy, it is particularly important, I think, to separate the essential institution itself from the operating devices that are commonly associated with it—mechanisms like written constitutions, the separation of powers or "checks and balances" (including an independent judiciary), and even elections. Any definition of democracy is inadequate, I think, if it can logically be taken to suggest that Britain (which has neither a written constitution nor separation of powers) is not a democracy or that Switzerland did not become one until 1971 (when women were finally given the vote)....

In my view, democracy is characterized by government that is necessarily and routinely responsive—although this responsiveness is not always even, fair, or equal. It comes into effect when the people effectively agree not to use violence to replace the leadership, and the leadership effectively leaves them free to criticize, to pressure, to organize, and to try to dislodge it by any other means. This approach can be used to set up a sort of sliding scale of governmental forms. An *authoritarian* government may effectively and sometimes intentionally allow a degree of opposition—a limited amount of press disagreement, for example, or the freedom to complain privately, something sometimes known as the freedom of conversation. But it will not tolerate organized attempts to replace it, even if they are peaceful. A *totalitarian* government does not allow even those limited freedoms. On the other end of the scale is *anarchy*: a condition which holds when a government "allows" the use of violence to try to overthrow it—presumably mainly out of weakness or ineffectiveness.

Authoritarian and even totalitarian governments can sometimes be responsive as well, of course. But their responsiveness depends on the will and the mindset of the leadership. By contrast, democracy is *routinely, necessarily* responsive: because people are free to develop and use peaceful methods to criticize, pressure, and replace the leadership, the leaders must pay attention to their critics and petitioners.

It seems to me that the formal and informal institutional mechanisms variously applied in democracies to facilitate this core consideration are secondary—though this does not mean that all institutions are equally fair or efficient. One can embellish this central democratic relationship with concerns about ethos, way of life, social culture, shared goals, economic correlates, common purposes, customs, preferred policy outcomes, norms, patriotism, shared traditions, and the like. These issues are interesting, but ... they don't seem to be essential or necessary to the functioning of democracy....

Apathy

... One of the great, neglected aspects of free speech is the freedom not to listen. As Hubert Humphrey reportedly put it, "The right to be heard doesn't automatically include the right to be taken seriously."[1] It is no easy task to persuade free people to agree with one's point of view, but as any experienced demagogue is likely to point out with some exasperation, what is most difficult of all is to get them to pay attention at all. People, particularly those in a free, open society, are regularly barraged by shysters and schemers, by people with new angles and neglected remedies, with purveyors of panaceas and palliatives. Very few are successful—and even those who do succeed, including Adolf Hitler, owe their success as much to luck as to skill.

... [Such] apathy helps importantly with the problem that is usually called the tyranny of the majority. It is not difficult to find a place where the majority harbors a considerable hatred for a minority—indeed, it may be difficult to find one where this is not the case. Polls in the United States regularly have found plenty of people who would cheerfully restrict not only the undeserving rich, but also homosexuals, atheists, accused Communists, Nazi paraders, flag burners, and people who like to shout unpleasant words and perpetrate unconventional messages. But it is not easy to get this majority to do anything about it—after all, that would require a certain amount of work.

Because of apathy, therefore, people, sometimes despite their political predispositions, are effectively tolerant. For democracies the danger is not so much that agile demagogues will play on hatreds and weaknesses to fabricate a vindictive mob-like tyranny of the majority: the perversions of the French Revolution have proved unusual. More to be feared, it seems, is the tyranny of a few who obtain bland acquiescence from the uninterested, and essentially unaffected, many....

---

1. Hubert Humphrey was a Democratic senator from Minnesota and served as vice president under President Lyndon B. Johnson.

The Quest for Political Equality

... The notion that all men are created equal suggests that people are *born* equal—that is, that none should necessarily be denied political opportunity merely because of their hereditary entrance into the wrong social or economic class or because they do not adhere to the visions or dictates of a particular ideological group. The notion does not, however, suggest that people must necessarily be equal in their impact on the political system, but this damaging extrapolation is often made by reformers, at least as a goal to be quested after.

An extensive study on the issue of equality by a team of political scientists finds, none too surprisingly, that people in a real democracy like the United States differ in the degree to which they affect the political system. Political effectiveness, the study concludes, depends on three varying factors: resources, especially time, money, and skills; psychological engagement with politics; and "access to networks through which individuals can be recruited to political life." The variance of effectiveness, the authors then conclude, poses a "threat to the democratic principle of equal protection of interests." Another analyst, reviewing their findings, makes a similar observation: "liberal democracies fail to live up to the norm of equal responsiveness to the interests of each citizen."

But instead of seeking to reform the system or the people who make it up, we may want instead to abandon, or at least substantially to modify, the principle and the norm. They clearly express a romantic perspective about democracy, a perspective which has now been fully and repeatedly disconfirmed in practice. Democracies are responsive and attentive to the interests of the citizenry—at least when compared to other forms of government—but they are nowhere near equally responsive to the interests of each citizen.

Related is the perennial clamor against "special interests." As the futile struggle for campaign finance reform in the United States suggests, people who want or need to influence public policy are very likely to find ways to do so no matter how clever the laws that seek to restrict them. As Gil Troy observes, "for all the pious hopes, the goal of the Watergate-era reforms—to remove the influence of money from presidential elections—was, in hard and inescapable fact, ridiculous." (He also notes that the entire cost of the 1996 election campaigns was about 25 percent of what Procter & Gamble routinely spends every year to market its products.) A rare voice of realism amid all the sanctimonious, politically correct bluster from politicians about campaign finance reform in the United States in the 1990s was that of Senator Robert Bennett of Utah: "rich people will always have influence in politics, and the solution is not to create barriers that cause the rich people to spend even more money to hire lawyers and consultants to find ways around the law to get the same results."

In the end, "special interests" can be effectively reined in only by abandoning democracy itself, because their activities are absolutely vital to the form. Indeed, it is quite incredible that two prominent Washington reporters merely deem it "simplistic" to argue that "people with common interests should not attempt to sway government policy." In a democracy the free, competitive play of "special interests" is fundamental. To reform this out of existence would be uncomprehending and profoundly antidemocratic.

Most of the agitation against political inequality is focused on the special privileges business is presumed to enjoy. For example, concern is voiced that the attention of public officials can be differently arrested: "a phone call from the CEO of a major employer in the district may carry considerably more weight than one from an unknown constituent." It is possible, of course, that the unweighty and unknown constituent has just come up with a plan which will achieve permanent worldwide bliss in the course of the next six months, but, since there are only twenty-four hours in a day, public officials (like the rest of us) are forced to ration their time, and they are probably correct to assume, as a first approximation at least, that the concerns of a major employer are likely to be of wider relevance to more people than are those of the hapless lone constituent.

But if the CEO's access advantage to a time-pressured politician is somehow reprehensible and must be reformed, what about other inequalities—that is, why focus only on economic ones? A telephone call from a big-time political columnist like David Broder of the *Washington Post* is likely to get the politician's attention even faster than that of the CEO. Should the influential David Broder hold off on his next column until the rest of us deserving unknowns have had a chance to put in our two cents in the same forum? Inequalities like these are simply and unavoidably endemic to the whole political system as, indeed, they are to life itself. It may be possible to reduce this inequality, but it is difficult to imagine a reform that could possibly raise the political impact of the average factory worker—or even of the average business executive—remotely to equal that enjoyed by Broder....

The Quest for Participation

Democratic theorists, idealists, and image-makers maintain that "democratic states require ... participation in order to flourish," or that "a politically active citizenry is a requisite of any theory of democracy," or that "democracy was built on the principle that political participation was not only the privilege of every man, but a necessity in ensuring the efficiency and prosperity of the democratic system," or that "high levels of electoral participation are essential for guaranteeing that government represents the public as a whole," or that "to make a democracy that works, we need citizens who are engaged."

But we now have over two hundred years of experience with living, breathing, messy democracy, and truly significant participation has almost never been achieved anywhere. Since democracy exists, *it simply can't be true* that wide participation is a notable requirement, requisite, need, or necessity for it to prosper or work. Routinely, huge numbers of citizens even—in fact, especially—in "mature" democracies simply decline to participate, and the trend in participation seems to be, if anything, mostly downward. In the United States, nearly half of those eligible fail to vote even in high-visibility elections and only a few percent ever actively participate in politics. The final winner of a recent election for the mayor of Rochester, N.Y., received only about 6 percent of the vote of the total electorate. (However, he is a very popular choice: if everybody had voted, he would almost certainly have achieved the same victory.) Switzerland is Europe's oldest democracy, and it also boasts the continent's lowest voter turnout.

Statistics like these frequently inspire a great deal of concern—after all, it is argued, "political participation" is one of the "basic democratic ideals." But it may be more useful to reshape democratic theories and ideals to take notice of the elemental fact that democracy works even though it often fails to inspire very much in the way of participation from its citizenry.

And it might also be asked, why, exactly, is it so important for citizens to participate? Most analyses suggest that nonvoters do not differ all that much from voters in their policy concerns, though there are some (controversial) suggestions that leftist parties might do a bit better in some countries if everyone were forced to vote. However, once in office, responsible leftist and rightist parties both face the same constraining conditions and, despite their ideologies and campaign promises, often do not differ all that much from each other in their policies—frequently to the disillusionment and disgust of their supporters who may come to feel they have been conned.

Some hold voting to be important because "of the problem of legitimacy." The idea is that "as fewer and fewer citizens participate in elections, the extent to which government truly rests on the consent of the governed may be called into question"; moreover the "quality of the link between elites and citizens" will erode. Actually, such callings into question seem to happen mostly when a candidate, like Bill Clinton in 1992, gets less than half of the recorded *vote*—and these are principally inspired by partisan maneuvering by the losers to undercut any claim that the winner has a mandate. And in local elections, the often exceedingly low turnout and participation levels rarely even cause much notice: I have yet to hear anyone suggest that the mayor of Rochester is illegitimate or "unlinked" because hardly anybody managed to make it to the polls when he was elected.

Moreover, it really seems to strain credulity to suggest that "if people feel distant from the electoral process, they can take no pride in the successes of the government." *No* pride? It seems that even nonvoters celebrated victory in the Gulf War. Or that nonvoters "avoid responsibility for the problems facing the nation." But nonvoters seem to have no more difficulty than voters in routinely (and sometimes even correctly) blaming the politicians for whatever is wrong. And it is simply too glib to conclude that "if you don't vote, you don't count." If that were true, women would never have gotten the vote, slavery would still exist, and there would never have been prison reform or legislation aiding the homeless.

There are also claims that low turnout levels "contribute to the problem of an unrepresentative policy agenda." But it is difficult to understand what this could possibly mean—or, better, what a "representative policy agenda" would look like. Agendas are set by people actively trying to pursue their interests; they are not out there somewhere in the miasma waiting for us objectively to snap them up. As Steven Rosenstone and John Mark Hansen argue, "political participation is the product of strategic interactions of citizens and leaders." People "participate when politicians, political parties, interest groups, and activists persuade them to get involved." Thus, there will not be an "ideal" or even "normal" degree of participation. Rather, participation will increase when "salient issues reach the public agenda … when governments approach crucial decisions … when competitive election campaigns stimulate, when social movements inspire."

Hundreds of years of experience, then, suggest that the pursuit of participation for the sake of participation is rather quixotic. Instead, applying a philosophical observation attributed to impresario Sol Hurok, perhaps we should accept the fact that "if people don't want to come, nothing will stop them." Moreover, discontent and cynicism about the system itself (and consequently perhaps nonvoting) are increased when alarmists passionately lament that many people, as they have throughout democratic eternity, freely decide to pursue interests they find more pressing than politics, or manage to come up with more interesting things to do on election day than to go through the often inconsequential ritual of voting. (Sometimes, actually, nonvoters, by the very act of not voting, may be indicating their concerns and preferences more eloquently than those who actually do vote.)

The Quest for an Enlightened Citizenry

"If a nation expects to be ignorant and free," Thomas Jefferson once said, "it expects what never was and never will be." Pretty much ever since those memorable words were issued, the United States has managed to be both, and with considerable alacrity.

Fortunately for America, eternal vigilance has not proven to be the price of democracy—it can come quite a bit cheaper. In ideal democracies, James Bryce once suggested, "the average citizen will give close and constant attention to public affairs, recognizing that this is his interest as well as his duty"—but not in real ones.[2] And Horace Mann's ringing prediction that "with universal suffrage, there must be universal elevation of character, intellectual and moral, or there will be universal mismanagement and calamity" has proven untrue.[3]

Nonetheless, democratic idealists continue to insist that "democracies require responsibility." Or they contend that democracy "relies on informed popular judgment and political vigilance." Or they persist in defining democracy "as a political system in which people actively attend to what is significant." One would think it would be obvious by now that democracy works despite the fact that it often fails to inspire or require very much in the

---

2. James Bryce was a British writer who published a classic study, *The American Commonwealth*, in the late nineteenth century.

3. Horace Mann was a nineteenth-century educational reformer.

way of responsibility and knowledge from its citizenry. Democracy does feed on the bandying about of information, but that is going to happen pretty much automatically when people are free to ferret it out and to exchange it. Democracy clearly does not require that people generally be well informed, responsible, or actively attentive.

Recent surveys find that around half the American people haven't the foggiest idea which party controls the Senate or what the first ten amendments of the Constitution are called or what the Fifth Amendment does or who their congressional representative or senators are. Moreover, this lack of knowledge has generally increased (particularly when education is controlled for) since the 1940s. A month after the Republican victory in the 1994 election that propelled the vocal and energetic Newt Gingrich into the speakership of the House of Representatives and into the media stratosphere, a national poll found that 50 percent hadn't heard enough about Gingrich even to have an opinion about him. Four months later, after endless publicity over Gingrich's varying fortunes and after *Time* magazine had designated him its "Man of the Year," that number had not changed (so much for the power of the press). In a poll conducted two years later, half were still unable to indicate who the speaker was. Meanwhile, less than 20 percent guessed correctly that over the preceding twenty years air pollution and the number of the elderly living in poverty had declined, and most people were of the wildly distorted impression that foreign aid comprised a larger share of the federal budget than Medicare.

One recent analysis observes that "for the last 200 years the United States has survived as a stable democracy, despite continued evidence of an uninformed public." It also notes that "in theory, a democracy requires knowledgeable citizens." Although it then labels the contradictory condition "the paradox of modern democracy," it seems, rather, that it is the theory that should be called into question, not the reality.

Moreover, it may not be entirely clear why one should expect people to spend a lot of time worrying about politics when democratic capitalism not only leaves them free to choose other ways to get their kicks, but in its seemingly infinite quest for variety is constantly developing seductive distractions. Democratic theorists and idealists may be intensely interested in government and its processes, but it verges on the arrogant, even the self-righteous, to suggest that other people are somehow inadequate or derelict unless they share the same curious passion. Many studies have determined that it is the politically interested who are the most politically active. It is also doubtless true that those most interested in unidentified flying objects are the ones most likely to join UFO clubs. UFO enthusiasts, however, get no special credit by political theorists for servicing their particular obsession, while politics junkies are lauded because they seem to be fulfilling a higher, theory-sanctified function.

In the end, the insistence that terrible things will happen unless the citizenry becomes addicted to C-SPAN can inspire cynicism about the process when it is observed that the Beverly Hillbillies (or whatever) enjoy vastly higher ratings.

The Active Citizen

PAUL ROGAT LOEB

In the personal realm, most Americans are thoughtful, caring, generous. We try to do our best by family and friends. At times we'll even stop to help another driver stranded with a roadside breakdown, or give some spare change to a stranger. But increasingly, a wall now separates each of us from the world out-side, and from others who've likewise taken refuge in their own private sanctu-aries. We've all but forgotten that public participation is the very soul of democratic citizenship, and how much it can enrich our lives.

However, the reason for our wholesale retreat from social involvement is not, I believe, that most of us feel all is well with the world. I live in Seattle, a city with a seemingly unstoppable economy. Yet every time I go downtown I see men and women with signs saying "I'll work for food," or "Homeless vet. Please help." Their suffering diminishes me as a human being. I also travel extensively, doing research and giving lectures throughout the country. Except in the wealthiest of enclaves, people everywhere say, "Things are hard here." America's economic boom has passed many of us by. We struggle to live on meager paychecks. We worry about layoffs, random violence, the rising cost of health care, and the miseducation of our kids. Too stretched to save, uncertain about Social Security, many of us wonder just how we'll survive when we get old. We feel overwhelmed, we say, and helpless to change things.

Even those of us who are economically comfortable seem stressed. We spend hours commuting on crowded freeways, and hours more at jobs whose demands never end. We complain that we don't have enough time left for fami-lies and friends. We worry about the kind of world we'll pass on to our grand-children. Then we also shrug and say there's nothing we can do.

To be sure, the issues we now face are complex—perhaps more so than in the past. How can we comprehend the moral implications of a world in which Nike pays Michael Jordan more to appear in its ads than it pays all the workers at its Indonesian shoe factories combined? Today the five hundred richest people on the planet control more wealth than the bottom three billion, half of the human population. Is it possible even to grasp the process that led to this most extraordinary imbalance? More important, how do we even begin to redress it?

Yet what leaves too many of us sitting on the sidelines is not only a lack of understanding of the complexities of our world. It's not only an absence of readily apparent ways to begin or resume public involvement. Certainly we need to decide for ourselves whether particular causes are wise or foolish—be they the politics of campaign finance reform, attempts to address the growing gap between rich and poor, or efforts to safeguard water, air, and wilderness. We need to identify and connect with worthy groups that take on these issues, whether locally or globally. But first we need to believe that our individual involvement is worthwhile, that what we might do in the public sphere will not be in vain.

This means we face a challenge that is as much psychological as political. As the Ethiopian proverb says, "He who conceals his disease cannot be cured." We need to understand our cultural diseases of callousness, shortsightedness, and denial, and learn what it will take to heal our society and heal our souls. How did so many of us become convinced that we can do nothing to affect our common future? And how have some other Americans managed to remove the cataracts from their vision and work powerfully for change?

When we do take a stand, we grow psychologically and spiritually. Pete Knutson is one of my oldest friends. During his twenty-five years as a commercial fisherman in Washington and Alaska, he's been forced, time and again, to respond to the steady degradation of salmon spawning grounds. "You'd have a hard time spawning, too, if you had a bulldozer in your bedroom," he says, explaining the destruction of once-rich salmon habitat by commercial development and timber industry clear-cutting. Pete could have simply accepted this degradation as fate, focusing on getting a maximum share of the dwindling fish populations. Instead, he's gradually built an alliance between Washington State fishermen, environmentalists, and Native American tribes, persuading them to work collectively to demand that the habitat be preserved and restored.

The cooperation Pete created didn't come easy: Washington's fishermen were historically individualistic and politically mistrustful, more inclined, in Pete's judgment, "to grumble or blame the Indians than to act." Now, with their new allies, they began to push for cleaner spawning streams, preservation of the Endangered Species Act, and an increased flow of water over major regional dams to help boost salmon runs. But large industrial interests, such as the aluminum companies, feared that these measures would raise their electricity costs or restrict their opportunities for development. So a few years ago they bankrolled a statewide initiative to regulate fishing nets in a way that would eliminate small family fishing operations.

"I think we may be toast," said Pete, when Initiative 640 first surfaced. In an Orwellian twist, its backers even presented the initiative as environmentally friendly, to mislead casual voters. It was called "Save Our Sealife," although fishermen soon rechristened it "Save Our Smelters." At first, those opposing 640 thought they had no chance of success: They were outspent, outstaffed, outgunned. Similar initiatives had already passed in Florida, Louisiana, and Texas, backed by similar industrial interests. I remember Pete sitting in a Seattle tavern with two fisherman friends, laughing bitterly and saying, "The three of us are going to take on the aluminum companies? We're going to beat Reynolds and Kaiser?"

But they refused to give up. Instead, Pete and his coworkers systematically enlisted the region's major environmental groups to campaign against the initiative. They worked with the media to explain the larger issues at stake. And they focused public attention on the measure's powerful financial backers, and their interest in its outcome. On election night, November 1995, Initiative 640 was defeated throughout the state. White fishermen, Native American activists, and Friends of the Earth staffers threw their arms around each other in victory. "I'm really proud of you, Dad," Pete's twelve-year-old son kept repeating. Pete was stunned.

"Everyone felt it was hopeless," Pete said, looking back. "But if we were going to lose, I wanted at least to put up a good fight. And we won because of all the earlier work we'd done, year after year, to build up our environmental relationships, get some credibility, and show that we weren't just in it for ourselves."

We often think of social involvement as noble but impractical. Yet as Pete's story attests, it can serve enlightened self-interest and the interests of others simultaneously, while giving us a sense of connection and purpose nearly impossible to find in purely private life. "It takes energy to act," said Pete. "But it's more draining to bury your anger, convince yourself you're powerless, and swallow whatever's handed to you. The times I've compromised my integrity and accepted something I shouldn't, the ghosts of my choices have haunted me. When you get involved in something meaningful, you make your life count. What you do makes a difference. It blows my mind that we beat 640 starting out with just a small group of people who felt it was wrong to tell lies."

In fighting to save the environment and his economic livelihood, Pete strengthened his own soul. How the rest of us might achieve something similar is not always clear. We often don't know where to start. Most of us would like to see people treated more justly, to have the earth accorded the respect it deserves, and to feel less pressure in our lives. But we find it hard to imagine having much of a role in this process. We mistrust our own ability to make a difference. The magnitude of the issues at hand, coupled with this sense of powerlessness, has led far too many of us to conclude that social involvement isn't worth the cost.

Such resignation isn't an innate response, or the creation of some inevitable fate. Rather, it's what psychologists call learned helplessness. Society has systematically taught us to ignore the ills we see, and leave them to others to handle. Understandably, we find it unsettling even to think about crises as huge and profound in their implications as the extinction of species, depletion of the ozone layer, and destruction of the rainforests. Or the desperate poverty that blights entire neighborhoods in our nation's largest cities. We're led to believe that if we can't solve every one of these kinds of problems, we shouldn't bother to become socially active at all. We're also taught to doubt our voice—to feel we lack either the time to properly learn and articulate the issues we care about, or the standing to speak out and be heard. To get socially involved, we believe, requires almost saint-like judgment, confidence, and character—a standard we can never meet. Whatever impulses toward involvement we might have, they're dampened by a culture that demeans idealism, enshrines cynicism, and makes us feel naïve for caring about our fellow human beings or the planet we inhabit....

Learned Helplessness

America's prevailing culture of cynicism insists that nothing we do can matter. It teaches us not to get involved in shaping the world we'll pass on to our children. It encourages us to leave such important decisions to others—whether they be corporate and government leaders, or social activists whose lifestyles seem impossibly selfless or foreign. Sadly, and ironically, in a country born of a democratic political revolution, to be American today is to be apolitical. Civic withdrawal has become our norm. To challenge this requires courage. It also requires creating a renewed definition of ourselves as citizens—something closer to the nation of active stakeholders that leaders like Thomas Jefferson had in mind.

The importance of citizens' direct participation in a democracy was expressed thousands of years ago, by the ancient Greeks. In fact, they used the word "idiot" for people incapable of involving themselves in civic life. Now, the very word "political" has become so debased in our culture that we use it to describe either trivial office power plays or the inherently corrupt world of elected leaders. We've lost sight of its original roots in the Greek notion of the polis: the democratic sphere in which citizens, acting in concert, determine the character and direction of their society. "All persons alike," wrote Aristotle, should share "in the government to the utmost." ...

Bowling Alone

Creating any kind of activist community is harder when the civic associations and institutions that might once have offered a foundation have themselves eroded. In a much-discussed article, "Bowling Alone," the Harvard political theorist Robert Putnam observes that during the past thirty years Americans have steadily reduced their participation not only in voting, but also in traditional forms of community involvement, such as the PTA, the League of Women Voters, unions, mainstream churches, the Boy Scouts and Campfire Girls, and service clubs like the Lions and Kiwanis. We've squandered the "social capital" that allows people to work together effectively to pursue shared objectives. As a strangely poignant example of this trend, Putnam notes that local bowling leagues have seen a 40 percent decline in membership since 1980. During the same period, however, the number of individuals who actually bowl has risen until it now exceeds the number who vote in congressional elections. These trends bode ill for American democracy, Putnam argues, because the more socially isolated our citizens become, the fewer chances they have for the kinds of civic conversations that fuel involvement in crucial public concerns.

Putnam's critics, like *Atlantic Monthly* writer Nicholas Lemann, have argued that citizens are still just as likely to get involved in community social networks, but that as America's population shifts toward the suburbs, the networks have changed form. Youth soccer leagues, in which parents participate on the weekends, are booming, he says. So are Internet discussion groups and self-help associations like Alcoholics Anonymous. Organizations from NOW and the Sierra Club to the NRA and the Christian Coalition have taken the place of the old political machines.[1]

Such examples notwithstanding, I remain convinced by Putnam's basic proposition, that civic involvement has dropped off significantly. In a follow-up

---

1. NOW is an acronym for the National Organization for Women; NRA is an acronym for the National Rifle Association.

article, Putnam examines a number of possible causes for the decline, including suburbanization, the increased numbers of women in the work force, and the general demands of modern life. While most of these factors seem to play some role, they don't account for the fact that the decline cuts across cities and suburbs, the married and the single, working men, working women, and stay-at-home moms. The key change during the past fifty years, Putnam concludes, is the steadily increasing influence of television. Regardless of background or current circumstances, the more people watch TV, he finds, the less they involve themselves in civic activities of any kind, and the more mistrusting and pessimistic they become about human nature. As their sense of connectedness and common purpose erodes, they find it easy to scapegoat others, to view the world in prejudicial and unforgiving terms, and to believe that ordinary citizens can do nothing to shape the history of our time. This is all the more troubling given that extensive TV watching now begins in early childhood, taking up as much time among average kids aged nine to fourteen as all other discretionary activities combined. For many adults, TV has gradually replaced nearly every social activity outside the home.

It worries me that so many of us now sit alone for hours on end, passive spectators, paying more attention to the strangers on the screen than to the real people next door. What are the consequences for ourselves and our society? The greatest misfortune, in my view, is that by focusing so much on stories scripted by others, we forfeit the opportunity to create our own.

Fishing Together

Whatever the reasons for our declining civic involvement, we need to rebuild local communities even as we work to expand their vision. Pete Knutson took this approach in working with his fellow fishermen: First he helped create a cohesive community; then he involved its members in larger public issues. Pete, the son of a plainspoken Lutheran minister, grew up in the hardscrabble mill town of Everett, Washington. He had a Barry Goldwater poster on his wall, "because Goldwater spoke his mind."[2] At first Pete supported the Vietnam War, and even got a jingoistic letter published on the *Everett Herald*'s youth page. His views changed as friends who'd enlisted came back, feeling betrayed, and told him, "Don't believe anything the military tells you. They always lie." Before long, Pete was organizing an antiwar moratorium at his high school; then he went off to Stanford, and became the only draft-age man to testify before Congress. He even got his fifteen minutes of fame on the national news, after Strom Thurmond stormed out when Pete had the audacity to ask a Senate committee, "If you're so eager to fight this war, why don't you pick up an M16 and lead the first wave?"

Pete began fishing to work his way through school. Soon, fishing became a way of life, as he bought his own boat, with borrowed money, to support his wife and two young sons. Because he knew his fellow fishermen were powerless in

---

2. Barry Goldwater, a founder of modern American conservatism and a senator from Arizona, was the Republican candidate for president in 1964.

isolation, he helped build the Puget Sound Gillnetters' Association, which enabled members to market fish jointly, lobby on laws that affected them, and gain leverage against the giant canneries. "I felt we had to trust each other," he says. "If we didn't, we had no chance." The association became a base through which fishermen gradually became conversant with large ecological issues, such as the destruction of salmon habitat, upon whose outcome their livelihoods depended.

Pete worked steadily to bridge the gap between fishermen and the generally more middle-class environmentalists. That was no easy task, given long-standing mutual mistrust fed by class divides and stereotypes. Yet a coalition did in fact emerge, and the fishermen brought a powerful blue-collar presence to issues like the Endangered Species Act and habitat protection. When President Clinton visited Seattle for a Pacific Rim trade conference, a parade of fishing boats joined with Greenpeace activists to challenge his environmental timidity. Both Pete's ethical stand and pride in craft were evoked by the bumper sticker on his truck: "Jesus Was a Gillnetter."

This hard-won and unexpected alliance proved critical when Initiative 640 threatened to shut down the gillnetters' operations by banning the nets they used. The fishermen held joint press conferences with the now-supportive environmental groups, picketed a pleasure-boat company that was a prime initial backer of the initiative, and generally refused to succumb quietly to their opponents' well-financed campaign. They survived because Pete, along with a few others, had helped change their vision from one of enlightened self-interest to a more complex and sustainable ethic, best summed up when he spoke of nurturing the salmon habitat "so my kids can fish, too, and everyone's children can inherit a healthy planet." First the fishermen learned to work together, then to reach beyond their own ranks. Building their association's internal cohesion made it easier for them to tackle difficult issues later on....

The Fullness of Time

However we promote social change, we do so in time: We link past, present, and future in our attempts to create a better world. Some historical eras, however, seem more pregnant with possibility than others....

The 1960s were marked by a ... sense of urgency and creative ferment. Ordinary people worldwide challenged entrenched institutions and policies. They talked of realizing a more humane and generous future. These movements then collapsed because of powerful opposition, their participants' exhaustion, and some dangerous moments of arrogance. But for a time, people unleashed powerful dreams.

Our lives today are hardly stagnant. We have access to a world of food, music, sights, sounds, and healing traditions. We can log onto websites from Bangkok and Reykjavik to Nairobi and Calcutta. As technology changes by leaps and bounds, it alters our lives and the earth at an almost incomprehensible pace. So does the relentless global economy. Change happens so fast we can barely keep up.

But politically, we often feel powerless, incapable of moving forward. We may have witnessed citizens fighting for democracy in the streets of Prague,

Berlin, and Moscow, Tiananmen Square and Soweto, Manila, and Jakarta. But we saw them from a distance on TV. People risked their lives to have a say in their common future, but the lessons seemed remote from our world. They didn't apply to us. Not here, and certainly not now.

It's tempting to gaze back longingly toward the most dramatic periods of history, while disdaining our own era as unheroic and meaningless. "People seem so stuck these days," says Ginny Nicarthy. "But things looked pretty grim in the late 1950s too, when I first got involved. A dozen of us would picket the bomb shelters or stores that were racist in their hiring, and people would yell at us, tell us to 'Go back to Russia,' 'Go back to your kitchen, where you belong.' There were no clear reasons to believe that we could change things, but somehow we did. We leaped forward, started the ball rolling, and built enough political mass that it kept going. Maybe we need to do that again."

Seeding the ground for the next round of highly visible social progress will take work. Yet major gains for human dignity are possible, even in seemingly resistant times. Indeed, our efforts may be even more critical now than in periods when the whole world seems to be watching.

The Turnings of History

Historical contexts can change shape suddenly and dramatically. As Václav Havel wrote before the epochal Eastern European revolutions, "Hope is not prognostication."[3] Richard Flacks remembers visiting Berkeley in September 1964 and hearing members of the activist student group SDS complain that their fellow students were almost terminally apathetic, uncaring, and passive. They said that nothing they could try would work. A few weeks later, the free speech movement erupted.

We can never predict when a historical mood will suddenly shift and new hopes and possibilities emerge. But we do know that this shift won't occur unless someone takes action. Recall the struggle of Susan B. Anthony. She labored her entire life for women's suffrage, then died fourteen years before it was achieved. Thirty years ago, few would have thought that the Soviet bloc would crumble, thanks in part to the persistence of individuals from Havel to Lech Walesa and Andrei Sakharov, who voiced prophetic truths despite all costs. Few would have thought that South Africa would become a democracy, with Nelson Mandela its president. Few would have imagined that women throughout the world would begin to insist on shaping their own destiny. Major victories for human dignity rarely come easily or quickly. But they do come.

"When nothing seems to help," said the early twentieth-century reformer Jacob Riis, "I go and look at a stonecutter hammering away at his rock perhaps a hundred times without as much as a crack showing in it. Yet at the hundred

3. Václav Havel, a prominent playwright and a dissident during communist rule in Czechoslovakia, became president of the Czech Republic.

and first blow it will split in two, and I know it was not that blow that did it—but all that had gone before." ...

Faith and Hope

Even if the past holds no guarantees for the future, we can still take heart from previous examples of courage and vision. We can draw hope from those who came before us, to whom we owe so much. We can remember that history unfolds in ways we can never predict, but that again and again bring astounding transformations, often against the longest of odds. Our strength can come, as I've suggested, from a radical stubbornness, from savoring the richness of our journey, and from the victories we win and the lives that we change. We can draw on the community we build.

More than anything, activists religious and secular keep going because participation is essential to their dignity, to their very identity, to the person they see in the mirror. To stay silent, they say, would be self-betrayal, a violation of their soul. Plainly stated, it would feel cheap and tacky. "That's why we were put here on this earth," they stress again and again. "What better thing can you do with your life?" "There'll be nobody like you ever again," says veteran environmentalist David Brower. "Make the most of every molecule you've got, as long as you've got a second to go. That's your charge."

This means responding to the ills of our time with what Rabbi Abraham Heschel once called "a persistent effort to be worthy of the name human." A technical editor who chaired her local Amnesty International chapter felt demeaned just by knowing about incidents of torture. To do something about it helped her recover her spirit. "When you stand in front of the Creator," says Carol McNulty, "you want to say, 'I tried to make a difference.' It isn't going to be what kind of car I had or how big a house. I'd like to think I tried."

Being true to oneself in this fashion doesn't eradicate human destructiveness. We need to live, as Albert Camus suggests, with a "double memory—a memory of the best and the worst."[4] We can't deny the cynicism and callousness of which humans are capable. We also can't deny the courage and compassion that offer us hope. It's our choice which characteristics we'll steer our lives by....

Discussion Questions

1. What are the most important differences between the elite democratic perspective and the popular democratic perspective? In your view, which side has the stronger case?

2. Mueller argues that "'special interests' can be effectively reined in only by abandoning democracy itself." Do you agree?

---

4. Albert Camus was a French philosopher and novelist who won the Nobel Prize for Literature in 1957.

3. Mueller believes that there is no greater intrinsic value in being a "politics junkie" than in pursuing any other interest or hobby, whereas Loeb sees public involvement as essential for personal growth. Is there anything distinctive about political participation that makes it especially worthy of our time and commitments?

4. Are most Americans too preoccupied with their private affairs to pay much attention to public ones, or can they be taught to see critical links between their own needs and interests and the shared pursuit of public goods?

Suggested Readings and Internet Resources

The classic work on the meaning, practices, and dilemmas of American democracy remains Alexis de Tocqueville, *Democracy in America*, vols. 1 and 2 (New York: Vintage Books, 1990). Two provocative histories of American democracy are Robert H. Wiebe, *Self-Rule: A Cultural History of American Democracy* (Chicago: University of Chicago Press, 1995), and Michael Schudson, *The Good Citizen: A History of American Civic Life* (Cambridge, Mass.: Harvard University Press, 1999). Perhaps the greatest work of modern political science in the elite democratic vein is Robert A. Dahl, *Who Governs? Democracy and Power in an American City* (New Haven, Conn.: Yale University Press, 1961). For a fascinating study of the 1960s experiment with participatory democracy, see James Miller, *"Democracy Is in the Streets": From Port Huron to the Siege of Chicago* (Cambridge, Mass.: Harvard University Press, 1994). For critical accounts of the current status of democracy in America, see Theda Skocpol, *Diminished Democracy: From Membership to Management in American Civic Life* (Norman: University of Oklahoma Press, 2003), and Matthew A. Crenson and Benjamin Ginsberg, *Downsizing Democracy: How America Sidelined Its Citizens and Privatized Its Public* (Baltimore, Md.: Johns Hopkins University Press, 2004).

Center for Democracy and Citizenship
www.publicwork.org
The Center for Democracy and Citizenship offers information about various citizenship projects as well as information about the center's own publications; it provides links to other sites on citizenship.

Institute for the Study of Civic Values
www.iscv.org
The Institute for the Study of Civic Values is a nonprofit organization in Philadelphia. Its website provides classic articles and lectures on American democratic values as well as information on civic values projects.

The Democracy Collaborative
www.democracycollaborative.org
The Democracy Collaborative's website provides scholarly materials "in support of democratic renewal, civic participation, and community building."

Chapter 3

✳

The New Federalism: Does It Create Laboratories of Democracy or a Race to the Bottom?

Addressing the National Governors Association in Philadelphia in December 2008, President-elect Barack Obama quoted Justice Louis Brandeis's famous dissent in a 1932 Supreme Court case celebrating the ability of "a single courageous state" to "serve as a laboratory experimenting with innovative solutions to our economic problems." In the 2008 presidential campaign Obama did not articulate a theory of federalism, outlining how power should be divided between the federal government and the states. Obama's speech to the National Governors Association suggests that he favors giving more power to the states to experiment with new policies. In fact, Obama, like most presidents, is more of a pragmatist, favoring state power only when it favors his goals. Shortly after assuming office, for example, Obama reversed a Bush administration policy that had forbidden states, such as California, to have more stringent auto emissions standards than the federal government.

American politics often takes a peculiar form: instead of debating *what* policy should be enacted, people argue about *where* the policy decision should be made—at the federal, state, or local level. One side will proclaim its adherence to "states' rights" or "community control," invoking Brandeis's metaphor of states as laboratories of democracy. Critics of decentralization argue that giving states too much power can

---

Note: Both phrases in the chapter title, "laboratories of democracy" and "race to the bottom," were coined by Louis Brandeis, U.S. Supreme Court justice from 1916 to 1939.

lead to a "race to the bottom" in which states favor wealthy investors over the poor, in order to attract investment, or violate the rights of minorities. Proponents of federal power argue that that it is needed to guarantee fairness and equal protection of the laws. Usually the two sides are sincere in their defense of different levels of democracy. As you might suspect, however, the debate is not just about ideals but about who will win and who will lose. This is because where decisions are made greatly affects who wins and who loses. This peculiar quality of the "game" of politics in the United States is determined by a system we call *federalism*.

Federalism is a system of government that divides power between a central government and state and local governments. As a theory of government, federalism was born in compromise during the struggle over the U.S. Constitution. Some of the framers of the Constitution favored a unitary system in which all significant powers would be placed in the hands of a central government. Realizing that such a system would never be approved by the voters, the framers compromised on a system that divided power between the two levels of government. As we saw in Chapter 1, the opponents of the Constitution, the Anti-Federalists, still feared that too much power had been given to the federal government at the expense of the states.

The ratification of the Constitution in 1789 did not settle the federalism issue, primarily because the language in the Constitution is exceedingly vague. The framers were themselves divided, so they left it up to future generations to settle the issue. The biggest crisis of federalism occurred over slavery. In 1861, the southern states decided they had the right to secede from the United States if they did not agree with the policies of the federal government. The issue was settled in a bloody civil war: States do *not* have the right to secede unilaterally from the union; they have to work out their differences within the federal system.

Until Franklin Roosevelt's New Deal of the 1930s, the federal government was remarkably uninvolved in a wide range of domestic policy functions where we now take for granted vigorous federal action. The halting response of states and localities to the Great Depression changed all that. Roosevelt swiftly moved the federal government into a wide range of functions, including Social Security, welfare, and regulation of the economy, that had previously been considered off limits. For the most part, however, Washington did not take over these functions but instead funded new programs with grants that were administered by state and local governments under varied federal rules. In the 1960s, under President Lyndon Johnson's leadership, the system of intergovernmental grants expanded tremendously.

Richard Nixon's election in 1968 began a period of reaction against the expanded powers of the federal government that has continued to this day. For the most part, Nixon did not try to roll back the functions of the federal government but instead deregulated the federal grant system and gave more power over grants to states and localities. The election of Ronald Reagan inaugurated a more radical phase of this new federalism in which efforts were made to return to the system that had existed before the New Deal when the federal government left many domestic policy functions to the states. Although confidence in all levels of government has fallen since the 1960s, the drop in confidence has been most severe for the federal government. A 2009 Pew Research Center poll found that only

42 percent of Americans had a "very or mostly favorable" opinion of the federal government compared to 50 and 60 percent favorable ratings for state and local governments, respectively.

The 1994 Republican takeover of Congress accelerated the trend toward devolution of federal powers to the states. In 1996, Congress passed, and President Bill Clinton signed, the Personal Responsibility and Work Opportunity Act, which converted welfare from a federal entitlement for individuals to a block grant to states, leaving them significant freedom to set their own eligibility criteria and conditions for aid.

The Supreme Court is also moving in the direction of restricting federal power. In 1995, the Court ruled for the first time in sixty years that Congress had exceeded its authority under the Interstate Commerce Clause of the Constitution and declared the federal Gun-Free School Zone Act of 1990 unconstitutional (*U.S. v. Lopez*). In a series of cases decided in 1999, 2000, and 2001, the Supreme Court made it more difficult for the federal government to enforce uniform national standards by giving states immunity against lawsuits alleging violation of federal laws in areas such as labor rights, violence against women, and discrimination on the basis of age or disability.

In times of crisis, however, the federal government invariably expands its power as the public looks to it for decisive action. The September 11 terrorist attacks greatly strengthened the case for expanded federal responsibilities, especially in law enforcement, public health, and airline safety. The financial crisis and economic recession that began in 2008 prompted major expansions of the federal government under both Republican and Democratic presidents. Facing a possible financial panic following the collapse of the Wall Street firm Lehman Brothers, President Bush approved the $700 billion Troubled Assets Relief Program (TARP), which authorized the Secretary of the Treasury to buy up troubled securities in order to stabilize the financial system and encourage lending. In February 2009 President Obama signed the American Recovery and Reinvestment Act (ARRA), which authorized pumping $787 billion into many different sectors of the American economy in order to stimulate recovery. The *New York Times* called this act "a striking return of big government" and conservatives attacked the expansion of the federal government and ballooning deficit (a debate we cover in Chapter 12).

In their essay "Beyond the Beltway," William Eggers and John O'Leary identify themselves with the "devolution revolution" generally supported by conservatives. They stress that the purpose of devolution is not just to make the existing government programs work more efficiently but to raise the question of whether certain functions should be the responsibility of government at all. Such decisions, they maintain, are better left with those governments that are closest to the grass roots, where citizens can see immediately the costs as well as the benefits of government programs. Shrink the federal government, Eggers and O'Leary say, and grassroots organizations will flourish, becoming "laboratories of democracy." Moreover, argue Eggers and O'Leary in a section of their book not reprinted here, the expanded powers of the federal government violate the U.S. Constitution, which in the Tenth Amendment reserves all powers not specifically given to the federal government "to the States respectively, or to the people."

John Donahue, the author of "The Devil in Devolution," argues that the words of the Constitution are much more ambiguous about the division of power between the federal government and the states than Eggers and O'Leary acknowledge. Moreover, Donahue argues, it is up to each generation to adapt the federal system to the needs of the time. Donahue criticizes the trend toward devolution. Whereas Eggers and O'Leary base their argument primarily on what we call (in the introduction) negative freedom—getting the government out of individuals' lives—Donahue stresses positive freedom, or the idea that by acting together, we can accomplish things we cannot accomplish separately. Donahue argues that when each state acts separately, those things that we all share, what he calls the "commons," can be damaged. For example, states may pursue economic development knowing that much of the pollution produced by it will drift to neighboring states. Instead of devolution resulting in "laboratories of democracy," Donahue suggests, the more likely result will be a "race to the bottom."

An intriguing aspect of this debate is that each side argues that its position is reinforced by modern technology. The reader will have to sort this out. Do you think that new technologies make it easier for decision making to be decentralized, or do they increase the interdependencies in society, thus requiring more central coordination? Note that the two sides in the debate stress different values. Eggers and O'Leary emphasize individual freedom and local democracy, whereas Donahue puts more stress on national values and equality. In this debate, are we forced to choose among competing values, or is there some way to slip between the horns of the dilemma of devolution and serve all values?

The contemporary debate on federalism reverberates with the same issues and arguments that have been made since the country's founding. It is unlikely that this debate will ever be completely settled. It seems as though each generation is doomed to decide anew the proper balance between Washington, D.C., and the states and localities. Even though there is no one neat answer, this does not mean there is not a *better* answer for our time. It is up to the reader to decide which position will best serve the core values of American democracy.

Beyond the Beltway

WILLIAM D. EGGERS AND JOHN O'LEARY

Our swollen federal government is in large measure incompatible with the demands of a modern society. In today's Information Age, there is little rationale for the federal government to control as much as it does. Large, centralized bureaucracies—whether that be IBM headquarters, the Kremlin, or Washington, D.C.—aren't well suited to an age of rapid technological change. In business, companies are decentralizing, empowering workers, and establishing autonomous business units. (It's not just trendy, it's an economic necessity.) In politics, economic reality is relegating central planning to the dustbin of history.

Washington, D.C., is becoming increasingly irrelevant. Explain authors Alvin and Heidi Toffler:

> It is not possible for a society to de-massify economic activity, communications and many other crucial processes without also, sooner or later, being compelled to decentralize government decision making as well. There is no possibility of restoring sense, order, and management "efficiency" to many governments without a substantial devolution of central power.

In today's rapidly changing world, the performance of the federal government looks worse and worse. There is a reason for this. As technology advances, decentralized decision making becomes more efficient in more and more cases. The problems of centralized decision making are inherent to *any* central authority, whether corporate or governmental, and are based on the relationship between knowledge, decision-making power, and technology.

As technology advances, productivity increasingly depends on knowledge. And, as communications technology advances, *general* knowledge—the kind that can be written down—becomes widely accessible. But *specific* knowledge—the kind that requires firsthand experience and that is difficult to communicate—is as difficult to obtain today as it has ever been. Other things being equal, *specific* knowledge—the kind that is dispersed throughout society—is growing in importance relative to *general* knowledge. Thus, as technology advances, it makes less and less sense to bottle up decision-making authority in a distant, centralized bureaucracy. Dictating the "one best way" from Washington, whether in education, welfare, or crime fighting, makes less and less sense. In particular cases, there may be a compelling reason for maintaining centralized control, such as the need for a coordinated national defense. But as a general principle, for efficiency's sake we should be increasingly devolving power *away* from centralized bureaucracies.

More than simply efficiency is at stake, however. We need to return to our roots as self-governing people. Democracy is not a spectator sport. In a healthy democracy, citizens are actively involved in their own governance—and not simply on election day. Americans need to reconnect with the political process. Numerous functions now handled (and mishandled) by the federal government should be transferred back to the states and, wherever possible, to communities and individuals. Radical devolution brings government closer to home.

The Revolt Against Washington

In 1992, a highly respected economist wrote, "The federal government should eliminate most of its programs in education, housing, highways, social services, economic development, and job training."

These radical sentiments come from Alice Rivlin, then a Brookings Institution scholar and currently President Clinton's director of the Office of Management and Budget. Writing as an independent scholar, Rivlin called for a massive, radical devolution of federal programs to states.

Devolution is not a partisan issue. It is a recognition that centralized control and centralized decision making carry unacceptably high costs, in terms of both efficiency and democratic accountability. It is not a question of Democratic dictates from Washington versus Republican dictates. Following the election of 1994, Republican governors seem ready to oppose federal usurpation even when orchestrated by their fellow party members. "My priority is for Texans to be running Texas," says Texas Governor George W. Bush. "We're pretty good at what we do in Texas, and we like to be left alone by the federal government as much as possible." It's time to end the unequal partnership and the whole idea of one-size-fits-all national prescriptions. The American people have said it's time to move power and responsibility out of Washington—for good.

Devolution would restore clearer lines of responsibility between state and federal tasks. By bringing government closer to home, citizens could once again understand what each level of government does and hold the appropriate officials accountable at election time. Radical devolution will make much of what goes on inside the Beltway redundant or unnecessary. "You have to get rid of a lot of those vested interests in Washington," says Mayor [Stephen] Goldsmith [of Indianapolis]. "There are tens of thousands of people there whose only job in life is to control what I do."

The Department of Education, for example, spends about $15 billion a year on 150 different elementary and secondary programs. Since the department was created in 1979, Washington has become fond of imposing top-down solutions on local schools. Ohio Governor George Voinovich says his state's school superintendents spend nearly half their time filling out federal forms to get money that makes up only 5 to 6 percent of their school budgets.

... Joann Wysocki, [a] first-grade teacher from the Los Angeles Unified School District, ... told us that the federal government was providing money for school days lost due to the 1994 earthquake. The rules required a special form, so every teacher had to copy *by hand* the attendance register. Photocopies were not acceptable. That's the rule. Wysocki doesn't like to jump through hoops for money from Washington, "That 'federal money' is our money to begin with, on the local level," she says. "Please don't insult anyone's intelligence saying anything else. The money comes back to us with strings attached. Why should the money go in the first place? Let it stay!"

Former Education Secretary William J. Bennett concurs: "We really do not need a Department of Education. We were educating our kids better before we had a Department of Education. Why do we have to pass the dollars from the states and locales to Washington and back out again?"

Sending housing, welfare, and social service programs to the states, as Rivlin proposes, would mean that Health and Human Services (HHS) and the Department of Housing and Urban Development (HUD) can also be dramatically downsized or eliminated. Even [former] Housing Secretary Henry Cisneros has admitted that much of what HUD does is expendable. "Many aspects of this department are simply indefensible," said Cisneros. "Change is necessary."

As for the Environmental Protection Agency (EPA), state environmental agencies are better positioned to know the problems of their states. "We don't need an EPA in Washington, D.C.," says [Arizona] Governor [Fife] Symington. "We have a Department of Environmental Quality in Arizona that is better at dealing with environmental problems in our state. You don't need an EPA in Washington with a command-and-control structure dictating environmental policies to the states." Though we believe the EPA's powers should be greatly curtailed, we're not as radical as Governor Symington in this regard. There are certain cross-border pollution issues that may require some form of federal involvement.

No More Federal Santa Claus

For radical devolution to become a reality will require a fundamental change in mind-set not only in Washington, but also among state and local politicians. Since the beginning of the Great Society, state and local officials have come to see the federal government as a kind of Santa Claus, doling out money for all sorts of programs. Many mayors and governors became professional beggars at the Capitol's steps. Programs that would never be funded with local tax dollars become "vital" so long as they are paid for with "federal" dollars.

Even more than states, big cities turned to Washington for help. Today, most cities are addicted to federal funds. Local politicians fear the loss of federal funds, but where do they imagine this money comes from in the first place? France, perhaps? Jersey City Mayor Bret Schundler, one of the few big-city mayors to oppose the crime bill, did so because he recognized that all "federal money" comes from people living in one of the 50 states to begin with. Says Schundler:

> Clinton wants to shift the burden of policing to the federal government
> and increase taxes. After he takes his big cut, he'll give us a portion of
> the money back for local policing. What a bonehead idea. The solution
> is not to shift taxes and make us pay more. The solution is reducing the
> cost of local policing.

Washington doesn't add any value to the tax dollars it receives and then sends back down to cities and states; in fact, the federal bureaucracy subtracts value as it takes its cut before sending money back to local governments.

Less federal money flowing out of Washington should mean less money flowing into Washington from the residents of cities and states. Keeping the money closer to home will also mean more flexibility, control, and accountability. "We understand this is going to mean less dollars from Washington," says New Jersey Governor Christine Todd Whitman, "but if you relieve us of some of the most onerous mandates, we will live with that." State and local officials need to stop judging the worth of joint federal/state programs merely in terms of whether they are funded by "federal dollars." "We as Governors need to begin to ask a new question about programs," says Utah Governor Mike Leavitt. "Instead of asking is this a funded program, we should ask, should there be a federal role?"

In the transportation arena, for example, the federal government could get out of highway and airport funding by forgoing the gasoline tax and letting states raise construction money themselves—whether through a state gasoline tax, by raising landing fees or highway tolls, or by securing private debt. This approach would allow states to avoid a host of federal mandates—including the 55-mile-per-hour speed limit, the Davis Bacon Act, and the minimum drinking age—that accompany acceptance of federal highway funds.

Local Money for Local Problems

In many areas the ultimate goal of policy must be to transfer as much power, authority, and responsibility as possible from government to individuals and local communities. Once citizens see the true cost of local programs now being financed from Washington, they may not think they're worth the tax dollars spent on them.

Consider, for example, the uproar that ensued in Manhattan Beach, California (where one of us lives), after the city council voted to spend money expanding a parking garage that residents felt would benefit only merchants. A front-page story in *The Beach Reporter* noted that "three dozen residents ... bombarded the Manhattan Beach City Council on Tuesday...." Another story noted:

> [M]any residents complained that they were continually having to come down to City Hall to protect their interests. District 4 Council-member Bob Pinzler told the residents that they should continue voicing their opinions and concerns. "You have to keep coming down here to protect your interests," Pinzler said, "because the special interest groups are here all the time."

This is democracy at its local, messy best, with vigilant residents watching over elected officials spending their tax dollars. Chances are no one in Manhattan Beach even knew that the federal government spent $2.5 million of tax money to build a parking garage in Burlington, Iowa. That little item didn't make the front page of *The Beach Reporter*, and no Manhattan Beach residents drove the 3,000-odd miles to Washington, D.C., to testify before a congressional committee. At the federal level, organized interests have an enormous advantage. Former Education Secretary William Bennett estimates that 285 education lobbying groups have offices within walking distance of the Department of Education headquarters. The average Manhattan Beach parent doesn't have a prayer.

The parking garage story illustrates the phenomenon known as "bill averaging." Imagine going out to dinner by yourself. When ordering, you'll closely watch the cost of each menu selection because you'll be paying the entire bill. Even if you were going out to dinner with one or two friends, you still wouldn't spend outrageously because you'd still be footing a good portion of the bill.

Now imagine that you are going out to dinner with 75 strangers, and that the bill is to be divided evenly. If you are like most people, you are going to order liberally, enjoy an extra drink, maybe even dessert and coffee. And why not? Your order will only affect your bill a minuscule amount; besides, you can bet that everyone else will be ordering big. The only way to get your "fair share" is to order lobster and Lowenbrau.

The federal government is like going to dinner with 250 million strangers. Rather than everyone paying his own way, a complex tangle of cross-subsidies obscures everyone's actual bill.

It's time to ask for separate checks. The good folks of Burlington, Iowa, got a new parking garage because Uncle Sam took about one penny from every Manhattan Beach resident—and every other American. Because local taxpayers don't feel the bite, local officials love to spend "federal dollars." Would Altoonans have approved Altoona, Pennsylvania's multimillion dollar moving sidewalk if Altoonan taxes were going to pay for it? Unlikely. But since the folks in Burlington, Iowa, and Manhattan Beach, California, are footing the bill, the Altoonans are happy to be carried along.

The Devil in Devolution

JOHN D. DONAHUE

The shift in government's center of gravity away from Washington and toward the states—a transition propelled by both popular sentiment and budget imperatives, and blessed by leaders in both major parties—reflects an uncommon pause in an endless American argument over the balance between nation and state.

This moment of consensus in favor of letting Washington fade while the states take the lead is badly timed. The public sector's current trajectory—the devolution of welfare and other programs, legislative and judicial action circumscribing Washington's authority, and the federal government's retreat to a domestic role largely defined by writing checks to entitlement claimants, creditors, and state and local governments—would make sense if economic and cultural ties reaching across state lines were *weakening* over time. But state borders are becoming more, not less, permeable.

From a vantage point three-fifths of the way between James Madison's day and our own, Woodrow Wilson wrote that the "common interests of a nation brought together in thought and interest and action by the telegraph and the telephone, as well as by the rushing mails which every express train carries, have a scope and variety, an infinite multiplication and intricate interlacing, of which a simpler day can have had no conception." Issues in which other states' citizens have no stakes, and hence no valid claim to a voice, are becoming rarer still in an age of air freight, interlinked computers, nonstop currency trading, and site-shopping global corporations. Our current enchantment with devolution will be seen one day as oddly discordant with our era's challenges.

The concept of "the commons" can help to cast in a sharper light the perils of fragmented decision making on issues of national consequence. In a much-noted 1968 article in *Science*, biologist Garrett Hardin invoked the parable of a herdsman pondering how many cattle to graze on the village commons. Self-interest will lead the herdsman to increase the size of his herd even if the commons is already overburdened, since he alone benefits from raising an extra animal, but shares the consequent damage to the common pasture. As each farmer follows the same logic, overgrazing wrecks the commons.

Where the nation as a whole is a commons, whether as an economic reality or as a political ideal, and states take action that ignores or narrowly exploits that fact, the frequent result is the kind of "tragedy" that Hardin's metaphor predicts: Collective value is squandered in the name of a constricted definition of gain. States win advantages that seem worthwhile only because other states bear much of the costs. America's most urgent public challenges—shoring up the economic underpinnings of an imperiled middle-class culture; developing and deploying productive workplace skills; orchestrating Americans' engagement with increasingly global capital—involve the stewardship of common interests. The fragmentation of authority makes success less likely. The phenomenon is by no means limited to contemporary economic issues, and a smattering of examples from other times and other policy agendas illustrate the theme.

Environmental Regulation

Antipollution law is perhaps the most obvious application of the "commons" metaphor to policymaking in a federal system. If a state maintains a lax regime of environmental laws it spares its own citizens, businesses, and government agencies from economic burdens. The "benefits" of environmental recklessness, in other words, are collected in-state. Part of the pollution consequently dumped into the air or water, however, drifts away to do its damage elsewhere in the nation. If states held all authority over environmental rule making, the predictable result would be feeble regulations against any kinds of pollution where in-state costs and benefits of control are seriously out of balance. Even in states whose citizens valued the environment—even if the citizens of *all* states were willing to accept substantial economic costs in the name of cleaner air and water—constituents and representatives would calculate that their sacrifice could not on its own stem the tide and reluctantly settle for weaker rules than they would otherwise prefer.

A state contemplating tough antipollution rules might calculate that its citizens will pay for environmental improvements that will be enjoyed, in part, by others. Even worse, by imposing higher costs on business than do other states, it risks repelling investment, and thus losing jobs and tax revenues to states with weak environmental laws. Congress explicitly invoked the specter of a "race for the bottom"—competitive loosening of environmental laws in order to lure business—to justify federal standards that would "preclude efforts on the part of states to compete with each other in trying to attract new plants." In a series of legislative changes starting in the early 1970s, the major choices about how aggressively to act against pollution were moved to the federal government. While aspects of enforcement remained state responsibilities—introducing another level of complications that continues to plague environmental policy—the trade-off between environmental and economic values moved much closer to a single national standard.

National regulation in a diverse economy does have a downside. States differ in their environmental problems, and in the priorities of their citizens. Requiring all states to accept the same balance between environmental and economic values imposes some real costs and generates real political friction. Yet even if the tilt toward national authority is, on balance, the correct approach to environmental regulation, there is reason to doubt we got all the details right. Moreover, logic suggests that the federal role should be stronger for forms of pollution that readily cross state borders, and weaker for pollution that stays put. But federal authority is actually weaker under the Clean Air Act and the Clean Water Act than under the "Superfund" law covering hazardous waste. Toxic-waste sites are undeniably nasty things. But most of them are situated within a single state, and stay there.

Governmental Efficiency

There is an alluring a priori case for predicting that public-sector efficiency will increase as responsibilities flow to lower levels of government. Yet this *potential* advantage largely fails to pan out; there is little evidence of a significant or systematic state efficiency edge. The states share with Washington the basic operational handicaps of the public sector.

The devolution debate, moreover, is almost wholly irrelevant to the debt service and middle-class entitlements causing most of the strain on citizens' tolerance for taxation. It is safe to assert that the ascendancy of the states will have, at best, a limited impact on the cost of American government. This is not an argument based on ideology, or economic theory, or learned predictions about comparative administrative behavior. It is a matter of arithmetic. In 1996 total public spending came to about $2.3 trillion. State and local activities, funded by state and local taxes, *already* accounted for about one-third of this total. Another one-third consisted of check-writing programs like Social Security and Medicare. National defense (12 percent of the total), interest on the national debt (10 percent), and federal grants to state and local governments (another 10 percent) accounted for most of the remaining third of the public sector. All other federal domestic undertakings, taken together, claimed between 4 and 5 percent of total government spending. Suppose every last thing the federal government does, aside from running defense and foreign affairs and writing checks (to entitlement claimants, debt holders, and state and local governments) were transferred to the states—national parks and museums, air-traffic control, the FBI, the border patrol, the Centers for Disease Control, the National Weather Service, student loans, the space program, and all the rest. Suppose, then, that the states proved able to do *everything* that the federal government used to do a full 10 percent more efficiently. The cost of government would fall by a little under one-half of one percent.

Beyond the low ceiling on cost savings—and more pertinent to the hidden issue of the *quality* of government—is the similarity between most federal agencies and most state agencies on the core characteristics of scale, complexity, and administration by legislative statute and formal rules. It is rare that economic or managerial imperatives will call for the reassignment of authority away from central government, but then stop at the states. State boundaries have been drawn by a capricious history, and only occasionally (and then by accident) does a state constitute the most logical economic unit for either making policy or delivering services. The coalition between the state-sovereignty constitutionalists and the efficient-scale de-centralizers is based on a misunderstanding, and will break down as soon as it begins to succeed.

More promising strategies for improving the efficiency with which public purposes are pursued usually involve going *beyond* devolution to the states. The array of options includes privatization, to enlist private-sector efficiency advantages in the service of public goals; vouchers, to assign purchasing power while letting individuals choose how to deploy it; and the empowerment (through authority and resources) of levels of government smaller than the state, including cities, towns, and school districts. None of these strategies is without its risks and limits, but together they form a far richer menu of reform possibilities than the simple switch from federal to state bureaucracy.

Devolution is often, though misleadingly, cast as a way station toward such fundamental reforms. Its popularity among those convinced of American government's shortcomings, and committed to repairing them, diverts reformist energy that could be put to better use. State governments are only slightly, if any, less bureaucratic than Washington, and no less jealous of power or resistant to change. Power dislodged from federal bureaus is likely to stick at the state level instead of diffusing further. The characteristic pattern of American intergovernmental relations is rivalry between state and local officials, and Washington more often acts as local government's shield against state hegemony than as the common oppressor of cities and states. The ascendancy of the states is thus unlikely either to liberate local governments or to unleash fundamental reform in how government operates.

Rising Inequality

It is by no means certain that America will prove able to reverse growing economic inequality and the erosion of the middle class, no matter how we structure our politics. Devolution, however, will worsen the odds. Shared prosperity, amid the maelstrom of economic change tearing away at the industrial underpinnings of middle-class culture, is an artifact of policy. Policies to shore up the middle class include work-based antipoverty efforts that become both more important and more expensive as unskilled jobs evaporate; relentless investments in education and job training; measures to strengthen employees' leverage in the workplace; and a more progressive tilt in the overall burden of taxation. The individual states—each scrambling to lure mobile capital, fearful of losing businesses and well-off residents to lower-tax rivals, anxious to minimize their burden of needy citizens—will find such policies nearly impossible to sustain. As Washington sheds responsibilities and inter-state rivalry intensifies, only a small-government agenda becomes realistic. But even for principled small-government conservatives, devolution is likely to prove less sat-isfying than many expect. Since it has been justified in terms of improving, not shrinking, government, the ascendancy of the states represents no conclusion to the debate over the public sector's proper size and scope.

Like the run-up in federal debt in the 1980s and early 1990s, devolution short-circuits (rather than settles) deliberation over government's purpose by mak-ing activism impossible—for a time. America's federal system is sufficiently resilient that unless citizens are convinced of small government's merits, the tilt toward the states that suppress public-sector ambition will eventually be reversed, though only after an unpredictable price has been paid. The conservative intellectual Herbert Storing has argued that a strategy of crippling the activist impulse through devolu-tion, instead of discrediting it through reasoned appeal, was "not only contrary to the best conservative tradition but also hopelessly unrealistic." By attempting to enthrone the states as the sole locus of legitimate government, conservatives muffle their own voices in the conversation over the country's future.

By the standards of those who credit any diagnosis of what ails America *other than* "big government," shifting authority to competing states is likely to solve minor problems while causing, or perpetuating, far graver ills. As states gain a greater share of governmental duties but prove reluctant or unable to tax mobile firms or well-off individuals, the burden of funding the public sector will tilt even more heavily toward middle-class taxpayers. Their resentment of government can be expected to intensify. Efforts to use state laws or regulations to strengthen employees' leverage in the workplace will often be rendered unworkable by in-terstate competition for business. America's largest source of fiscal imbalance—the unsustainability of middle-class entitlement programs as the baby boom generation ages—will be untouched by devolution, feeding cynicism about the impervious-ness to solution of America's public problems. And the fragmentation of taxing and spending authority puts in peril the education and training agenda that defines our single most promising tactic for shoring up the middle class.

The global marketplace both gives new fuel to America's culture of oppor-tunity *and* allows the range of economic conditions experienced within this erst-while middle-class country to reflect, with less and less filtering, the whole planet's disparate array of fates. A middle-class national economy, within a world of economic extremes, is a precious but unnatural thing. The policies that sustain shared prosperity will be difficult, perhaps impossible, to pursue if America's cen-ter of gravity in economic policymaking continues its precipitous shift toward the separate states. Federal officials, as a class, are certainly no wiser, more farsighted, or defter at implementation than their state counterparts. But our country as a whole remains much less subject to the flight of wealth and the influx of need than are its constituent states. Policies to shrink the underclass and solidify the middle class are thus far more sustainable at the federal level.

Fixing the federal government is an intimidating proposition in the late 1990s. The trajectory of fiscal and political trends suggests that devolution will remain the focus of politicians' promises and citizens' hopes for some time to come. But the inherent limits of a fragmented approach to national adaptation will eventually inspire America to reappraise the ascendancy of the states. Not too far into the new century we will again collect the resolve to confront together our common fate. And we will once more take up, in the two-century tradition of Americans before us, the echoing challenge of George Washington's 1796 farewell address: "Is there a doubt whether a common government can embrace so large a sphere? Let experience solve it."

Discussion Questions

1. Think of a policy issue that you are interested in. Which level of government do you think is the most appropriate one to make decisions on this issue? Why?

2. Which level of government do you think is the most democratic—federal, state, or local? Can privileged elites more easily dominate at the local level or at the national level?

3. Many people argue that justice should be the same no matter where you live and therefore the federal government should establish minimal standards of fairness on certain issues. Do you agree or disagree? Do you think the federal government should guarantee every American medical care or a minimum income?

4. One of the problems with decentralizing decision making is that some local governments have much larger tax resources than others. Many inner cities and small towns, for example, are poor. How would Eggers and O'Leary respond to this problem? What can be done about it?

5. Do you think that marriage law (divorce, child custody, and so on) should be decided by the federal government or the states? What about educational policy? Should the federal government establish national standards in education?

Suggested Readings and Internet Resources

In *From New Federalism to Devolution* (Washington, D.C.: Brookings Institution Press, 1998) Timothy Conlan argues that Nixon and Reagan actually had very different approaches to federalism. Jeffrey M. Berry, Kent E. Portney, and

Ken Thomson in *The Rebirth of Urban Democracy* (Washington, D.C.: Brookings Institution Press, 1993) present evidence that decentralizing some positions all the way to neighborhood governments makes sense. Grant McConnell, in *Private Power and American Democracy* (New York: Vintage Books, 1966), argues, in contrast, that decentralization of power leads to tyranny by elites. Probably the best book on the possibilities and limits of state economic development efforts is Paul Brace, *State Government and Economic Performance* (Baltimore, Md.: Johns Hopkins University Press, 1993). In *Tense Commandments: Federal Prescriptions and City Problems* (Washington, D.C.: Brookings Institution Press, 2002), Pietro S. Nivola argues that federal programs often tie the hands of local administrators, making city renewal even more difficult. For a comprehensive, up-to-date treatment of the issues, see Laurence J. O'Toole Jr., ed., *American Intergovernmental Relations: Foundations, Perspectives, and Issues* (Washington, D.C.: Congressional Quarterly Press, 2007). For an intriguing change of pace, read Ernest Callenbach's *Ecotopia* (New York: Bantam Books, 1975), an entertaining novel about environmentalists who take over part of the Northwest and secede from the United States.

James Madison Institute
www.jamesmadison.org
The James Madison Institute is a public policy research organization dedicated to promoting economic freedom, limited government, federalism, the rule of law, and individual liberty coupled with individual responsibility. The site includes a list of current books and policy studies.

The Council of State Governments
www.csg.org
The website of the Council of State Governments has information on state governments and state-level public policies.

Close Up Foundation
www.closeup.org
The Close Up Foundation Special Topic Page on federalism in the United States features an overview, a timeline, a teaching activity, and an annotated list of links to additional sources of information.

Chapter 4

＊

Immigration: Does It Strengthen or Threaten American Democracy?

On April 23, 2010 Arizona Republican Governor Jan Brewer signed into law the nation's most restrictive bill on illegal immigration. The law makes it a crime not to carry immigration papers and gives the police broad powers to detain anyone suspected of being in the county illegally. Proponents argued that the federal government was not adequately policing the border and the state needed to do something to discourage illegal immigration. Opponents of the law staged noisy demonstrations across the country charging that the law would encourage racial and ethnic profiling by police who could harass Hispanics without any evidence that they had committed a crime. Even before the bill was signed into law President Obama criticized it as threatening "to undermine basic notions of fairness that we cherish as Americans." The immigration issue was sure to play into the Fall 2010 elections with Republicans using their support of the Arizona law to mobilize voters concerned about jobs lost to illegal immigrations, while Democrats used Republican support of the law to rally Hispanic voters to their side.

Americans are deeply ambivalent about immigration. On the one hand, with the exception of Native Americans, all Americans are descendants of immigrants. Since its founding, the United States has probably been the most welcoming nation in the world for immigrants. The Statue of Liberty, a gift from France in 1886, is an enduring symbol of this welcoming attitude toward immigrants. At its base are written the famous words "Give me your tired, your poor, your huddled masses yearning to breathe free." Throughout most of American history, no limits were placed on the number of immigrants who could enter. Unlike other nations, there is no "blood" requirement to becoming an American citizen. The road to citizenship is easy: basically, a person must pass a simple civics test and take an oath of allegiance to the United States and the Constitution. According to the Fourteenth Amendment, anyone born in the United States, even if both parents are noncitizens, is automatically a U.S. citizen.

On the other hand, Americans have always been fearful of immigrants who are different from most Americans—ethnically, racially, religiously. Four years before the Statue of Liberty arrived Congress passed the Chinese Exclusion Act, prohibiting immigration by anyone of Chinese origin. Opposition to immigrants from non-European countries culminated in laws passed in the 1920s that established quotas for immigrants from each nation based on their percentage in the U.S. population at the time. Because most Americans were of Northern European stock (English, German, or Scandinavian), this meant the number of immigrants from Southern Europe (such as Italian or Slavic) and the rest of the world was strictly limited.

Strict limits on immigration ended in 1965 with the passage of the Immigration and Nationality Act, which eliminated quotas and based immigration for the most part on family reunification. This meant that someone with a close relative living in the United States could probably immigrate here legally. More immigrants entered the United States in the 1990s than at any other decade in American history. In 2008 fully 12.5 percent of the population was foreign-born.

Not only has there been a huge surge in immigration since 1965, but there has also been an enormous diversification of the immigrant stream. Instead of emigrating from Europe, most immigrants now come from Asia, Central America, Latin America, and, to a lesser extent, Africa and Eastern Europe. Increasingly, the population of the United States resembles that of the world in general. This diversification of the immigrant stream coincided with the rise of multiculturalism, the idea that instead of a "melting pot" we should celebrate the diversity of cultures that make up the "mosaic" of America.

September 11, 2001, cast a pall over the celebration of diversity and the faith in liberal immigration laws. The terrorists who crashed planes into the World Trade Center and the Pentagon had entered the United States under either a student visa or a visa waiver program. Americans demanded tighter border controls, especially in light of the estimated 11 million illegal immigrants already living in the country. In 2003 the Immigration and Naturalization Service (INS) was abolished and its functions were taken over by the newly formed Department of Homeland Security, which proceeded to deport thousands of illegal immigrants and make it more difficult for those wishing to study in the United States to acquire a student visa.

During the Bush administration, Congress failed to pass comprehensive immigration reform. "Comprehensive" reform means legislation that would both create a process for illegal, or undocumented, workers to become citizens and reduce the number of illegal immigrants though stricter border controls and harsher penalties on those who attempt to cross. (In 1986, Congress passed a controversial law that enabled millions of illegal immigrants to become citizens.) Although Democrats tend to be more pro-immigrant (some say to let in more Democratic-leaning voters) and Republicans generally support greater restrictions, positions on immigration do not follow strictly partisan lines. In the 2008 presidential campaign, President Obama promised he would pursue comprehensive immigration reform, but the economic crisis put that on the back burner.

The two essays that follow illustrate conflicting attitudes on immigration. Ben Wattenberg, a Senior Fellow at the conservative American Enterprise Institute, an author, and a frequent commentator on public television, argues that the declining birthrate in the United States requires large numbers of immigrants to meet the future demand for labor. The idea that immigrants will refuse to learn English or assimilate into American culture is false, Wattenberg maintains. In the long run, immigration will make America a stronger nation, one that can project its universal Western values around the globe.

Newt Gingrich, former Speaker of the House of Representatives and possible future candidate for the presidency, is much more critical of U.S. open immigration policies. Although Gingrich is not opposed to legal immigration, he is concerned that too many immigrants refuse to assimilate into American culture and he proposes several programs to encourage them to become patriotic Americans. Above all, Gingrich argues, immigration is a national security issue and America has to do whatever is necessary to protect itself from terrorists.

As you read through the two selections, think about the distinction made in the book's introduction between elite and popular democracy. How do these two approaches to democracy line up on immigration? On the one hand, the pro-immigration side would appear to be more popular democratic because it promotes easier paths to citizenship and voting rights for immigrants who are often poor. On the other hand, many argue that immigration harms working-class Americans by forcing them to compete with cheap labor at the same time that wealthy elites benefit from lower wages paid to many service workers such as maids, gardeners, and construction workers. You decide: Is immigration good or bad for average Americans?

Immigration Strengthens
American Democracy

BEN WATTENBERG

Many leading thinkers tell us we are now in a culture clash that will determine the course of history, that today's war is for Western civilization itself. There is a demographic dimension to this "clash of civilizations." While certain of today's demographic signals bode well for America, some look very bad. If we are to assess America's future prospects, we must start by asking, "Who are we?" "Who will we be?" and "How will we relate to the rest of the world?" The answers all involve immigration.

As data from the 2000 census trickled out, one item hit the headline jackpot. By the year 2050, we were told, America would be "majority nonwhite." The census count showed more Hispanics in America than had been expected, making them "America's largest minority." When blacks, Asians, and Native Americans are added to the Hispanic total, the "nonwhite" population emerges as a large minority, on the way to becoming a small majority around the middle of this century.

The first thing worth noting is that these rigid racial definitions are absurd. The whole concept of race as a biological category is becoming evermore dubious in America. Consider:

Under the Clinton administration's census rules, any American who checks both the black and white boxes on the form inquiring about "race" is counted as black, even if his heritage is, say, one eighth black and seven eighths white. In effect, this enshrines the infamous segregationist view that one drop of black blood makes a person black.

Although most Americans of Hispanic heritage declare themselves "white," they are often inferentially counted as non-white, as in the erroneous *New York Times* headline which recently declared: "Census Confirms Whites Now a Minority" in California.

If those of Hispanic descent, hailing originally from about 40 nations, are counted as a minority, why aren't those of Eastern European descent, coming from about 10 nations, also counted as a minority? (In which case the Eastern European "minority" would be larger than the Hispanic minority.)

But within this jumble of numbers there lies a central truth: America is becoming a *universal nation*, with significant representation of nearly all human hues, creeds, ethnicities, and national ancestries. Continued moderate immigration will make us an even more universal nation as time goes on. And this process may well play a serious role in determining the outcome of the contest of civilizations taking place across the globe.

And current immigration rates *are* moderate, even though America admitted more legal immigrants from 1991 to 2000 than in any previous decade—between 10 and 11 million. The highest previous decade was 1901–1910, when 8.8 million people arrived. In addition, each decade now, several million illegal immigrants enter the U.S., thanks partly to ease of transportation.

Critics like Pat Buchanan say that absorbing all those immigrants will "swamp" the American culture and bring Third World chaos inside our borders. I disagree. Keep in mind: Those 8.8 million immigrants who arrived in the U.S. between 1901 and 1910 increased the total American population by 1 percent per year. (Our numbers grew from 76 million to 92 million during that decade.) In our most recent decade, on the other hand, the 10 million legal immigrants represented annual growth of only 0.36 percent (as the U.S. went from 249 million to 281 million).

Overall, nearly 15 percent of Americans were foreign-born in 1910. In 1999, our foreign-born were about 10 percent of our total. (In 1970, the foreign-born portion of our population was down to about 5 percent. Most of the rebound resulted from a more liberal immigration law enacted in 1965.) Or look at the "foreign stock" data. These figures combine Americans born in foreign lands *and* their offspring, even if those children have only one foreign-born parent. Today, America's "foreign stock" amounts to 21 percent of the population and heading up. But in 1910, the comparable figure was 34 percent—one-third of the entire country—and the heavens did not collapse.

We can take in more immigrants, if we want to. Should we?

Return to the idea that immigrants could swamp American culture. If that is true, we clearly should not increase our intake. But what if, instead of swamping us, immigration helps us become a stronger nation and a *swamper of others* in the global competition of civilizations?

Immigration is now what keeps America growing. According to the UN, the typical American woman today bears an average of 1.93 children over the course of her childbearing years. That is mildly below the 2.1 "replacement" rate required to keep a population stable over time, absent immigration. The "medium variant" of the most recent Census Bureau projections posits that the U.S. population will grow from 281 million in 2000 to 397 million in 2050 with expected immigration, but only to 328 million should we choose a path of zero immigration. That is a difference of a population growth of 47 million versus 116 million. (The 47 million rise is due mostly to demographic momentum from previous higher birthrates.) If we have zero immigration with today's low birthrates indefinitely, the American population would eventually begin to *shrink*, albeit slowly.

Is more population good for America? When it comes to potential global power and influence, numbers can matter a great deal. Taxpayers, many of them, pay for a fleet of aircraft carriers. And on the economic side it is better to have a customer boom than a customer bust. (It may well be that Japan's stagnant demography is one cause of its decade-long slump.) The environmental case could be debated all day long, but remember that an immigrant does not add to the global population—he merely moves from one spot on the planet to another.

But will the current crop of immigrants acculturate? Immigrants to America always have. Some critics, like Mr. Buchanan, claim that this time, it's different. Mexicans seem to draw his particular ire, probably because they are currently our largest single source of immigration.

Yet only about a fifth (22 percent) of legal immigrants to America currently come from Mexico. Adding illegal immigrants might boost the figure to 30 percent, but the proportion of Mexican immigrants will almost surely shrink over time. Mexican fertility has diminished from 6.5 children per woman 30 years age to 2.5 children now, and continues to fall. If high immigration continues under such circumstances, Mexico will run out of Mexicans.

California hosts a wide variety of immigrant groups in addition to Mexicans. And the children and grandchildren of Koreans, Chinese, Khmer, Russian Jews, Iranians, and Thai (to name a few) will speak English, not Spanish. Even among Mexican-Americans, many second- and third-generation offspring speak no Spanish at all, often to the dismay of their elders (a familiar American story).

Michael Barone's book *The New Americans* theorizes that Mexican immigrants are following roughly the same course of earlier Italian and Irish immigrants. Noel

Ignatiev's book *How the Irish Became White* notes that it took a hundred years until Irish-Americans (who were routinely characterized as drunken "gorillas") reached full income parity with the rest of America.

California recently repealed its bilingual education programs. Nearly half of Latino voters supported the proposition, even though it was demonized by opponents as being anti-Hispanic. Latina mothers reportedly tell their children, with no intent to disparage the Spanish language, that "Spanish is the language of busboys"—stressing that in America you have to speak English to get ahead.

The huge immigration wave at the dawn of the twentieth century undeniably brought tumult to America. Many early social scientists promoted theories of what is now called "scientific racism," which "proved" that persons from Northwest Europe were biologically superior. The new immigrants— Jews, Poles, and Italians—were considered racially apart and far down the totem pole of human character and intelligence. Blacks and Asians were hardly worth measuring. The immigration wave sparked a resurgence of the Ku Klux Klan, peaking in the early 1920s. At that time, the biggest KKK state was not in the South; it was Indiana, where Catholics, Jews, and immigrants, as well as blacks, were targets.

Francis Walker, superintendent of the U.S. Bureau of the Census in the late 1890s, and later president of MIT, wrote in 1896 that "The entrance of such vast masses of peasantry degraded below our utmost conceptions is a matter which no intelligent patriot can look upon without the gravest apprehension and alarm. They are beaten men from beaten races. They have none of the ideas and aptitudes such as belong to those who were descended from the tribes that met under the oak trees of old Germany to make laws and choose chiefs." (Sorry, Francis, but Germany did not have a good twentieth century.)

Fast-forward to the present. By high margins, Americans now tell pollsters it was a very good thing that Poles, Italians, and Jews emigrated to America. Once again, it's the *newcomers* who are viewed with suspicion. This time, it's the Mexicans, Filipinos, and people from the Caribbean who make Americans nervous. But such views change over time. The newer immigrant groups are typically more popular now than they were even a decade ago.

Look at the high rates of intermarriage. Most Americans have long since lost their qualms about marriage between people of different European ethnicities. That is spreading across new boundaries. In 1990, 64 percent of Asian Americans married outside their heritage, as did 37 percent of Hispanics. Black-white intermarriage is much lower, but it climbed from 3 percent in 1980 to 9 percent in 1998. (One reason to do away with the race question on the census is that within a few decades we won't be able to know who's what.)

Can the West, led by America, prevail in a world full of sometimes unfriendly neighbors? Substantial numbers of people are necessary (though not sufficient) for a country, or a civilization, to be globally influential. Will America and its Western allies have enough people to keep their ideas and principles alive?

On the surface, it doesn't look good. In 1986, I wrote a book called *The Birth Dearth*. My thesis was that birth rates in developed parts of the world—Europe,

North America, Australia, and Japan, nations where liberal Western values are rooted—had sunk so low that there was danger ahead. At that time, women in those modern countries were bearing a lifetime average of 1.83 children, the lowest rate ever absent war, famine, economic depression, or epidemic illness. It was, in fact, 15 percent below the long-term population replacement level.

Those trendlines have now plummeted even further. Today, the fertility rate in the modern countries averages 1.5 children per woman, 28 percent below the replacement level. The European rate, astonishingly, is 1.34 children per woman—radically below replacement level. The Japanese rate is similar. The United States is the exceptional country in the current demographic scene.

As a whole, the nations of the Western world will soon be less populous, and a substantially smaller fraction of the world population. Demographer Samuel Preston estimates that even if European fertility rates jump back to replacement level immediately (which won't happen) the continent would still lose 100 million people by 2060. Should the rate not level off fairly soon, the ramifications are incalculable, or, as the Italian demographer Antonio Golini likes to mutter at demographic meetings, "unsustainable … unsustainable." (Shockingly, the current Italian fertility rate is 1.2 children per woman, and it has been at or below 1.5 for 20 years—a full generation.)

The modern countries of the world, the bearers of Western civilization, made up one third of the global population in 1950, and one fifth in 2000, and are projected to represent one eighth by 2050. If we end up in a world with nine competing civilizations, as Samuel Huntington maintains, this will make it that much harder for Western values to prevail in the cultural and political arenas.

The good news is that fertility rates have also plunged in the less developed countries—from 6 children in 1970 to 2.9 today. By the middle to end of this century, there should be a rough global convergence of fertility rates and population growth.

Since September 11, immigration has gotten bad press in America. The terrorist villains, indeed, were foreigners. Not only in the U.S. but in many other nations as well, governments are suddenly cracking down on illegal entry. This is understandable for the moment. But an enduring turn away from legal immigration would be foolhardy for America and its allies.

If America doesn't continue to take in immigrants, it won't continue to grow in the long run. If the Europeans and Japanese don't start to accept more immigrants they will evaporate. Who will empty the bedpans in Italy's retirement homes? The only major pool of immigrants available to Western countries hails from the less developed world, i.e., non-white, and non-Western countries.

The West as a whole is in a deep demographic ditch. Accordingly, Western countries should try to make it easier for couples who want to have children. In America, the advent of tax credits for children (which went from zero to $1,000 per child per year over the last decade) is a small step in the direction of fertility reflation. Some European nations are enacting similar pronatal policies. But their fertility rates are so low, and their economies so constrained, that any such actions can only be of limited help.

That leaves immigration. I suggest America should make immigration safer (by more carefully investigating new entrants), but not cut it back. It may even be wise to make a small increase in our current immigration rate. America needs to keep growing, and we can fruitfully use both high- and low-skill immigrants. Pluralism works here, as it does in Canada and Australia.

Can pluralism work in Europe? I don't know, and neither do the Europeans. They hate the idea, but they will depopulate if they don't embrace pluralism, via immigration. Perhaps our example can help Europeans see that pluralism might work in the admittedly more complex European context. Japan is probably a hopeless case; perhaps the Japanese should just change the name of their country to Dwindle.

Our non-pluralist Western allies will likely diminish in population, relative power, and influence during this century. They will become much grayer. Nevertheless, by 2050 there will still be 750 million of them left, so the U.S. needs to keep the Western alliance strong. For all our bickering, let us not forget that the European story in the second half of the twentieth century was a wonderful one; Western Europeans stopped killing each other. Now they are joining hands politically. The next big prize may be Russia. If the Russians choose our path, we will see what [nineteenth-century French theorist Alexis de] Tocqueville saw: that America and Russia are natural allies.

We must enlist other allies as well. America and India, for instance, are logical partners—pluralist, large, English-speaking, and democratic. We must tell our story. And our immigrants, who come to our land by choice, are our best salesmen. We should extend our radio services to the Islamic world, as we have to the unliberated nations of Asia through Radio Free Asia. The people at the microphones will be U.S. immigrants.

We can lose the contest of civilizations if the developing countries don't evolve toward Western values. One of the best forms of "public diplomacy" is immigration. New immigrants send money home, bypassing corrupt governments—the best kind of foreign aid there is. They go back home to visit and tell their families and friends in the motherland that American modernism, while not perfect, ain't half-bad. Some return home permanently, but they bring with them Western expectations of open government, economic efficiency, and personal liberty. They know that Westernism need not be restricted to the West, and they often have an influence on local politics when they return to their home countries.

Still, because of Europe and Japan, the demographic slide of Western civilization will continue. And so, America must be prepared to go it alone. If we keep admitting immigrants at our current levels there will be almost 400 million Americans by 2050. That can keep us strong enough to defend and perhaps extend our views and values. And the civilization we will be advancing may not just be Western, but even more universal: American.

Patriotic Immigration

NEWT GINGRICH

A chilling hearing before the Senate Intelligence Committee last year provides the starting point of our national debate on immigration reform. Former CIA Chief Porter Goss set the stage by testifying that "it may be only a matter of time" before al Qaeda or another terrorist group attempts to use a chemical, biological, or nuclear weapon against the United States. And then Admiral James Loy, the Deputy Secretary of Homeland Security, added the detail that should have every American demanding immediate action about our uncontrolled borders: Loy testified that evidence "strongly suggests" that the same terrorists who are planning on using a weapon of mass destruction against the United States have considered using our south-west border as an entry point.

Nearly five years after 9/11, our bureaucratic system is so broken we don't even know who is in our country. In the age of terrorism, no nation can afford to have uncontrolled borders with millions crossing illegally. There is no point in having a war on terrorism—much less a $9 billion a year national missile defense program—when the same terrorists can rent a truck in Mexico and drive a weapon of mass destruction over the border. A government team recently proved that it was easy to do.

And the threat of uncontrolled borders isn't confined to terrorism. Gangs, drug dealers, and common criminals are drawn to our border as lawlessness breeds more lawlessness. The sheriff of Val Verde County, Texas, reports that people crossing the U.S.–Mexico border illegally no longer bother running from the authorities. "They make it known to the deputies," he said. 'We're going through; you're not going to stop us.'"

When our government fails to enforce immigration law, it sends a signal that our laws don't matter. And when people learn that we won't enforce some laws, they don't respect other laws. The failure to control our borders has led to a dramatic increase in violent crime in our country. One government study found that in 2003 there were 74,000 criminals in state prisons who are here illegally and 147,000 in local jails.

Our immigration debate is about many things: how we see ourselves as a people; our compassion for those seeking a better life; and our respect for the rule of law. But first and foremost, we must treat immigration as a national security issue. We have an absolute obligation to control our borders. Not to close them, but to control them. The safety of our people depends on it. But many Americans believe their leaders in Washington are not serious about stopping illegal immigration and are rightly frustrated.

I don't worry about people who want to come to the United States to obey the law, work hard, pay taxes, and become Americans. In fact, I am delighted to have new Americans join our country, because historically they have been a source of enormous talent, energy, and courage. From Alexander Hamilton to Andrew Carnegie to Albert Einstein to Henry Kissinger to Arnold Schwarzenegger, people who wanted to improve their lives, and in the process improve the country, have enriched America.

America has a long history of absorbing and blending peoples of many languages and backgrounds. There have always been non-English newspapers in America and now we have non-English radio and television. I am also not worried that some immigrants come here only to earn money and then go home (Italian immigrants, in particular, did that in the late 19th century).

What worries me is the breakdown of will on the part of America's leaders to control our borders and to ensure that new immigrants learn to be American.

A Continent of Hope

Pope John Paul II had a beautiful and inspiring vision for America. From his first trip abroad to Mexico in 1979 to the mass he celebrated in Mexico City's Basilica of Our Lady of Guadalupe in 1999, he consistently spoke of America as a "Continent of Hope." By America, John Paul was referring to both North *and* South America to express his desire for greater unity and mutual respect.

The United States has a special place in this vision of a Continent of Hope. We are a very special nation because we are founded on a revolutionary idea: That we are all created equal—citizen and non-citizen alike—and endowed by our Creator with inalienable rights to life, liberty, and the pursuit of happiness.

The idea of America as a Continent of Hope carries both privileges and responsibilities for the people of the United States. It means that every person has an inherent human dignity that must be respected, including those who are in our country illegally. But it also means that all of us must respect the laws that have been passed to ensure freedom and security. As Pope John Paul II recognized, "The rule of law is the necessary condition for establishing true democracy."

In fulfilling a vision of America as a Continent of Hope, two values are inextricably linked: our compassion for those who come to our country for a better life and our commitment to the rule of law. Just as we would betray this vision by turning our backs on the poverty and injustice suffered by our neighbors, we would also undermine the very foundation of our nation by tolerating eleven million people in our midst in open violation of our laws. If we fail to abide by either of these values, we risk becoming less of the nation our Founders and Pope John Paul II believed we could be, and which we have been for 230 years.

But how do we reconcile this inspiring vision of America with the day-to-day demands of controlling our borders? To build a Continent of Hope we need a system of "patriotic immigration." Patriotic immigration means knowing that all immigrants to our country are legal and accounted for, and that once they're here, they learn to be Americans before they can become citizens. It means using the technology we have—today—to enforce our immigration laws. And it means that immigrants become Americans. Not that they simply mimic American popular culture, but that they learn the language, history, and values that bind us together as a nation.

The way forward lies in a logical set of step-by-step, sustainable solutions that build a momentum and over time will result in a rational and orderly immigration policy acceptable to a majority of the American people.

Controlling Our Borders

In Los Angeles, police are prohibited from asking about the immigration status of people they arrest. In Denver, police aren't allowed to enforce laws against employing workers who are illegal. And in Seattle, law enforcement officials can't report violent criminals that they believe are here illegally to federal immigration authorities.

All of these cities, and many more from Anchorage, Alaska, to Cambridge, Massachusetts, have declared themselves "sanctuary cities" and prohibit their police from enforcing federal immigration law. But maybe we shouldn't be surprised that these cities have thrown up a white flag. The lack of respect for the law that began at the border and spread to American businesses routinely employing those here illegally was bound to infiltrate our cities.

Sanctuary cities—what should be called "lawless cities"—should lose their federal funding if they continue to refuse to enforce our immigration laws. Cracking down on these "don't ask, don't enforce" havens of lawlessness would be an important part of controlling our borders.

Our standard must be absolute: complete control of our borders and coasts. We have the technology and the capability to control border crossing. We simply need the will to use it. Secure card technology used very effectively by companies like Visa, MasterCard and American Express is one example we should adopt.

A comprehensive border control program should begin with demanding that everyone entering the United States provide a biometric identifier, like a thumbprint or an embedded retinal scan, along with a photograph. Background checks should screen out those with criminal records. Foreign governments that want their citizens to participate should turn over up-to-date records of convicted felons so they can be prohibited from entering the United States.

Saying No to Amnesty

Every parent knows that if you reward a behavior, you get more of it. That's why amnesty would be a disaster both for the United States and for immigrants: By rewarding breaking the law to enter our country, amnesty sends the signal that we will not enforce our laws. Moreover, the word would quickly spread that it will only be a matter of time before another amnesty is granted.

But more than the temptation it poses to would-be illegal immigrants, amnesty makes a fool out of the cousin back home or the hopeful Asian or African who is playing by the rules and waiting in line to enter the United States legally. It tells them that they are wasting their time trying to obey our laws. And it tells their governments that they don't need to reform their economies to provide more jobs and opportunity. All they have to do is allow or encourage emigration and rely on the economic engine of the United States to provide jobs for their workers—and checks sent back home.

Maybe the most compelling moral argument against amnesty is that it actually harms those who enter our country illegally. By encouraging more illegal immigration, amnesty encourages more people to come to our country only to live on the margins of society. It means more—not fewer—immigrants subject to exploitation by unscrupulous employers, criminals, and predatory businesses. Amnesty means more families living fearfully in the shadows instead of participating fully in their communities.

Instead of sending the message that our laws are meaningless, we should send the message that they are non-negotiable and at the heart of our system. Along with total border control, we must make it easier for people to enter the United States legally, to work for a set period of time, obey the law, and return home. The requirements for participation in a worker visa program should be tough and uncompromising. The first is essential: Everyone currently working in the United States illegally must return to their home country to apply for the worker visa program. Anything less than requiring those who are here illegally to return home to apply for legal status is amnesty, plain and simple.

Our out-of-control borders didn't get that way overnight, and transitioning from a pattern of illegal immigration to a legal system will take some time. Besides the obvious fact that it will become harder and harder to find work without participating in the worker visa program, those here illegally would have other incentives to return home to apply. If an individual working here illegally knows that improved border control will make it nearly impossible to cross the border again, that stepped up law enforcement and removal will dramatically increase the chances of being picked up and returned home, that there is a legal way to work here, and that there is a very reasonable transition period in which to return home and apply, then we should expect people will chose to participate in a dramatically improved immigration system that will save lives and protect the rule of law.

Work visa holders should have to fulfill other requirements as well. All work visa holders must sign an agreement to pay taxes, obey the law, and waive any rights to appeal their removal from the United States within seventy-two hours if they violate their agreement.

Also, critically, all work visa holders would have to carry a tamperproof, electronic "smart card" with their photo and the thumbprint or iris scan they provided when they entered the United States. This would be their passport to legal employment. And to make sure that the program is administered effectively, it should be outsourced to a company like Visa, MasterCard, or American Express that has a proven track record of preventing fraud and ensuring accountability in a card program. Most Americans have zero confidence that the federal bureaucracy could run such a program competently, so we should give the job to those who can.

And finally, because it takes two to break the law by working here illegally—both an illegal worker and an illegal employer—we must get serious about penalizing employers who hire illegal workers. Astonishingly, the federal government did not levy a single fine on a single employer for hiring illegal workers in 2004. This must change, and under a worker visa program it would change. Employers who hire workers without smart cards that verify their legal status would receive staggering financial penalties that would escalate dramatically with a second and third offense. We must recognize that our failure to enforce our laws against employers who hire illegal workers has contributed to the explosion of illegal immigration into our country.

Making New Americans

For much of our history, America has absorbed waves of immigrants by helping newcomers assimilate into American culture. After all, there is no such thing as a genetic American. To become an American means becoming an American in values, culture, and historic understanding.

But in the last two generations the Left-liberal establishment has undermined and ridiculed American values, American history, and even the idea of American citizenship. Today, Left-liberals want voting opened to non-citizens, including those who are here illegally. That is why the Left-liberal fights against a voter identity card even though Americans overwhelmingly support the idea of limiting their elections to legal citizens. The Left-liberal regards national identity and patriotic commitment to America as irrelevant.

An essential part of encouraging patriotic immigration is a renewal of our commitment to what Senator Lamar Alexander calls patriotic integration: education about American citizenship based on American history; the English language; and the core values of American civilization. American citizenship is not just a piece of paper to be granted but a set of values to be understood and accepted. We must insist that permanent immigrants to this country are encouraged to become citizens, and that the path to citizenship is through a comprehensive understanding of the value, history, language, and culture of our country.

Eighty-eight percent of Americans agree that "schools should make a special effort to teach new immigrants about American values." American feel so strongly about teaching America's language and culture to new immigrants that 65 percent believe schools should help immigrants learn America's language and culture even if it means their native culture is neglected. When asked "what should be the bigger priority; teaching students to be proud of being part of this country and learning the rights and responsibilities of citizenship, or focusing on instilling pride in their ethnic group's identity and heritage," 79 percent of parents chose pride and learning about America.

Similarly, foreign-born parents know how important it is for their children to learn about their new country. In the same Public Agenda 2000 survey, 80 percent of Hispanic parents chose pride and learning about America and 73 percent of foreign-born parents preferred learning about America to their country of origin.

What We Can Do

At the federal and state levels, we can take a number of steps to encourage the teaching of American history to immigrants. The U.S. Department of Education should cooperate with state governments to create online American studies programs in every major city. The Office of Migrant Education should have an American studies program. Every English language instruction course should be required by federal law to base its instruction on patriotic American history.

One of the more sensitive and contentious questions surrounding assimilation of new immigrants is language. English is not and never has been the only language in America. We have a long tradition of people speaking many languages in their local community and with other immigrants. But English has been and should remain our language of government and public discourse.

Americans instinctively know that English matters—81 percent believe immigrants should learn English. Ninety percent believe speaking and writing English should be a primary characteristic of American citizenship. But instead of listening to the American people, the liberal establishment has done everything it can to diminish the importance of English and to promote bilingual education. We cannot let Left-liberals divide the country this way. One proposal to accelerate English fluency is to create a National Program for English Instruction. The program would be modeled after the highly successful "Ulpan Studies" program in Israel. Former Congressman Chris Cox of California describes the program in a bill he introduced in Congress:

> Like the United States, Israel has a polyglot immigrant mix, including Eastern Europeans, Central Asians and Ethiopians. Every new immigrant to Israel is entitled to 500 hours of intensive Hebrew language training, which is designed to give them the language and practical skills to participate in everyday Israeli life. Although the program is not compulsory, participants receive a small stipend to defray expenses and receive a certificate upon successful completion of the program.

This certificate has real value, since many employers require an "Ulpan certificate" for a job and many schools require one for admission.

Chris Cox's proposal is the kind of innovative solution that is a "win–win" for new immigrants and the future of America. Like the Israeli program, it would provide highly intensive English, American history, and civics training for immigrants so they can acquire the practical skills to participate fully in their communities and workplaces. To encourage participation, immigrants could be given a modest stipend. In addition, the time required for naturalization could be shortened for those who successfully complete the program.

And hand-in-hand with this focus on English language education should be a requirement that a written test in English of American history be passed by those wishing to become citizens. What's more, Executive Order 13166 requiring federal documents to be published in many different languages should be rescinded. We must put an end to providing ballots and election materials in foreign languages. And we should renew our efforts to help immigrants learn English. And in return, we should ask immigrants to commit to learning and using the English language as part of being an American.

For four hundred years, from the founding of the Jamestown colony in 1607, people who believe their rights come from God have been building an exciting, prosperous, and free society in America. They have been open to people of many backgrounds and many languages but they have insisted that they become American.

We must return to that great tradition of being pro-immigration and pro-legality, being pro-newcomer and pro-integration into American history, American traditions, and American civic values.

This is the only path which will sustain American civilization for the next generation.

Discussion Questions

1. Do you have any relatives who were immigrants? If so, ask them what their experience was like. Did they feel welcome, and how long did it take before they began to participate in the political process?
2. Should illegal immigrants be eligible for welfare, food stamps, or Medicaid (government health insurance)?
3. How is being an immigrant today different from a hundred years ago? Is it more difficult today or easier?
4. Should employers who hire illegal immigrants be punished?

5. Should the United States construct a wall along the entire U.S.–Mexican border?

6. Instead of erecting a wall, should the United States provide economic development aid to Mexico so that Mexicans can find decent-paying jobs there?

7. In your experience, do most immigrants want to assimilate into American culture or do they want to maintain a separate culture?

8. Should legal immigrants be given the right to vote even before they become naturalized citizens?

Suggested Readings and Internet Resources

In *Who Are We? The Challenges to America's National Identity* (New York: Simon & Schuster, 2004), Samuel Huntington argues that the recent wave of non-European immigrants threatens Americans' identity and cultural consensus. Patrick J. Buchanan sounds the alarm about current high levels of immigration in his *State of Emergency: The Third World Invasion and Conquest of America* (New York: St. Martin's Press, 2006). Aviva Chomsky attacks what she calls "myths" about immigration in *"They Take Our Jobs!" and 20 Other Myths About Immigration* (Boston: Beacon Press, 2007). In *Heaven's Door: Immigration Policy and the American Economy* (Princeton, N.J.: Princeton University Press, 1999) George Borjas documents the negative effects of immigration on low-wage-earning Americans. For a scholarly and critical analysis of efforts to restrict immigration, see Roger Daniels, *Guarding the Golden Door: American Immigration Policy Since 1882* (New York: Hill and Wang, 2004). In *Remaking the American Mainstream: Assimilation and Contemporary Immigration* (Cambridge, Mass.: Harvard University Press, 2003), Richard Alba and Victor Nee argue that as immigrants assimilate into American culture, they also change it.

National Immigration Forum
www.immigrationforum.org
Considered the nation's foremost immigrant rights organization, the National Immigration Forum does research and promotes policies to curb illegal immigration and help immigrants assimilate into American society.

Federation for American Immigration Reform (FAIR)
www.fairus.org
FAIR promotes the view that excessive immigration imposes burdens on governments and schools and creates greater income inequality in American society.

U.S. Citizenship and Immigration Service (USCIS)
www.uscis.gov
Part of the Department of Homeland Security, the USCIS website provides comprehensive and up-to-date information on immigration and naturalization news, applications, forms, and announcements.

Chapter 5

✳

Political Economy: How Democratic Is the Free Market Economy?

At first glance, democratic politics and free market economics seem to go together. The liberty to speak, to practice any religion or none at all, and to participate in politics has often come to be associated with the right to make as much money as we can, to succeed or fail according to our own merits in a free marketplace. Free enterprise seems as unintimidating as a yard sale or a bazaar, with many buyers and sellers, colorful haggling, and a variety of products from which to choose. In contrast, big, intrusive government, with its taxes, police, laws, and bureaucracy, appears to present the greatest threat to all these rights. The equation of democracy with free market capitalism seems, especially since the demise of communism, the best and now the only economic game in town. After all, aren't the most prosperous countries in the world also the most free from governmental control? And even if there are sometimes problems, what alternative do we have?

Upon closer inspection, though, the marriage between democracy and contemporary capitalism continues to be a contentious one. In Singapore and China, and arguably in many states of the former USSR, the rise of the market economy has certainly not led to political freedom; and in America, free enterprise capitalism and political democracy may exist at the same time, but their relationship is hardly cozy. Everywhere, free market capitalism seems to generate enormous wealth, but also wrenching instability and inequalities. *Political economy* is the study of the relationship between politics and economics in different countries around the globe. The two essays that follow ask what the roles of government, citizens, corporations, workers, and consumers actually are in America and also what they *should be* to best serve the public interest.

Perhaps the most important debate in political economy concerns the relationship among democracy, equality, and economic efficiency. Aristotle wrote that democracy could not tolerate extremes of wealth and poverty; large inequalities destroyed the spirit of self-sacrifice and fellowship necessary in a democracy. Politics became less the search for the common good than the single-minded pursuit of material interests by rich and poor alike. While the wealthy fell into luxury and decadence, the poor would sink into ignorance and envy.

For those who believe that economic equality and social equality are important for democratic politics, recent trends in America's political economy are indeed ominous. As we go to press, the economy is locked in a recession caused by greed and excessive risk-taking by the mortgage industry and Wall Street. Unemployment is hovering around 10 percent. The income and wealth gap has widened continually at the expense of what was once a very large and politically predominant middle class. In 2003, nearly half the national income went to just 20 percent of the population, and the top 20,000 income earners accumulated as much as the bottom 96 million. (The inequality debate is covered in Chapter 16.) Most U.S. wage earners face increased insecurity, as waves of corporate mergers, downsizing, outsourcing, and other "innovations" make companies leaner but also meaner. Is the free market really free? If it produces such results, can democracy survive such new extremes?

Many corporations and individuals as well as ordinary Americans defend such inequalities by pointing to the efficiency, growth, and technological innovation that are the products of the free enterprise system. They argue that it is better to divide a very large economic pie unequally than to have less pie to divide; they go on to say that many of the changes represent necessary and inevitable adjustments to the realities of the new global economy. The market, its many defenders claim, also preserves liberty by allowing each individual to compete fairly and consumers to choose among a wide range of new products. Free market economies are said to be meritocracies, rewarding the industrious with wealth and punishing the lazy with hardship. In George Gilder's words, "A successful economy depends on the proliferation of the rich, on creating a large class of risk-taking men who are willing to shun the easy channels of a comfortable life in order to create new enterprise, win huge profits, and invest them again."

The two essays that follow not only offer opposing views about the meanings of American democracy and capitalism; they also differ about the meaning of freedom, individual liberty, and equality. They disagree profoundly about what role government actually does play in relationship to the U.S. market economy as well as about what role it should play.

The first essay is excerpted from *Capitalism and Freedom,* by Nobel Prize-winner Milton Friedman, who died in 2006. It was originally written in 1962 and has since been reissued in many editions. Friedman describes himself as a "classic liberal" and tries to restore the original doctrine's political and moral meanings. Classic liberals like Friedman advocate maximum individual freedom in the face of government's tendency to tyrannize. The market economy, Friedman argues, "remov[es] the organization of economic activity from the control of political authority," thereby "eliminat[ing] this source of coercive power." Because liberty is synonymous with democracy, Friedman argues that government has only two legitimate roles: It must defend the national territory and act as an umpire, deciding the rules of the market "game" and interpreting them as necessary when free individuals compete with one another.

In the second essay, Samuel Bowles, Frank Roosevelt, and Richard Edwards deny Friedman's claim that market capitalism and small government go together. They argue that "the expansion of the role of government in the United States is not something that happened in *opposition* to capitalism" but something that happened "in *response* to the development of capitalism." Bowles, Roosevelt, and Edwards go on to claim that a capitalist market economy is hardly a meritocracy; political power and economic power are linked through biased rules. Unlike Friedman, they say that the marketplace concentrates both kinds of power. Hierarchical corporations determine the investments and life circumstances for workers and communities and severely limit the meaning and scope of democratic government and citizenship themselves. For these writers, growing economic inequality spells the effective denial of liberty to the many. Corporate power often buys undue political influence, whether through campaign contributions or corporate ownership of the mass media.

The authors of both essays base their arguments on a defense of democracy. While reading them, ask the following questions: How would Friedman have defended himself against the charge that the market economy produces corporations that exercise unchecked and undemocratic power? What would Bowles, Roosevelt, and Edwards say to Friedman's charge that government often poses a threat to individual freedom and choice and thus to democratic liberty? How do both essays deal with voters and citizens and their potential role in controlling the production and distribution of economic resources? How would the U.S. political economy change if each author had his way? How would it stay the same?

Capitalism and Freedom
MILTON FRIEDMAN

Introduction

The free man will ask neither what his country can do for him nor what he can do for his country.[1] He will ask rather "What can I and my compatriots do through government" to help us discharge our individual responsibilities, to

---

1. Friedman is referring to John F. Kennedy's 1961 inaugural address.

achieve our several goals and purposes, and above all, to protect our freedom? And he will accompany this question with another: How can we keep the government we create from becoming a Frankenstein that will destroy the very freedom we establish it to protect? Freedom is a rare and delicate plant. Our minds tell us, and history confirms, that the great threat to freedom is the concentration of power. Government is necessary to preserve our freedom, it is an instrument through which we can exercise our freedom; yet by concentrating power in political hands, it is also a threat to freedom. Even though the men who wield this power initially be of good will and even though they be not corrupted by the power they exercise, the power will both attract and form men of a different stamp.

How can we benefit from the promise of government while avoiding the threat to freedom? Two broad principles embodied in our Constitution give an answer that has preserved our freedom so far, though they have been violated repeatedly in practice while proclaimed as precept.

First, the scope of government must be limited. Its major function must be to protect our freedom both from the enemies outside our gates and from our fellow-citizens: to preserve law and order, to enforce private contracts, to foster competitive markets. Beyond this major function, government may enable us at times to accomplish jointly what we would find it more difficult or expensive to accomplish severally. However, any such use of government is fraught with danger. We should not and cannot avoid using government in this way. But there should be a clear and large balance of advantages before we do. By relying primarily on voluntary co-operation and private enterprise, in both economic and other activities, we can insure that the private sector is a check on the powers of the governmental sector and an effective protection of freedom of speech, of religion, and of thought.

The second broad principle is that government power must be dispersed. If government is to exercise power, better in the county than in the state, better in the state than in Washington. If I do not like what my local community does, be it in sewage disposal, or zoning, or schools, I can move to another local community, and though few may take this step, the mere possibility acts as a check. If I do not like what my state does, I can move to another. If I do not like what Washington imposes, I have few alternatives in this world of jealous nations....

Government can never duplicate the variety and diversity of individual action. At any moment in time, by imposing uniform standards in housing, or nutrition, or clothing, government could undoubtedly improve the level of living of many individuals; by imposing uniform standards in schooling, road construction, or sanitation, central government could undoubtedly improve the level of performance in many local areas and perhaps even on the average of all communities. But in the process, government would replace progress by stagnation, it would substitute uniform mediocrity for the variety essential for that experimentation which can bring tomorrow's laggards above today's mean....

The Relation between Economic Freedom
and Political Freedom

It is widely believed that politics and economics are separate and largely unconnected; that individual freedom is a political problem and material welfare an
economic problem; and that any kind of political arrangements can be combined
with any kind of economic arrangements.... The thesis of this chapter is ... that
there is an intimate connection between economics and politics, that only certain
combinations of political and economic arrangements are possible, and that in
particular, a society which is socialist cannot also be democratic, in the sense of
guaranteeing individual freedom.

Economic arrangements play a dual role in the promotion of a free society.
On the one hand, freedom in economic arrangements is itself a component of
freedom broadly understood, so economic freedom is an end in itself. In the second place, economic freedom is also an indispensable means toward the achieve-
ment of political freedom.

The first of these roles of economic freedom needs special emphasis because
intellectuals in particular have a strong bias against regarding this aspect of freedom as important. They tend to express contempt for what they regard as material aspects of life, and to regard their own pursuit of allegedly higher values as on
a different plane of significance and as deserving of special attention. For most
citizens of the country, however, if not for the intellectual, the direct importance
of economic freedom is at least comparable in significance to the indirect importance of economic freedom as a means to political freedom....

Viewed as a means to the end of political freedom, economic arrangements
are important because of their effect on the concentration or dispersion of
power. The kind of economic organization that provides economic freedom directly, namely, competitive capitalism, also promotes political freedom because it
separates economic power from political power and in this way enables the one
to offset the other.

Historical evidence speaks with a single voice on the relation between political freedom and a free market. I know of no example in time or place of a
society that has been marked by a large measure of political freedom, and that
has not also used something comparable to a free market to organize the bulk of
economic activity.

Because we live in a largely free society, we tend to forget how limited is
the span of time and the part of the globe for which there has ever been anything like political freedom: the typical state of mankind is tyranny, servitude,
and misery. The nineteenth century and early twentieth century in the Western
world stand out as striking exceptions to the general trend of historical development. Political freedom in this instance clearly came along with the free market
and the development of capitalist institutions. So also did political freedom in the
golden age of Greece and in the early days of the Roman era.

History suggests only that capitalism is a necessary condition for political
freedom. Clearly it is not a sufficient condition. Fascist Italy and Fascist Spain,

Germany at various times in the last seventy years, Japan before World Wars I and II, tzarist Russia in the decades before World War I—are all societies that cannot conceivably be described as politically free. Yet, in each, private enterprise was the dominant form of economic organization. It is therefore clearly possible to have economic arrangements that are fundamentally capitalist and political arrangements that are not free.

Even in those societies, the citizenry had a good deal more freedom than citizens of a modern totalitarian state.[2] ... Even in Russia under the Tzars, it was possible for some citizens, under some circumstances, to change their jobs without getting permission from political authority because capitalism and the existence of private property provided some check to the centralized power of the state....

Historical evidence by itself can never be convincing. Perhaps it was sheer coincidence that the expansion of freedom occurred at the same time as the development of capitalist and market institutions. Why should there be a connection? What are the logical links between economic and political freedom? In discussing these questions we shall consider first the market as a direct component of freedom, and then the indirect relation between market arrangements and political freedom. A by-product will be an outline of the ideal economic arrangements for a free society.

As liberals, we take freedom of the individual, or perhaps the family, as our ultimate goal in judging social arrangements. Freedom as a value in this sense has to do with the interrelations among people; it has no meaning whatsoever to a Robinson Crusoe on an isolated island.... Robinson Crusoe on his island is subject to "constraint," he has limited "power," and he has only a limited number of alternatives, but there is no problem of freedom in the sense that is relevant to our discussion. Similarly, in a society freedom has nothing to say about what an individual does with his freedom; it is not an all-embracing ethic. Indeed, a major aim of the liberal is to leave the ethical problem for the individual to wrestle with. The "really" important ethical problems are those that face an individual in a free society—what he should do with his freedom. There are thus two sets of values that a liberal will emphasize—the values that are relevant to relations among people, which is the context in which he assigns first priority to freedom; and the values that are relevant to the individual in the exercise of his freedom, which is the realm of individual ethics and philosophy.

The liberal conceives of men as imperfect beings. He regards the problem of social organization to be as much a negative problem of preventing "bad" people from doing harm as of enabling "good" people to do good; and, of course, "bad" and "good" people may be the same people, depending on who is judging them.

The basic problem of social organization is how to co-ordinate the economic activities of large numbers of people. Even in relatively backward societies, extensive division of labor and specialization of function is required to make effective use of available resources. In advanced societies, the scale on which co-ordination is needed, to take full advantage of the opportunities offered by

---

2. A totalitarian state is a political order in which state power is held by a single political party, with no political rights accorded to individuals. Friedman here is referring to the former Soviet Union and to other communist countries.

modern science and technology, is enormously greater. Literally millions of people are involved in providing one another with their daily bread, let alone with their yearly automobiles. The challenge to the believer in liberty is to reconcile this widespread interdependence with individual freedom.

Fundamentally, there are only two ways of co-ordinating the economic activities of millions. One is central direction involving the use of coercion—the technique of the army and of the modern totalitarian state. The other is voluntary co-operation of individuals—the technique of the market place.

The possibility of co-ordination through voluntary co-operation rests on the elementary—yet frequently denied—proposition that both parties to an economic transaction benefit from it, *provided the transaction is bilaterally voluntary and informed.*

Exchange can therefore bring about co-ordination without coercion. A working model of a society organized through voluntary exchange is a *free private enterprise exchange economy*—what we have been calling competitive capitalism.

In its simplest form, such a society consists of a number of independent households—a collection of Robinson Crusoes, as it were. Each household uses the resources it controls to produce goods and services that it exchanges for goods and services produced by other households, on terms mutually acceptable to the two parties to the bargain. It is thereby enabled to satisfy its wants indirectly by producing goods and services for others, rather than directly by producing goods for its own immediate use. The incentive for adopting this indirect route is, of course, the increased product made possible by division of labor and specialization of function. Since the household always has the alternative of producing directly for itself, it need not enter into any exchange unless it benefits from it. Hence, no exchange will take place unless both parties do benefit from it. Co-operation is thereby achieved without coercion.

Specialization of function and division of labor would not go far if the ultimate productive unit were the household. In a modern society, we have gone much further. We have introduced enterprises which are intermediaries between individuals in their capacities as suppliers of service and as purchasers of goods. And similarly, specialization of function and division of labor could not go very far if we had to continue to rely on the barter of product for product. In consequence, money has been introduced as a means of facilitating exchange, and of enabling the acts of purchase and of sale to be separated into two parts.

Despite the important role of enterprises and of money in our actual economy, and despite the numerous and complex problems they raise, the central characteristic of the market technique of achieving co-ordination is fully displayed in the simple exchange economy that contains neither enterprises nor money. As in that simple model, so in the complex enterprise and money-exchange economy, co-operation is strictly individual and voluntary *provided*: (a) that enterprises are private, so that the ultimate contracting parties are individuals and (b) that individuals are effectively free to enter or not to enter into any particular exchange, so that every transaction is strictly voluntary....

So long as effective freedom of exchange is maintained, the central feature of the market organization of economic activity is that it prevents one person from interfering with another in respect of most of his activities. The consumer is protected from coercion by the seller because of the presence of other sellers with whom he can deal. The seller is protected from coercion by the consumer because of other consumers to whom he can sell. The employee is protected from coercion by the employer because of other employers for whom he can work, and so on. And the market does this impersonally and without centralized authority.

Indeed, a major source of objection to a free economy is precisely that it does this task so well. It gives people what they want instead of what a particular group thinks they ought to want. Underlying most arguments against the free market is a lack of belief in freedom itself.

The existence of a free market does not of course eliminate the need for government. On the contrary, government is essential both as a forum for determining the "rules of the game" and as an umpire to interpret and enforce the rules decided on. What the market does is to reduce greatly the range of issues that must be decided through political means, and thereby to minimize the extent to which government need participate directly in the game. The characteristic feature of action through political channels is that it tends to require or enforce substantial conformity. The great advantage of the market, on the other hand, is that it permits wide diversity. It is, in political terms, a system of proportional representation. Each man can vote, as it were, for the color of tie he wants and get it; he does not have to see what color the majority wants and then, if he is in the minority, submit.

It is this feature of the market that we refer to when we say that the market provides economic freedom. But this characteristic also has implications that go far beyond the narrowly economic. Political freedom means the absence of coercion of a man by his fellow men. The fundamental threat to freedom is power to coerce, be it in the hands of a monarch, a dictator, an oligarchy, or a momentary majority. The preservation of freedom requires the elimination of such concentration of power to the fullest possible extent and the dispersal and distribution of whatever power cannot be eliminated—a system of checks and balances. By removing the organization of economic activity from the control of political authority, the market eliminates this source of coercive power. It enables economic strength to be a check to political power rather than a reinforcement.

Economic power can be widely dispersed. There is no law of conservation which forces the growth of new centers of economic strength to be at the expense of existing centers. Political power, on the other hand, is more difficult to decentralize. There can be numerous small independent governments. But it is far more difficult to maintain numerous equipotent small centers of political power in a single large government than it is to have numerous centers of economic strength in a single large economy. There can be many millionaires in one large economy. But can there be more than one really outstanding leader, one person on whom the energies and enthusiasms of his countrymen are centered? If the central government gains power, it is likely to be at the expense of local governments. There seems to be something like a fixed total of political power to be distributed. Consequently, if economic power is joined to political power, concentration seems almost inevitable. On the other hand, if economic power is kept in separate hands from political power, it can serve as a check and a counter to political power....

In a capitalist society, it is only necessary to convince a few wealthy people to get funds to launch any idea, however strange, and there are many such persons, many independent foci of support. And, indeed, it is not even necessary to persuade people or financial institutions with available funds of the soundness of the ideas to be propagated. It is only necessary to persuade them that the propagation can be financially successful; that the newspaper or magazine or book or other venture will be profitable. The competitive publisher, for example, cannot afford to publish only writing with which he personally agrees; his touchstone must be the likelihood that the market will be large enough to yield a satisfactory return on his investment....

The Role of Government in a Free Society

... From this standpoint, the role of the market is that it permits unanimity without conformity.... On the other hand, the characteristic feature of action through explicitly political channels is that it tends to require or to enforce substantial conformity.... The typical issue must be decided "yes" or "no"; at most, provision can be made for a fairly limited number of alternatives....

The use of political channels, while inevitable, tends to strain the social cohesion essential for a stable society. The strain is least if agreement for joint action need be reached only on a limited range of issues on which people in any event have common views. Every extension of the range of issues for which explicit agreement is sought strains further the delicate threads that hold society together. If it goes so far as to touch an issue on which men feel deeply yet differently, it may well disrupt the society. Fundamental differences in basic values can seldom if ever be resolved at the ballot box; ultimately they can only be decided, though not resolved, by conflict. The religious and civil wars of history are a bloody testament to this judgment.

The widespread use of the market reduces the strain on the social fabric by rendering conformity unnecessary with respect to any activities it encompasses. The wider the range of activities covered by the market, the fewer are the issues on which explicitly political decisions are required and hence on which it is necessary to achieve agreement. In turn, the fewer the issues on which agreement is necessary, the greater is the likelihood of getting agreement while maintaining a free society....

Government as Rule-Maker and Umpire

... Just as a good game requires acceptance by the players both of the rules and of the umpire to interpret and enforce them, so a good society requires that its members agree on the general conditions that will govern relations among them, on some means of arbitrating different interpretations of these conditions, and on some device for enforcing compliance with the generally accepted rules.... In both games and society also, no set of rules can prevail unless most participants most of the time conform to them without external sanctions; unless that is, there is a broad underlying social consensus. But we cannot rely on custom or on this consensus alone to interpret and to enforce the rules; we need an umpire. These then are the basic roles of government in a free society: to provide a means whereby we can modify the rules, to mediate differences among us on the meaning of the rules, and to enforce compliance with the rules on the part of those few who would otherwise not play the game.

The need for government in these respects arises because absolute freedom is impossible. However attractive anarchy may be as a philosophy, it is not feasible in a world of imperfect men. Men's freedoms can conflict, and when they do, one man's freedom must be limited to preserve another's—as a Supreme Court Justice once put it, "My freedom to move my fist must be limited by the proximity of your chin."...

Action through Government on Grounds of Technical Monopoly and Neighborhood Effects

The role of government ... is to do something that the market cannot do for itself, namely, to determine, arbitrate, and enforce the rules of the game. We may also want to do through government some things that might conceivably be done through the market but that technical or similar conditions render it difficult to do in that way. These all reduce to cases in which strictly voluntary exchange is either exceedingly costly or practically impossible. There are two general classes of such cases: monopoly and similar market imperfections, and neighborhood effects.

Exchange is truly voluntary only when nearly equivalent alternatives exist. Monopoly implies the absence of alternatives and thereby inhibits effective freedom of exchange. In practice, monopoly frequently, if not generally, arises from government support or from collusive agreements among individuals. With respect to these, the problem is either to avoid governmental fostering of monopoly or to stimulate the effective enforcement of rules such as those embodied in our anti-trust laws. However, monopoly may also arise because it is technically efficient to have a single producer or enterprise. I venture to suggest that such cases are more limited than is supposed but they unquestionably do arise....

A second general class of cases in which strictly voluntary exchange is impossible arises when actions of individuals have effects on other individuals for which it is not feasible to charge or recompense them. This is the problem of "neighborhood effects." An obvious example is the pollution of a stream. The man who pollutes a stream is in effect forcing others to exchange good water for bad. These others might be willing to make the exchange at a price. But it is not feasible for them, acting individually, to avoid the exchange or to enforce appropriate compensation....

Parks are an interesting example because they illustrate the difference between cases that can and cases that cannot be justified by neighborhood effects, and because almost everyone at first sight regards the conduct of national parks as obviously a valid function of government. In fact, however, neighborhood effects may justify a city park; they do not justify a national park, like Yellowstone National Park or the Grand Canyon. What is the fundamental difference between the two? For the city park, it is extremely difficult to identify the people who benefit from it and to charge them for the benefits which they receive. If there is a park in the middle of the city, the houses on all sides get the benefit of the open space, and people who walk through it or by it also benefit. To maintain toll collectors at the gates or to impose annual charges per window overlooking the park would be very expensive and difficult. The entrances to a national park like Yellowstone, on the other hand, are few; most of the people who come stay for a considerable period of time and it is perfectly feasible to set up toll gates and collect admission charges. This is indeed now done, though the charges do not cover the whole costs. If the public wants this kind of an activity enough to pay for it, private enterprises will have every incentive to provide such parks. And, of course, there are many private enterprises of this nature now in existence. I cannot myself conjure up any neighborhood effects or important monopoly effects that would justify governmental activity in this area.

Considerations like those I have treated under the heading of neighborhood effects have been used to rationalize almost every conceivable intervention. In many instances, however, this rationalization is special pleading rather than a legitimate application of the concept of neighborhood effects. Neighborhood effects cut both ways. They can be a reason for limiting the activities of government as well as for expanding them....

Action through Government on Paternalistic Grounds

Freedom is a tenable objective only for responsible individuals. We do not believe in freedom for madmen or children. The necessity of drawing a line between responsible individuals and others is inescapable, yet it means that there is an essential ambiguity in our ultimate objective of freedom. Paternalism is inescapable for those whom we designate as not responsible.

The clearest case, perhaps, is that of madmen. We are willing neither to permit them freedom nor to shoot them. It would be nice if we could rely on voluntary activities of individuals to house and care for the madmen. But I think we cannot rule out the possibility that such charitable activities will be inadequate, if only because of the neighborhood effect involved in the fact that I benefit if another man contributes to the care of the insane. For this reason, we may be willing to arrange for their care through government.

Children offer a more difficult case. The ultimate operative unit in our society is the family, not the individual. Yet the acceptance of the family as the unit rests in considerable part on expediency rather than principle. We believe that parents are generally best able to protect their children and to provide for their development into responsible individuals for whom freedom is appropriate. But we do not believe in the freedom of parents to do what they will with other people. The children are responsible individuals in embryo, and a believer in freedom believes in protecting their ultimate rights.

To put this in a different and what may seem a more callous way, children are at one and the same time consumer goods and potentially responsible members of society. The freedom of individuals to use their economic resources as they want includes the freedom to use them to have children—to buy, as it were, the services of children as a particular form of consumption. But once this choice is exercised, the children have a value in and of themselves and have a freedom of their own that is not simply an extension of the freedom of the parents.

The paternalistic ground for governmental activity is in many ways the most troublesome to a liberal; for it involves the acceptance of a principle—that some shall decide for others—which he finds objectionable in most applications and which he rightly regards as a hallmark of his chief intellectual opponents, the proponents of collectivism in one or another of its guises, whether it be communism, socialism, or a welfare state. Yet there is no use pretending that problems are simpler than in fact they are. There is no avoiding the need for some measure of paternalism....

Conclusion

A government which maintained law and order, defined property rights, served as a means whereby we could modify property rights and other rules of the economic game, adjudicated disputes about the interpretation of the rules, enforced contracts, promoted competition, provided a monetary framework, engaged in activities to counter technical monopolies and to overcome neighborhood effects widely regarded as sufficiently important to justify government intervention, and which supplemented private charity and the private family in protecting the irresponsible, whether madman or child—such a government would clearly have important functions to perform. The consistent liberal is not an anarchist....

Is it an accident that so many of the governmental reforms of recent decades have gone awry, that the bright hopes have turned to ashes? Is it simply because the programs are faulty in detail?

I believe the answer is clearly in the negative. The central defect of these measures is that they seek through government to force people to act against their own immediate interests in order to promote a supposedly general interest. They seek to resolve what is supposedly a conflict of interest, or a difference in view about interests, not by establishing a framework that will eliminate the conflict, or by persuading people to have different interests, but by forcing people to act against their own interest. They substitute the values of outsiders for the values of participants; either some telling others what is good for them, or the government taking from some to benefit others. These measures are therefore countered by one of the strongest and most creative forces known to man—the attempt by millions of individuals to promote their own interests, to live their lives by their own values. This is the major reason why the measures have so often had the opposite of the effects intended. It is also one of the major strengths of a free society and explains why governmental regulation does not strangle it.

Corporate Capitalism Hurts American Democracy

SAMUEL BOWLES, FRANK ROOSEVELT, AND RICHARD EDWARDS

A capitalist economy operates on the basis of a set of principles—rules of the game—designed to organize commodity production for profit using wage labor and privately owned capital goods. Governments, on the other hand, are organized according to different principles, a different set of rules. These rules make possible collective action, and involve a compulsory relationship between citizens and their government. Governments—or government leaders—act on behalf of the entire population of a nation, and their actions can be enforced on all of its residents.

The principles of democratic government are very different from those that govern the capitalist economy. Generally, the employees of a corporation do not elect its leaders—the management—and neither does the community in which the corporation is located. In fact, corporate leaders are not elected at all in the sense that is usually attached to the word *election*. The people who own the corporation select them, with each owner having as many votes as the number of shares of stock he or she owns. Similarly, freedom of speech and other civil liberties guaranteed in the political sphere are often limited in the workplace. Many businesses enforce dress codes, and employees are generally not free to post information such as appeals from labor unions.

These two sets of rules—the rules of democratic government and the rules of a capitalist economy—exist side by side in our society. Both affect the economy, and they each conflict. Why has government grown and what does it have to do with the capitalist economy? Do citizens or capitalists have power in politics? Below, we address these questions.

The Expansion of Government Economic Activity

During the past century, the economic importance of the government has grown dramatically. Because its role has expanded qualitatively as well as quantitatively, and because not all government activities are equally important in relation to the economy, there is no single measure by which the expansion of the government's role can be adequately gauged. Measured in dollars, however, federal, state, and local government spending in the United States increased from 7.7 percent of the total output of the economy in 1902 to 31 percent of it in 2002.

In the United States, increases in military, Social Security, and health-related programs in the twentieth century led to substantial growth of expenditures at the level of the federal government. Expansion of such direct services as public schools, municipal hospitals, and police and fire protection led to even more rapid growth of employment at the state and local levels.

Although government expenditures at all levels in the United States increased greatly during the past century, the sum of such expenditures, as a share of the nation's total output of goods and services, is smaller than the comparable percentages of national output spent by governments in other advanced capitalist countries.

The reasons for the increased economic importance of the government are much debated. Some people see growing government as a triumph by the ordinary citizen over the self-serving interests of business. Others see the growth as a triumph of the bureaucratic mentality, which assumes that if there is a problem its solution must take the form of a government program. Still others see big government and the free market economy as opposites.

But there is a more persuasive explanation for the increasing role of government in economic life: **The survival and workability of capitalism as an economic system has required the government to grow.** The ceaseless search for extra profits and the ensuing social, technical, and other changes ... have created conditions that have led to demands for a more active government. These demands, as we will see, have come as often from businesspeople as from workers, as often from the Chamber of Commerce as from the AFL–CIO, as often from Republicans as from Democrats. The expansion of the role of government in the United States is not something that happened in *opposition* to capitalism; rather, it is something that has happened in *response* to the development of capitalism. In what specific ways did this expansion occur?

Economic Concentration

Much of the growth of governmental economic activity can be explained by the growth of large corporations and the decline of small producers. The enormous power of modern corporations in the United States has allowed their owners to lobby the government for favors and to influence the formation of public opinion. Thus, big business is able to induce the government to do things that enhance profit making. Examples of this would include subsidies for the nuclear power industry and exorbitant purchases of military hardware. U.S. corporate leaders have also supported the expansion of government regulation in those many situations in which they wanted protection from competitive pressures that might lower profits. Examples of such situations include regulation of the quality of meat and other food to prevent competition from companies that would lower the quality of such products. In addition, consumers and workers have supported the expansion of the economic role of the government, in part to protect themselves from the power of the giant corporations. Passage of the Sherman Antitrust Act (1890), the Clean Air Act (1970), and the Consumer Product Safety Act (1973) are examples of this.

International Expansion

The increasingly global reach of large American corporations has contributed to the development of a conception of "U.S. interests" around the world. As corporations expanded from national to international businesses, they changed from wanting the government to impose tariffs to keep out goods made abroad to insisting that the government protect U.S. investments around the world. They have promoted the development of an increasingly expensive military establishment to defend these interests. Preparations for war and the payment of interest on the national debt—much of which was borrowed to pay for past wars—have accounted for much of the growth in federal expenditures. Capitalism did not invent war, but the degree of international economic interdependence and rivalry produced by the expansion of capitalism did make *world* wars more likely. After World War II, high levels of military expenditure became a permanent feature of the U.S. economy. In 2002 military expenditures amounted to nearly one-half of the "discretionary spending" part of the U.S. federal budget—the part not already committed to paying for "entitlements" such as Social Security and Medicare. In the aftermath of the terrorist attack on the World Trade Center in 2001 the role of government has increased still further with the creation of the Department of Homeland Security and with the government now empowered to monitor private individuals' e-mail communications and to bypass some of the rights of privacy that Americans had long taken for granted.

Economic Instability

The increasing instability of the economy, marked by periods of severe unemployment and dramatized by the worldwide Great Depression of the 1930s, has been another reason for the growing economic importance of the government. The stabilization of the U.S. economy was a major objective of the businessmen who promoted the formation of the Federal Reserve System in 1913 and the Securities and Exchange Commission in 1935. An even more significant impetus for governmental intervention was the persistence of the Great Depression until military expenditures brought about full employment at the beginning of World War II. During the depressed 1930s, radical political movements of both the left and the right spread around the world generating political instability as people responded in different ways to the failure of capitalist economies to provide for their livelihoods.

In many countries, broad coalitions of employers and workers pushed the government to take greater responsibility for maintaining economic growth, profits, and employment through its activities as a macroeconomic regulator. Immediately following World War II, organizations such as the Committee for Economic Development in the United States were successful in gaining congressional passage of the Employment Act of 1946. This legislation committed the U.S. federal government, at least in principle, to insuring that there would be adequate job opportunities for everyone in the labor force.

The post–World War II growth of total government expenditures has increased the ability of the government to stabilize employment. Some government programs (such as unemployment insurance) act as built-in stabilizers that auto-matically raise government spending when the economy slows down, thus help-ing to maintain enough total demand to avoid severe recessions. Other more deliberate macroeconomic regulation such as new tax policies or changes in the rate of interest may also counteract the economy's tendency to provide too few jobs. Except during the Korean War, the Vietnam War, and the late 1990s, however, such policies have not succeeded in bringing about full employment in the United States. In part this is because, despite the Employment Act of 1946, the elimination of unemployment has never actually been the objective of the government's macroeconomic regulation. Alben Barkley, a U.S. senator at the time of its passage, drew attention to the inadequacy of the Full Employ-ment Act by saying that the new law "promised anyone needing a job the right to go out and look for one."

Income Support

During the Great Depression, many Americans became convinced that those un-able to make an adequate living should be supported, at least at some minimal level, by the government. Government programs to support poor people re-placed informal support systems and private charity, both because people who fell on hard times could no longer count on their families or neighbors to tide them over and because private charities did not have sufficient funds to take care of them. In the 1930s unemployment compensation, general relief, and Social Security were established. With the numerical growth and political mobilization of the aged population and of single parent families during the 1960s and early 1970s, benefits and beneficiaries expanded.

In recent years, however, the idea of government support for those in need has come under serious attack from political forces on the right. From the early 1970s through the 1990s, the expansion of income support programs was halted and, in some cases, reversed. In the 1990s, for example, the average weekly un-employment insurance benefit payment was lower in real terms (corrected for inflation) than it had been twenty years earlier.

With the 1996 "welfare reform" legislation passed by the Republican-dom-inated Congress and signed into law by President Clinton, the federal role in maintaining income support through Aid to Families with Dependent Children (AFDC) was eliminated altogether. Under the Temporary Assistance to Needy Families (TANF) legislation, blocks of aid were granted to states, which then became solely responsible for providing relief. From 1996 to 2002 welfare rolls were further cut back by new regulations requiring all able-bodied former reci-pients to work at menial jobs in order to qualify for aid. It is too soon to judge whether this recent curtailment of federal support will have beneficial or harmful economic consequences for America's neediest citizens over the long term.

Changing Patterns of Family Life

The combination in the late 1960s of a slowdown in the growth of real wages and an upsurge of women's demands for equality had the effect of altering relationships between women and men both in the household and in the economy as a whole. The two developments have made it less likely that men will be the sole "breadwinners" while their wives stay home to take care of the children, cook the meals, and clean the house. In 1900, only 20 percent of American women worked outside the home; by 2000, the percentage of women between the ages of 25 and 64 in the paid labor force had increased to 73.5 percent.

In the face of wage stagnation from the late 1960s to the mid-1990s, more and more families found that they needed to have both husband and wife in the paid labor force in order to support their living standards. At the same time, the women's movement changed people's consciousness in ways that led at least some men to take more responsibility for household tasks and allowed many more women to take full-time jobs and have careers. Of course these changes have been accompanied by an increasing commodification of household tasks: more children are now taken care of in daycare centers or by paid "nannies," more meals are eaten out or ordered in, and more housecleaning is done by paid "help."

Increases in the labor force participation of women and the broader changes in society's gender roles became yet another set of factors making for expansion of the government's role in the economy. To break down barriers to women's equality in the workplace, new laws and new enforcement activities were required. In the United States, the Civil Rights Act of 1964 created the Equal Employment Opportunity Commission (EEOC) to secure the rights of women as well as members of minority groups to equal opportunities in the workplace. To help both women and men combine paid work with family responsibilities, the U.S. Congress passed and President Clinton signed the 1993 Family and Medical Leave Act. Although compliance with these laws has been less than perfect, they are both significant in bringing U.S. policies closer to those in other advanced industrial nations.

However, citizens in Japan and many Western nations have long had rights to government-funded childcare, to health care for children as well as adults, and to paid parental leave as well as generous required vacation time. In contrast, the U.S. government has been reluctant to formulate comprehensive policies for the support of families, the only exception being for families at or below the poverty line.

Still, the passage of the U.S. Family and Medical Leave Act in 1993 was at least a small step in the direction of governmental support for working families. The Act requires that all workers in firms with more than fifty employees be allowed to take up to twelve weeks of unpaid leave at the time of the birth or adoption of a child or when an ill family member needs to be cared for. Both women and men are covered by the Act. Although their leave is unpaid, employees retain their health benefits while they are on leave and are assured of an equivalent position within their firm when they return to work. What both the Equal Employment Opportunity Commission and the Family and Medical Leave Act do, then, is to assign greater responsibility to the U.S. government for regulating relationships between employers and their employees.

Public Safety

Many groups have demanded that government mediate the conflict between profitability and public safety. While competition generally pushes firms to develop the most profitable technology, the resulting technological advancements do not always result in net benefits to society. The pharmaceutical industry provides an example of the danger of leaving economic decision making solely up to firms seeking to maximize their profits. Certain drugs may be very profitable for the companies, but their side effects, though often complicated and long delayed, may ultimately be damaging to people's health. The chemical industry offers another example of the conflict between profit making and public safety. Some highly profitable production processes in this industry may cause brain damage, sterility, or cancer in the workers who run them; such effects may become known only after many years of exposure....

Environmental Protection

Another issue that has aroused public demands for governmental intervention is the growing need to protect the natural environment from the effects of industrial production. Our natural surroundings—our land, fresh water, air, and oceans—are not only being used, they are being used up or contaminated as corporations compete to produce goods more cheaply. Historically, there have been no prices charged for the use—or misuse—of air and water, and the result has been the pollution of the elements that sustain life. In many cases the most profitable way of disposing of wastes—even very hazardous ones—has been simply to throw them away, using our natural environment as a free dumping ground. Incidents such as the burning of Ohio's Cuyahoga River in 1969, the poisoning of the Love Canal residential area outside of Buffalo in the 1970s, and the 1989 Exxon *Valdez* oil spill off the coast of Alaska have dramatized the need for more adequate controls. The creation of the Environmental Protection Agency and the passage of the Clean Air Act and the Water Pollution Control Act in the early 1970s were important steps in this direction.

Discrimination

Over the last three decades people have come to realize that the unrestricted exercise of private property rights can result in racial and sexual discrimination against both customers and workers. The lunch-counter sit-ins that set off the civil rights movement in the early 1960s brought the issue into sharp relief: should the owners of restaurants and lunch counters have the right to do whatever they please with their property, even if it involves the exclusion of black customers? Or do black people have a right to be treated equally in public places? Since 1964 the U.S. Civil Rights Commission has brought suits against companies, unions, and other institutions to force them to abandon discriminatory practices.

Many of the causes of expanded government economic activity discussed above may be understood as responses to particular aspects of the accumulation process of the capitalist economy. Thus the growth of government regulation has been as much a part of capitalist economic development as the growth of investment or the growth of technology.

But if government has had to grow to repair the problems and hardships caused by the development of the economy, it does not follow that such growth has always succeeded in meeting human needs. It is debatable whether people are today more secure economically than they were a hundred years ago, or better protected from the arbitrary power of giant corporations, or less susceptible to environmental or natural disaster, or less likely to encounter health hazards in their workplace or in their food. Many of the political battles during the last century have been about the extent to which the government can or should be called on to solve social problems caused by economic forces beyond the control of individuals.

Just as we should not overrate the impact of the government's economic activities, we should not exaggerate their extent. Government employment, including the military, is only 15 percent of the total labor force, and of greater significance is the fact that the most important determinant of the future course of the economy—investment—is still almost entirely in private hands....

Government and Corporate Profits

While there is much controversy over the amount of government participation in the economy, the more essential question might be the ways in which government activity and taxation policy affect corporate profits. In general, when it comes to governmental intervention and the corporate profit rate, the power of ordinary citizens and workers is often sacrificed to the needs and political power of large companies and their biggest shareholders. Government can have a huge impact on both the pre-tax profit rate and, through taxation, on how much the after-tax profit rate of corporations rewards shareholders.

Government can improve corporate profits through relatively noncontroversial means, such as promoting research. Yet most other activities provide benefits to some groups and classes and harm others. Consider work regulations and the minimum hourly wage; minimal work regulation and a low minimum wage—both current policies—provide a higher profit rate by cutting corners with safety and by causing higher levels of job insecurity. Current policies permit employers to pay relatively low wages compared to other wealthy countries, speed up work, and obtain other concessions from workers without the time and expense of bargaining with them. These measures are all contrary to what workers generally want—higher wages, safer and less stressful working conditions, and more job opportunities....

Businesses themselves may have contradictory goals for government. Each firm is not so concerned about the economy-wide profit rate as it is about its own profit rate. Thus businesses are often ready to urge the government to adopt policies that will raise their own profit rates even though such policies may push down the profit rates of other businesses. Individual firms lobby the government to reduce their own taxes, to obtain subsidies, or to be allowed to set high prices for their output. Big oil companies benefit enormously from tax credits for foreign royalties paid. The Boeing Corporation has regularly obtained support through government-subsidized cheap credit for the company's foreign customers. Companies in the oil industry were quite happy when the government lifted its controls on oil prices, permitting the price of oil (a raw material input for most other companies) to go up, not down. The oil companies' support of decontrol seemed unaffected by the fact that this policy inflicted big losses on the auto industry, whose high-profit gas guzzlers fell from favor among consumers as gasoline prices rose. Most businesses would be happy to promote government policies that would allow them to pay their own workers less while forcing other firms to pay more. In all these ways, businesses lobby for special benefits that are often in conflict with policies to raise the general profit rate.

Workers, too, have divided interests concerning what the government should do, although often for quite different reasons. Workers in the automobile industry, for example, may want government policies to limit imports of cars produced elsewhere; other workers may want to save money by purchasing a cheaper automobile made in, say, Japan. To take another example, unions that have mainly white male members may be less enthusiastic about government programs designed to secure equal employment opportunities for women and minority workers than unions with substantial minority and female memberships.

Our understanding of government policy is further complicated by the fact that employers and workers are not the only players in the game. Government leaders have their own objectives and face their own constraints. Most of all, they must find ways of getting reelected or reappointed. Such concerns may necessitate appealing to large numbers of voters, an objective that itself may require a combination of two strategies: adopting policies that are in the interest of a majority of voters, and instituting policies that appeal to individuals who can make substantial financial contributions to election campaigns. Only a combination of these strategies would improve one's chance of being reelected: politicians who faithfully serve the interests of the majority but cannot finance election campaigns are just as surely losers as the ones who too blatantly favor the few at the expense of the many.

Government leaders, like businesspeople, may thus find that their objectives work at cross-purposes. To gain favor with business, government leaders may want to cut taxes on profits or high incomes. But raising other taxes to maintain sufficient government revenues may incur the wrath of the broader electorate. And with lower taxes all around, it may be impossible for government leaders to offer public services that are considered essential by a majority of voters.

The three-way tug of war among government leaders, citizens (including workers), and business executives is illustrated, in the following section, by the problem of macroeconomic regulation of the unemployment rate....

The Limits of Democratic Control of the
Capitalist Economy

If government has often grown in response to the needs of the capitalist economy, might the economic powers of government be used instead to achieve economic growth that would benefit everyone? Can the citizens of a democratic society control the economy in ways that will promote their own well-being?

... The ability of voters—even large majorities of them—to alter the course of economic events is quite limited as long as the economy remains capitalist.

To understand the limits on government, think of our economy as a game in which there are two different sets of rules. One set of rules—the rules of a capitalist economy—confers power and privilege on those who own and control the capital goods used in production, particularly on the owners and managers of the largest corporations. The other set of rules—the rules of democratic government—confers substantial power on the electorate, that is, on the majority of adult citizens. Thus our social system gives rise to two types of power: the *power of capital* and the *power of the citizenry*.

Those powers are often at loggerheads, as when citizens want to restrict the power of capitalists to sell dangerous or environmentally destructive products. In most such conflicts, capitalists have immense and often overwhelming advantages, despite the fact that the owners of businesses (and particularly the owners of large businesses) are greatly outnumbered in the political arena. There are three explanations for their political power—one obvious, the other two not so obvious.

One reason capitalists have a significant amount of political power is that economic resources can often be translated *directly* into political power. Businesses or wealthy individuals can contribute to political campaigns; they can buy advertisements to alter public opinion; they can hire lawyers, expert witnesses, and others to influence the detailed drafting and implementation of legislation; and they can use their economic resources in other ways—engaging in outright bribery, for example—to influence the political system. In all these ways corporate control of economic resources makes it possible for businesspeople to influence government officials and economic policies.

A second reason for the disproportionate political power of business leaders is more indirect. The owners of today's media conglomerates control the TV stations, newspapers, publishing houses, and other capital goods used in the media that shape public opinion. Even "public" radio and TV now depend heavily on corporate contributions. The constitutional rights to freedom of speech and of the press (which includes TV and radio) guarantee that people can say, and journalists can write, whatever they please. However, the private ownership of the capital goods used in the TV industry, for example, guarantees that what is broadcast is in the end controlled by corporate leaders—either the owners of the stations or the owners of the major corporations that buy the advertising for the programs. These are people who generally have little interest in promoting citizen power because increases in such power may jeopardize their profits.

A third way in which money brings power has to do with the fact that capitalists control investment and therefore can influence what happens in the economy of any particular area. If businesspeople see an area as having a bad investment climate, meaning that they may have difficulty making profits there, they will not invest in that area but will choose instead to invest somewhere else (if they invest at all). If they do not invest in a particular area, the result will be unemployment, economic stagnation, and probably a decline in living standards. This explains why political leaders in particular areas are apt to be easily influenced by the demands of business leaders. If the former do not go along with the wishes of the latter, the population of the area will suffer economic hardships and, placing at least part of the blame for their difficulties on their political leaders, will vote the incumbents out in the next election.

Something like the same process plays a role in the political business cycle. When there has been a long expansion, government leaders are usually willing to go along with the demands of business leaders to bring about a recession that will raise the rate of unemployment. Why is this? It is because, in this situation, government officials can anticipate that business leaders will blame them for any decline in profit rates that might result from increases in the power of workers. If the profit rate was in fact threatened, business leaders would not only withhold their investment, thereby causing economic hardships that would lead people to express their anger in the next election; they would also deny the current political leaders the financial support the latter would need in order to finance a reelection campaign.

When business leaders refuse to invest in a particular area, whether it is a locality, an area such as a state in the United States, or an entire nation, the area will experience what is referred to as a *capital strike*. When workers strike, they refuse to do their part in the economy: they do not work. When capitalists strike, they also refuse to do their part: they do not invest. But here the similarity between the strikes of workers and those of capitalists ends. When workers strike they must organize themselves so that they all strike together. A single worker cannot go on strike (that would be called quitting). By contrast, when capital goes on strike, no coordination is needed.... Each corporation routinely studies the economic and other conditions relevant to its decision to invest. If the executives of the corporation do not like what they see, they will not invest. Nobody organizes a capital strike. Such strikes happen through the independent decisions of corporate leaders. If things look bad to a significant number of corporations, the effect of their combined withholding of investment will be large enough to change the economic conditions of a whole area.

The potential for a capital strike severely limits what citizen power can accomplish when citizen power conflicts with the power of capital. A hypothetical scenario will make this clear. It is currently the policy in the United States that unemployed workers are entitled to receive unemployment insurance checks for 26 weeks after they lose their jobs. But imagine what would happen if the government of a particular state—let's call it "Anystate, USA"—were to decide to provide longer-lasting unemployment benefits so that workers could continue to receive unemployment insurance checks as long as they are unemployed. And let's say that these payments are financed by heavy taxes on the profits of firms that pollute the environment. If a majority of Anystate's citizens support these policies, the state government will adopt them, paying the additional benefits to unemployed workers and collecting the "pollution taxes" to pay for them.

Now imagine that you are the chief executive officer (CEO) of a large multinational corporation—let's call it "MNC Enterprises, Inc."—that employs large numbers of workers in Anystate. Assume that you are considering investing in Anystate, say, by building a new plant there. Not only will you worry about the potential taxes (applicable to any production process that pollutes the environment); you will also be uncertain, first, about how much power you will have over your employees and, second, about how hard they will work, knowing that they are entitled to receive unemployment insurance checks for a long period if you fire them.

You may even ask yourself what the citizenry will vote for next—and you will certainly think twice before investing in Anystate, not necessarily because you personally do not like the new laws, but because your profit rate, both before and after taxes, would most likely be lower in Anystate than it might be elsewhere. Not only would a low profit rate make it difficult for MNC Enterprises to maintain its competitive position relative to other corporations; it would also have additional consequences. Once it became known that the company's profit rate was falling, the price of the company's stock in the stock market would fall. This, in turn, might cause the stockholders to sell their shares, putting more downward pressure on the price of the stock. It is also possible that the Board of Directors of the company, in response to its poor "performance," would begin thinking about replacing you with a new CEO. Anticipating all this, you will probably put any new plant somewhere else, perhaps in a state that actively advertises its favorable investment climate.

Quite independently, other businesspeople will, no doubt, come to the same conclusion. Some may even close plants or offices in Anystate and move them elsewhere. The cumulative effect of these independently made decisions will be increasing unemployment and lower incomes for the people of Anystate.

The hard times may bring on a state financial crisis. As unemployment increases, state expenditures on unemployment insurance will rise, as will the costs of other income support programs. As people's incomes fall, the state's tax revenues will also fall, and a deficit will appear in the state's budget. (Most states are required by their state constitutions to balance their budgets.)

But the problems have only just begun. In order to spend more money than taxes are currently bringing in, the state government will be forced to raise taxes further or to borrow money from banks or individuals willing to make loans to the state or buy bonds (IOUs) issued by the state government. Because of the decline in Anystate's economy, the banks cannot be sure that their loans will be paid back promptly or that they will ever be paid back. If they agree to lend money to the state, they will do so only at high interest rates (to cover the risk of lending to the state). Similarly, investors will be willing to buy the state's newly issued bonds only if they are guaranteed high rates of interest. If the loans are granted and the bonds are bought, the state will have more money to finance its current expenditure, but its fundamental problems will only be put off. They will return with greater intensity when the high interest charges have to be paid, adding to the other demands on state revenues. The resulting vicious cycle, now evident in many U.S. states, is called a *state fiscal crisis*.

There are two likely outcomes. First, with repayment increasingly uncertain, the banks may refuse further loans until the state government changes its policy. If the state government is on the verge of bankruptcy—which means breaking contracts with state employees and not paying wages or bills—the bank's policy recommendations may be quite persuasive. Second, the sovereign citizens of Anystate may decide to elect a new government, in order to have the laws revoked. In either case the new laws will be repealed.

Our example was for a single state, but in fact the process we have outlined could well occur in any state or even in any nation. After all, MNC Enterprises did not have to locate any of its factories in the United States.

Let's go back over our "Anystate" example. Were the citizens' voting rights or civil liberties violated? No. Did capitalists collude to deliberately undermine citizen power? No, they acted independently and in competition with each other. Did they use campaign contributions or lobbyists to influence government officials or elections? They might have but they did not need to.

Did the citizens exercise control over the economy? That is a much harder question. The capitalist economy certainly imposed limits on what they could do. The citizens could vote for any policy they wanted, but they could not force businesses to invest in Anystate, and that fact severely limited the political outcomes.

Where did they go wrong? The example could have turned out very differently.

One course the citizens of Anystate could have followed would have been to limit their expectations; they could have instructed their government to concentrate only on those programs that would benefit citizens but at the same time *raise*—or at least not lower—the profit rates of companies in the state. In other words, they might have accepted from the outset the fact that they were not "sovereign" in economic matters. This would have allowed them to make the best of a less-than-ideal situation.

Thus, for example, the citizens might have concentrated solely on eliminating the forms of air pollution that push down property values by reducing profits in recreation businesses. They might have designed programs to give economic security to the elderly, but not to current workers. They might have tried to increase employment and equality of opportunity by giving all children more business-oriented schooling. And they might have voted to finance these programs by taxes that did not affect profits. If they had adopted any or all of these policies, many Anystate citizens would have benefited, and those who were adversely affected might not have been in a position to block the adoption of them. Specifically, capitalists might have looked favorably or at least indifferently at such policies and might not have brought about economic decline in the state by withholding or withdrawing their investments.

Again, our Anystate example is hypothetical, but it is in fact similar to a process that actually occurred in Wisconsin early in the twentieth century. Wisconsin was a leader in trying out programs to make the most of citizen power while operating within the limits of a capitalist economy. Moreover, the federal government and a number of state and local governments now engage in many beneficial economic activities that also fit this description. Providing for social needs within the general framework of a capitalist economy has been the aim of European nations such as Sweden and Austria, where social democratic governments have been in power during much of the last century. As beneficial as these programs have been, however, they are severely limited by the fact that many of the ways to improve living standards and the quality of life sooner or later also threaten the rate of profit.

There is yet another course that Anystate citizens could have followed, which, if not likely, is at least conceivable. When MNC Enterprises (or other companies) decided to close down their operations in Anystate, the plants could have been bought by their local communities, by their workers, or by the state government itself. When a business leaves a community, what it takes with it, usually, is just its money. The plant, equipment and machinery—not to mention the workers—are left behind. If a way could be found to purchase the firm and sell its output, there is no reason why the workers who held jobs in the MNC Enterprises plant could not continue working there. They could do this by forming a community-owned enterprise, a worker-owned firm, or some other type of democratic organization.

We may conclude from our Anystate example that citizen power is severely limited in its ability to alter fundamental economic policies. These limits can only be overcome if citizens commit themselves to altering the rules of a capitalist economy.... The rules of a capitalist economy are not the same as those of democratic government. To achieve a democratic *society*—not just a democratic *government*—decision making in the economy, as well as in the government, would have to be made accountable to a majority of its participants.

Discussion Questions

1. Friedman stresses that the market economy is made up of *voluntary exchanges*. No one is forced to buy a particular product or to work for a particular company. What would Bowles, Roosevelt, and Edwards say about Friedman's argument?

2. There is a substantial amount of income inequality in the United States. As long as all citizens still maintain equal political rights, is such inequality necessarily harmful to democracy? Where would you draw the line between acceptable and unacceptable levels of economic inequality in a democracy?

3. Friedman argues that the free market promotes individual liberty. Yet many citizens in democratic countries use their liberty to support government programs that limit and regulate the scope and power of the marketplace itself. How might Friedman have responded to this reality?

4. "If you work hard and play the rules, *anyone*, regardless of race, religion, educational or class background, can achieve the American Dream." Agree or disagree. Be sure to define what you mean by the American Dream.

Suggested Readings and Internet Resources

How democratic is the U.S. capitalist system? What are and what should be the roles of government and democratic citizens in the creation and distribution of economic resources? How "free" is our market system and how "equal" its citizens? Two excellent introductions to the answers of these questions are Joseph Schumpeter, *Capitalism, Socialism, and Democracy* (New Haven, Conn.: Yale University Press, 1984), and Charles Lindblom, *The Market System: What It Is, How It Works, and What to Make of It* (New Haven, Conn.: Yale University Press, 2002). In a highly accessible book written with his wife, Rose Friedman, Milton Friedman defends free market capitalism: *Free to Choose: A Personal Statement* (San Diego, Calif.: Harcourt, 1980). For a mainstream account of a new, healthy globalized economy, see Thomas Friedman, *The Lexus and the Olive Tree* (New York: Anchor Books, 2000). *New York Times* Pulitzer-Prize-winning journalist David Cay Johnston documents how the wealthy distort the rules in *Perfectly Legal: The Covert Campaign to Rig Our Tax System to Benefit the Super Rich—and Cheat Everybody Else* (New York: Penguin, 2003).

The Policy Action Network
www.movingideas.org
This is the best site for extensive data on and analyses of current economic policy issues from a liberal perspective. Click on the internal links to the Economic Policy Institute or the Center on Budget and Policy Priorities for an analysis of current issues, or use the topic search engine. This site is sponsored by *0*, a liberal opinion magazine.

The Heritage Foundation
www.heritage.org
This site contains economic news and policy prescriptions from the premier right-wing think tank, as well as good links to other conservative foundations and public policy lobbies.

The Left Business Observer
www.leftbusinessobserver.com
A spirited, iconoclastic newsletter by corporate critic Doug Henwood, this website has interesting statistics and many links to unconventional left- and right-wing websites.

The Cato Institute
www.cato.org
Here are speeches, research, and opinion from the leading libertarian think tank in the United States. This site provides economic data and opinion supportive of privatization of now-public functions, from Social Security to environmental protection and education.

Chapter 6

✳

Civil Liberties: Is Corporate Spending on Elections the Equivalent of Free Speech?

Citizens United is a conservative advocacy group dedicated to restoring "traditional values" and the free market in American society. After producing a documentary film, *Hillary: The Movie*, highly critical of then-Senator Hillary Clinton, Citizens United sought to run television ads for the movie shortly before the Democratic primaries for president. According to the Bipartisan Campaign Reform Act (BCRA) of 2002, commonly known as McCain-Feingold (after the two senators who co-sponsored it), corporations may not spend money that expressly advocates the election or defeat of a candidate for 30 days before a primary (or 60 days before a general election). The Federal Election Commission (FEC) concluded that *Hillary* was being distributed for no other reason than to discredit Clinton in the upcoming presidential primaries and ruled that the ads could not be aired. This ruling was upheld by the U.S. District Court for the District of Columbia. Citizens United appealed the decision and the Supreme Court agreed to hear the case.

The Supreme Court could have ruled narrowly on the case, for example, by simply deciding whether television ads for distributing a film by DirectTV were prohibited under BCRA. Instead, the Supreme Court decided to broaden the case to examine the constitutionality of the system of campaign finance regulations established by BCRA. On January 21, 2010 the Supreme Court announced its momentous decision overturning over a century of law and declared that profit and nonprofit corporations can spend unlimited funds to elect or defeat candidates for public office. Corporate spending, the Court ruled in a close 5-4 vote, was free speech protected under the First Amendment: "If the First Amendment has any force, it prohibits Congress from fining or jailing citizens, or associations of citizens, for simply engaging in political speech."

The announcement immediately unleashed a torrent of free speech for and against the ruling in *Citizens United v. Federal Election Commission*. Defenders extolled the Supreme Court for eliminating an egregious example of government censorship. As David Bossie, the president of Citizens United, put it, "The Supreme Court stopped a 100-year slide down a very slippery and dangerous slope last week, and I am proud to have played a role." The *New York Times*, on the other hand, attacked the decision in an editorial: "The Supreme Court has handed lobbyists a new weapon. A lobbyist can now tell any elected official: if you vote wrong, my company, labor union or interest group will spend unlimited sums explicitly advertising against your re-election." In his weekly radio address, President Obama charged that the ruling "strikes at our democracy itself," adding "I can't think of anything more devastating to the public interest."

In order to evaluate this debate, you need to understand the system of campaign finance regulations that has grown up since the Watergate scandal of the Nixon administration. Congress has sought to limit the role of big contributors in elections by placing rules on who can give money for what purposes. The original legislation passed in 1974, the Federal Election Campaign Act (FECA), made a distinction between hard and soft money. If corporations wanted to contribute money directly to a candidate, they had to do it with hard money, which means money contributed to Political Action Committees (PACs), which are regulated by the FEC. However, soft money, or contributions that were independent of the candidate or party, were unregulated. The result was a flood of soft money into elections, supposedly independent of the campaign, but which might as well have been controlled by the party or the candidate because they had the effect of directly supporting the election of particular candidates. The 2002 BCRA, or McCain-Feingold Act, attempted to fill this hole by banning independent expenditures financing television advertising right before an election. Thus, before *Citizens United* corporations could not independently fund ads to defeat or elect specific candidates.

Citizens United makes it difficult for the government to regulate corporate spending on elections because it gives corporations the same free speech rights as individuals. By striking down the ban on independent corporate contributions the Court overturned federal law going back to the Tillman Act of 1907 that enabled the government to distinguish between expenditures by individuals and expenditures by corporations. The former were protected as free speech while corporate spending could be regulated. *Citizens United* eliminated this distinction, which had been upheld in *McConnell v. Federal Election Commission* (2003) and *Austin v. Michigan Chamber of Commerce* (1990), and equated corporate spending with individual free speech. The Supreme Court ruling potentially strikes down similar state laws, but at the same time that it strikes down limits on corporate spending it upholds the authority of government to require disclosure of who is paying for the ads.

What follow are excerpts from the majority opinion, written by Justice Anthony Kennedy, and from the minority dissenting opinion, written by Justice John Paul Stevens. We have edited out the extensive citations and footnotes that are found in the original opinions. (Readers are encouraged to read the full original opinions which are easily accessible online.) Both opinions are splendid examples of careful reasoning on a crucial issue facing modern democracies—whether and how to regulate corporate spending on elections. Justice Kennedy argues that the Constitution does not allow the government to make a distinction between different types of speakers, regulating some and not regulating others. He sees no evidence that independent corporate expenditures will corrupt politicians. Justice Stevens, on the other hand, argues that there is no evidence that the framers of the Constitution wanted no distinctions between corporations and individuals. Clearly, Stevens argues, corporations are different from individuals and more dangerous to democracy; Congress has every right to regulate corporate expenditures.

When you read the democratic debate between Justice Kennedy and Justice Stevens you should consider a number of issues that have been raised. Conservatives pride themselves on upholding precedent in judicial decision making (called *stare decisis*) and judicial restraint (not overturning laws passed by Congress). In this case, the majority opinion overturns longstanding legal decisions and laws. Should the conservative justices have been more deferential to judicial precedent and the will of Congress? It is difficult to know the intent of the framers of the Constitution with regard to corporations because large private corporations, as we know them today, did not exist in 1789. If so, how does Justice Kennedy argue that the framers actually would have approved of regulating corporate spending on elections?

Corporate Spending on Elections Is Free Speech and Should Not Be Regulated (Excerpts from the Majority Opinion)

JUSTICE ANTHONY KENNEDY

The First Amendment provides that "Congress shall make no law... abridging the freedom of speech." Laws enacted to control or suppress speech may operate at different points in the speech process....

The law before us is an outright ban, backed by criminal sanctions. Section 441b[1] makes it a felony for all corporations—including nonprofit advocacy

---

1. The relevant section of the Bipartisan Campaign Reform Act of 2002.

corporations—either to expressly advocate the election or defeat of candidates or to broadcast electioneering communications within 30 days of a primary election and 60 days of a general election. Thus, the following acts would all be felonies under §441b: The Sierra Club runs an ad, within the crucial phase of 60 days before the general election, that exhorts the public to disapprove of a Congressman who favors logging in national forests; the National Rifle Association publishes a book urging the public to vote for the challenger because the incumbent U. S. Senator supports a handgun ban; and the American Civil Liberties Union creates a Web site telling the public to vote for a Presidential candidate in light of that candidate's defense of free speech. These prohibitions are classic examples of censorship.

Section 441b is a ban on corporate speech notwithstanding the fact that a PAC created by a corporation can still speak. A PAC is a separate association from the corporation. So the PAC exemption from §441b's expenditure ban, does not allow corporations to speak. Even if a PAC could somehow allow a corporation to speak—and it does not—the option to form PACs does not alleviate the First Amendment problems with §441b. PACs are burdensome alternatives; they are expensive to administer and subject to extensive regulations. For example, every PAC must appoint a treasurer, forward donations to the treasurer promptly, keep detailed records of the identities of the persons making donations, preserve receipts for three years, and file an organization statement and report changes to this information within 10 days.

And that is just the beginning. PACs must file detailed monthly reports with the FEC, which are due at different times depending on the type of election that is about to occur:

> These reports must contain information regarding the amount of cash on hand; the total amount of receipts, detailed by 10 different categories; the identification of each political committee and candidate's authorized or affiliated committee making contributions, and any persons making loans, providing rebates, refunds, dividends, or interest or any other offset to operating expenditures in an aggregate amount over $200; the total amount of all disbursements, detailed by 12 different categories; the names of all authorized or affiliated committees to whom expenditures aggregating over $200 have been made; persons to whom loan repayments or refunds have been made; the total sum of all contributions, operating expenses, outstanding debts and obligations, and the settlement terms of the retirement of any debt or obligation.

PACs have to comply with these regulations just to speak. This might explain why fewer than 2,000 of the millions of corporations in this country have PACs.

PACs, furthermore, must exist before they can speak. Given the onerous restrictions, a corporation may not be able to establish a PAC in time to make its views known regarding candidates and issues in a current campaign.

Section 441b's prohibition on corporate independent expenditures is thus a ban on speech. As a "restriction on the amount of money a person or group can spend on political communication during a campaign," that statute "necessarily reduces the quantity of expression by restricting the number of issues discussed, the depth of their exploration, and the size of the audience reached." Were the Court to uphold these restrictions, the Government could repress speech by silencing certain voices at any of the various points in the speech process. (Government could repress speech by "attacking all levels of the production and dissemination of ideas," for "effective public communication requires the speaker to make use of the services of others.") If §441b applied to individuals, no one would believe that it is merely a time, place, or manner restriction on speech. Its purpose and effect are to silence entities whose voices the Government deems to be suspect.

Speech is an essential mechanism of democracy, for it is the means to hold officials accountable to the people. ("In a republic where the people are sovereign, the ability of the citizenry to make informed choices among candidates for office is essential.") The right of citizens to inquire, to hear, to speak, and to use information to reach consensus is a precondition to enlightened self-government and a necessary means to protect it. The First Amendment "'has its fullest and most urgent application' to speech uttered during a campaign for political office... "

For these reasons, political speech must prevail against laws that would suppress it, whether by design or inadvertence. Laws that burden political speech are "subject to strict scrutiny," which requires the Government to prove that the restriction "furthers a compelling interest and is narrowly tailored to achieve that interest." While it might be maintained that political speech simply cannot be banned or restricted as a categorical matter, the quoted language provides a sufficient framework for protecting the relevant First Amendment interests in this case. We shall employ it here.

Premised on mistrust of governmental power, the First Amendment stands against attempts to disfavor certain subjects or viewpoints. Prohibited, too, are restrictions distinguishing among different speakers, allowing speech by some but not others. As instruments to censor, these categories are interrelated: Speech restrictions based on the identity of the speaker are all too often simply a means to control content.

Quite apart from the purpose or effect of regulating content, moreover, the Government may commit a constitutional wrong when by law it identifies certain preferred speakers. By taking the right to speak from some and giving it to others, the Government deprives the disadvantaged person or class of the right to use speech to strive to establish worth, standing, and respect for the speaker's voice. The Government may not by these means deprive the public of the right and privilege to determine for itself what speech and speakers are worthy of consideration. The First Amendment protects speech and speaker, and the ideas that flow from each...

We find no basis for the proposition that, in the context of political speech, the Government may impose restrictions on certain disfavored speakers. Both history and logic lead us to this conclusion...

If the First Amendment has any force, it prohibits Congress from fining or jailing citizens, or associations of citizens, for simply engaging in political speech. If the antidistortion rationale were to be accepted, however, it would permit

Government to ban political speech simply because the speaker is an association that has taken on the corporate form. The Government contends that *Austin* permits it to ban corporate expenditures for almost all forms of communication stemming from a corporation. If *Austin* were correct, the Government could prohibit a corporation from expressing political views in media beyond those presented here, such as by printing books. The Government responds "that the FEC has never applied this statute to a book," and if it did, "there would be quite [a] good as-applied challenge." This troubling assertion of brooding governmental power cannot be reconciled with the confidence and stability in civic discourse that the First Amendment must secure.

Political speech is "indispensable to decision making in a democracy, and this is no less true because the speech comes from a corporation rather than an individual." ("[T]he concept that government may restrict the speech of some elements of our society in order to enhance the relative voice of others is wholly foreign to the First Amendment....")

It is irrelevant for purposes of the First Amendment that corporate funds may "have little or no correlation to the public's support for the corporation's political ideas." All speakers, including individuals and the media, use money amassed from the economic marketplace to fund their speech. The First Amendment protects the resulting speech, even if it was enabled by economic transactions with persons or entities who disagree with the speaker's ideas...

Austin interferes with the "open marketplace" of ideas protected by the First Amendment.[2] It permits the Government to ban the political speech of millions of associations of citizens. Most of these are small corporations without large amounts of wealth...

This fact belies the Government's argument that the statute is justified on the ground that it prevents the "distorting effects of immense aggregations of wealth." It is not even aimed at amassed wealth.

The censorship we now confront is vast in its reach. The Government has "muffle[d] the voices that best represent the most significant segments of the economy." And "the electorate [has been] deprived of information, knowledge and opinion vital to its function." By suppressing the speech of manifold corporations, both for-profit and nonprofit, the Government prevents their voices and viewpoints from reaching the public and advising voters on which persons or entities are hostile to their interests. Factions will necessarily form in our Republic, but the remedy of "destroying the liberty" of some factions is "worse than the disease." The Federalist No. 10, p. 130 (B. Wright ed. 1961) (J. Madison). Factions should be checked by permitting them all to speak and by entrusting the people to judge what is true and what is false....

When Government seeks to use its full power, including the criminal law, to command where a person may get his or her information or what distrusted source he or she may not hear, it uses censorship to control thought. This is unlawful. The First Amendment confirms the freedom to think for ourselves....

---

2. Austin v. Michigan Chamber of commerce (1990) which upheld regulation of corporate spending on elections.

The appearance of influence or access, furthermore, will not cause the electorate to lose faith in our democracy. By definition, an independent expenditure is political speech presented to the electorate that is not coordinated with a candidate. The fact that a corporation, or any other speaker, is willing to spend money to try to persuade voters presupposes that the people have the ultimate influence over elected officials. This is inconsistent with any suggestion that the electorate will refuse "to take part in democratic governance" because of additional political speech made by a corporation or any other speaker....

Austin is undermined by experience since its announcement. Political speech is so ingrained in our culture that speakers find ways to circumvent campaign finance laws. Our Nation's speech dynamic is changing, and informative voices should not have to circumvent onerous restrictions to exercise their First Amendment rights. Speakers have become adept at presenting citizens with sound bites, talking points, and scripted messages that dominate the 24-hour news cycle. Corporations, like individuals, do not have monolithic views. On certain topics corporations may possess valuable expertise, leaving them the best equipped to point out errors or fallacies in speech of all sorts, including the speech of candidates and elected officials.

Rapid changes in technology—and the creative dynamic inherent in the concept of free expression—counsel against upholding a law that restricts political speech in certain media or by certain speakers. Today, 30-second television ads may be the most effective way to convey a political message. Soon, however, it may be that Internet sources, such as blogs and social networking Web sites, will provide citizens with significant information about political candidates and issues. Yet, §441b would seem to ban a blog post expressly advocating the election or defeat of a candidate if that blog were created with corporate funds. The First Amendment does not permit Congress to make these categorical distinctions based on the corporate identity of the speaker and the content of the political speech.

When word concerning the plot of the movie *Mr. Smith Goes to Washington* reached the circles of Government, some officials sought, by persuasion, to discourage its distribution.[3] Under *Austin*, though, officials could have done more than discourage its distribution—they could have banned the film. After all, it, like *Hillary*, was speech funded by a corporation that was critical of Members of Congress. *Mr. Smith Goes to Washington* may be fiction and caricature; but fiction and caricature can be a powerful force.

Modern day movies, television comedies, or skits on Youtube.com might portray public officials or public policies in unflattering ways. Yet if a covered transmission during the blackout period creates the background for candidate endorsement or opposition, a felony occurs solely because a corporation, other than an exempt media corporation, has made the "purchase, payment, distribution, loan, advance, deposit, or gift of money or anything of value" in order to engage in political speech. Speech would be suppressed in the realm where its necessity is most evident: in the public dialogue preceding a real election. Governments

---

3. A 1939 film starring James Stewart as an idealistic young man who dramatically confronts corruption in Congress.

are often hostile to speech, but under our law and our tradition it seems stranger than fiction for our Government to make this political speech a crime. Yet this is the statute's purpose and design.

Some members of the public might consider *Hillary* to be insightful and instructive; some might find it to be neither high art nor a fair discussion on how to set the Nation's course; still others simply might suspend judgment on these points but decide to think more about issues and candidates. Those choices and assessments, however, are not for the Government to make. "The First Amendment underwrites the freedom to experiment and to create in the realm of thought and speech. Citizens must be free to use new forms, and new forums, for the expression of ideas. The civic discourse belongs to the people, and the Government may not prescribe the means used to conduct it."

The judgment of the District Court is reversed with respect to the constitutionality of 2 U. S. C. §441b's restrictions on corporate independent expenditures.

Corporate Spending on Elections Is Not Free Speech and Can Be Regulated (Excerpts from Minority Opinion)

JUSTICE JOHN PAUL STEVENS

The basic premise underlying the Court's ruling is its iteration, and constant reiteration, of the proposition that the First Amendment bars regulatory distinctions based on a speaker's identity, including its "identity" as a corporation. While that glittering generality has rhetorical appeal, it is not a correct statement of the law. Nor does it tell us when a corporation may engage in electioneering that some of its shareholders oppose. It does not even resolve the specific question whether Citizens United may be required to finance some of its messages with the money in its PAC. The conceit that corporations must be treated identically to natural persons in the political sphere is not only inaccurate but also inadequate to justify the Court's disposition of this case.

In the context of election to public office, the distinction between corporate and human speakers is significant. Although they make enormous contributions to our society, corporations are not actually members of it. They cannot vote or run for office. Because they may be managed and controlled by nonresidents, their interests may conflict in fundamental respects with the interests of eligible voters. The financial resources, legal structure, and instrumental orientation of corporations raise legitimate concerns about their role in the electoral process. Our lawmakers have a compelling constitutional basis, if not also a democratic duty, to take measures designed to guard against the potentially deleterious effects of corporate spending in local and national races....

The Court's ruling threatens to undermine the integrity of elected institutions across the Nation. The path it has taken to reach its outcome will, I fear, do damage to this institution....

The So-Called "Ban"

Pervading the Court's analysis is the ominous image of a "categorical ba[n]" on corporate speech. Indeed, the majority invokes the specter of a "ban" on nearly every page of its opinion. This characterization is highly misleading, and needs to be corrected....

Under BCRA, any corporation's "stockholders and their families and its executive or administrative personnel and their families" can pool their resources to finance electioneering communications. A significant and growing number of corporations avail themselves of this option; during the most recent election cycle, corporate and union PACs raised nearly a billion dollars. Administering a PAC entails some administrative burden, but so does complying with the disclaimer, disclosure, and reporting requirements that the Court today upholds, and no one has suggested that the burden is severe for a sophisticated for-profit corporation. To the extent the majority is worried about this issue, it is important to keep in mind that we have no record to show how substantial the burden really is, just the majority's own unsupported factfinding. Like all other natural persons, every shareholder of every corporation remains entirely free under *Austin* and *McConnell* to do however much electioneering she pleases outside of the corporate form.[1] The owners of a "mom & pop" store can simply place ads in their own names, rather than the store's....

So let us be clear: Neither *Austin* nor *McConnell* held or implied that corporations may be silenced; the FEC is not a "censor"; and in the years since these cases were decided, corporations have continued to play a major role in the national dialogue....

Identity-Based Distinctions

The second pillar of the Court's opinion is its assertion that "the Government cannot restrict political speech based on the speaker's ... identity...."

"Our jurisprudence over the past 216 years has rejected an absolutist interpretation" of the First Amendment. The First Amendment provides that "Congress shall make no law ... abridging the freedom of speech, or of the

---

1. McConnell v. FEC (2003) which upheld regulation of corporate spending on elections.

press." Apart perhaps from measures designed to protect the press that text might seem to permit no distinctions of any kind. Yet in a variety of contexts, we have held that speech can be regulated differentially on account of the speaker's identity, when identity is understood in categorical or institutional terms. The Government routinely places special restrictions on the speech rights of students, prisoners, members of the Armed Forces, foreigners, and its own employees. When such restrictions are justified by a legitimate governmental interest, they do not necessarily raise constitutional problems. In contrast to the blanket rule that the majority espouses, our cases recognize that the Government's interests may be more or less compelling with respect to different classes of speakers....

As we have unanimously observed, legislatures are entitled to decide "that the special characteristics of the corporate structure require particularly careful regulation" in an electoral context. Not only has the distinctive potential of corporations to corrupt the electoral process long been recognized, but within the area of campaign finance, corporate spending is also "furthest from the core of political expression, since corporations' First Amendment speech and association interests are derived largely from those of their members and of the public in receiving information," Campaign finance distinctions based on corporate identity tend to be less worrisome, in other words, because the "speakers" are not natural persons, much less members of our political community, and the governmental interests are of the highest order....

If taken seriously, our colleagues' assumption that the identity of a speaker has *no* relevance to the Government's ability to regulate political speech would lead to some remarkable conclusions. Such an assumption would have accorded the propaganda broadcasts to our troops by "Tokyo Rose" during World War II the same protection as speech by Allied commanders.[2] More pertinently, it would appear to afford the same protection to multinational corporations controlled by foreigners as to individual Americans: To do otherwise, after all, could "enhance the relative voice" of some (*i.e.*, humans) over others (*i.e.*, nonhumans). Under the majority's view, I suppose it may be a First Amendment problem that corporations are not permitted to vote, given that voting is, among other things, a form of speech.

In short, the Court dramatically overstates its critique of identity-based distinctions, without ever explaining why corporate identity demands the same treatment as individual identity. Only the most wooden approach to the First Amendment could justify the unprecedented line it seeks to draw.

Our First Amendment Tradition

The Framers took it as a given that corporations could be comprehensively regulated in the service of the public welfare. Unlike our colleagues, they had little trouble distinguishing corporations from human beings, and when they

---

2. The name given to Japanese broadcasters of anti-American propaganda during world war II.

constitutionalized the right to free speech in the First Amendment, it was the free speech of individual Americans that they had in mind. While individuals might join together to exercise their speech rights, business corporations, at least, were plainly not seen as facilitating such associational or expressive ends. Even "the notion that business corporations could invoke the First Amendment would probably have been quite a novelty," given that "at the time, the legitimacy of every corporate activity was thought to rest entirely in a concession of the sovereign."

In light of these background practices and understandings, it seems to me implausible that the Framers believed "the freedom of speech" would extend equally to all corporate speakers, much less that it would preclude legislatures from taking limited measures to guard against corporate capture of elections....

Having explained why ... *Austin* and *McConnell* sit perfectly well with "First Amendment principles," I come at last to the interests that are at stake. The majority recognizes that *Austin* and *McConnell* may be defended on anticorruption, antidistortion, and shareholder protection rationales. It badly errs both in explaining the nature of these rationales, which overlap and complement each other, and in applying them to the case at hand.

The Anticorruption Interest

Undergirding the majority's approach to the merits is the claim that the only "sufficiently important governmental interest in preventing corruption or the appearance of corruption" is one that is "limited to *quid pro quo* corruption...."[3] While it is true that we have not always spoken about corruption in a clear or consistent voice, the approach taken by the majority cannot be right, in my judgment. It disregards our constitutional history and the fundamental demands of a democratic society.

On numerous occasions we have recognized Congress' legitimate interest in preventing the money that is spent on elections from exerting an "undue influence on an officeholder's judgment" and from creating "the appearance of such influence," beyond the sphere of *quid pro quo* relationships. Corruption can take many forms. Bribery may be the paradigm case. But the difference between selling a vote and selling access is a matter of degree, not kind. And selling access is not qualitatively different from giving special preference to those who spent money on one's behalf. Corruption operates along a spectrum, and the majority's apparent belief that *quid pro quo* arrangements can be neatly demarcated from other improper influences does not accord with the theory or reality of politics. It certainly does not accord with the record Congress developed in passing BCRA, a record that stands as a remarkable testament to the energy and ingenuity with which corporations, unions, lobbyists, and politicians may go about scratching each other's backs—and which amply supported Congress' determination to target a limited set of especially destructive practices....

---

3. Corruption in which someone pays off a politician in exchange for political favors.

Our "undue influence" cases have allowed the American people to cast a wider net through legislative experiments designed to ensure, to some minimal extent, "that officeholders will decide issues ... on the merits or the desires of their constituencies," and not "according to the wishes of those who have made large financial contributions"—or expenditures—"valued by the officeholder." When private interests are seen to exert outsized control over officeholders solely on account of the money spent on (or withheld from) their campaigns, the result can depart so thoroughly "from what is pure or correct" in the conduct of Government....

At stake in the legislative efforts to address this threat is therefore not only the legitimacy and quality of Government but also the public's faith therein, not only "the capacity of this democracy to represent its constituents [but also] the confidence of its citizens in their capacity to govern themselves." "Take away Congress' authority to regulate the appearance of undue influence and 'the cynical assumption that large donors call the tune could jeopardize the willingness of voters to take part in democratic governance....'"

In short, regulations impose only a limited burden on First Amendment freedoms not only because they target a narrow subset of expenditures and leave untouched the broader "public dialogue," but also because they leave untouched the speech of natural persons....

In addition to this immediate drowning out of noncorporate voices, there may be deleterious effects that follow soon thereafter. Corporate "domination" of electioneering, can generate the impression that corporations dominate our democracy. When citizens turn on their televisions and radios before an election and hear only corporate electioneering they may lose faith in their capacity, as citizens, to influence public policy. A Government captured by corporate interests, they may come to believe, will be neither responsive to their needs nor willing to give their views a fair hearing. The predictable result is cynicism and disenchantment: an increased perception that large spenders "call the tune" and a reduced "willingness of voters to take part in democratic governance." To the extent that corporations are allowed to exert undue influence in electoral races, the speech of the eventual winners of those races may also be chilled. Politicians who fear that a certain corporation can make or break their reelection chances may be cowed into silence about that corporation. On a variety of levels, unregulated corporate electioneering might diminish the ability of citizens to "hold officials accountable to the people," and disserve the goal of a public debate that is "uninhibited, robust, and wide-open." At the least, I stress again, a legislature is entitled to credit these concerns and to take tailored measures in response....

All of the majority's theoretical arguments turn on a proposition with undeniable surface appeal but little grounding in evidence or experience, "that there is no such thing as too much speech." If individuals in our society had infinite free time to listen to and contemplate every last bit of speech uttered by anyone, anywhere; and if broadcast advertisements had no special ability to influence elections apart from the merits of their arguments (to the extent they make any); and if legislators always operated with nothing less than perfect virtue; then I suppose the majority's premise would be sound. In the real world, we have seen, corporate domination of the airwaves prior to an election may decrease the average listener's exposure to relevant viewpoints, and it may diminish citizens' willingness and capacity to participate in the democratic process.

In a democratic society, the longstanding consensus on the need to limit corporate campaign spending should outweigh the wooden application of judge-made rules.

At bottom, the Court's opinion is a rejection of the common sense of the American people, who have recognized a need to prevent corporations from undermining self-government since the founding, and who have fought against the distinctive corrupting potential of corporate electioneering since the days of Theodore Roosevelt. It is a strange time to repudiate that common sense. While American democracy is imperfect, few outside the majority of this Court would have thought its flaws included a dearth of corporate money in politics.

Discussion Questions

1. Do you think that *Citizens United* will unleash a torrent of corporate spending that will corrupt the political process? Will elected officials now be afraid to vote against the interests of large corporations?

2. Opponents of *Citizens United* argue that corporations spend funds that ultimately belong to shareholders without getting the permission of shareholders. Is this a problem? If you owned stock in a corporation, would you object to that company spending money to defeat an elected official whom you supported?

3. Do you think full disclosure of who paid for an ad, including the name of the chief elected officer (CEO), will cause corporations to limit their campaign spending for fear of offending customers or investors?

4. Do you favor a system of public financing of elections in which candidates who receive a minimum of support can opt for public funding of their campaigns, paid for by voluntary dues checked-off on income tax returns, and thus avoid all private contributions?

Suggested Readings and Internet Resources

For a comprehensive examination of campaign finance laws before *Citizens United* see Michael Malbin, ed., *Life After Reform: When the Bipartisan Campaign Finance Reform Act Meets Politics* (New York: Rowman and Littlefield, 2003). Revealing examinations of the effects of private money on electoral politics are found in Charles Lewis, *The Buying of the President, 2004* (New York: Perennial, 2004) and in Robert G. Kaiser, *So Damn Much Money: The Triumph of Lobbying and the Corrosion of American Government* (New York: Alfred A. Knopf, 2009). For a critical analysis of attempts to regulate campaign finance, see Bradley Smith, *Unfree Speech: The Folly of Campaign Finance Reform* (Princeton, N.J.: Princeton University Press, 2001).

Federal Election Commission (FEC)
www.fec.gov
The FEC's official government site provides access to data on campaign contributions and information on campaign regulations.

Center for Responsive Politics
www.opensecrets.org
This site provides accessible data, based on FEC reports, on campaign contributions to candidates across the country.

Campaign Finance Institute
www.cfinst.org
The Campaign Finance Institute is a non-partisan, non-profit institute, affiliated with George Washington University, that conducts research and makes recommendations for policy change in the field of campaign finance.

Chapter 7

*

Civil Rights: Debating Same-Sex Marriage

The civil-rights revolution has been perhaps the most dramatic modern chapter in the story of American democracy. Starting in the 1950s for African Americans and in the 1960s for women, victories won in the courts, the legislatures, and the streets have overcome long-standing discrimination and brought the nation closer to its ideal of equality for all citizens. For one group, though—gays and lesbians—the gains so far have been more limited.

The U.S. Supreme Court has been more equivocal on equal rights for gays and lesbians than for racial minorities and women. Its first major decision in this field—*Bowers v. Hardwick* (1986)—upheld a Georgia sodomy law, with the Court majority arguing that the right of privacy in sexual behavior belonged only to heterosexuals. Seventeen years later, in *Lawrence v. Texas*, the Court reversed itself and guaranteed equal treatment for gays and lesbians in their private lives. The rights of gays and lesbians were also advanced in *Romer v. Evans* (1996), when the Court majority denied the right of a state to single out homosexuals as the only group ineligible for protection by antidiscrimination laws. Nonetheless, in *Boy Scouts of America v. Dale* (2000), the Court supported the right of an association to expel a gay member on the grounds that his homosexuality was contrary to the values it was propagating.

Of all of the issues concerning the rights of lesbian, gay, bisexual, and transgender individuals, same-sex marriage has become the most visible and controversial. The right of same-sex couples to marry has faced a formidable opposition. Once the possibility of establishing same-sex marriage was raised, opponents responded with the Defense of Marriage Act (DOMA), passed by Congress and signed into law by President Bill Clinton in 1996. DOMA exempts states from having to recognize same-sex marriages sanctified by law in other states, and it puts the federal government on record as defining marriage as a legal union between one man and one woman. A majority of states have enacted prohibitions on marriage between individuals of the same sex.

However, in the last few years, same-sex marriage has been gaining ground. A state supreme court decision made Massachusetts the first legal jurisdiction to recognize same-sex marriage in 2004. Since that year, same-sex marriage has been legalized by judicial action in Iowa and by legislative action in Vermont, Connecticut, New Hampshire, and the District of Columbia. In two additional states, California and Maine, the right of same-sex couples to marry was legally established only to be overturned shortly afterwards by narrow margins in popular referenda.

The debate over same-sex marriage brings into play conflicting values. For proponents, the right of same-sex couples to wed is a matter of equal treatment under law. This side of the debate often brings up the analogy of earlier state laws forbidding men and women of different races from marrying, a practice outlawed as unconstitutional by the U.S. Supreme Court in *Loving v. Virginia* (1967). Proponents of same-sex marriage also point to the practical consequences of denying this right to gay and lesbian couples. Marriage carries with it many legal and financial benefits that unmarried couples do not enjoy. For example, only couples who are legally wed can claim the special marital advantages in the federal income tax code.

Opponents of same-sex marriage more often view the issue through a moral prism. In their eyes, marriage lies at the heart of a decent social order that counters individual selfishness by bonding together men and women in lasting unions and providing for the care and protection of children. Rewriting the definition of marriage, they suggest, will open the door to its unraveling as an anchor of family life and social harmony. Some opponents base their position on their religious convictions, with many Christian groups condemning same-sex marriage as contrary to God's will.

The author of our first selection, political scientist Evan Gerstmann, argues that marriage is a constitutional right and that there are no legitimate grounds to restrict this right to opposite-sex couples. Gerstmann denies that the right to marry hinges on a capacity for procreation, pointing out that no one challenges the freedom of infertile heterosexual couples to wed. He questions the claim that legal recognition of the marriages of same-sex couples will create a precedent for legalizing other kinds of marriage that our society currently prohibits, such as polygamy. For Gerstmann, the heart of the issue is America's commitment to equality for all of its citizens.

Writer Sam Schulman, the author of our second selection, acknowledges that the case for same-sex marriage appeals to Americans' sense of fairness. Nevertheless, he believes that redefining marriage to include same-sex couples will inflict harm that we have barely begun to realize. The legal institution of marriage is especially important as a protection for women, Schulman writes. It permits women to restrict who has access to their bodies and to make legally and financially responsible the men who have fathered their children. If marriage is stripped of its traditional meaning and given a loose definition that incorporates couples of the same sex, he concludes, we will lose "an arrangement that has to do with empowering women to avoid ... unhappiness and with sustaining the future history of the species."

How do you view the issue of same-sex marriage? Should we approach this issue mainly as a matter of constitutional rights? Or should we adopt the position that changing the meaning of marriage will undermine its strength as the most important moral bond in our society? Can the interests of gays and lesbians be served through civil unions, arrangements short of marriage that still bestow legal and financial benefits on same-sex couples, or does marriage alone ensure genuine equality? Will the institution of same-sex marriage harm traditional marriage, or will it have no impact whatsoever on marriages between men and women?

Same-Sex Marriage as a Constitutional Right

EVAN GERSTMANN

[This essay] argues [that] the most powerful argument in favor of [same-sex marriage is]: *The Constitution guarantees every person the right to marry the person of his or her choice.* This is not to say that the right is limitless; nobody has the right to marry a nine-year-old, to mention just one example. No constitutional right is absolute, as all are balanced against other societal interests. Few rights are more intensely protected in this country than is freedom of speech, but the Constitution allows limitations on obscene speech, libel, perjury, shouting "Fire!" in a crowded theater, and many other forms of speech in which the harm outweighs the First Amendment interest of the speaker.

Recognizing the constitutional right to marry, then, does not send us plunging down a slippery slope to a purely libertarian, "anything goes" view in which society loses all control over the definition of marriage. Marriage is not an exclusively personal decision, for the government has an interest in what is called "marriage" and is not prevented from preferring some forms of it to others. The First Amendment right of association may protect one's right to join the Ku Klux Klan, but the government has not lost its power to endorse, fund, and promote organizations that fight racism, or to teach schoolchildren that certain associations are worthier than others and that the Klan is not a worthy organization. Similarly, legalizing same-sex marriage will not end the social debate over issues such as what to teach children about unconventional families, how adoption agencies should treat same-sex couples, or whether civil rights laws should protect such couples from discrimination when they buy or lease property. The fundamental right to marry, however, means that legislatures will have to articulate the necessity for placing certain restrictions on marriage. If same-sex marriage truly represents a threat to society or cannot really be considered a form of marriage, the government may ban it, just as government may ban libelous and obscene speech. As with speech, though, mere unpopularity or disdain cannot justify a ban. Gays and lesbians will be entitled to demand that the government justify the same-sex marriage ban by reference to social interests other than pure majoritarian moral preference.

In contemporary constitutional parlance, there is a "fundamental right" to marry that is protected under the Constitution. Nothing is radical or shocking about this position, which is in keeping with the broad range of protections of personal and family life that the Supreme Court has been enforcing for some time. The government has long been held to a heightened level of judicial scrutiny with regard to its treatment of many aspects of family life. Courts have not permitted the government free rein in treatment of unconventional family structures, illegitimacy, or divorce, and freedom of personal association is a cherished constitutional value. Indeed, it is the position denying the existence of the fundamental marriage right that is extreme. Does anyone believe that the government could simply ban divorce, forbid remarriage by divorced people, or prevent people who have genetic disorders from marrying one another? Most people would undoubtedly be alarmed over the idea of this sort of unchecked power...

The Court has long held that the Constitution protects numerous "fundamental" rights that are not explicitly mentioned therein; sometimes they are called "unenumerated" rights. These rights have been elevated to a par with those rights enumerated in the Bill of Rights, including freedom of speech, assembly, and religion. Fundamental rights, many people know, include the right to abortion and contraception and the right to vote. These rights also include such lesser-known rights as the right to receive welfare payments immediately upon moving to a new state and the right of genetically related people to live in a neighborhood zoned for single-family housing, even if the people living in the house do not meet the law's definition of a single family. In addition, the Court has implied, if not firmly held, that fundamental rights might include access to public education (although not to an equal public education). Understanding this system of unenumerated rights is difficult because the Court has left so many questions unanswered or only partly answered. It is extremely unclear what part of the Constitution the Court believes is the basis for these rights. On this point, the justices have been free ranging, sometimes holding that fundamental rights originate in the due process clause, at other times holding that these rights arise from the equal protection clause, and have also said that at least one fundamental right, the right to travel, derives from the privileges and immunities clause. The Court has also held that these rights do not come from any single part of the Constitution, but "emanate" from the Bill of Rights as a whole ....

[T]he Court has repeatedly and unequivocally held that there is a constitutionally protected fundamental right to marry... [I]t was among the first fundamental rights the Court recognized, included in opinions at the very dawn of the era of unenumerated constitutional rights and recognized by liberal and conservative courts alike. [T]he right to marry is broad indeed. Far from being limited to a racial context, it has been applied to individuals whom society has every reason to punish, individuals whose fitness for marriage and parenthood could be doubted: a "deadbeat dad" ... [and] "convicted criminals."

But this is merely the beginning of the inquiry. Many important questions remain: Is there some good reason to believe that same-sex marriage is an exception to this fundamental right to marry? If the right to marry is not limited to traditional marriages, what is the logical stopping point? Does it protect polygamous or incestuous marriages?

Why would same-sex marriage *not* be included under the fundamental right to marry? In a nation in which the right to marry is constitutionally protected for convicted criminals and parents who fail to make court-ordered child support payments, the right to marry must mean, at a minimum, that the state bears the burden of explaining why gays and lesbians cannot exercise this right.

Three related explanations have been proffered for the exclusion of same-sex marriage from the right to marry:

1. The right to marry is a predicate of the right to procreate and raise children in a traditional family setting.
2. The ability to have children is at the core of marriage.
3. Marriage is by definition dualgendered.

It has been suggested that the right to marry is a predicate to other rights, rather than a right in and of itself. The idea that the right to marry is simply the logical predicate to procreation and childbearing has been an important and influential part of the debate on same-sex marriage. In this view, marriage is not a freestanding constitutional right, but a right that results from society's interest in the bearing and raising of children in a traditional family setting ...

It is not only academic commentators who subscribe to this view of the right to marry. Even the Supreme Court of Hawaii, which held that the same-sex marriage ban is a form of gender discrimination, saw the marriage right as the "logical predicate" to the right to procreate and raise children. It therefore held that the right to marry does not apply to same-sex marriages ....

Procreation and children, of course, are part of the reason that many people want to marry, and part of the reason that society has an interest in the institution of marriage. But that is very different from the idea that the marriage right is *solely* concerned with children, and that the right does not protect couples who cannot conceive children or raise them in a "traditional family setting." A reference to the right of free speech can help illustrate this point. Courts and scholars have often linked the right of free speech to democratic debate and deliberation, yet it is well settled that freedom of speech covers a great deal of speech that is completely unrelated to democratic debate and deliberation. The sexual images of the Playboy Channel are protected speech, despite their lack of political content; so is advertising the price of liquor. Speech is related to democracy, but *related to* does not mean "the same as." Similarly, marriage might be related to child rearing, but it is far more than a mere child-rearing arrangement. As is obvious to any childless married couple, there are powerful reasons for being married that are completely unrelated to children. Unsurprisingly, the Supreme Court has never held that the fundamental right to marry is dependent upon or ancillary to a couple's intention or ability to have children ...

Related to the argument that the marriage right is reserved only for dual-gendered, child-raising couples is the notion that regardless of what the Court has said, having children is so central to marriage that it makes no sense to protect the right for couples who obviously cannot have them. The state of Vermont, for example, argued that procreation is the defining feature of marriage when it defended its same-sex marriage ban to the state Supreme Court. This argument has been accepted in federal court as well; in *Adams v. Howerton*, the judge held that "the main justification in this age for societal recognition and protection of the institution, of marriage is procreation, perpetuation of the race..." This is perhaps the least supportable of the reasons proffered for denying same-sex couples the right to marry.

The idea that marriage inherently requires the ability to reproduce is utterly foreign to Western traditions. Even John Finnis, who strongly opposes same-sex marriage, concedes that

> the ancient philosophers do not much discuss the case of sterile marriages, or the fact (well known to them) that for long periods of time (e.g. throughout pregnancy) the sexual acts of a married couple are naturally incapable of resulting in reproduction. They appear to take for granted what the subsequent Christian tradition certainly did, that such sterility does not render the conjugal sexual acts of the spouses nonmarital. (Plutarch indicates that intercourse with a sterile spouse is a desirable mark of marital esteem and affection.)

Even the Christian moralist St. Augustine stated that companionship is an important goal of marriage and never indicated that sterility voided a marriage.

The idea that marriage requires reproductive ability has no support in contemporary law either. "Opposite-sex couples may marry without showing that they possess either the ability or the intention to have children," William Hohengarten observes. Why, then, does the issue of fertility prevent same-sex marriages but not infertile dual-gendered marriages...

As far back as 1898, moreover, the law was clear that infertile women are eligible to marry: "It cannot be held, as a matter of law, that the possession of the organs necessary to conception are essential to entrance to the marriage state, so long as there is no impediment to the indulgence of the passions incident to that state." It is not logically possible that procreational ability is a vital component of marriage, whereas the lack of it is not a ground for dissolving that marriage...

In sum, nothing in the law indicates that the ability to have children is a vital component of marriage. The courts, frankly, have made up this standard out of thin air and have applied it only to same-sex couples. Additionally, it is not true that same-sex couples cannot have children; they simply cannot have them via conventional means. Like many heterosexual couples, lesbians can have children through means such as third-party artificial insemination. Courts have scrupulously protected the parental rights of heterosexual fathers whose wives conceived children via third-party insemination. The heterosexual couples are allowed to marry so the nongenetic parent receives full legal recognition as the child's parent. This legal provision cannot justify allowing only dual-gendered couples to marry, as it is the *result* of the fact that only dual-gendered couples are allowed to marry. The argument that only dual-gendered couples can marry because only they can have children is a tautology...

[N]umerous courts and commentators have relied upon traditional and dictionary definitions of marriage to show that same-sex couples cannot be married. There are several fatal problems with their arguments. First, definitions themselves are not beyond the reach of judicial review ... Even if dictionaries in the 1950s and 1960s had defined marriage as a union between persons of the same race, they would not have saved the Virginia statute at issue in *Loving*.

Courts have consistently ignored the dictionary in defining constitutional rights. Constitutional law would be very different if the courts used dictionary definitions to shape the contours of our rights. The First Amendment protection for freedom of speech is an illuminating example. *Webster's New Collegiate Dictionary* defines *speech* as "the communication or expression of thoughts in *spoken words*," "something that is *spoken*," "public *discourse*," "an individual manner or style of *speaking*," or "the power of expressing or communicating thoughts through *speaking*." All these definitions make clear that speech is something that is spoken, yet freedom of speech protects much more than the spoken word. For constitutional purposes, speech includes wearing black armbands to school, picketing silently, donating money to political candidates, burning the American flag, and printing pornographic cartoons. If the Court relied upon the dictionary to define the right to free speech, that right would be drastically narrower.

The Court has also explicitly rejected the dictionary definition of *search* in interpreting the Fourth Amendment. In a case involving a thermal imaging device that measured heat radiating from a private home, the majority opinion rejected *Webster's American Dictionary of the English Language*. Citing *Webster's*, Justice Antonin Scalia observed that "when the Fourth Amendment was adopted, as now, to 'search' meant 'to look over or through for the purpose of finding something; to explore; to examine by inspection; as to search the house for a book; to search the wood for a thief.'" Scalia noted that the Court pays this definition no heed: "One might think that the new validating rationale would be that examining the portion of a house that is in plain public view, while it is a 'search' [according to the dictionary] despite the absence of trespass, is not an 'unreasonable' one under the Fourth Amendment. But in fact we have held that visual observation is no 'search' at all."

With the argument about fertility, however, the dictionary definition argument is used to reject same-sex marriage and then tucked away again in other contexts. Even if we were to refer sometimes to dictionaries to define constitutional rights, it would be particularly inappropriate in the case of marriage ... The law of marriage was once deeply sexist, with the husband as master of the wife. Of course, marriage was defined as dual gendered; without a woman, who would occupy the legally subordinate role? Rigid reliance on long-standing dictionary definitions makes even less sense in the case of marriage than it does in the other examples discussed previously.

The Court consistently defines rights according to their underlying purposes. *Speech* is defined as that which has a specific expressive intent and which is likely to be so understood; a *search* is defined by reference to a person's expectation of privacy. As discussed, there is nothing about same-sex couples that precludes them from enjoying many of what the Court has defined as the purposes of marriage, even if one regards homosexuality as immoral. Unless the Court drastically alters its method of constitutional interpretation, dictionary definitions do not justify the disqualification of same-sex couples from the fundamental right to marriage.

If the arguments against same-sex marriage discussed in this chapter are so weak, why have the courts been so reluctant to hold that the long-established fundamental right to marry applies to same-sex marriage? Judges are reluctant to speak publicly about cases that might again come before them, so the answer here is necessarily speculative.

One probable answer is the overwhelming intuition that marriage is *naturally* heterosexual. Intuitions about what God or nature intended can be very powerful for us, although they can also be disastrously misleading, and we should be skeptical of them, even when they are our own. The Virginia judge who upheld that state's antimiscegenation laws in *Loving* opined. "Almighty God created the races white, black, yellow, malay and red, and he placed them on separate continents... The fact that he separated the races shows that he did not intend for the races to mix." The idea that interracial marriage is unnatural or against God's will because God put the races on different continents had an internal logic for its proponents—just as the idea that same-sex marriage is unnatural has logic for the heterosexual majority. "Was there ever any domination which did not appear natural to those who possessed it?" asked the great political thinker John Stuart Mill.

But intuitions about nature are not the only reasons cited for opposition to same-sex marriage. Judges, political leaders, and commentators have expressed more substantive concerns, among them the specters of polygamy and incest, which haunted the debate over same-sex marriage even before it really started. If there is a fundamental right to marry that is not confined by tradition, nature, and so forth, what is the logical stopping point? Will society go down the slippery slope to marital anarchy, in which the public will be forced to accept marriages to many spouses or to one's brother or sister?...

The argument that there is a fundamental right to marriage that applies to same-sex marriage threatens conventional morality in ways that extend beyond the issue of homosexuality. Polygamists and practitioners of incest could argue that such a right protects them as well, a possibility very much on Justice Potter Stewart's mind when he declined to join the majority in *Zablocki [v. Redhail]*. He warned that the Court's support for a fundamental right to marry could open the door to all three forms of prohibited marriage, writing that "a 'compelling state purpose' inquiry would cast doubt on the network of restrictions that the States have fashioned to govern marriage and divorce."

Stewart was not alone in these fears. Many opponents of same-sex marriage have expressed concerns that if society allowed same-sex marriage, it would have to allow polygamy. Numerous Republican congressmen, in addition to the noted political commentators William Bennett, George Will, Robert Bork, and William Safire, have made similar arguments. Also, during congressional hearings on the Defense of Marriage Act, the analogy between polygamy and same-sex marriage was a dominant theme. Many prominent liberal academics have been circumspect on this point, perhaps because polygamists, mostly associated with Mormons in the public mind, are not as popular in the academy or with the political Left as are gays and lesbians...

When the Supreme Court was asked to rule upon polygamy, its holding was steeped in racism and nativism. "Polygamy has always been odious among the northern and western nations of Europe, and, until the establishment of the Mormon Church, was almost exclusively a feature of the life of Asiatic and of African people," justices wrote. The Court apparently assumed that a practice's association with nonwhites was convincing evidence of its degraded nature.

It must be emphasized that my argument here is *not* that polygamy is a positive institution or that it should be legalized. My argument, first, is that the position that gays and lesbians have the fundamental right to marry someone of their own gender leads many people to worry that polygamists would be protected as well; this concern may better account for judicial hostility to same-sex marriage than do the very weak explanations offered by the courts themselves. Second, liberal and left-leaning academics and lawyers have responded by avoiding the fundamental rights argument, preferring the analytically weaker gender discrimination argument because it helps gays and lesbians but not polygamists or other groups to whom they may be unsympathetic. Third, advocates of same-sex marriage should take the same hard look at the reasons for banning polygamy that they are asking heterosexuals to take with same-sex marriage. In evaluating ways of living, we must not rely upon mere speculation or intuitions that support our prejudices; we should hold ourselves to stringent standards of evidence. Gays, lesbians, and their allies should not compromise these high standards when critiquing nontraditional families that are vilified even more than are same-sex couples.

Nonetheless, it is quite possible to distinguish same-sex marriage from polygamy without resorting to unsupported, stereotype-based attacks. There certainly seems to be a difference between a right to marry *whomever* you want and marrying *however many* people you want.

Multiple marriages raise several legitimate state concerns that same-sex marriages do not. First and foremost, legalizing polygamy, unlike legalizing same-sex marriage, would profoundly alter the legal structure of *every* couple's marriage. Every married person's spouse would suddenly have the right to marry another person without exiting the current marriage. This would be a very significant alteration in the marriage of every couple in America. Same-sex marriage is a completely different situation. It would have no legal impact whatsoever on opposite-sex marriages. Rather, it would merely entitle a relatively small group of people who currently cannot marry to marry legally. Admittedly, some argue that same-sex marriage would alter the way opposite-sex couples *feel* about their marriage, but ... there is little evidence of this ...

There are other important differences between same-sex marriage and polygamy as well. Crucially for equal protection analysis, gay men and lesbians are only seeking the same right everyone already has: the right to marry the person they love most. Polygamists are seeking a right that no one else has: the right to marry as many people as they please. This is no mere semantic difference or word game. Unless one believes that gay men and lesbians could simply decide to fall in love with someone of the opposite gender, they are foreclosed from the institution of marriage. The same thing certainly could not be said of frustrated polygamists.

So, even without resort to stereotypes, there is a world of difference between polygamy and same-sex marriage. Protecting the latter would not lead to protecting the former...

Same-sex marriage is an issue that truly tests America's commitment to genuine legal equality. Many have raised concerns that America's focus on groups and group rights threatens our unity and democracy. If we hope to move past the current discourse of "gay rights" as well as "women's rights," "minority rights," and so forth, then we must be willing to take a fresh look at the question of what rights we *all* share as people and as Americans. Although reasonable people can disagree on the merits of same-sex marriage, much of the response to the claims of same-sex couples has been callow and dismissive. The courts' repeated reliance upon reasons that have so little analytic substance does serious damage to the ideal that all are equal before the law. At an absolute minimum, the courts must refrain from relying upon arguments that they would never accept in other contexts. The same is true for the heterosexual majority. If we find it charming when 80-year-olds marry, we cannot tell same-sex couples that they cannot marry because they cannot have children or because marriage is reserved for traditional families...

We can do better than this. Neither our personal beliefs about sexuality, nor cynicism about legal principles, nor doubts about judicial efficacy should prevent judges, lawyers, professors, teachers, and engaged citizens from vigorously engaging the question of which rights we all share and what the contours of those rights should be. Rights-based discourse is not the *only* form of reasoned discussion and should not replace religious, moral, and other forms of discourse. The Court's protection of the rights of dissidents to burn the American flag did not stop millions of Americans from proudly flying that flag in the wake of the terrorist attacks of 2001; nor did it diminish the power of the flag in the hearts of the people. Nor would judicial protection of same-sex marriage diminish the power of marriage in American life. But it would stand as a potent symbol of the depth of our commitment to genuine equality under the law.

Gay Marriage—and Marriage

SAM SCHULMAN

The feeling seems to be growing that gay marriage is inevitably coming our way in the United States, perhaps through a combination of judicial fiat and legislation in individual states. Growing, too, is the sense of a shift in the climate of opinion. The American public seems to be in the process of changing its mind—not actually in favor of gay marriage, but toward a position of slightly revolted tolerance for the idea. Survey results suggest that people have forgotten why they were so opposed to the notion even as recently as a few years ago.

It is curious that this has happened so quickly. With honorable exceptions, most of those who are passionately on the side of the traditional understanding of marriage appear to be at a loss for words to justify their passion; as for the rest, many seem to wish gay marriage had never been proposed in the first place, but also to have resigned themselves to whatever happens. In this respect, the gay-marriage debate is very different from the abortion debate, in which few with an opinion on either side have been so disengaged.

I think I understand why this is the case: as someone passionately and instinctively opposed to the idea of homosexual marriage, I have found myself disappointed by the arguments I have seen advanced against it. The strongest of these arguments predict measurable harm to the family and to our arrangements for the upbringing and well-being of children. I do not doubt the accuracy of those arguments. But they do not seem to get at the heart of the matter.

To me, what is at stake in this debate is not only the potential unhappiness of children, grave as that is; it is our ability to maintain the most basic components of our humanity. I believe, in fact, that we are at an "Antigone moment." Some of our fellow citizens wish to impose a radically new understanding upon laws and institutions that are both very old and fundamental to our organization as individuals and as a society. As Antigone said to Creon, we are being asked to tamper with "unwritten and unfailing laws, not of now, nor of yesterday; they always live, and no one knows their origin in time." I suspect, moreover, that everyone knows this is the case, and that, paradoxically, this very awareness of just how much is at stake is what may have induced, in defenders of those same "unwritten and unfailing laws," a kind of paralysis.

Admittedly, it is very difficult to defend that which is both ancient and "unwritten"—the arguments do not resolve themselves into a neat parade of documentary evidence, research results, or citations from the legal literature. Admittedly, too, proponents of this radical new understanding have been uncommonly effective in presenting their program as something that is not radical at all but as requiring merely a slight and painless adjustment in our customary arrangements. Finally, we have all learned to practice a certain deference to the pleas of minorities with a grievance, and in recent years no group has benefited more from this society-wide dispensation than homosexuals. Nevertheless, in the somewhat fragmentary notes that follow, I hope to rearticulate what I am persuaded everyone knows to be the case about marriage, and perhaps thereby encourage others with stronger arguments than mine to help break the general paralysis.

Let us begin by admiring the case *for* gay marriage. Unlike the case for completely unrestricted abortion, which has come to be something of an embarrassment even to those who advance it, the case for gay marriage enjoys the decided advantage of appealing to our better moral natures as well as to our reason. It deploys two arguments. The first centers on principles of justice and fairness and may be thought of as the civil rights argument. The second is at once more personal and more utilitarian, emphasizing the degradation and unhappiness attendant upon the denial of gay marriage and, conversely, the human and social happiness that will flow from its legal establishment.

Both arguments have been set forth most persuasively by two gifted writers, Bruce Bawer and Andrew Sullivan, each of whom describes himself as a social conservative. In their separate ways, they have been campaigning for gay marriage for over a decade. Bawer's take on the subject is succinctly summarized in his 1993 book, *A Place at the Table*; Sullivan has held forth on the desirability of legalizing gay marriage in numerous articles, on his Web site (andrewsullivan.com), and in an influential book. *Virtually Normal* (1995).

The civil rights argument goes like this. Marriage is a legal state conferring real, tangible benefits on those who participate in it: specifically, tax breaks as well as other advantages when it comes to inheritance, property ownership, and employment benefits. But family law, since it limits marriage to heterosexual couples over the age of consent, clearly discriminates against a segment of the population. It is thus a matter of simple justice that, in Sullivan's words, "all public (as opposed to private) discrimination against homosexuals be ended and that every right and responsibility that heterosexuals enjoy as public citizens be extended to those who grow up and find themselves emotionally different." Not to grant such rights, Sullivan maintains, is to impose on homosexuals a civil deprivation akin to that suffered by black Americans under Jim Crow.

The utilitarian argument is more subtle; just as the rights argument seems aimed mainly at liberals, this one seems mostly to have in mind the concerns of conservatives. In light of the disruptive, anarchic, violence-prone behavior of many homosexuals (the argument runs), why should we not encourage the formation of stable, long-term, monogamous relationships that will redound to the health of society as a whole? In the apt words of a letter writer in *Commentary* in 1996:

> [H]omosexual marriage ... preserves and promotes a set of moral values that are essential to civilized society. Like heterosexual marriage, it sanctions loyalty, unselfishness, and sexual fidelity; it rejects the promiscuous, the self-serving, the transitory relationship. Given the choice between building family units and preventing them, any conservative should favor the former.

Bawer, for his part, has come close to saying that the inability of many male homosexuals to remain faithful in long-term relationships is a consequence of the lack of marriage rights—a burning sign of the more general stigma under which gays labor in our society and which can be redressed by changes in law. As it happens, though, this particular line of argument is already somewhat out of date and is gradually being phased out of the discussion. The toleration of gay styles of life has come about on its own in American society, without the help of legal sanctions, and protecting gay couples from the contempt of bigots is not the emergency Bawer has depicted. Quite the contrary: with increasing numbers of gay partners committing themselves to each other for life, in full and approving view of their families and friends, advocates of gay marriage need no longer call upon the law to light (or force) the way; they need only ask it to ratify a trend.

In brief, legalizing gay marriage would, in Andrew Sullivan's summary formulation,

> offer homosexuals the same deal society now offers heterosexuals: general social approval and specific legal advantages in exchange for a deeper and harder-to-extract-yourself-from commitment to another human being. Like straight marriage, it would foster social cohesion, emotional security, and economic prudence.

The case is elegant, and it is compelling. But it is not unanswerable. And answers have indeed been forthcoming, even if, as I indicated at the outset, many of them have tended to be couched somewhat defensively. Thus, rather than repudiating the very idea of an abstract "right" to marry, many upholders of the traditional definition of marriage tacitly concede such a right, only going on to suggest that denying it to a minority amounts to a lesser hurt than conferring it would impose on the majority, and especially on children, the weakest members of our society.

Others, to be sure, have attacked the Bawer/Sullivan line more forthrightly. In a September 2000 article in *Commentary*, "What Is Wrong with Gay Marriage," Stanley Kurtz challenged the central contention that marriage would do for gay men what it does for straights—that is, "domesticate" their natural male impulse to promiscuity. Citing a number of academic "queer theorists" and radical gays, Kurtz wrote:

> In contrast to moderates and "conservatives" like Andrew Sullivan, who consistently play down [the] difference [between gays and straights] in order to promote their vision of gays as monogamists-in-the-making, radical gays have argued—more knowledgeably, more powerfully, and more vocally than any opponent of same-sex marriage would dare to do—that homosexuality, and particularly male homosexuality, is by its very nature incompatible with the norms of traditional monogamous marriage.

True, Kurtz went on, such radical gays nevertheless support same-sex marriage. But what motivates them is the hope of "eventually undoing the institution [of marriage] altogether," by delegitimizing age-old understandings of the family and thus (in the words of one such radical) "striking at the heart of the organization of Western culture and societies."

Nor are radical gays the only ones to entertain such destructive ambitions. Queuing up behind them, Kurtz warned, are the proponents of polygamy, polyandry, and polyamorism, all ready to argue that their threesomes, foursomes, and other "nontraditional" arrangements are entitled to the same rights as everyone else's. In a recent piece in the *Weekly Standard*, Kurtz has written that the "bottom" of this particular slippery slope is "visible from where we stand":

> Advocacy of legalized polygamy is growing. A network of grassroots organizations seeking legal recognition for group marriage already exists. The cause of legalized group marriage is championed by a powerful faction of family-law specialists. Influential legal bodies in both the

United States and Canada have presented radical programs of marital reform,... [even] the abolition of marriage. The ideas behind this movement have already achieved surprising influence with a prominent American politician [Al Gore].

Like other critics of same-sex marriage, Kurtz has himself been vigorously criticized, especially by Sullivan. But he is almost certainly correct as to political and legal realities. If we grant rights to one group because they have demanded it—which is, practically, how legalized gay marriage will come to pass—we will find it exceedingly awkward to deny similar rights to others ready with their own dossiers of "victimization." In time, restricting marriage rights to couples, whether straight or gay, can be made to seem no less arbitrary than the practice of restricting marriage rights to one man and one woman. Ultimately, the same must go for incestuous relationships between consenting adults—a theme to which I will return.

A different defense of heterosexual marriage has proceeded by circling the wagons around the institution itself. According to this school of thought, ably represented by the columnist Maggie Gallagher, the essential purpose of that institution is to create stable families:

> Most men and women are powerfully drawn to perform a sexual act that can and does generate life. Marriage is our attempt to reconcile and harmonize the erotic, social, sexual, and financial needs of men and women with the needs of their partner and their children.

Even childless marriages protect this purpose, writes Gallagher, by ensuring that, as long as the marriage exists, neither the childless husband nor the childless wife is likely to father or mother children outside of wedlock.

Gallagher is especially strong on the larger, social meaning of heterosexual marriage, which she calls "inherently normative":

> The laws of marriage do not create marriage, but in societies ruled by law they help trace the boundaries and sustain the public meanings of marriage.... Without this shared, public aspect, perpetuated generation after generation, marriage becomes what its critics say it is: a mere contract, a vessel with no particular content, one of a menu of sexual lifestyles, of no fundamental importance to anyone outside a given relationship.

Human relationships are by nature difficult enough, Gallagher reminds us, which is why communities must do all they can to strengthen and not to weaken those institutions that keep us up to a mark we may not be able to achieve through our own efforts. The consequences of not doing so will be an intensification of all the other woes of which we have so far had only a taste in our society and which are reflected in the galloping statistics of illegitimacy, cohabitation, divorce, and fatherlessness. For Gallagher, the modest request of gay-marriage advocates for "a place at the table" is thus profoundly selfish as well as utterly destructive—for gay marriage "would require society at large to gut marriage of its central presumptions about family in order to accommodate a few adults' desires."

James Q. Wilson, Maggie Gallagher, Stanley Kurtz, and others—including William J. Bennett in *The Broken Hearth* (2001)—are right to point to the deleterious private and public consequences of instituting gay marriage. Why, then, do their arguments fail to satisfy completely? Partly, no doubt, it is because the damage they describe is largely prospective and to that degree hypothetical; partly, as I remarked early on, the defensive tone that invariably enters into these polemics may rob them of the force they would otherwise have. I hardly mean to deprecate that tone: anyone with homosexual friends or relatives, especially those participating in longstanding romantic relationships, must feel abashed to find himself saying, in effect, "You gentlemen, you ladies, are at one and the same time a fine example of fidelity and mutual attachment—and the thin edge of the wedge." Nevertheless, in demanding the right to marry, that is exactly what they are.

To grasp what is at the other edge of that wedge—that is, what stands to be undone by gay marriage—we have to distinguish marriage itself from a variety of other goods and values with which it is regularly associated by its defenders and its aspirants alike. Those values—love and monogamous sex and establishing a home, fidelity, childbearing and childrearing, stability, inheritance, tax breaks, and all the rest—are not the same as marriage. True, a good marriage generally contains them, a bad marriage is generally deficient in them, and in law, religion, and custom, even under the strictest of moral regimes, their absence can be grounds for ending the union. But the essence of marriage resides elsewhere, and those who seek to arrange a kind of marriage for the inherently unmarriageable are looking for those things in the wrong place.

The largest fallacy of all arises from the emphasis on romantic love. In a book published in 2002, Tipper and Al Gore defined a family as those who are "joined at the heart"—"getting beyond words, legal formalities, and even blood ties." The distinction the Gores draw in this sentimental and offhand way is crucial, but they utterly misconstrue it. Hearts can indeed love, and stop loving, but what exactly does this have to do with marriage, which can follow, precede, or remain wholly independent of that condition?

It is a truism that many married people feel little sexual or romantic attraction to each other—perhaps because they have been married too long, or perhaps, as some men have always claimed, because the death of sexual desire is coincident with the wedding ceremony. ("All comedies are ended by a marriage," Byron wittily and sadly remarked.) Many people—in ages past, certainly most people—have married for reasons other than sexual or romantic attraction. So what? I could marry a woman I did not love, a woman I did not feel sexually attracted to or want to sleep with, and our marriage would still be a marriage, not just legally but in its essence.

The truth is banal, circular, but finally unavoidable: by definition, the essence of marriage is to sanction and solemnize that connection of opposites which alone creates new life. (Whether or not a given married couple does in fact create new life is immaterial.) Men and women *can* marry only because they belong to different, opposite sexes. In marriage, they surrender those separate and different sexual allegiances, coming together to form a new entity. Their union is not a formalizing of romantic love but represents a certain idea—a construction, an abstract thought—about how best to formalize the human condition. This thought, embodied in a promise or a contract, is what holds marriage together, and the creation of this idea of marriage marks a key moment in the history of human development, a triumph over the alternative idea, which is concubinage.

Let me try to be more precise. Marriage can only concern my connection to a woman (and not to a man) because, as my reference to concubinage suggests, marriage is an institution that is built around female sexuality and female procreativity. (The very word "marriage" comes from the Latin word for mother, *mater*.) It exists for the gathering-in of a woman's sexuality under the protective net of the human or divine order, or both. This was so in the past and it is so even now, in our supposedly liberated times, when a woman who is in a sexual relationship without being married is, and is perceived to be, in a different state of being (not just a different legal state) from a woman who is married.

Circumstances have, admittedly, changed. Thanks to contraception, the decision to marry no longer precedes sexual intercourse as commonly as it did fifty years ago, when, for most people, a fully sexual relationship could begin only with marriage (and, when, as my mother constantly reminds me, one married *for* sex). Now the decision can come later; but come it almost certainly must. Even with contraception, even with feminism and women's liberation, the feeling would appear to be nearly as strong as ever that, for a woman, a sexual relationship must either end in marriage, or end.

This is surely understandable, for marriage benefits women, again not just in law but essentially. A woman can control who is the father of her children only insofar as there is a civil and private order that protects her from rape; marriage is the bulwark of that order. The 1960s feminists had the right idea: the essential thing for a woman is to control her own body. But they were wrong that this is what abortion is for; it is, rather, what marriage is for. It is humanity's way of enabling a woman to control her own body and to know (if she cares to) who is the father of her children.

Yes, marriage tends to regulate or channel the sexual appetite of men, and this is undoubtedly a good thing for women. But it is not the ultimate good. A husband, no matter how unfaithful, cannot introduce a child who is not his wife's own into a marriage without her knowledge; she alone has the power to do such a thing. For a woman, the fundamental advantage of marriage is thus not to regulate her husband but to empower herself—to regulate who has access to her person, and to marshal the resources of her husband and of the wider community to help her raise her children.

Every human relationship can be described as an enslavement, but for women the alternative to marriage is a much worse enslavement—which is why marriage, for women, is often associated as much with sexual freedom as with sexual constraint. In the traditional Roman Catholic cultures of the Mediterranean and South America, where virginity is fiercely protected and adolescent girls are hardly permitted to "date," marriage gives a woman the double luxury of controlling her sexuality and, if she wishes, extending it.

For men, by contrast, the same phenomenon—needing to be married in order to feel safe and free in a sexual relationships—simply does not exist. Men may wish to marry, but for more particular reasons: because they want to have children, or because they want to make a woman they love happy, or because they fear they will otherwise lose the woman they love. But it is rare for a man to feel essentially incomplete, or unprotected, in a sexual relationship that has not been solemnized by marriage. In fact, a man desperate to marry is often considered to have something wrong with him—to be unusually controlling or needy.

Because marriage is an arrangement built around female sexuality, because the institution has to do with women far more than it has to do with men, women will be the victims of its destruction. Those analysts who have focused on how children will suffer from the legalization of gay marriage are undoubtedly correct—but this will not be the first time that social developments perceived as advances for one group or another have harmed children. After all, the two most important (if effortless) achievements of the women's movement of the late 1960s were the right to abort and the right—in some social classes, the commandment—to join the professional workforce, both manifestly harmful to the interests of children.

But with the success of the gay liberation movement, it is women themselves, all women, who will be hurt. The reason is that gay marriage takes something that belongs essentially to women, is crucial to their very freedom, and empties it of meaning.

Why should I not be able to marry a man? The question addresses a class of human phenomena that can be described in sentences but nonetheless cannot be. However much I might wish to, I cannot be a father to a pebble—I cannot be a brother to a puppy—I cannot make my horse my consul. Just so, I cannot, and should not be able to, marry a man. If I want to be a brother to a puppy, are you abridging my rights by not permitting it? I may say what I please; saying it does not mean that it can be.

In a gay marriage, one of two men must play the woman, or one of two women must play the man. "Play" here means travesty—burlesque. Not that their love is a travesty; but their participation in a ceremony that apes the marriage bond, with all that goes into it, is a travesty. Their taking over of the form of this crucial and fragile connection of opposites is a travesty of marriage's purpose of protecting, actually and symbolically, the woman who enters into marriage with a man. To burlesque that purpose weakens those protections, and is essentially and profoundly antifemale.

Radical feminists were right, to an extent, in insisting that men's and women's sexuality is so different as to be inimical. Catharine MacKinnon has proclaimed that in a "patriarchal" society, all sexual intercourse is rape. Repellent as her view is, it is formed around a kernel of truth. There is something inherently violative about sexual intercourse—and there is something dangerous about being a woman in a sexual relationship with a man to whom she is not yet married. Among the now-aging feminists of my generation, no less than among their mothers, such a woman is commonly thought to be a victim.

Marriage is a sign that the ever-so-slight violation that is involved in a heterosexual relationship has been sanctioned by some recognized authority. That sanction is also what makes divorce a scandal—for divorce cannot truly undo the sanction of sexual intercourse, which is to say the sanction to create life, with one's original partner. Even in the Jewish tradition, which regards marriage (but not love) in a completely unsacralized way, divorce, though perfectly legal, does not erase the ontological status of the earlier marriage. (The Talmud records that God weeps when a man puts aside his first wife.) This sanction does not exist for homosexual couples. They are not opposites; they are the same. They live in a world of innocence, and neither their union nor their disunion partakes of the act of creation.

This brings us back to the incest ban, with which marriage is intimately and intricately connected. Indeed, marriage exists for the same reason that incest must not: because in our darker, inhuman moments we are driven toward that which is the same as ourselves and away from that which is fundamentally different from ourselves. Therefore we are enjoined from committing incest, negatively, and commanded to join with our opposite, positively—so that humanity may endure.

Homosexuals are, of course, free to avoid the latter commandment—and those who choose to do so are assuredly capable of leading rich and satisfying lives. The same goes for all those nonhomosexuals who have decided or been advised not to marry in certain circumstances—for example, if they wish to be members of celibate religious communities, or ascetic soldiers in a cause, or geniuses (as Cyril Connolly warned, "there is no more somber enemy of good art than the pram in the hall"). Men and women alike now spend more time as sexually mature adults outside of marriage than ever before, and some number of them live together in unreal or mock marriages of one kind or another. The social status of homosexuals is no better and no worse than that of anyone else who lives in an unmarried condition.

What of simple compassion? What do we owe to our fellow beings who wish, as they might put it, to achieve a happiness they see we are entitled to but which we deny to them? From those of us who oppose gay marriage, Andrew Sullivan demands *some* "reference to gay people's lives or relationships or needs." But the truth is that many people have many needs that are not provided for by law, by government, or by society at large—and for good reason.

Insofar as I care for my homosexual friend as a friend, I am required to say to him that, if a lifelong monogamous relationship is what you want, I wish you that felicity, just as I hope you would wish me the same. But insofar as our lives as citizens are concerned, or even as human beings, your monogamy and the durability of your relationship are, to be blunt about it, matters of complete indifference. They are of as little concern to our collective life as if you were to smoke cigars or build model railroads in your basement or hang glide, and of less concern to society than the safety of your property when you leave your house or your right not to be overcharged by the phone company.

That is not because you are gay. It is because, in choosing to conduct your life as you have every right to do, you have stepped out of the area of shared social concern—in the same sense as has anyone, of whatever sexuality, who chooses not to marry. There are millions of lonely people, of whom it is safe to say that the majority are in heterosexual marriages. But marriage, though it may help meet the needs of the lonely, does not exist because it is an answer to those needs; it is an arrangement that has to do with empowering women to avoid even greater unhappiness, and with sustaining the future history of the species.

Marriage, to say it for the last time, is what connects us with our nature and with our animal origins, with how all of us, heterosexual and homosexual alike, came to be. It exists not because of custom, or because of a conspiracy (whether patriarchal or matriarchal), but because, through marriage, the *world* exists. Marriage is how we are connected backward in time, through the generations, to our creator (or, if you insist, to the primal soup), and forward to the future beyond the scope of our own lifespan. It is, to say the least, bigger than two hearts beating as one.

Severing this connection by defining it out of existence—cutting it down to size, transforming it into a mere contract between chums—sunders the natural laws that prevent concubinage and incest. Unless we resist, we will find ourselves entering on the path to the abolition of the human. The gods move very fast when they bring ruin on misguided men.

Discussion Questions

1. Should the issue of same-sex marriage be viewed primarily as a matter of constitutional rights or as a matter of traditional social bonds?

2. Should the issue of same-sex marriage be decided by courts or legislatures, or should the electorate have the final say?

3. How would Gerstmann respond to the argument that allowing same-sex couples to wed will empty the institution of marriage of its meaning as the foundation of a decent society?

4. How would Schulman respond to the argument that marriages today between men and women are threatened by many economic and social pressures, but that same-sex marriage, entered into by the minority that is gay or lesbian, is not among these threats?

Suggested Readings and Internet Resources

For anthologies that present the opposing sides in the debate over same-sex marriage, see Andrew Sullivan, ed., *Same-Sex Marriage: Pro and Con* (New York: Vintage Books, 2004) and Robert M. Baird and Stuart E. Rosenbaum, eds., *Same-Sex Marriage: The Moral and Legal Debate*, Second Edition (Amherst, N.Y.: Prometheus Books, 2004). An array of political scientists examine the issues in same-sex marriage in Craig A. Rimmerman and Clyde Wilcox, eds., *The Politics of Same-Sex Marriage* (Chicago: University of Chicago Press, 2007). Martha Nussbaum, a prominent philosopher, probes the bases for moral and psychological opposition to gay and lesbian rights in *From Disgust to Humanity: Sexual Orientation and Constitutional Law* (New York: Oxford University Press, 2010).

National Conference of State Legislatures
www.ncsl.org
The website of the National Conference of State Legislatures provides a useful overview of the status of same-sex marriage in each state.

Freedom to Marry
www.freedomtomarry.org
An activist organization that seeks to build support for same-sex marriage across the United States.

Chapter 8

✳

Church–State Relations: Was the United States Founded as a Christian Nation?

The United States is one of the most religious nations in the world. About 85 percent of Americans tell pollsters that they identify with a specific religious faith, and 40 percent report they attend religious services at least once a week. By these measures the United States is more religious than every European nation except Poland and Ireland.

In recent decades religion has played an ever more prominent role in American public life. When Jimmy Carter publicly proclaimed his Evangelical faith in 1976, it was viewed as something of a curiosity. Now, "God talk" is common in presidential campaigns. In a Republican debate during the 2000 campaign, George W. Bush declared that Jesus Christ was his favorite political philosopher, and several of his opponents quickly followed suit. Barack Obama speaks often and openly about his religious commitments. Although the Constitution forbids any religious test for office, today the United States essentially has a de facto religious requirement for the presidency: no one who admits to being an unbeliever could ever be elected president.

Notwithstanding their deep religious commitments, Americans are reluctant to force their beliefs on anyone. Unlike most nations in the world, the United States is home to people from many different religious traditions. Although overwhelmingly Christian, Americans are divided among Catholics, mainline Protestants, white Evangelical Protestants, and African-American Protestants (with many different denominations within each broad group of Protestants). Jews make up only about 2 percent of the population. Other religious groups such as Mormons, Orthodox Christians, Christian Scientists, Muslims, Buddhists, and Hindus are small but growing.

Many immigrants fled to America to escape religious persecution. The United States was a religious sanctuary where the "free exercise of religion" was guaranteed by the Constitution. Conversely, the Constitution also forbade the "establishment of religion." In recent history the courts have ruled this to mean that religion should be kept strictly separate from government. Conservatives have complained bitterly that this has gone too far and interfered with their free exercise of religion. Conservatives have called for permitting prayer in public schools and Christian symbols on public property, such as crucifixes or the Ten Commandments.

The diversity of religious beliefs has made it impossible for any one group to impose its beliefs on others. Americans are quite religiously tolerant. A joke about a priest, minister, and rabbi is common at public gatherings—testament to our tolerance for different beliefs, at least within the Judeo-Christian tradition. Polls show that Americans support the separation of church and state. On the other hand, in a 2007 poll by the First Amendment Center, 55 percent said they believed the Constitution established the country as a Christian nation.

The debate about the proper role of religion in American life is broad and deep. In this chapter we look at only one narrow slice of that debate: Were the framers of the U.S. Constitution in 1787 motivated by Christian beliefs? Although this may seem like an academic debate about a distant historical period, given Americans' reverence for the founders it clearly has great resonance for contemporary debates about the proper role of religion in politics. How Americans view the framers of the Constitution affects not only how we interpret that document but our very identity as a nation.

At the time of the Constitutional Convention the main example the delegates had before them was England, which had an established church, the Church of England. Following the Glorious Revolution of 1688, when Parliament asserted its authority over the monarchy, other Christian faiths were given the right to worship more or less as they saw fit. When the framers met to write the Constitution, eleven out of thirteen states had a specific religion recognized in their state constitutions, but the framers based their document on Virginia's example, with its Statute for Religious Freedom.

The framers were religious men deeply steeped in the Bible. However, they were also followers of the Enlightenment, a philosophical movement peaking in the eighteenth century that stressed the role of reason over revelation. Great Enlightenment thinkers, like Isaac Newton and especially the political philosopher John Locke, influenced the thinking of the framers. Enlightenment philosophers believed that we could understand the laws of nature through careful observation and reason, and this knowledge could help us bring order and justice to human societies. Government should not be based on the divine right of kings but on natural rights and reason. The U.S. Constitution, with its ideas of limited government, checks and balances, and a Bill of Rights, embodies many of the ideas of the Enlightenment.

Whether the Enlightenment was hostile to or supportive of religion is a topic of continued debate. On the one hand, the French Enlightenment was quite hostile to religion, and the French Revolution attacked the Catholic Church, destroying many religious structures and killing many believers or forcing them to flee. On the other hand, many Enlightenment philosophers were believers, just like many scientists are today. The English Enlightenment tended to be less hostile to religion. Reason and science were viewed as ways to discover God through the workings of nature. Some framers were deists, who believed that God created the world to run on natural laws that could be discovered by human reason. However, once these laws were set in motion, God did not intervene in history.

The two essays that follow represent diametrically opposed views on the relationship of religion and the founding. Newt Gingrich, former Speaker of the House of Representatives and holder of a doctorate in American history, argues passionately that the founders were Christian men who were inspired by their religious faith. Like many conservatives, he is especially unhappy with the judiciary, which has consistently ruled against public displays of religion. Secular humanists, Gingrich believes, have tried to subvert freedom *of* religion into freedom *from* religion.

Brooke Allen, a scholar and freelance writer, would probably be considered one of those secular leftists whom Gingrich rails against. Allen argues that the widespread belief, promoted by the Christian right, that the founders were motivated by Christian beliefs is simply wrong. Like politicians today, the framers were aware of the need to defer to the religious beliefs of common Americans, but in private they expressed more skeptical views of religion. They believed that reason, not revelation, should guide public policy—much like those scientists today who defend the teaching of evolution against creationists.

As you read the debate between Gingrich and Allen, think about the proper role of religion in American politics. On the one hand, liberals usually advocate positive freedom. As defined in the introduction of this book, *positive freedom* means that governments actively help people to realize their goals. On the other hand, conservatives usually believe in negative freedom—that is, that governments should leave people alone. In this case, the two sides seem to have reversed themselves: Gingrich wants government to play a positive role in promoting religion, and Allen wants government to leave religion alone. Which stance do you think is best for religion? For American politics?

The Centrality of Our Creator in Defining America

NEWT GINGRICH

... The secular Left has been inventing law and grotesquely distorting the Constitution to achieve a goal that none of the Founding Fathers would have thought reasonable. History is vividly clear about the importance of God in the founding of our nation. To prove that our Creator is so central to understanding

America, I have developed a walking tour of Washington, D.C., to show how often the Founding Fathers and other great Americans, and the institutions they created, refer to God and call upon Him. Indeed, to study American history is to encounter God again and again. A tour like this should be part of every school class's visit to Washington, D.C.

Religion is the fulcrum of American history. People came to America's shores to be free to practice their religious beliefs. It brought the Pilgrims with their desire to create a "city on a hill" that would be a beacon of religious belief and piety. The Pilgrims were but one group that poured into the new colonies. Quakers in Pennsylvania were another, Catholics in Maryland yet a third. A religious revival, the Great Awakening in the 1730s, inspired many Americans to fight the Revolutionary War to secure their God-given freedoms. Another great religious revival in the nineteenth century inspired the abolitionists' campaign against slavery.

It was no accident that the marching song of the Union Army during the Civil War included the line "as Christ died to make men holy let us die to make men free." That phrase was later changed to "let us live to make men free." But for the men in uniform who were literally placing their lives on the line to end slavery, they knew that the original line was the right one.

First Principles

For the colonists the argument with the British government was an argument about first principles. Where did power come from? What defined loyalty? Who defined rights between king and subject?

It was in this historic context that America proclaimed in the Declaration of Independence that all people "are endowed by their Creator with certain inalienable rights, that among these are life, liberty and the pursuit of happiness." This turned on its head the notion that power came from God through the monarch to the people.

Beginning with King John in 1215, the English had gradually been restricting and confining the power of their monarchs. But Americans went further, asserting that God granted rights directly to everyone. Moreover, these rights were "inalienable." The government could not deny man's God-given rights.

Those who came aboard the Mayflower in 1620 in search of religious freedom wrote a compact expressing that,

> We whose names are underwritten ... by the grace of God ... having undertaken, for the glory of God, and advancement of the Christian faith ... a voyage to plant the first colony in the Northern parts of Virginia, do by these presents solemnly and mutually in the presence of God, and one of another, covenant and combine ourselves together into a civil body politic, for our better ordering and preservation and furtherance of the ends aforesaid; and by virtue hereof to enact, constitute, and frame such just and equal laws, ordinances, acts, constitutions, and offices, from time to time, as shall be thought most meet and convenient for the general good of the colony, unto which we promise all due submission and obedience.

At America's Founding, religion was central. The very first Continental Congress in 1774 had invited the Reverend Jacob Duché to begin each session with a prayer. When the war against Britain began, the Continental Congress provided for chaplains to serve with the military and be paid at the same rate as majors in the Army.

During the Constitutional Convention of 1787, Benjamin Franklin (often considered one of the least religious of the Founding Fathers) proposed that the Convention begin each day with a prayer. As the oldest delegate, at age eighty-one, Franklin insisted that "the longer I live, the more convincing proofs I see of this truth—that God governs in the Affairs of Men."

Because of their belief that power had come from God to the individual, they began the Constitution "we the people." Note that the Founding Fathers did not write "we the states." Not did they write "we the government." Nor did they write "we the lawyers and judges."

These historic facts pose an enormous problem for secular liberals. How can they explain America without getting into the area of religion? If they dislike and in many cases fear religion, how then can they communicate the core nature of the people in America? ...

[T]he Founding Fathers, from the very birth of the United States, saw God as central to defining America. Professor Donald Lutz reviewed an estimated 15,000 items and 2,200 books, pamphlets, and newspaper articles with explicitly political content printed between 1760 and 1805. He counted 3,154 citations in the writings of the Founders; of these, nearly 1,100 references (34 percent) are to the Bible, and about 300 each are to Montesquieu and Blackstone, followed at considerable distance by Locke, Hume, and Plutarch. Quite clearly, the original intent of the Founding Fathers in adopting *both* the Free Exercise and Establishment Clause was to promote religious freedom, not to suppress it.

Our first president, George Washington, at his first inauguration on April 30, 1789, "put his right hand on the Bible ... [after taking the oath] adding 'So help me God.' He then bent forward and kissed the Bible before him." In his inaugural address, Washington remarked that

> ... it would be peculiarly improper to omit in this first official act my fervent supplications to that Almighty Being who rules over the universe, who presides in the councils of nations, and whose providential aids can supply every human defect, that His benediction may consecrate to the liberties and happiness of the people of the United States a Government instituted by themselves for these essential purposes, and may enable every instrument employed in its administration to execute with success the functions allotted to his charge.... No people can be bound to acknowledge and adore the Invisible Hand which conducts the affairs of men more than those of the United States.... You will join with me, I trust, in thinking that there are none under the influence of which the proceedings of a new and free government can more auspiciously commence.

Then in the Thanksgiving Proclamation of October 3, 1789, Washington declared "it is the duty of all Nations to acknowledge the Providence of Almighty

God, to obey His will, to be grateful for His benefits, and humbly to implore His protection and favor." Note that Washington was not just imploring that individuals have an obligation to God, but *nations* do as well. The United States government was not yet a year old.

Freedom of Religion: Not Freedom from Religion

The Bill of Rights was designed to protect freedom *of* religion not freedom *from* religion. Any serious look at the Founding Fathers and their behavior would reveal how much they believed in freedom *of* religion and how deeply they would have opposed government trying to create freedom *from* religion.

In writing the Northwest Ordinance in 1787, the Congress asserted "Religion, Morality, and knowledge being necessary to good government and the happiness of mankind, schools and the means of education shall be forever encouraged." Note that religion and morality precede knowledge as the purposes of school. Compare that with the secular, moral relativism of the modern education establishment.

Washington's successor, John Adams, warned that "it is Religion and Morality alone, which can establish the Principles upon which Freedom can securely stand."

The third and fourth presidents, Thomas Jefferson and James Madison, are usually considered the least religious of the early presidents, yet both attended church services in the Capitol. In fact, services were held in the House chamber until after the Civil War. At one point some 2,000 people were attending church in the Capitol, making our capitol building probably the largest church in the country. Jefferson also allowed executive branch buildings to be used for church services.

Jefferson was opposed to an official national religion but he was supportive of religion. The key was the term "Establishment of Religion." The secular Left looks to Jefferson's letter to the Danbury Baptists (January 1, 1802) in which he said there should be "a wall of separation between church and state." They then ignore the fact that two days later he went to the United States House of Representatives to attend church services. In fact one observer wrote that "Jefferson during his whole administration was a most regular attendant."

Church did not just take place in the House chamber. During Jefferson's presidency church was also held in the Treasury building and in the Supreme Court. For those secular liberals who believe Jefferson did not believe in God, I always urge them to visit the Jefferson Memorial and read around the top: "I have sworn upon on the altar of God eternal hostility against every form of tyranny over the mind of man."

The issue of the Establishment Clause and its interpretation is at the heart of the question of God in American public life. The First Amendment is actually quite clear. It states, "Congress shall make no law respecting an establishment of religion, or prohibiting the free exercise thereof; or abridging the freedom of speech, or of the press; or the right of the people peaceably to assemble, and to petition the Government for a redress of grievances."

This language plainly refers to the question of establishing an official religion. Jefferson and Madison, by attending church in public buildings, clearly saw no conflict between opposing an official, state religion, and favoring religious observance in public places.

Jefferson took additional steps to indicate government support for religion in general. While president, Jefferson chaired the school board for the District of Columbia. He wrote the first plan of education adopted by the City of Washington, which used the Bible and Isaac Watt's Hymnal as the principal books to teach reading to students.

Jefferson recommended that Congress extend a treaty with the Kaskaskia Indians, which provided for annual support ($100) to a Catholic missionary priest to be paid out of the federal treasury. Similar treaties were made with the Wyandotte and the Cherokee tribes. Jefferson extended three times the "Resolution granting lands to Moravian Brethren," a 1787 act of Congress in which special lands were designated "for the sole use of Christian Indians and the Moravian Brethren missionaries for civilizing the Indians and promoting Christianity."

Jefferson not only signed bills that appropriated financial support for chaplains in Congress and in the armed services, but he also signed the Articles of War on April 10, 1806, in which he "Earnestly recommended to all officers and soldiers, diligently to attend divine services."

In establishing the University of Virginia, Jefferson encouraged the teaching of religion, and also set aside a place inside the Rotunda for chapel services. He also spoke highly of the use, in his hometown, of the local courthouse for religious services.

On one occasion, Jefferson declared that religion is "deemed in other countries incompatible with good government and yet proved by our experience to be its best support."...

James Madison authored the Bill of Rights in the First Congress. At the very time Congress was considering the First Amendment, which blocked "an establishment of religion," the same members of Congress were also hiring and paying for chaplains for the House and Senate. If the members who authored the First Amendment did not believe it blocked them from paying public money for a chaplain and offering public prayers in a public building, then it is an absurdity for the Supreme Court to interpret the behavior of the Founding Fathers in writing the First Amendment as an antireligious action. Everything we know about the Founders' individual and collective behavior indicates they were comfortable with God in public life and determined to recognize the religious basis of American liberty....

[Samuel] Huntington believes it is possible for the vast majority to reassert American exceptionalism and insist on respect for and reinforcement of America's values and institutions. As Huntington suggests:

> America was founded in large part for religious reasons and religious movements have shaped its evolution for almost four centuries. By every indicator, Americans are far more religious than the people of

other industrialized countries. Overwhelming majorities of white Americans, of black Americans, and of Hispanic Americans are Christians. In a world in which culture and particularly religion shape the allegiances, the alliances and the antagonisms of people on every continent, Americans could again find their national identity and their national purpose in their culture and religion.

The two primary battlefields of this cultural struggle are the courts and the classrooms. Those are the arenas in which the secular Left has imposed change against the wishes of the overwhelming majority of Americans. Those are the arenas in which believing in the Founding Fathers and the classic interpretation of the Constitution can be disastrous to a career and lead to social ostracism.

If we insist on courts that follow the facts of American history in interpreting the Constitution, we will reestablish the right that every American has to acknowledge our Creator as the source of our rights, our well-being, and our wisdom. And if we insist on patriotic education both for our children and for new immigrants, we will rebuild the cultural bond of historic memory that has made America the most exceptional nation in history.

Our Godless Constitution

BROOKE ALLEN

It is hard to believe that George Bush has ever read the works of George Orwell, but he seems, somehow, to have grasped a few Orwellian precepts. The lesson the President has learned best—and certainly the one that has been the most useful to him—is the axiom that if you repeat a lie often enough, people will believe it. One of his Administration's current favorites is the whopper about America having been founded on Christian principles. Our nation was founded not on Christian principles but on Enlightenment ones. God only entered the picture as a very minor player, and Jesus Christ was conspicuously absent.

Our Constitution makes no mention whatever of God. The omission was too obvious to have been anything but deliberate, in spite of Alexander Hamilton's flippant responses when asked about it: According to one account, he said that the new nation was not in need of "foreign aid"; according to another, he simply said "we forgot." But as Hamilton's biographer Ron Chernow points out, Hamilton never forgot anything important.

In the eighty-five essays that make up *The Federalist*, God is mentioned only twice (both times by Madison, who uses the word, as Gore Vidal has remarked, in the "only Heaven knows" sense). In the Declaration of Independence, He gets two brief nods: a reference to "the Laws of Nature and Nature's God," and the famous line about men being "endowed by their Creator with certain inalienable rights." More blatant official references to a deity date from long after the founding period: "In God We Trust" did not appear on our coinage until the Civil War, and "under God" was introduced into the Pledge of Allegiance during the McCarthy hysteria in 1954.

In 1797 our government concluded a "Treaty of Peace and Friendship between the United States of America and the Bey and Subjects of Tripoli, or Barbary," now known simply as the Treaty of Tripoli. Article 11 of the treaty contains these words:

> As the Government of the United States ... is not in any sense founded on the Christian religion—as it has in itself no character of enmity against the laws, religion, or tranquillity of Musselmen—and as the said States never have entered into any war or act of hostility against any Mehomitan nation, it is declared by the parties that no pretext arising from religious opinions shall ever produce an interruption of the harmony existing between the two countries.

This document was endorsed by Secretary of State Timothy Pickering and President John Adams. It was then sent to the Senate for ratification; the vote was unanimous. It is worth pointing out that although this was the 339th time a recorded vote had been required by the Senate, it was only the third unanimous vote in the Senate's history. There is no record of debate or dissent. The text of the treaty was printed in full in the *Philadelphia Gazette* and in two New York papers, but there were no screams of outrage, as one might expect today.

The Founding Fathers were not religious men, and they fought hard to erect, in Thomas Jefferson's words, "a wall of separation between church and state." John Adams opined that if they were not restrained by legal measures, Puritans—the fundamentalists of their day—would "whip and crop, and pillory and roast." The historical epoch had afforded these men ample opportunity to observe the corruption to which established priesthoods were liable, as well as "the impious presumption of legislators and rulers," as Jefferson wrote, "civil as well as ecclesiastical, who, being themselves but fallible and uninspired men, have assumed dominion over the faith of others, setting up their own opinions and modes of thinking as the only true and infallible, and as such endeavoring to impose them on others, hath established and maintained false religions over the greatest part of the world and through all time."

If we define a Christian as a person who believes in the divinity of Jesus Christ, then it is safe to say that some of the key Founding Fathers were not Christians at all. Benjamin Franklin, Thomas Jefferson, and Tom Paine were deists—that is, they believed in one Supreme Being but rejected revelation and all the supernatural elements of the Christian Church; the word of the Creator, they believed, could best be read in Nature. John Adams was a professed liberal

Unitarian, but he, too, in his private correspondence seems more deist than Christian.

George Washington and James Madison also leaned toward deism, although neither took much interest in religious matters. Madison believed that "religious bondage shackles and debilitates the mind and unfits it for every noble enterprize." He spoke of the "almost fifteen centuries" during which Christianity had been on trial: "What have been its fruits? More or less in all places, pride and indolence in the Clergy, ignorance and servility in the laity, in both, superstition, bigotry, and persecution." If Washington mentioned the Almighty in a public address, as he occasionally did, he was careful to refer to Him not as "God" but with some nondenominational moniker like "Great Author" or "Almighty Being." It is interesting to note that the Father of our Country spoke no words of a religious nature on his deathbed, although fully aware that he was dying, and did not ask for a man of God to be present; his last act was to take his own pulse, the consummate gesture of a creature of the age of scientific rationalism.

Tom Paine, a polemicist rather than a politician, could afford to be perfectly honest about his religious beliefs, which were baldly deist in the tradition of Voltaire: "I believe in one God, and no more; and I hope for happiness beyond this life ... I do not believe in the creed professed by the Jewish church, by the Roman church, by the Greek church, by the Turkish church, by the Protestant church, nor by any church that I know of. My own mind is my own church." This is how he opened *The Age of Reason*, his virulent attack on Christianity. In it he railed against the "obscene stories, the voluptuous debaucheries, the cruel and torturous executions, the unrelenting vindictiveness" of the Old Testament, "a history of wickedness, that has served to corrupt and brutalize mankind." The New Testament is less brutalizing but more absurd, the story of Christ's divine genesis a "fable, which for absurdity and extravagance is not exceeded by any thing that is to be found in the mythology of the ancients." He held the idea of the Resurrection in especial ridicule: Indeed, "the wretched contrivance with which this latter part is told, exceeds every thing that went before it." Paine was careful to contrast the tortuous twists of theology with the pure clarity of deism. "The true deist has but one Deity; and his religion consists in contemplating the power, wisdom, and benignity of the Deity in his works, and in endeavoring to imitate him in every thing moral, scientifical, and mechanical."

Paine's rhetoric was so fervent that he was inevitably branded an atheist. Men like Franklin, Adams, and Jefferson could not risk being tarred with that brush, and in fact Jefferson got into a good deal of trouble for continuing his friendship with Paine and entertaining him at Monticello. These statesmen had to be far more circumspect than the turbulent Paine, yet if we examine their beliefs it is all but impossible to see just how theirs differed from his.

Franklin was the oldest of the Founding Fathers. He was also the most worldly and sophisticated, and was well aware of the Machiavellian principle that if one aspires to influence the masses, one must at least profess religious sentiments. By his own definition he was a deist, although one French acquaintance claimed that "our free-thinkers have adroitly sounded him on his religion, and they maintain that they have discovered he is one of their own, that is that he has none at all." If he did have a religion, it was strictly utilitarian: As his biographer Gordon Wood has said, "He praised religion for whatever moral effects it had, but for little else." Divine revelation, Franklin freely admitted, has "no weight with me," and the covenant of grace seemed "unintelligible" and "not beneficial." As for the pious hypocrites who have ever controlled nations, "A man compounded of law and gospel is able to cheat a whole country with his religion and then destroy them under color of law"—a comment we should carefully consider at this turning point in the history of our Republic.

Here is Franklin's considered summary of his own beliefs, in response to a query by Ezra Stiles, the president of Yale. He wrote it just six weeks before his death at the age of 84.

> Here is my creed. I believe in one God, Creator of the universe. That he governs it by his providence. That he ought to be worshipped. That the most acceptable service we render to him is doing good to his other children. That the soul of Man is immortal, and will be treated with justice in another life respecting its conduct in this. These I take to be the fundamental points in all sound religion, and I regard them as you do in whatever sect I meet with them.
>
> As for Jesus of Nazareth, my opinion of whom you particularly desire, I think his system of morals and his religion, as he left them to us, the best the world ever saw or is likely to see; but I apprehend it has received various corrupting changes, and I have, with most of the present dissenters in England, some doubts as to his divinity; though it is a question I do not dogmatize upon, having never studied it, and think it needless to busy myself with now, when I expect soon an opportunity of knowing the truth with less trouble. I see no harm, however, in its being believed, if that belief has the good consequence, as it probably has, of making his doctrines more respected and better observed, especially as I do not perceive that the Supreme takes it amiss, by distinguishing the unbelievers in his government of the world with any particular marks of his displeasure.

Jefferson thoroughly agreed with Franklin on the corruptions the teachings of Jesus had undergone. "The metaphysical abstractions of Athanasius, and the maniacal ravings of Calvin, tinctured plentifully with the foggy dreams of Plato, have so loaded [Christianity] with absurdities and incomprehensibilities" that it was almost impossible to recapture "its native simplicity and purity." Like Paine, Jefferson felt that the miracles claimed by the New Testament put an intolerable strain on credulity. "The day will come," he predicted (wrongly, so far), "when the mystical generation of Jesus, by the supreme being as his father in the womb of a virgin, will be classed with the fable of the generation of Minerva in the brain of Jupiter." The Revelation of St. John he dismissed as "the ravings of a maniac."

Jefferson edited his own version of the New Testament, "The Life and Morals of Jesus of Nazareth," in which he carefully deleted all the miraculous passages from the works of the Evangelists. He intended it, he said, as "a document in proof that I am a real Christian, that is to say, a disciple of the doctrines of Jesus." This was clearly a defense against his many enemies, who hoped to blacken his reputation by comparing him with the vile atheist Paine. His biographer Joseph Ellis is undoubtedly correct, though, in seeing disingenuousness here: "If [Jefferson] had been completely scrupulous, he would have described himself as a deist who admired the ethical teachings of Jesus as a man rather than as the son of God. (In modern-day parlance, he was a secular humanist.)" In short, not a Christian at all.

The three accomplishments Jefferson was proudest of—those that he requested be put on his tombstone—were the founding of the University of Virginia and the authorship of the Declaration of Independence and the Virginia Statute for Religious Freedom. The latter was a truly radical document that would eventually influence the separation of church and state in the U.S. Constitution; when it was passed by the Virginia legislature in 1786, Jefferson rejoiced that there was finally "freedom for the Jew and the Gentile, the Christian and the Mohammeden, the Hindu and infidel of every denomination"—note his respect, still unusual today, for the sensibilities of the "infidel." The University of Virginia was notable among early-American seats of higher education in that it had no religious affiliation whatever. Jefferson even banned the teaching of theology at the school.

If we were to speak of Jefferson in modern political categories, we would have to admit that he was a pure libertarian, in religious as in other matters. His real commitment (or lack thereof) to the teachings of Jesus Christ is plain from a famous throwaway comment he made: "It does me no injury for my neighbor to say there are twenty gods or no god. It neither picks my pocket nor breaks my leg." This raised plenty of hackles when it got about, and Jefferson had to go to some pains to restore his reputation as a good Christian. But one can only conclude, with Ellis, that he was no Christian at all.

John Adams, though no more religious than Jefferson, had inherited the fatalistic mindset of the Puritan culture in which he had grown up. He personally endorsed the Enlightenment commitment to Reason but did not share Jefferson's optimism about its future, writing to him, "I wish that Superstition in Religion exciting Superstition in Polliticks … may never blow up all your benevolent and phylanthropic Lucubrations," but that "the History of all Ages is against you." As an old man he observed, "Twenty times in the course of my late reading have I been upon the point of breaking out, 'This would be the best of all possible worlds, if there were no religion in it!'" Speaking ex cathedra, as a relic of the founding generation, he expressed his admiration for the Roman system whereby every man could worship whom, what, and how he pleased. When his young listeners objected that this was paganism, Adams replied that it was indeed, and laughed.

In their fascinating and eloquent valetudinarian correspondence, Adams and Jefferson had a great deal to say about religion. Pressed by Jefferson to define his personal creed, Adams replied that it was "contained in four short words, 'Be just and good.'" Jefferson replied, "The result of our fifty or sixty years of religious reading, in the four words, 'Be just and good,' is that in which all our inquiries must end; as the riddles of all priesthoods end in four more, 'ubi panis, ibi deus.' What all agree in, is probably right. What no two agree in, most probably wrong."

This was a clear reference to Voltaire's *Reflections on Religion*. As Voltaire put it:

> There are no sects in geometry. One does not speak of a Euclidean, an Archimedean. When the truth is evident, it is impossible for parties and factions to arise.... Well, to what dogma do all minds agree? To the worship of a God, and to honesty. All the philosophers of the world who have had a religion have said in all ages: "There is a God, and one must be just." There, then, is the universal religion established in all ages and throughout mankind. The point in which they all agree is therefore true, and the systems through which they differ are therefore false.

Of course all these men knew, as all modern presidential candidates know, that to admit to theological skepticism is political suicide. During Jefferson's presidency a friend observed him on his way to church, carrying a large prayer book. "You going to church, Mr. J," remarked the friend. "You do not believe a word in it." Jefferson didn't exactly deny the charge. "Sir," he replied, "no nation has ever yet existed or been governed without religion. Nor can be. The Christian religion is the best religion that has been given to man and I as chief Magistrate of this nation am bound to give it the sanction of my example. Good morning Sir."

Like Jefferson, every recent President has understood the necessity of at least paying lip service to the piety of most American voters. All of our leaders, Democrat and Republican, have attended church, and have made very sure they are seen to do so. But there is a difference between offering this gesture of respect for majority beliefs and manipulating and pandering to the bigotry, prejudice, and millennial fantasies of Christian extremists. Though for public consumption the Founding Fathers identified themselves as Christians, they were, at least by today's standards, remarkably honest about their misgivings when it came to theological doctrine, and religion in general came very low on the list of their concerns and priorities—always excepting, that is, their determination to keep the new nation free from bondage to its rule.

Discussion Questions

1. Is the U.S. Constitution based on Christian values? If so, name them.

2. Poll your class or your friends. How many are Christian and how many different types of Christianity are represented? How many are non-Christian or nonbelievers? Does knowing people from different religious backgrounds increase tolerance?

3. According to polls, Americans are evenly divided on whether God gives their country special protection. Do you think God intervenes in history to help your county? If so, give an example.

4. Does religious faith tend to pull people into civic participation or does it tend to cause people to withdraw into spiritual contemplation? Give examples.

5. Would you favor a constitutional amendment to allow prayer or the display of Christian symbols in public schools?

6. Do you like it when candidates for public office openly discuss their religious beliefs, or would you prefer that they keep their religious beliefs to themselves?

Suggested Readings and Internet Resources

For a careful scholarly argument that the founders intended a separation of church and state, see Isaac Kramnick and R. Laurence Moore, *Our Godless Constitution: The Case Against Religious Correctness* (New York: W. W. Norton, 1996). One of best-known American political philosophers, Martha Nussbaum, examines the role of religion in American political life in *Liberty of Conscience: In Defense of America's Tradition of Religious Toleration* (New York: Basic Books, 2008). For a contrasting argument about how important religion was for the founders, see Michael Novak, *On Two Wings: Humble Faith and Common Sense in the American Founding* (San Francisco: Encounter Books, 2003). In *Thomas Jefferson and the Wall of Separation Between Church and State* (New York: New York University Press, 2002) Daniel L. Dreisbach argues that the Jefferson never intended a "wall" that would keep religion out of the public life. A. James Reichley's *Faith in Politics* (Washington, D.C.: Brookings Institution Press, 2002) argues that the founders believed in the complementary goals of a secular government and a society shaped by religion. In a much-discussed book, *The Culture of Disbelief: How American Law and Politics Trivializes Religious Devotion* (New York: Basic Books, 1993), Stephen L. Carter, a political moderate, argues that American culture is biased against public expressions of faith.

Beliefnet
www.beliefnet.com
Beliefnet is an award-winning website designed to promote religion generally and includes discussion of the relationship of religion and politics.

Americans United for Separation of Church and State
www.au.org
Started by Barry Lynn, Americans United advocates a wall of separation between religion and government.

Britannica Blog
http://www.britannica.com/blogs/2007/03/the-us-founding-fathers-their-religious-beliefs-cont/
Sponsored by the same company that publishes the encyclopedia, the Britannica Blog contains spirited exchanges by scholars debating the religious beliefs of the founders.

Pew Forum on Religion & Public Life
http://pewforum.org
Founded in 2001 by the Pew Charitable Trusts, the Pew Forum takes an objective approach, conducting surveys and seeking to promote a deeper understanding of issues at the intersection of religion and public affairs.

Chapter 9

✳

Digital Media: Do They Expand or Shrink Democracy?

It is a cliché to say that we live in an age saturated with information. A billion websites are available to the digerati at the click of a mouse. Hundreds of cable television stations compete with satellite radio and the long-established television networks, newspapers, and magazines for mass attention. Individuals can now access a world of information with a tiny smartphone that they pull out of their pockets or purses.

Yet this information doesn't come to us unmediated: even on a website, someone is structuring a particular version of facts, is setting an agenda for discussion, is including some information while excluding a vast tidal wave of those facts that may conflict with a particular viewpoint. Most of us are dependent on the mass media for knowledge of phenomena with which we have little direct experience. In a democratic society, we can only hope that all citizens are exposed to a variety of information and ideas. Yet we also hope that the media somehow mirrors ourselves as well as others, that it reflects and expresses a wide range of views, and that at some level at least parts of the media speak "truth to power." While any single media source can be deemed biased and incorrect, a diverse mass media is supposed to provide assurance that conflicting versions of political truth emerge and can be rationally debated.

Just how have the mass media performed these democratic tasks? According to a chorus of critics, not all that well. The media's most vocal critics lampoon the media for liberal or conservative biases. Others accuse the news media of crass commercialism and "cheerleading." During the early days of the Iraq war, leading news commentators donned U.S.–flag lapel pins, frankly supported the invasion, and, perhaps more seriously, rarely challenged what turned out to be the Bush administration's false assertions about Iraq's weapons of mass destruction. The rationale was often the ratings race; network news was more interested in pleasing the audience than in informing it. Conversely, "new media" and "streaming" fueled the antiwar movement. Activists streamed the BBC and searched out dissident websites to supply information counter to that found on the U.S. networks. Is the media "glass" half empty or half full?

Contemporary U.S. and global media are dominated by two major trends, which seem to run at cross-purposes. First, and as noted above, there seem to be more media outlets to choose from than at any other time in human history. However, concentrated corporate ownership of the mass media means that most people see programming, read books, and listen to music produced by a handful of mega-corporations with a global reach. The paradox of diversity and increased corporate concentration in firms like the News Corporation, Disney, and Viacom raises fundamental questions about how noncommercial, non-self-interested voices can ever be heard.

Still, the case for a wide and increasingly democratic and participatory market-place of ideas seems bolstered by the growth of digital communication. On the Internet, or even through Twittering, every person and group can set up as a media source, sending out opinion and fact seemingly at the speed of light. Low start-up costs allow millions of people to exchange ideas and information below the radar screen of corporate life and government—those using such sites as moveon.org and meetup.com can even arrange impromptu demonstrations if they so desire.

Perhaps the most dramatic demonstration of the digital age's prospects for political mobilization was the Obama presidential campaign of 2007–2008. The unsuccessful effort of Democrat Howard Dean in 2003–2004 was the first presidential campaign truly to exploit the possibilities of digital communication, but the hugely successful Obama campaign used digital media in a far more extensive and productive manner. Obama's digital campaigners, many of them very young, were savvy about building and sustaining a passionate political following through e-mail, text messaging, social networking, blogging, and YouTube videos. As one Obama activist proudly put it, the campaign's "brilliant use of technology to build relationships, transmit information, and organize offline action has redefined modern politics." Ironically, conservatives have awakened to their technological disadvantage since the 2008 campaign and are using many of the same digital techniques to mount an opposition to the Obama presidency.

In the essays that follow, two prominent authors arrive at different perspectives on the democratic potential of the new digital media. Cass Sunstein, a law professor at the University of Chicago at the time he wrote the essay contained here, and currently director of the White House Office of Information and Regulatory Affairs in the Obama administration, heralds the World Wide Web, but he worries that individuals and groups will use it to insulate themselves from the larger realm of public life and political dialogue. Sunstein argues that personal choices mesh with digital technologies to produce a "Daily Me." Many individuals gravitate only to sites where their existing beliefs are echoed; as they communicate online only with like-minded people, their views become more extreme and their hostility to different perspectives hardens. Without having to attend to alternative viewpoints, or to share common experiences with fellow citizens, Sunstein warns, democratic life is undermined.

The author of our second essay, political scientist W. Lance Bennett, a leading scholar in the field of media and politics, also sees several problems in the contemporary digital environment. Yet, in his focus on the role of young citizens in a digital age, he has a more hopeful outlook. Bennett notes that scholars are divided over whether young people today are disengaged from politics or are engaged in new and personal ways through media activities of their own choosing. Proponents of the former position point to low rates of voting or newspaper readership among the young. Proponents of the latter position point to online activism in areas like environmental protection or online mobilization for political protests. Attempting to bridge this divide, Bennett suggests how the traditional world of politics and education can learn to speak more effectively through digital media in terms that young people respect, while young people can move beyond current digital preoccupation with friendship networks or gaming and begin to find their voices as citizens in the processes of democratic governance.

Although they differ on how the new media currently affect democracy, both Sunstein and Bennett point to public policies and ideas that can enhance democracy for a digital age. While reading these two essays, you might ask the following questions: How would each author define a democratic standard for digital media? How might Sunstein respond to the idea that young people will become more engaged in democratic governance if older generations learn to speak through digital forums in ways that interest young people? How might Bennett respond to the concern that digital media inherently allow individuals to find comfortable niches with like-minded people, thereby encouraging polarization in place of democratic debate?

The Daily We

CASS R. SUNSTEIN

Is the Internet a wonderful development for democracy? In many ways it certainly is. As a result of the Internet, people can learn far more than they could before, and they can learn it much faster. If you are interested in issues that bear on public policy—environmental quality, wages over time, motor vehicle safety—you can find what you need to know in a matter of seconds. If you are suspicious of the mass media, and want to discuss issues with like-minded people, you can do that, transcending the limitations of geography in ways that could barely be imagined even a decade ago. And if you want to get information to a wide range of people, you can do that via email and websites; this is another sense in which the Internet is a great boon for democracy.

But in the midst of the celebration, I want to raise a note of caution. I do so by emphasizing one of the most striking powers provided by emerging technologies: the growing power of consumers to "filter" what they see. As a result of the Internet and other technological developments, many people are increasingly engaged in a process of "personalization" that limits their exposure to topics and points of view of their own choosing. They filter in, and they also filter out, with unprecedented powers of precision. Consider just a few examples:

1. Broadcast.com has "compiled hundreds of thousands of programs so you can find the one that suits your fancy.... For example, if you want to see all the latest fashions from France 24 hours of the day you can get them. If you're from Baltimore living in Dallas and you want to listen to WBAL, your hometown station, you can hear it."

2. Sonicnet.com [now part of VH1] allows you to create your own musical universe, consisting of what it calls "Me Music." Me Music is "A place where you can listen to the music you love on the radio station YOU create.... A place where you can watch videos of your favorite artists and new artists."

3. Zatso.net allows users to produce "a personal newscast." Its intention is to create a place "where you decide what's news." Your task is to tell "what TV news stories you're interested in," and Zatso.net turns that information into a specifically designed newscast....

4. George Bell, the chief executive officer of the search engine Excite, exclaims, "We are looking for ways to be able to lift chunks of content off other areas of our service and paste them onto your personal page so you can constantly refresh and update that 'newspaper of me.'"...

Of course, these developments make life much more convenient and in some ways much better: we all seek to reduce our exposure to uninvited noise. But from the standpoint of democracy, filtering is a mixed blessing. An understanding of the mix will permit us to obtain a better sense of what makes for a well-functioning system of free expression. In a heterogeneous society, such a system requires something other than free, or publicly unrestricted, individual choices. On the contrary, it imposes two distinctive requirements. First, people should be exposed to materials that they would not have chosen in advance. *Unanticipated encounters*, involving topics and points of view that people have not sought out and perhaps find irritating, are central to democracy and even to freedom itself. Second, many or most citizens should have a range of *common experiences*. Without shared experiences, a heterogeneous society will have a more difficult time addressing social problems and understanding one another.

Individual Design

Consider a thought experiment—an apparently utopian dream, that of complete individuation, in which consumers can entirely personalize (or "customize") their communications universe.

Imagine, that is, a system of communications in which each person has unlimited power of individual design. If some people want to watch news all the time, they would be entirely free to do exactly that. If they dislike news, and want to watch football in the morning and situation comedies at night, that would be fine too. If people care only about America, and want to avoid international issues entirely, that would be very simple; so too if they care only about New York or Chicago or California. If people want to restrict themselves to certain points of view, by limiting themselves to conservatives, moderates, liberals, vegetarians, or Nazis, that would be entirely feasible with a simple point-and-click. If people want to isolate themselves, and speak only with like-minded others, that is feasible too.

At least as a matter of technological feasibility, our communications market is moving rapidly toward this apparently utopian picture. A number of newspapers' websites allow readers to create filtered versions, containing exactly what they want, and no more ... To be sure, the Internet greatly increases people's ability to expand their horizons, as millions of people are now doing; but many people are using it to produce narrowness, not breadth. Thus MIT professor Nicholas Negroponte refers to the emergence of the "Daily Me"—a communications package that is personally designed, with components fully chosen in advance.

Of course, this is not entirely different from what has come before. People who read newspapers do not read the same newspaper; some people do not read any newspaper at all. People make choices among magazines based on their tastes and their points of view. But in the emerging situation, there is a difference of degree if not of kind. What *is* different is a dramatic increase in individual control over content, and a corresponding decrease in the power of general interest intermediaries, including newspapers, magazines, and broadcasters. For all their problems, and their unmistakable limitations and biases, these intermediaries have performed some important democratic functions.

People who rely on such intermediaries have a range of chance encounters, involving shared experience with diverse others and exposure to material that they did not specifically choose. You might, for example, read the city newspaper and in the process come across a range of stories that you would not have selected if you had the power to control what you see. Your eyes may come across a story about Germany, or crime in Los Angeles, or innovative business practices in Tokyo, and you may read those stories although you would hardly have placed them in your "Daily Me." ... Reading *Time* magazine, you might come across a discussion of endangered species in Madagascar, and this discussion might interest you, even affect your behavior, although you would not have sought it out in the first instance. A system in which you lack control over the particular content that you see has a great deal in common with a public street, where you might encounter not only friends, but a heterogeneous variety of people engaged in a wide array of activities (including, perhaps, political protests and begging).

In fact, a risk with a system of perfect individual control is that it can reduce the importance of the "public sphere" and of common spaces in general. One of the important features of such spaces is that they tend to ensure that people will encounter materials on important issues, whether or not they have specifically chosen the encounter. When people see materials that they have not chosen, their interests and their views might change as a result. At the very least, they will know a bit more about what their fellow citizens are thinking. As it happens, this point is closely connected with an important, and somewhat exotic, constitutional principle.

Public (and Private) Forums

In the popular understanding, the free speech principle forbids government from "censoring" speech of which it disapproves. In the standard cases, the government attempts to impose penalties, whether civil or criminal, on political dissent, and on speech that it considers dangerous, libelous, or sexually explicit. The question is whether the government has a legitimate and sufficiently weighty basis for restricting the speech that it seeks to control.

But a central part of free speech law, with large implications for thinking about the Internet, takes a quite different form. The Supreme Court has also held that streets and parks must be kept open to the public for expressive activity. Governments are obliged to allow speech to occur freely on public streets and in public parks—even if many citizens would prefer to have peace and quiet, and even if it seems irritating to come across protesters and dissidents whom one would like to avoid....

The public forum doctrine serves three important functions. First, it ensures that speakers can have access to a wide array of people. If you want to claim that taxes are too high, or that police brutality against African Americans is common, you can press this argument on many people who might otherwise fail to hear the message. Those who use the streets and parks are likely to learn something about your argument; they might also learn the nature and intensity of views held by one of their fellow citizens. Perhaps their views will be changed; perhaps they will become curious, enough to investigate the question on their own.

Second, the public forum doctrine allows speakers not only to have general access to heterogeneous people, but also to specific people, and specific institutions, with whom they have a complaint. Suppose, for example, that you believe that the state legislature has behaved irresponsibly with respect to crime or health care for children. The public forum ensures that you can make your views heard by legislators simply by protesting in front of the state legislature building.

Third, the public forum doctrine increases the likelihood that people generally will be exposed to a wide variety of people and views. When you go to work, or visit a park, it is possible that you will have a range of unexpected encounters, however fleeting or seemingly inconsequential. You cannot easily wall yourself off from contentions or conditions that you would not have sought out in advance, or that you would have chosen to avoid if you could. Here, too, the public forum doctrine tends to ensure a range of experiences that are widely shared—streets and parks are public property—and also a set of exposures to diverse circumstances....

... Society's general interest intermediaries—newspapers, magazines, television broadcasters—can be understood as public forums of an especially important sort, perhaps above all because they expose people to new, unanticipated topics and points of view.

When you read a city newspaper or a national magazine, your eyes will come across a number of articles that you might not have selected in advance, and if you are like most people, you will read some of those articles. Perhaps you did not know that you might have an interest in minimum wage legislation, or Somalia, or the latest developments in the Middle East. But a story might catch your attention. And what is true for topics of interest is also true for points of view. You might think that you have nothing to learn from someone whose view you abhor; but once you come across the editorial pages, you might read what they have to say, and you might benefit from the experience....

Television broadcasters have similar functions. Most important in this regard is what has become an institution: the evening news. If you tune into the evening news, you will learn about a number of topics that you would not have chosen in advance. Because of their speech and immediacy, television broadcasts perform these public forum–type functions more than general interest intermediaries in the print media. The "lead story" on the networks is likely to have a great deal of public salience; it helps to define central issues and creates a kind of shared focus of attention for millions of people....

None of these claims depends on a judgment that general interest intermediaries are unbiased, or always do an excellent job, or deserve a monopoly over the world of communications. The Internet is a boon partly because it breaks that monopoly. So too for the proliferation of television and radio shows, and even channels, that have some specialized identity. (Consider the rise of Fox News, which appeals to a more conservative audience.) All that I am claiming is that general interest intermediaries expose people to a wide range of topics and views and at the same time provide shared experiences for a heterogeneous public. Indeed, intermediaries of this sort have large advantages over streets and parks precisely because they tend to be national, even international. Typically they expose people to questions and problems in other areas, even other countries.

Specialization and Fragmentation

In a system with public forums and general interest intermediaries, people will frequently come across materials that they would not have chosen in advance—and in a diverse society, this provides something like a common framework for social experience. A fragmented communications market will change things significantly.

Consider some simple facts. If you take the ten most highly rated television programs for whites, and then take the ten most highly rated programs for African Americans, you will find little overlap between them. Indeed, more than half of the ten most highly rated programs for African Americans rank among the ten *least* popular programs for whites. With respect to race, similar divisions can be found on the Internet. Not surprisingly, many people tend to choose like-minded sites and like-minded discussion groups. Many of those with committed views on a topic—gun control, abortion, affirmative action—speak mostly with each other. It is exceedingly rare for a site with an identifiable point of view to provide links to sites with opposing views; but it is very common for such a site to provide links to like-minded sites.

With a dramatic increase in options, and a greater power to customize, comes an increase in the range of actual choices. Those choices are likely, in many cases, to mean that people will try to find material that makes them feel comfortable, or that is created by and for people like themselves. This is what the Daily Me is all about. Of course, many people seek out new topics and ideas. And to the extent that people do, the increase in options is hardly bad on balance; it will, among other things, increase variety, the aggregate amount of information, and the entertainment value of actual choices. But there are serious risks as well. If diverse groups are seeing and hearing different points of view, or focusing on different topics, mutual understanding might be difficult, and it might be hard for people to solve problems that society faces together....

We can sharpen our understanding of this problem if we attend to the phenomenon of *group polarization*. The idea is that after deliberating with one another, people are likely to move toward a more extreme point in the direction to which they were previously inclined, as indicated by the median of their predeliberation judgments. With respect to the Internet, the implication is that groups of people, especially if they are like-minded, will end up thinking the same thing that they thought before—but in more extreme form.

Consider some examples of this basic phenomenon, which has been found in over a dozen nations. (a) After discussion, citizens of France become more critical of the United States and its intentions with respect to economic aid. (b) After discussion, whites predisposed to show racial prejudice offer more negative responses to questions about whether white racism is responsible for conditions faced by African Americans in American cities. (c) After discussion, whites predisposed not to show racial prejudice offer more positive responses to the same question. (d) A group of moderately profeminist women will become more strongly profeminist after discussion....

The phenomenon of group polarization has conspicuous importance to the current communications market, where groups with distinctive identities increasingly engage in within-group discussion. If the public is balkanized, and if different groups design their own preferred communications packages, the consequence will be further balkanization, as group members move one another toward more extreme points in line with their initial tendencies. At the same time, different deliberating groups, each consisting of like-minded people, will be driven increasingly far apart, simply because most of their discussions are with one another....

Group polarization is a human regularity, but social context can decrease, increase, or even eliminate it. For present purposes, the most important point is that group polarization will significantly increase if people think of themselves ... as part of a group having a shared identity and a degree of solidarity. If ... a group of people in an Internet discussion group think of themselves as opponents of high taxes, or advocates of animal rights, their discussions are likely to move toward extreme positions. As this happens to many different groups, polarization is both more likely and more extreme. Hence significant movements should be expected for those who listen to a radio show known to be conservative, or a television program dedicated to traditional religious values or to exposing white racism....

Group polarization is occurring every day on the Internet. Indeed, it is clear that the Internet is serving, for many, as a breeding ground for extremism, precisely because like-minded people are deliberating with one another, without hearing contrary views. Hate groups are the most obvious example. Consider one extremist group, the so-called Unorganized Militia, the armed wing of the Patriot movement, "which believes that the federal government is becoming increasingly dictatorial with its regulatory power over taxes, guns and land use." A crucial factor behind the growth of the Unorganized Militia "has been the use of computer networks," allowing members "to make contact quickly and easily with like-minded individuals to trade information, discuss current conspiracy theories, and organize events."...

Of course we cannot say, from the mere fact of polarization, that there has been a movement in the *wrong* direction. Perhaps the more extreme tendency is better; indeed, group polarization is likely to have fueled many movements of great value, including the movement for civil rights, the antislavery movement, the movement for sex equality. All of these movements were extreme in their time, and within-group discussion bred greater extremism; but extremism need not be a word of opprobrium. If greater communications choices produce greater extremism, society may, in many cases, be better off as a result....

The basic issue here is whether something like a "public sphere," with a wide range of voices, might not have significant advantages over a system in which isolated consumer choices produce a highly fragmented speech market. The most reasonable conclusion is that it is extremely important to ensure that people are exposed to views other than those with which they currently agree, that doing so protects against the harmful effects of group polarization on individual thinking and on social cohesion. This does not mean that the government should jail or fine people who refuse to listen to others. Nor is what I have said inconsistent with approval of deliberating "enclaves," on the Internet or elsewhere, designed to ensure that positions that would otherwise be silenced or squelched have a chance to develop. Readers will be able to think of their own preferred illustrations....

Consider in this light the ideal of "consumer sovereignty," which underlies much of contemporary enthusiasm for the Internet. Consumer sovereignty means that people can choose to purchase, or to obtain, whatever they want. For many purposes this is a worthy ideal. But the adverse effects of group polarization show that, with respect to communications, consumer sovereignty is likely to produce serious problems for individuals and society at large—and these problems will occur by a kind of iron logic of social interactions.

The phenomenon of group polarization is [also] closely related to the widespread phenomenon of "social cascades." Cascade effects are common on the Internet, and we cannot understand the relationship between democracy and the Internet without having a sense of how cascades work.

It is obvious that many social groups, both large and small, seem to move both rapidly and dramatically in the direction of one or another set of beliefs or actions. These sorts of "cascades" often involve the spread of information; in fact they are driven by information. If you lack a great deal of private information, you may well rely on information provided by the statements or actions of others. A stylized example: If Joan is unaware whether abandoned toxic waste dumps are in fact hazardous, she may be moved in the direction of fear if Mary seems to think that fear is justified. If Joan and Mary both believe that fear is justified, Carl may end up thinking so too, at least if he lacks reliable independent information to the contrary. If Joan, Mary, and Carl believe that abandoned toxic waste dumps are hazardous, Don will have to have a good deal of confidence to reject their shared conclusion.

The example shows how information travels, and often becomes quite entrenched, even if it is entirely wrong. The view, widespread in some African-American communities, that white doctors are responsible for the spread of AIDS among African Americans is a recent illustration. Often cascades of this kind are local, and take different form in different communities. Hence one group may end up believing something and another group the exact opposite, and the reason is the rapid transmission of one piece of information within one group and a different piece of information in the other. In a balkanized speech market, this danger takes a particular form: different groups may be led to quite different perspectives, as local cascades lead people in dramatically different directions. The Internet dramatically increases the likelihood of rapid cascades, based on false information. Of course, low-cost Internet communication also makes it possible for truth, and corrections, to spread quickly as well. But sometimes this happens much too late. In the event, balkanization is extremely likely. As a result of the Internet, cascade effects are more common than they have ever been before....

I hope that I have shown enough to demonstrate that for citizens of a heterogeneous democracy, a fragmented communications market creates considerable dangers. There are dangers for each of us as individuals; constant exposure to one set of views is likely to lead to errors and confusions, or to unthinking conformity (emphasized by John Stuart Mill). And to the extent that the process makes people less able to work cooperatively on shared problems, by turning collections of people into non-communicating confessional groups, there are dangers for society as a whole.

Common Experiences

In a heterogeneous society, it is extremely important for diverse people to have a set of common experiences. Many of our practices reflect a judgment to this effect. National holidays, for example, help constitute a nation, by encouraging citizens to think, all at once, about events of shared importance. And they do much more than this. They enable people, in all their diversity, to have certain memories and attitudes in common. At least this is true in nations where national holidays have a vivid and concrete meaning. In the United States, many national holidays have become mere days-off-from-work, and the precipitating occasion—President's

Day, Memorial Day, Labor Day—has come to be nearly invisible. This is a serious loss. With the possible exception of the Fourth of July, Martin Luther King Day is probably the closest thing to a genuinely substantive national holiday, largely because that celebration involves something that can be treated as concrete and meaningful—in other words, it is *about* something.

Communications and the media are, of course, exceptionally important here. Sometimes millions of people follow the presidential election, or the Super Bowl, or the coronation of a new monarch; many of them do so because of the simultaneous actions of others. The point very much bears on the historic role of both public forums and general interest intermediaries. Public parks are places where diverse people can congregate and see one another. General interest intermediaries, if they are operating properly, give a simultaneous sense of problems and tasks.

Why are these shared experiences so desirable? There are three principal reasons:

1. Simple enjoyment is probably the least of it, but it is far from irrelevant. People like many experiences more simply because they are being shared. Consider a popular movie, the Super Bowl, or a presidential debate....

2. Sometimes shared experiences ease social interactions, permitting people to speak with one another, and to congregate around a common issue, task, or concern, whether or not they have much in common with one another. In this sense they provide a form of social glue. They help make it possible for diverse people to believe that they live in the same culture. Indeed they help constitute that shared culture, simply by creating common memories and experiences, and a sense of common tasks.

3. A fortunate consequence of shared experiences—many of them produced by the media—is that people who would otherwise see one another as unfamiliar can come to regard one another as fellow citizens, with shared hopes, goals, and concerns. This is a subjective good for those directly involved. But it can be objectively good as well, especially if it leads to cooperative projects of various kinds....

How does this bear on the Internet? An increasingly fragmented communications universe will reduce the level of shared experiences having salience to a diverse group of Americans. This is a simple matter of numbers. When there were three television networks, much of what appeared would have the quality of a genuinely common experience. The lead story on the evening news, for example, would provide a common reference point for many millions of people. To the extent that choices proliferate, it is inevitable that diverse individuals, and diverse groups, will have fewer shared experiences and fewer common reference points. It is possible, for example, that some events that are highly salient to some people will barely register on others' viewscreens. And it is possible that some views and perspectives that seem obvious for many people will, for others, seem barely intelligible.

This is hardly a suggestion that everyone should be required to watch the same thing. A degree of plurality, with respect to both topics and points of view, is highly desirable. Moreover, talk about "requirements" misses the point. My only claim is that a common set of frameworks and experiences is valuable for a heterogeneous society, and that a system with limitless options, making for diverse choices, could compromise the underlying values.

Changing Filters

My goal here has been to understand what makes for a well-functioning system of free expression, and to show how consumer sovereignty, in a world of limitless options, could undermine that system. The point is that a well-functioning system includes a kind of public sphere, one that fosters common experiences, in which people hear messages that challenge their prior convictions, and in which citizens can present their views to a broad audience. I do not intend to offer a comprehensive set of policy reforms or any kind of blueprint for the future.... But it will be useful to offer a few ideas, if only by way of introduction to questions that are likely to engage public attention in coming years.

In thinking about reforms, it is important to have a sense of the problems we aim to address, and some possible ways of addressing them. If the discussion thus far is correct, there are three fundamental concerns from the democratic point of view. These include:

(a) the need to promote exposure to materials, topics, and positions that people would not have chosen in advance, or at least enough exposure to produce a degree of understanding and curiosity;

(b) the value of a range of common experiences;

(c) the need for exposure to substantive questions of policy and principle, combined with a range of positions on such questions....

Drawing on recent developments in regulation generally, we can see the potential appeal of five simple alternatives. Of course, different proposals would work better for some communications outlets than others. I will speak here of both private and public responses, but the former should be favored: they are less intrusive, and in general they are likely to be more effective as well.

Disclosure: Producers of communications might disclose important information on their own, about the extent to which they are promoting democratic goals. To the extent that they do not, they might be subject to disclosure requirements (though not to regulation). In the environmental area, this strategy has produced excellent results. The mere fact that polluters have been asked to disclose toxic releases has produced voluntary, low-cost reductions. Apparently fearful of public opprobrium, companies have been spurred to reduce toxic emissions on their own....

The same idea could be used far more broadly. Television broadcasters might, for example, be asked to disclose their public interest activities. On a quarterly basis, they might say whether and to what extent they have provided educational programming for children, free air time for candidates, and closed captioning for the hearing impaired. They might also be asked whether they have covered issues of concern to the local community and allowed opposing views a chance to speak. The Federal Communications Commission has already taken steps in this direction; it could do a lot more....

Self-Regulation: Producers of communications might engage in *voluntary self-regulation*. Some of the difficulties in the current speech market stem from relentless competition for viewers and listeners, competition that leads to a situation that many broadcast journalists abhor about their profession, and from which society does not benefit. The competition might be reduced via a "code" of appropriate conduct, agreed upon by various companies, and encouraged but not imposed by government. In fact, the National Association of Broadcasters maintained such a code for several decades, and there is growing interest in voluntary self-regulation for both television and the Internet. The case for this approach is that it avoids government regulation while at the same time reducing some of the harmful effects of market pressures. Any such code could, for example, call for an opportunity for opposing views to speak, or for avoiding unnecessary sensationalism, or for offering arguments rather than quick sound-bites whenever feasible....

Subsidy: The government might *subsidize speech*, as, for example, through publicly subsidized programming or publicly subsidized websites. This is, of course, the idea that motivates the Public Broadcasting System. But it is reasonable to ask whether the PBS model is not outmoded. Other approaches, similarly designed to promote educational, cultural, and democratic goals, might well be ventured. Perhaps government could subsidize a "Public.net" designed to promote debate on public issues among diverse citizens—and to create a right of access to speakers of various sorts.

Links: Websites might use links and hyperlinks to ensure that viewers learn about sites containing opposing views. A liberal magazine's website might, for example, provide a link to a conservative magazine's website, and the conservative magazine might do the same. The idea would be to decrease the likelihood that people will simply hear echoes of their own voices. Of course many people would not click on the icons of sites whose views seem objectionable; but some people would, and in that sense the system would not operate so differently from general interest intermediaries and public forums....

Public Sidewalk: If the problem consists in the failure to attend to public issues, the most popular websites in any given period might offer links and hyperlinks, designed to ensure more exposure to substantive questions. Under such a system, viewers of especially popular sites would see an icon for sites that deal with substantive issues in a serious way. It is well established that whenever there is a link to a particular webpage from a major site, such as MSNBC, the traffic is huge. Nothing here imposes any requirements on viewers. People would not be required to click on links and hyperlinks. But it is reasonable to expect that many viewers would do so, if only to satisfy their curiosity. The result would be to create a kind of Internet "sidewalk" that promotes some of the purposes of the public forum doctrine....

These are brief thoughts on some complex subjects. My goal has not been to evaluate any proposal in detail, but to give a flavor of some possibilities for those concerned to promote democratic goals in a dramatically changed media environment....

Beyond Anticensorship

My principal claim here has been that a well-functioning democracy depends on far more than restraints on official censorship of controversial ideas and opinions. It also depends on some kind of public sphere, in which a wide range of speakers have access to a diverse public—and also to particular institutions, and practices, against which they seek to launch objections.

Emerging technologies, including the Internet, are hardly an enemy here. They hold out far more promise than risk, especially because they allow people to widen their horizons. But to the extent that they weaken the power of general interest intermediaries and increase people's ability to wall themselves off from topics and opinions that they would prefer to avoid, they create serious dangers. And if we believe that a system of free expression calls for unrestricted choices by individual consumers, we will not even understand the dangers as such. Whether such dangers will materialize will ultimately depend on the aspirations, for freedom and democracy alike, by whose light we evaluate our practices. What I have sought to establish here is that in a free republic, citizens aspire to a system that provides a wide range of experiences—with people, topics, and ideas—that would not have been selected in advance.

Changing Citizenship in the Digital Age

W. LANCE BENNETT

Democracy is not a sure thing. Governments and party systems often strain against changes in societies, and some fall prey to corruption and bad policies. Under the right conditions, people may reassert their rights to govern, and produce remarkable periods of creative reform, realignment, and change. In these times, politics becomes a focus of personal life itself, restoring the sense that participation makes a difference. The challenges of influencing the course of nations and addressing global issues may inspire creative solutions from the generations of young citizens who have access to digital communication tools. The cascading advance of media platforms and social software enables unprecedented levels of production and distribution of ideas, public deliberation, and network organization.

It is clear that many young citizens of this digital and global age have demonstrated interests in making contributions to society. Yet the challenge of engaging effectively with politics that are linked to spheres of government remains, for most, a daunting prospect. The reasons are numerous. A casual look at world democracies suggests that many of the most established ones are showing signs of wear. Parties are trying to reinvent themselves while awkwardly staying the course that keeps them in power. In the press, in everyday conversation, and often from the mouths of politicians, politics has become a dirty word rather than a commonly accepted vocabulary for personal expression. Perhaps most notably, younger generations have disconnected from conventional politics and government in alarming numbers. These trends in youth dissatisfaction with conventional political engagement are not just occurring in the United States, but have parallels in other democracies as well, including Germany, Sweden, and the United Kingdom. The pathways to disconnection from government are many: adults are frequently negative about politics, the tone of the press is often cynical, candidates seldom appeal directly to young voters on their own terms about their concerns, politicians have poisoned the public well (particularly in the United States) with vitriol and negative campaigning, and young people see the media filled with inauthentic performances from officials who are staged by professional communication managers. Paralleling these developments has been a notable turning away from public life into online friendship networks, gaming and entertainment environments, and consumer pursuits. Where political activity occurs, it is often related to lifestyle concerns that seem outside the realm of government.

Many observers properly note that there are impressive signs of youth civic engagement in these nongovernmental areas, including increases in community volunteer work, high levels of consumer activism, and impressive involvement in social causes from the environment to economic injustice in local and global arenas. Some even ascribe civic engagement qualities to many activities that occur in online social networking and entertainment communities....

Many of the spontaneous and creative forms of collective expression online seem more appealing than the options typically offered in youth engagement sites sponsored by governments and nongovernmental organizations (NGOs) in efforts to invigorate public life for young people.... [M]any well-intentioned youth engagement sites have clear ideas about what constitute proper citizen activities. As a result, these *managed* environments seem inauthentic and irrelevant to many young people.... [Y]oung citizens find more authentic experiences in edgier political sites and in entertainment media and games. The dilemma is that many of the political sites that young people build and operate themselves may avoid formal government channels for communication and action and may lack the resources needed to sustain and grow them.

A key question thus becomes how to nurture the creative and expressive actions of a generation in change, while continuing to keep some positive engagement with government on their screens.

Two Paradigms of Youth Engagement

...[T]here seem to be two different paradigms that contrast young citizens (roughly in the fifteen to twenty-five age range) as either reasonably active and *engaged* or relatively passive and *disengaged*. Like all paradigms, each foregrounds different core organizing values and principles, prompting proponents to weigh and select different sets of supporting facts and reasons. Each paradigm thus comes equipped with its own arguments and evidence, making it convincing to adherents and elusive and often maddening to those operating from the other constructed reality.

The *engaged youth* paradigm implicitly emphasizes generational changes in social identity that have resulted in the growing importance of peer networks and online communities. In this view, if there is an attendant decline in the credibility or authenticity of many public institutions and discourses that define conventional political life, the fault lies more with the government performances and news narratives than with citizens who cannot engage with them. In an important sense, this paradigm emphasizes the empowerment of youth as expressive individuals and symbolically frees young people to make their own creative choices. In the bargain, the engaged youth paradigm also eases the overriding duty to participate in conventional government-centered activities. In many cases, researchers in this school are only dimly aware of (and may tend to discount) research on declines and deficits in more conventional political participation among young citizens. As a result, the *engaged youth* paradigm opens the door to a new spectrum of civic actions in online arenas from MySpace to *World of Warcraft*. By contrast, the *disengaged youth* paradigm may acknowledge the rise of more autonomous forms of public expression such as consumer politics, or the occasional protest in MySpace, while keeping the focus on the generational decline in connections to government (e.g., voting patterns) and general civic involvement (e.g., following public affairs in the news) as threats to the health of democracy itself....

[T]he two paradigms reflect different normative views of what the good citizen ought to do when she grows up. The *engaged youth* viewpoint, in a sense, empowers young people by recognizing personal expression and their capacity to project identities in collective spaces. As Cathy Davidson noted "... I think we have a unique opportunity to take advantage of peer-to-peer sites for creative, imaginative, activist learning purposes. That is a lot harder mission than critiquing the young.... I want to be attuned to what youth themselves say about the alternative forms of learning and social networking afforded by Web 2.0."

By contrast, those who lean toward the disengaged youth perspective often worry about this very personalization or privatization of the political sphere and focus more on how to promote public actions that link to government as the center of democratic politics, and to other social groups and institutions as the foundations of civic life. As David Buckingham put it...:

> OK, young people may well be participating and engaging in all sorts of very active and interesting ways online.... But in what ways is this CIVIC engagement?...
>
> I would suggest that "civic" implies some notion of the public (the polis or the public sphere, even)—by which I suppose I mean an open debate about issues of general social concern between people who may not agree with each other. In this respect, there are certainly tendencies? in the internet towards an individualisation, or at least a fragmentation, of social/political debate (a settling into established niche groups). So there may be ways in which the internet promotes participation, but undermines the "civic."...

And so the debate goes, often with real consequences in the worlds in which young people work, play, learn, and vote…. [T]he disengaged youth viewpoint leads to something of a narrative of despair or decline about young citizens, one that travels all too easily in the news and leads to overlooking the many innovations that young people have brought to our public communication spaces. At the same time … traditional activities such as voting continue to matter, and young people hold the future of our democratic life insofar as citizens can still shape their political institutions….

These divergent views of youth engagement shape the thinking of policymakers and educators concerned about getting young people involved in civic life. When set side by side, the broader picture seems to point to changing the institutional and communication environments in which young people encounter politics, rather than somehow fixing the attitudes of youth themselves. Yet the institutional and communication environments themselves are politically contested, and often produce anemic and restricted … experiences with credible or authentic politics. How many textbooks (or classroom teachers, who are monitored by school officials and parents) acknowledge that it makes sense for young people to follow the political lead of a rock star, such as Coldplay's Chris Martin, who encouraged concert goers to join Oxfam's *Make Trade Fair* campaign? Yet many Coldplay fans actually connected with government on their own: the band's 2003 U.S. tour included Oxfam workers at concerts gathering some 10,000 postcards to send to President Bush, asking him to stop dumping subsidized exports such as rice on poor countries where farmers could no longer profit from growing the same crops. For those who were not at the concerts, a visit to the band's Web site contained a link off the home page to the fair trade campaign materials.

Such pathways to political engagement are often not accommodated in traditional civic education and government sponsored e-citizen sites, leaving many young citizens at odds with brittle conceptions of proper citizenship imposed upon them by educators, public officials, and other institutional authorities. Even when more creative civic education and engagement approaches enable young people to trace their own personal concerns through the governmental process, the end result may crash against the palpable failure of governments, parties, and candidates to recognize the communication and identity preferences of young citizens….

(Mis)Communicating with Young Citizens

Perhaps one of the most obvious factors contributing to the relatively passive, disengaged stance of many young people toward government and formal elements of politics is the withering away of civic education in schools. Not only have civics offerings been in decline, notably the United States, but, where offered, the curriculum is often stripped of independent opportunities for young people to embrace and communicate about politics on their own terms…. The result is that there is often little connection between the academic presentation of politics and the acquisition of skills that might help develop engaged citizens. A massive International Education Association (IEA) survey of 90,000 fourteen-year-olds in twenty-eight nations suggested that civic education, where it is offered, remains largely a textbook based experience, largely severed from the vibrant experiences of politics that might help young people engage with public life.

Even in nations that do reasonably well at imparting some basic civic knowledge to young citizens, there are signs of relatively little carryover to participation in public life. For example, a study of Australian civic education in the late 1990s concluded that "the importance of civic knowledge has been well established.... Yet knowledge itself will be of little relevance if it does not lead to action in the civic sphere...." What emerges from different national surveys is something of a generational shift in which young citizens tend to express areas of interest and concern but often see those interests as unconnected, or even negatively related, to government....

We know that digital media provide those young people who have access to it an important set of tools to build social and personal identity and to create the on- and offline environments in which they spend their time. However, as Howard Rheingold notes ... many young people live online, but they may lack the skills to communicate their common concerns in effective ways to larger (public) audiences. Rheingold suggests building a public communication digital media skill set....

Perhaps the major puzzle running through all of this is how to create the media environments in which online communities can build the kinds of social capital—those bonds of trust and commitment to shared values—that lead to participation in civic life and the political world beyond....

Signs of Political Life in the Digital Age

The future of democracy is in the hands of these young citizens of the so-called digital age. Many young citizens in more economically prosperous societies already have in their hands the tools of change: digital media, from laptops, pagers, and cell phones to the convergences of the next new things. These new media reposition their users in society, making them both producers and consumers of information. Perhaps more important, they enable rapid formation of large-scale networks that may focus their energies in critical moments....

Sometimes those technologies enable large and more sustained political networks, as in the formation of Indymedia, a global political information network. Indymedia was created through the distribution of open source software enabling the production and sharing of information by young activists under the motto: Be the Media. This network began during the now iconic Battle of Seattle protests against the World Trade Organization in 1999 as a means for protesters to communicate among themselves and produce their own news coverage to counter what they perceived as the filtering of corporate media aligned with the targets of protest. Other, more issue-specific networks have emerged via the application of networking technologies to spark protests such as those that emerged around the world against war in Iraq on February 12, 2003. Estimated at between thirteen and twenty million participants, they were the largest coordinated protests in human history. They were organized in a matter of months through the integrated use of on- and offline network mobilization.

Digital media also show signs of successful adaptation to the work of conventional politics, as happened with the American presidential primary campaign of Howard Dean, whose early followers (many of whom were not so young) organized online networks to share their perceptions of the candidate. They eventually created unprecedented levels of bottom-up communication within the notoriously centralized *war room* communication model of election campaigns. However, the growth of semiautonomous supporter networks, with their pressures for some degree of bottom-up steering of the campaign, ultimately clashed with the centralized bureaucracy of the professionally managed campaign. The cautionary tale here is that the integration of horizontal digital networks with other organizational forms is not always seamless.

In other cases, applications of digital media do seem to bridge, and at times, transcend the conventional boundaries between different kinds of political organizations such as parties, interest groups, and social movements. This boundary jumping happened, for example, when the (mostly) online networking operation MoveOn.org became involved in Democratic Party politics in the United States, acting as a check on the party, and even running its own commercials. In other configurations, MoveOn acts more as an interest organization, mobilizing pressure on specific issues moving through legislative processes. In other moments, the organization joins many issue constituencies in protest actions as might happen in a social movement. The attractiveness of these loosely tied organizational forms to young people has not been lost on many conventional political organizations as they witness the graying of their conventional membership rosters.

Despite these and other signs of potential to revive and perhaps reinvent politics among next generation citizens, two overall trends seem to hold:

- The majority of those communicating with young people about conventional politics continue to do so in tired top-down, highly managed ways that most young people find inauthentic and largely irrelevant.

- What young people do online tends to be largely social and entertainment oriented, with only tangential pathways leading to the conventional civic and political worlds.

These two patterns are most likely related to each other. For example, in order to learn how to expand youth involvement in aspects of public life pertaining to governance, politicians, policymakers, and educators need to communicate differently with young citizens. And in order for young citizens to feel comfortable engaging in more conventional politics, they need to feel invited to participate on their own terms, and to learn how to use their digital tools to better express their public voices....

Where Are They? What Are They Doing?

The news headlines signaled a battle raging between television networks and Nielsen, the company that provided the audience ratings on which their income depended. In releasing their fall ratings sweeps for 2005, Nielsen reported a shocking trend. It was so shocking that the TV networks disputed it, as it seemed to make no sense to them. Moreover, they would lose huge amounts of ad revenues for their fall programs. The young male demographic was missing. The much sought after eighteen- to twenty-four-year-old male demographic (only 12 percent of the total audience, yet accounting for $4.1 billion in ad revenues) had dropped nearly 8 percent from TV viewing the year before, with an even larger drop in prime time. Every minute less TV watched by this group meant a $77 million loss in revenues across broadcast and cable. It was a trend that had been developing slowly for a dozen years, but suddenly soared to crisis levels for the television industry. Where did the young men go? It turned out that many of them were still watching TV, but they were more likely to be playing an Xbox on it. This same demographic group accounted for more than half of video game sales in a booming multibillion dollar market. Creating and interacting with one's entertainment programming was just more interesting than watching it passively.

Gamers are joined by even more young people who gravitate to social network environments that change almost as quickly as adults can learn their names: Friendster, Facebook, MySpace. When media mogul Rupert Murdoch saw the writing on the wall, he hedged his bets on the television networks that had been aimed at young audiences and bought MySpace, then the largest recorded social networking site, attracting upwards of sixty million youth. Early on, large online communities also formed around music file-sharing sites that indicated the creativity with which young people approached digital media....

A quick visit to any of the social sites suggests that what happens there mainly revolves around the formation of loosely connected networks dedicated to sharing music, movies, photos, and, above all, current and prospective friends. In what may be an eternal generational response, many older observers look disapprovingly on all this, seeing these environments as dangerous magnets for sexual predators, and as outlets for young people to indulge in inappropriate and edgy displays.... The importance of these networks for forging generational identity and solidarity cannot be underestimated. Moreover, lurking just beneath the surface is the potential for vast networks of public voice on contemporary issues. This potential has barely been tapped. Surprisingly large demonstrations against congressional immigration legislation in the spring of 2006 spread through organizing networks within MySpace. And, the recognition by the Dean campaign that supporters were gathering in Meetups quickly moved the Dean network (which attracted a broad age demographic) past Chihuahua owners and Elvis fans to become the most populous Meetup. Presidential candidates in 2008 gathered friends in MySpace.

A challenging question is how to better integrate the social and public worlds of young people online. Unlike classic accounts of civil society in which social bonds strengthened political participation in the golden age of dutiful citizens, the separation of the social and the civic in the youth online world often seems stark. There are, however, some curious signs of the integration of politics and social experience within these virtual worlds. For example, there have been reports of political protest in game environments. *World of Warcraft* was disrupted by demonstrations over vaguely defined class issues facing the warriors, resulting in protesters being banned under game rules established by Blizzard Entertainment, owner of the game.... [M]usic file sharers raised property ownership and copyright issues that eventually brought legal sanctions, and in many ways changed how file sharing was regulated and used....

[T]he very ways in which people use digital media present fundamental challenges to established understandings of property, which in turn, lie at the foundation of the political order. For these and other reasons, it is important to expand our conception of politics and the political, as young people, both wittingly and unwittingly, push those bounds through their applications of digital technologies. In what ways are these activities political? Do the communication skills involved transfer to more conventional areas of politics? Do political and legal responses concerning ownership and copyright enforcement make for formative early contacts between young people and the often distant world of power and government? These are among the important questions that abound in the grey zones of digital life.

Yet for all the tangential incursions of politics into the social and play environments of digital media, the sphere of more explicitly youth-oriented politics remains comparatively isolated and underdeveloped. Youth sites often seem less social, more moderated, less open to posting and sharing media content, and more top-down compared to those pertaining to dating, friends, games, music, or video....

Finding productive answers to the many questions about better integrating the public and private worlds of youth involves different kinds of learning for different kinds of players:

1. The politicians and public officials who represent the official world of politics to young people must learn more about their citizenship and communication preferences and how to engage with them.

2. The educators and other youth workers who design civic education programs, often based on unexamined assumptions about what citizenship should be, can benefit from learning how generational social identities and political preference formation are changing so they can design more engaging civic education models.

3. The government agencies, foundations, and NGOs that design and operate youth engagement communities online can benefit from learning more about how those sites may be networked and how they may be opened to partnership with young people who must see them as authentic if they are to participate in them.

4. News organizations and other public information producers can learn how to develop information formats that appeal to the young citizen's interest in interacting and coproducing digital content and in better integrating the information and action dimensions of citizenship.

5. Young people themselves can better learn how to use information and media skills in ways that give them stronger and more effective public voices.

6. And academic researchers can learn how to bridge the paradigms in order to better motivate and inform all of these players.

Understanding Changing Citizenship Across Paradigms

Learning about communities, networks, and civic life can take place at different levels and in different ways among the groups of key players in youth civic engagement identified above: politicians and public officials, educators and youth workers, operators of youth engagement communities, information producers, young people searching for public voice, and researchers trying to understand how these players can interact more effectively to promote engagement that is both personally satisfying and mindful of democracy.

A starting point for civic learning among all of these groups is to recognize the shifts in social and political identity processes resulting from the last several decades of global economic and social change.... The collection of nations once known as the industrial democracies have gone through a period of rapid and, in some cases, wrenching economic change, with the result that they may now more properly be called postindustrial democracies. Manufacturing is moving to the periphery of economic focus, as design, distribution, marketing, and management of information have come to the fore. Several results of this process, among others, include careers have changed from relatively secure life-long bonds with a single employer and type of work to several different employers and kinds of work; women have become fully engaged in the work force, changing the organization of family life; more work and more working parents means less discretionary time and more stress for most members of families. As a result, the experiences of childhood and transitions to adulthood are different for recent generations. One casualty associated with these changes is that the group based society that was the foundation of Putnam's fabled pluralist civic life has transformed into a network society in which individuals seek various kinds of support and recognition based on different conceptions of membership, identification, and commitment.[*]

In the network society, individuals may belong to many loosely tied associational chains that connect them to their social and occupational worlds. A major consequence of the uprooting from the broad social influence of groups is that individuals have become more responsible for the production and management of their own social and political identities. Contemporary young people enjoy unprecedented levels of freedom to define and manage their self-identities in contrast with earlier generations' experiences with stronger groups (denominational church, labor, class, party) that essentially assigned broad social identities to their members. This transformation of the relationship between individual and society places increasing strains on parties and governments to appeal to highly personalized political preferences that are more difficult to address, much less satisfy, than the broad group or class interests of an earlier era. At the same time, individual citizens—particularly younger generations who have grown up in this new social and economic matrix—feel that their personalized expectations of politics are perfectly reasonable (reflecting who they are) and often find that politics and politicians either ignore them or are far off the mark in their communication appeals.

---

[*]Political scientist Robert Putnam advances the thesis that a society with a rich mixture of civic associations fosters the sense of mutual trust and reciprocity that is favorable to the functioning of democracy.

As politicians and parties use marketing techniques to target ever more refined demographics, the democratic result is that ever larger groups of citizens are excluded from the discourses of elections and policy as they are deemed unnecessary by consultants. Young citizens are among those most blatantly excluded from the public discourses of government, policy arenas and elections. The result is that the world of politics and government seems distant, irrelevant, and inauthentic to many citizens, particularly younger demographics.

T A B L E   1.1   The Changing Citizenry: The Traditional Civic Education Ideal of the Dutiful Citizen (DC) versus the Emerging Youth Experience of Self-Actualizing Citizenship (AC)

Actualizing Citizen (AC)	Dutiful Citizen (DC)
Diminished sense of government obligation—higher sense of individual purpose	Obligation to participate in government centered activities
Voting is less meaningful than other, more personally defined acts such as consumerism, community volunteering, or transnational activism	Voting is the core democratic act
Mistrust of media and politicians is reinforced by negative mass media environment	Becomes informed about issues and government by following mass media
Favors loose networks of community action—often established or sustained through friendships and peer relations and thin social ties maintained by interactive information technologies	Joins civil society organizations and/or expresses interests through parties that typically employ one-way conventional communication to mobilize supporters

The challenge for civic education and engagement here is to begin by recognizing the profound generational shift in citizenship styles that seems to be occurring to varying degrees in most of the postindustrial democracies. The core of the shift is that young people are far less willing to subscribe to the notion held by earlier generations that citizenship is a matter of duty and obligation. This earlier sense of common commitment to participate at some level in public affairs was supported, indeed forged, within a group- and class-based civil society. The underlying sense of citizenship has shifted in societies in which individuals are more responsible for defining their own identities, using the various tools offered by social networks and communication media.

In short, there is a broad, cross-national generational shift in the postindustrial democracies from a *dutiful citizen* model (still adhered to by older generations and many young people who are positioned in more traditional social settings) to an *actualizing citizen* model favoring loosely networked activism to address issues that reflect personal values. In some cases, this brand of politics may be tangential to government and conventional political organization, and may even emerge in parallel cyberspaces such as games. This citizenship transformation is by no means uniform within societies. Where traditional institutions of church or labor remain strong, more conventional patterns of civic engagement prevail, and moral conflict may erupt. Other citizens lack the skills and background to engage civic life at either the group or the individual level, and actively avoid politics altogether. However, two broad patterns do seem to mark a change in citizenship among younger demographics coming of age in the recent decades of globalization. Table 1 illustrates some of the defining qualities of this shift in citizenship styles.

Bridging the Paradigm

The tendency to either explicitly or implicitly anchor political opportunities and offerings to young people in one conception of citizenship or the other helps to explain the rise of the two paradigms of youth engagement discussed earlier. Those paradigms support our dissonant public conversation about whether young people are engaged or disengaged. Given their value premises and empirical references, the paradigms are (by definition) both right, but they are also equally responsible for confounding much of our theoretical, empirical and practical approaches to youth engagement in the digital age.

Trying to keep both the actualizing citizen (AC) and dutiful citizen (DC) clusters of citizenship qualities in mind when we discuss learning goals for different players may help bridge the paradigms, while helping all of the players in the civic engagement process think about youth engagement in a more holistic way. In other words, recognizing the shift in emphasis from DC to AC citizenship among younger citizens, and then deciding how to accommodate both dimensions of citizenship in theory and practice may have important implications for what the various players in citizenship production can (and, dare I say should?) learn about youth civic engagement in the digital age...

If nothing is done to bridge the paradigms, the default scenario will likely be persistent youth disconnection from conventional politics, with little reconciliation of the gap between AC and DC citizenship styles, and continuing unproductive paradigm battles in the academic world. The flip side of this scenario is the continued growth of youth (AC) politics "by other means": political consumerism, pressures on entertainment product ownership and distribution, and issue networks spanning local and global concerns. This scenario will do little to bring young citizens meaningfully back to government, and it will continue to provoke unproductive debates about engagement and disengagement that talk past each other in academia, education, foundations, and government policy circles.

A second scenario utilizes the possibilities for convergence of technologies and political practices to bring vibrant experiences of politics into classrooms, youth programs, and yes, even elections, showing young people how their concerns can gain public voice within the conventional arenas of power and decision making. This scenario requires more creative research paradigms that combine AC and DC citizen qualities into realistic scenarios for engagement that can be implemented and assessed.

The most important question before us is: What kind of democratic experiences would we choose for future generations? This is a properly political question, yet it is one that often chills creativity among government officials, educators, and NGOs—the very players with the capacity to make a difference in the political futures of young people. The outcomes for youth engagement, insofar as they involve the restoration of positive engagement with government alongside creative and expressive personal communication, depend importantly on the adults who shape the early political impressions of young people. Are politicians, parents, educators, policymakers, and curriculum developers willing to allow young citizens to more fully explore, experience, and expand democracy, or will they continue to force them to just read all about it?

Discussion Questions

1. Is Sunstein persuasive in arguing that too many of us go online to seek out like-minded people as our sources for information, thus fostering dogmatism rather than enlightenment?

2. Is Bennett persuasive in his suggestion that young people in the digital age can become as interested in traditional democratic activities as in social networking or gaming?

3. Do you find Sunstein or Bennett more convincing on how to make digital media better vehicles for American democracy?

4. You have been asked to design an online social network site that will facilitate political participation by your peers. How will the site look? What features will it contain? How will it engage your fellow students?

Suggested Readings and Internet Resources

Bruce Bimber examines how information technologies from the Founding to the Internet have affected American democratic life in *Information and American Democracy* (New York: Cambridge University Press, 2003). Matthew Hindman argues that available data do not back up the enthusiastic claims of pundits that the Internet is transforming democracy in *The Myth of Digital Democracy* (Princeton, N.J.: Princeton University Press, 2008). How digital media might involve young people more actively in political life is the subject of W. Lance Bennett, ed., *Civic Life Online: Learning How Digital Media Can Engage Youth* (Cambridge, Mass.: The MIT Press, 2008). Costas Panagopoulos studies the role of new media in campaigns in *Politicking Online: The Transformation of Election Campaign Communications* (New Brunswick, N.J.: Rutgers University Press, 2009). For a first-hand account of the Obama campaign's use of digital media, see Rahaf Harfoush, *Yes, We Did: An Inside Look at How Social Media Built the Obama Brand* (Berkeley, Calif.: New Riders, 2009).

Media Reform—Free Press
www.freepress.net
This group is among the most active in efforts to roll back corporate concentration and commercialism in television and radio, and it has won several important

battles against the FCC's efforts to loosen ownership restrictions. There are great links to numerous groups who work on public media.

Fairness and Accuracy in Reporting (FAIR)
www.fair.org
This watchdog group reports inaccuracies and biases in mainstream news programs, with an emphasis on the undemocratic effects of corporate control.

Pew Research Center for the People & the Press
www.people-press.org
This website contains excellent polling information on the changing patterns of media use by Americans.

Chapter 10

✳

Political Polarization: How Divided Are We?

The success of American democracy has long been viewed as rooted in an underlying consensus. According to the consensus interpretation of American history, with the important exception of the Civil War, Americans have avoided the divisive conflicts that have wracked the political systems of Europe, sometimes leading to violent revolutions there. Political parties in the United States tend toward the center. Communist, socialist, extreme conservative, and monarchist parties are largely missing from the American political scene. The relative peacefulness of U.S. politics has been based on the fact that Americans agree on the fundamental law of the Constitution and the core values of individual freedom and limited government.

In recent years, as American politics has become more rancorous, the consensus view of American politics has been seriously questioned. The effort to impeach President Bill Clinton over the Monica Lewinsky affair and George W. Bush's contested victory in the 2000 presidential election turned up the heat in American politics to uncomfortable levels, causing citizens to characterize their opponents not just as wrong, but as immoral and corrupt as well. Barack Obama ran for president in 2008 on a promise to end the "broken and divided politics" in Washington and to govern in a bipartisan way. His approach was popular with voters, but Obama has found it much easier to call for bipartisanship than to actually achieve it. Despite highly publicized efforts, Obama won not a single Republican vote for his historic health care reform bill in 2010. The 65 percent gap between Democrats' (88 percent) and Republicans' (23 percent) average job approval rating of Obama was easily the largest for any modern president in the first year of office (Gallup Poll). In this chapter we examine the extent of this partisan divide and explore what it means for American democracy.

The underlying concept in this debate is *political polarization*. Polarization should not be confused with a closely divided electorate. Just because George

W. Bush won the 2000 election by the narrowest of margins does not mean the electorate was polarized. Voters may not have felt strongly about either candidate and could have been comfortable with either man in the White House.

Political polarization means that the two sides are deeply divided and far apart on their policy preferences. Polarized electorates view the victory of the other side as a disaster for the country. At the extreme, polarized electorates live in separate worlds and have little communication with or understanding of each other. We usually think of polarization as based on moral or cultural issues, such as abortion or gay rights, in which compromise on a middle position is especially difficult. However, polarization can also occur on foreign policy issues, such as the war in Iraq, or on economic issues, such as Franklin Roosevelt's New Deal.

Recent concern about political polarization is hardly unique in American history. In the early years of the Republic, when Thomas Jefferson rose up against the Federalists under the leadership of John Adams, there was a question about whether sharp criticism of the government would even be allowed. The Alien and Sedition Acts (1798) were used to throw political opponents in jail. But after he won the 1800 election, Jefferson took office peacefully and the right of citizens to criticize their government has largely been upheld ever since. Unlike in many other countries, in the United States political polarization has never become so severe that the losers try to prevent the winner of the election from assuming office. Polarization of beliefs around slavery tested this consensus, but the victory of the North in the Civil War established the principle that the losers of an election cannot choose to secede.

American politics has been characterized by periods of conflict followed by periods of relative calm and consensus. The populist rebellions of the late nineteenth and early twentieth centuries sorely tested the political system, as did the labor strife and conflict that grew out of the Great Depression. The Cold War that followed World War II ushered in a long period of relative calm. Wars, even "cold" wars, tend to suppress conflict as the nation unites against a common enemy. The decade of the 1950s was even heralded as marking an "end of ideology," with big ideological debates falling by the wayside as citizens united in the pursuit of economic prosperity.

All of this ended with the advent of the civil rights movement and the divisive Vietnam War. To a great extent, the heated politics of today are a continuation of the "culture wars" that erupted in the 1960s. Since *Roe v. Wade* guaranteed women's right to abortion in 1973, Catholic and Protestant opponents of abortion have bitterly opposed pro-choice politicians. In 2004 Archbishop Raymond Burke of St. Louis proclaimed that Catholics who voted for pro-choice politicians had committed a grave sin and should not receive communion unless they had their sins absolved. Burke's pronouncement is an example of extreme political polarization, but it reportedly had little effect on most Catholic voters.

The debate about the extent of polarization has revolved partly around the question of whether ordinary citizens have become bitterly divided or whether this is a phenomenon mostly confined to political elites. According to political scientists Jacob Hacker and Paul Pierson, the American electorate remains moderate but the

Republican Party, led by George Bush, tried to govern from the extreme right. Others argue that Democrats are equally guilty of pandering to their ideological extremists.

Another dimension of the issue is the extent to which the two parties have sorted themselves out geographically. Once highly contested, the South has now become securely Republican, just as New England has become a base for the Democrats. Not only are there "red" and "blue" states, but cities tend to be heavily Democratic, whereas small towns and rural areas lean heavily Republican. The concern is that as citizens move to partisan enclaves, they will stop communicating across the partisan divide, undermining the basis for healthy deliberation and compromise.

The two selections that follow on political polarization disagree both on the extent of polarization and on what it means. In the first selection, Jonathan Rauch, a freelance writer and outspoken supporter of gay rights, argues that the country is much less divided than most people think. The deep divisions are not among ordinary citizens but among party elites. And this is not all bad, Rauch argues, because polarized parties help to tame political extremists by giving them an outlet in the political process. In contrast, James Q. Wilson, Ronald Reagan Professor of Public Policy at Pepperdine University in California, argues that political polarization has increased in recent years and is a cause of concern. He is especially concerned that polarization will undermine America's ability to sustain a consistent, long-term foreign policy.

As you read the two essays, think about the role of conflict and debate in American democracy. A certain level of conflict is clearly healthy for a democracy. There is nothing like a good fight to motivate people to pay attention to politics and get involved. However, at what point does conflict pass over into paralyzing polarization, where the two sides stop listening to each other and begin to treat each other with disrespect? Democratic debate requires a certain level of civility to operate the way that it should. Is American politics passing over that divide into dangerous polarization, and, if so, what can be done about it?

Bipolar Disorder

JONATHAN RAUCH

Have fear, Americans. Ours is a country divided. On one side are those who divide Americans into two sides; on the other are all the rest. Yes, America today is divided over the question of whether America is divided.

All right, I'm joking. But the joke has a kernel of truth. In 1991 James Davison Hunter, a professor of sociology and religious studies at the University of Virginia, made his mark with an influential book called *Culture Wars: The Struggle to Define America*. The notion of a country deeply and fundamentally divided over core moral and political values soon made its way into politics; in 1992 Patrick Buchanan told the Republicans at their national convention that they were fighting "a cultural war, as critical to the kind of nation we will one day be as was the Cold War itself." By 1996, in his singeing dissent in the gay-rights case *Romer v. Evans*, Supreme Court Justice Antonin Scalia could accuse the Court of "tak[ing] sides in the culture wars," and everyone knew exactly what he meant.

In 2000 those ubiquitous election-night maps came along, with their red expanses of Bush states in the heartland and their blue blocks of Gore territory along the coasts and the Great Lakes. From then on everyone talked about red America and blue America as if they were separate countries. The 2004 post-election maps, which looked almost identical to the 2000 ones, further entrenched the conventional wisdom, to the point where most newspaper readers can recite the tropes: red America is godly, moralistic, patriotic, predominantly white, masculine, less educated, and heavily rural and suburban; blue America is secular, relativistic, internationalist, multicultural, feminine, college educated, and heavily urban and cosmopolitan. Reds vote for guns and capital punishment and war in Iraq, blues for abortion rights and the environment. In red America, Saturday is for NASCAR and Sunday is for church. In blue America, Saturday is for the farmers' market (provided there are no actual farmers) and Sunday is for *The New York Times*.

An odd thing, however, happened to many of the scholars who set out to map this culture war: they couldn't find it. If the country is split into culturally and politically distinct camps, they ought to be fairly easy to locate. Yet scholars investigating the phenomenon have often come back empty-handed. Other scholars have tried to explain why. And so, in the fullness of time, the country has arrived at today's great divide over whether there is a great divide.

One amusing example: In April of last year *The Washington Post* ran a front-page Sunday article headlined "POLITICAL SPLIT IS PERVASIVE." It quoted various experts as saying for example, "We have two parallel universes" and "People in these two countries don't even see each other." In June, *The New York Times* shot back with an article headlined "A NATION DIVIDED? WHO SAYS?" It quoted another set of experts who maintained that Americans' disagreements are actually smaller than in the past and shrinking.

Courageously, your correspondent set out into the zone of conflict. The culture-war hypothesis has generated some fairly rigorous scholarship in recent years, and I examined it. I wound up believing that a dichotomy holds the solution to the puzzle: American politics is polarized but the American public is not. In fact, what may be the most striking feature of the contemporary American landscape—a surprise, given today's bitterly adversarial politics—is not the culture war but the culture peace.

What, exactly, do people mean when they talk about a divided or polarized America? Often they mean simply that the country is evenly divided: split fifty-fifty, politically speaking. And so it indubitably and strikingly is. In 1979 Democratic senators, House members, governors, and state legislators commandingly outnumbered Republicans; since early in this decade the numbers have been close to equal, with Republicans slightly ahead. Opinion polls show that Republicans and Democrats are effectively tied for the public's loyalty. For the time being, America doesn't have a dominant party....[1]

To political analysts, who live in a world of zero-sum contests between two political parties, it seems natural to conclude that partisan division entails cultural division. Sometimes they elide the very distinction. In his book *The Two Americas* (2004), Stanley B. Greenberg, a prominent Democratic pollster, opens with the sentence "*America is divided*" (his italics) and goes on to say, "The loyalties of American voters are now almost perfectly divided between the Democrats and Republicans, a historical political deadlock that inflames the passions of politicians and citizens alike." In a two-party universe that is indeed how things look. But we do not live in a two-party universe. The fastest-growing group in American politics is independents, many of them centrists who identify with neither party and can tip the balance in close elections. According to the Pew Research Center for the People and the Press, since the Iraq War 30 percent of Americans have identified themselves as Republicans, 31 percent as Democrats, and 39 percent as independents (or "other"). Registered voters split into even thirds.

On election day, of course, independents who want to vote almost always have to choose between a Republican and a Democrat. Like the subatomic particles that live in a state of blurred quantum indeterminacy except during those fleeting moments when they are observed, on election day purple independents suddenly appear red or blue. Many of them, however, are undecided until the last moment and aren't particularly happy with either choice. Their ambivalence disappears from the vote tallies because the very act of voting excludes the non-partisan middle.

By no means, then, does partisan parity necessarily imply a deeply divided citizenry. People who talk about culture wars usually have in mind not merely a close division (fifty-fifty) but a wide or deep division—two populations with distinct and incompatible world views. It was this sort of divide that Hunter said he had found in 1991. One culture was "orthodox," the other "progressive." The disagreement transcended particular issues to encompass different conceptions of moral authority—one side anchored to tradition or the Bible, the other more relativistic. Not only does this transcendental disagreement reverberate throughout both politics and everyday life, Hunter said, but "*each side of the cultural divide can only talk past the other*" (his italics). In his book *The Values Divide* (2002) the political scientist John Kenneth White, of Catholic University, makes a similar case. "One faction emphasizes duty and morality; another stresses individual rights and self-fulfillment," he writes. The result is a "values divide"—indeed, a "chasm."

---

1. This article was written before the 2006 election in which the Democrats gained control of both the House and Senate.

Both authors make their observations about culture and values—many of which are quite useful—by aggregating the attitudes of large populations into archetypes and characteristic world views. The question remains, however, whether actual people are either as extreme or as distinct in their views as the analysts' cultural profiles suggest. Might the archetypes really be stereotypes?

In 1998 Alan Wolfe, a sociologist at Boston College, said yes. For his book *One Nation, After All*, Wolfe studied eight suburban communities. He found a battle over values, but it was fought not so much between groups as within individuals: "The two sides presumed to be fighting the culture war do not so much represent a divide between one group of Americans and another as a divide between sets of values important to everyone." Intellectuals and partisans may line up at the extremes, but ordinary people mix and match values from competing menus. Wolfe found his subjects to be "above all moderate," "reluctant to pass judgment," and "tolerant to a fault." Because opinion polls are designed to elicit and categorize disagreements, he concluded, they tend to obscure and even distort this reality.

I recently came across an interesting example of how this can happen: In an August 2004 article Jeffrey M. Jones and Joseph Carroll, two analysts with the Gallup Organization, took note of what they called an election-year puzzle. Frequent churchgoers and men were much more likely to support George W. Bush than John Kerry. Non-churchgoers and women leaned the other way. That all jibed with the familiar archetypes of religious-male reds and secular-female blues. But here was the puzzle: "Men—particularly white men—are much less likely to attend church than are women of any race or ethnicity." How, then, could churchgoers prefer Bush if women preferred Kerry?

The answer turns out to be that most individuals don't fit the archetypes. Men who go to church every week overwhelmingly favored Bush (by almost two to one), and women who stay home on Sundays favored Kerry by a similar margin. But these two archetypal categories leave out most of the population. Women who go to church weekly, men who stay home Sundays, and people of both sexes who go to church semi-regularly are all much more closely divided. The majority of actual Americans are in this conflicted middle.

To know how polarized the country is, then, we need to know what is happening with actual people, not with cultural or demographic categories. One thing we need to know, for example, is whether more people take extreme positions, such that two randomly chosen individuals would find less common ground today than in the past. In the fifty-fifty nation does the distribution of opinion look like a football, with Americans divided but clustered around the middle? Or has it come to look like a dumbbell, with more people at the extremes and fewer in the center?

In an impressive 1996 paper published in *The American Journal of Sociology*—"Have Americans' Social Attitudes Become More Polarized?"—the sociologists Paul DiMaggio, John Evans, and Bethany Bryson, of Princeton University, set out to answer that question using twenty years' worth of data from two periodic surveys of public opinion. They found no change in the "bimodality" of public opinion over the two decades. The football was not becoming a dumbbell.

DiMaggio and his colleagues then looked at particular issues and groups. On most issues (race and gender issues, crime and justice, attitudes toward liberals and conservatives, and sexual morality) Americans had become more united in their views, not more divided. (The exceptions were abortion and, to a lesser extent, poverty.) Perhaps more surprising, the authors found "dramatic *depolarization* in intergroup differences." That is, when they sorted people into groups based on age, education, sex, race, religion, and region, they found that the groups had become more likely to agree.

The authors did, however, find one group that had polarized quite dramatically: people who identified themselves as political partisans. There had been a "striking divergence of attitudes between Democrats and Republicans." In 2003 John Evans updated the study using data through 2000. He found, for the most part, no more polarization than before—except among partisans, who were more divided than ever.

Could it be that the structure of public opinion shows stability or convergence even as individuals hold their opinions in more vehement, less compromising ways? If so, that might be another kind of polarization. Getting inside individuals' heads is difficult, but scholars can look at so-called "feeling thermometers"—survey questions that ask respondents to rate other people and groups on a scale from "very cold" to "very warm." In his recent book *Culture War? The Myth of a Polarized America* the political scientist Morris P. Fiorina, of Stanford University (writing with Samuel J. Abrams and Jeremy C. Pope), finds little change in emotional polarization since 1980—except, again, among strong partisans.

A further possibility remains. Political *segregation* may be on the rise. Like-minded people may be clustering together socially or geographically, so that fewer people are exposed to other points of view. States, neighborhoods, and even bridge clubs may be turning all red or all blue. Is America becoming two countries living side by side but not together?

Fiorina and his associates approached that question by comparing blue-state and red-state opinion just before the 2000 election. What they found can only be described as a shocking level of agreement. Without doubt, red states were more conservative than blue ones; but only rarely did they actually disagree, even on such culturally loaded issues as gun control, the death penalty, and abortion. Rather, they generally agreed but by different margins. To take one example of many, 77 percent of red-state respondents favored capital punishment, but so did 70 percent of blue-state respondents. Similarly, 64 percent of those in blue states favored stricter gun control, but so did 52 percent of those in red states. Red-state residents were more likely to be born-again or evangelical Christians (45 percent, versus 28 percent in blue states), but strong majorities in both sets of states agreed that religion was very important in their lives. On only a few issues, such as whether to allow homosexuals to adopt children or join the military, did blue-state majorities part company with red-state majorities. Majorities in both red and blue states concurred—albeit by different margins—that Bill Clinton was doing a good job as president, that nonetheless they did not wish he could run again, that women's roles should be equal to men's, that the environment should take precedence over jobs, that English should be made the official language, that blacks should not receive preferences in hiring, and so on. This hardly suggests a culture war.

Red-state residents and blue-state residents agreed on one other point: most of them regarded themselves as centrists. Blue residents tipped toward describing themselves as liberal, and red residents tipped toward seeing themselves as conservative; but, Fiorina writes, "the distributions of self-placements in the red and blue states are very similar—both are centered over the 'moderate' or 'middle-of-the-road' position, whether we consider all residents or just voters." By the same token, people in both sets of states agreed, by very similar margins, that the Democratic Party was to their left and the Republican Party to their right. "In both red and blue states," Fiorina concludes, "a solid majority of voters see themselves as positioned between two relatively extreme parties."

Of course, one reason states look so centrist might be that most states aggregate so many people. A state could appear moderate, for example, even if it were made up of cities that were predominantly liberal and rural areas that were predominantly conservative. Indeed, media reports have suggested that a growing share of the population lives in so-called landslide counties, which vote for one party or the other by lopsided margins. Philip A. Klinkner, a professor of government at Hamilton College, examined this claim recently and found nothing in it. In 2000 the share of voters in landslide counties (36 percent) fell smack in the middle of the historical range for presidential elections going back to 1840. In 2000, Klinkner writes, "the average Democrat and the average Republican lived in a county that was close to evenly divided."

Of course, 36 percent of Americans living in landslide counties is a lot of people. But then, America has always been a partisan place. What John Adams's supporters said in 1796 about Thomas Jefferson, Bill Clinton pungently (and correctly) observed recently, would "blister the hairs off a dog's back." America is also no stranger to cultural fission. Think of Jeffersonians versus Hamiltonians, Jacksonians against the Establishment, the Civil War (now *there* was a culture war), labor versus capital a century ago, the civil-rights and Vietnam upheavals. No cultural conflict in America today approaches any of those. By historical standards America is racked with harmony.

My favorite indication of the culture peace came in a survey last July of unmarried Americans, conducted by the Gallup Organization for an online dating service called Match.com. Asked if they would be "open to marrying someone who held significantly different political views" from their own, 57 percent of singles said yes. Majorities of independents, Democrats, and (more narrowly) Republicans were willing to wed across political lines. Just how deep can our political disagreements be, I wonder, if most of us are willing to wake up next to them every morning?

A picture begins to emerge. A divide has opened, but not in the way most people assume. The divide is not within American culture but between politics and culture. At a time when the culture is notably calm, politics is notably shrill. Now, it bears emphasizing that culture peace, or war, is always a relative concept. America, with its cacophonous political schools and ethnic groups and religions and subcultures, will never be a culturally quiescent place, and thank goodness for that. Given the paucity of nation-splitting disagreements, however, what really needs explaining is the disproportionate polarization of American politics.

Reasons for it are not hard to find. They are almost bewilderingly numerous. When I burrow through the pile, I end up concluding that two are fundamental: America's politicians have changed, and so have America's political parties.

"Who sent us the political leaders we have?" Alan Ehrenhalt asked in 1991. Ehrenhalt is a respected Washington political journalist, the sort of person who becomes known as a "veteran observer," and the riddle is from his book *The United States of Ambition: Politicians, Power, and the Pursuit of Office*. "There is a simple answer," he continued. "They sent themselves." This, he argued persuasively, was something new and important.

Ehrenhalt, who was born in 1947, grew up in the dusk of a fading world that I, at age forty-four, am just a little too young to remember. In those days politicians and their supporters were like most other people, only more so. Ambition and talent always mattered, but many politicians were fairly ordinary people (think of Harry Truman) who were recruited into politics by local parties or political bosses and then worked their way up through the system, often trading on their ties to the party and on their ability to deliver patronage. Party machines and local grandees acted as gatekeepers. Bosses and elders might approach a popular local car dealer and ask him to run for a House seat, and they were frequently in a position to hand him the nomination, if not the job. Loyalty, not ideology, was the coin of the realm, and candidates were meant to be smart and ambitious but not, usually, *too* smart and ambitious.

In a society as rambunctious and egalitarian as America's, this system was probably bound to break down, and in the 1960s and 1970s it finally did. The smoke-filled rooms, despite their considerable (and often underappreciated) strengths, were too cozy and homogenous and, yes, unfair to accommodate the democratic spirit of those times. Reformers, demanding a more open style of politics, did away with the gatekeepers of old. The rise of primary elections was meant to democratize the process of nominating candidates, and so it did; but hard-core ideologues—with their superior hustle and higher turnouts—proved able to dominate the primaries as they never could the party caucuses and conventions. As the power of the machines declined, ideology replaced patronage as the prime motivator of the parties' rank and file. Volunteers who showed up at party meetings or campaign offices ran into fewer people who wanted jobs and more who shared their opinions on Vietnam or busing.

With parties and patrons no longer able to select candidates, candidates began selecting themselves. The party nominee, Ehrenhalt wrote, gave way to the "self-nominee." Holding office was now a full-time job, and running for office was if anything even more grueling than holding it. "Politics is a profession now," Ehrenhalt wrote. "Many people who would be happy to serve in office are unwilling to think of themselves as professionals, or to make the personal sacrifices that a full-time political career requires. And so political office—political power—passes to those who want the jobs badly enough to dedicate themselves to winning and holding them." Those people, of course, are often left-wing and right-wing ideologues and self-appointed reformers. In the 1920s the town druggist might be away serving in Congress while the local malcontent lolled around the drugstore grumbling about his pet peeve. Today there's a good chance that the druggist is minding the store and the malcontent is in Washington.

The parties, too, have changed. Whereas they used to be loose coalitions of interests and regions, they are now ideological clubs. Northeastern Republicans were once much more liberal than Southern Democrats. Today more or less all conservatives are Republicans and more or less all liberals are Democrats. To some extent the sorting of parties into blue and red happened naturally as voters migrated along the terrain of their convictions, but the partisans of the political class have been only too happy to prod the voters along. Whereas the old party machines specialized in mobilizing masses of partisans to vote for the ticket, the newer breed specializes in "activating" (as the political scientist Steven E. Schier has aptly put it) interest groups by using targeted appeals, often inflammatory in nature. (This past year the Republican National Committee sent mailings in Arkansas and West Virginia suggesting that the Democrats would try to ban the Bible.) Both parties, with the help of sophisticated computer software and block-by-block demographic data, have learned to target thinner and thinner slices of the population with direct mail and telephone appeals.

Perhaps more significant, both parties also got busy using their computer programs and demographic maps to draw wildly complicated new district boundaries that furnished their incumbents with safe congressional seats. Today House members choose their voters rather than the other way around, with the result that only a few dozen districts are competitive. In many districts House members are much less worried about the general election than they are about being challenged in the primary by a rival from their own party. Partisans in today's one-party districts feel at liberty to support right-wing or left-wing candidates, and the candidates feel free (or obliged) to cater to the right-wing or left-wing partisans.

It's not such a surprise, then, that the ideological divide between Democrats and Republicans in Congress is wider now than it has been in more than fifty years (though not wide by pre–World War I standards). The higher you go in the hierarchies of the parties, the further apart they lean. The top leaders on Capitol Hill are the bluest of blues and the reddest of reds—left and right not just of the country but even of their own parties. (This is especially true on the Republican side. *National Journal*, a nonpartisan public-policy magazine and a sister publication of *The Atlantic*, rated House Speaker Dennis Hastert the most conservative member of the House in 2003; Majority Leader Tom DeLay tied for second place.) As party lines have hardened and drawn apart, acrimony has grown between Democratic and Republican politicians, further separating the parties in what has become a vicious cycle. The political scientist Gary C. Jacobson, of the University of California at San Diego, finds that Democrats and Republicans not only enter Congress further apart ideologically, but also become more polarized the longer they stay in Congress's fiercely partisan environment.

Not all of this had to happen—and indeed, happenstance has made matters worse in recent years. It is interesting to wonder how much less polarized

American politics might be today if John McCain had won the presidency in 2000. Instead we got Bush, with his unyielding temperament and his strategy of mobilizing conservatives. Even more divisive was the fact that one party—the Republicans—has controlled the presidency and both chambers of Congress since 2003. In a fifty-fifty country, shutting one party out of the government can only lead to partisan excess on one side and bitter resentment on the other.

Centrist voters, of course, are unhappy, but what can they do? As Fiorina pithily puts it, "Given a choice between two extremes, they can only elect an extremist." Presented with a credible candidate who seemed relatively moderate, a McCain or a Ross Perot, many independents jumped at him; but the whole problem is that fewer moderates reach the ballot. The result, Fiorina writes, is that "the extremes are overrepresented in the political arena and the center underrepresented." The party system, he says, creates or inflames conflicts that are dear to the hearts of relatively small numbers of activists. "The activists who gave rise to the notion of a culture war, in particular, and a deeply polarized politics, in general, for the most part are sincere. *They* are polarized." But ordinary people—did someone say "silent majority"?—are not.

Well. A grim diagnosis. That it is largely correct is simply beyond question. I say this as one of the frustrated independent voters who feel left behind by two self-absorbed and overzealous major parties. In particular, the practice of gerrymandering congressional districts to entrench partisans (and thus extremists) is a scandal, far more insulting to popular sovereignty than anything to do with campaign finance. But that is not the note I wish to end on. Something may be going right as well.

It seems odd that cultural peace should break out at the same time that political contentiousness grows. But perhaps it is not so odd. America may be culturally peaceful *because* it is so politically polarized. The most irritating aspect of contemporary American politics—its tendency to harp on and heighten partisan and ideological differences—may be, as computer geeks like to say, not a bug but a feature.

America's polarized parties, whatever their flaws, are very good at developing and presenting crisp choices. How do you feel about abortion? A constitutional ban on same-sex marriage? Privatizing Social Security accounts? School vouchers? Pre-emptive war? Well, you know which party to vote for. Thanks to the sharply divided political parties, American voters—including the ones in the center—get clear alternatives on most issues that matter. By presenting those alternatives, elections provide a sense of direction.

Moreover, although party polarization may disgruntle the center (can't we be for stem-cell research *and* school vouchers?), it helps domesticate fanatics on the left and the right. Though you would be partly correct to say that the mainstream parties have been taken over by polarized activists, you could also say, just as accurately and a good deal more cheerfully, that polarized activists have been taken over by the mainstream parties. The Republican Party has acquired its distinctively tart right-wing flavor largely because it has absorbed—in fact, to a significant extent has organizationally merged with—the religious ... [R]eligious conservatives are becoming more uniformly Republican even as their faiths and backgrounds grow more diverse. On balance it is probably healthier if religious conservatives are inside the political system than if they operate as insurgents and provocateurs on the outside. Better they should write anti-abortion planks into the Republican platform than bomb abortion clinics. The same is true of the left. The clashes over civil rights and Vietnam turned into street warfare partly because activists were locked out by their own party establishments and had to fight, literally, to be heard. When Michael Moore receives a hero's welcome at the Democratic National Convention, we moderates grumble: but if the parties engage fierce activists while marginalizing tame centrists, that is probably better for the social peace than the other way around.

In the end what may matter most is not that the parties be moderate but that they be competitive—which America's parties are, in spades. Politically speaking, our fifty-fifty America is a divisive, rancorous place. The rest of the world should be so lucky.

How Divided Are We?

JAMES Q. WILSON

The 2004 election left our country deeply divided over whether our country is deeply divided. For some, America is indeed a polarized nation, perhaps more so today than at any time in living memory. In this view, yesterday's split over Bill Clinton has given way to today's even more acrimonious split between Americans who detest George Bush and Americans who detest John Kerry, and similar divisions will persist as long as angry liberals and angry conservatives continue to confront each other across the political abyss. Others, however, believe that most Americans are moderate centrists, who, although disagreeing over partisan issues in 2004, harbor no deep ideological hostility. I take the former view.

By polarization I do not have in mind partisan disagreements alone. These have always been with us. Since popular voting began in the 19th century, scarcely any winning candidate has received more than 60 percent of the vote, and very few losers have received less than 40 percent. Inevitably, Americans will differ over who should be in the White House. But this does not necessarily mean they are polarized.

By polarization I mean something else: an intense commitment to a candidate, a culture, or an ideology that sets people in one group definitively apart from people in another, rival group. Such a condition is revealed when a candidate for public office is regarded by a competitor and his supporters not simply as wrong but as corrupt or wicked; when one way of thinking about the world is assumed to be morally superior to any other way; when one set of political beliefs is considered to be entirely correct and a rival set wholly wrong. In extreme form, as defined by Richard Hofstadter in *The Paranoid Style in American Politics* (1965), polarization can entail the belief that the other side is in thrall to a secret conspiracy that is using devious means to obtain control over society. Today's versions might go like this: "Liberals employ their dominance of the media, the universities, and Hollywood to enforce a radically secular agenda"; or, "conservatives, working through the religious Right and the big corporations, conspired with their hired neocon advisers to invade Iraq for the sake of oil."

Polarization is not new to this country. It is hard to imagine a society more divided than ours was in 1800, when pro-British, pro-commerce New Englanders supported John Adams for the presidency while pro-French, pro-agriculture Southerners backed Thomas Jefferson. One sign of this hostility was the passage of the Alien and Sedition Acts in 1798; another was that in 1800, just as in 2000, an extremely close election was settled by a struggle in one state (New York in 1800, Florida in 2000).

The fierce contest between Abraham Lincoln and George McClellan in 1864 signaled another national division, this one over the conduct of the Civil War. But thereafter, until recently, the nation ceased to be polarized in that sense. Even in the half-century from 1948 to (roughly) 1996, marked as it was by sometimes strong expressions of feeling over whether the presidency should go to Harry Truman or Thomas Dewey, to Dwight Eisenhower or Adlai Stevenson, to John F. Kennedy or Richard Nixon, to Nixon or Hubert Humphrey, and so forth, opinion surveys do not indicate widespread detestation of one candidate or the other, or of the people who supported him.

Now they do. Today, many Americans and much of the press regularly speak of the President as a dimwit, a charlatan, or a knave. A former Democratic presidential candidate has asserted that Bush "betrayed" America by launching a war designed to benefit his friends and corporate backers. A senior Democratic Senator has characterized administration policy as a series of "lies, lies, and more lies" and has accused Bush of plotting a "mindless, needless, senseless, and reckless" war. From the other direction, similar expressions of popular disdain have been directed at Senator John Kerry (and before him at President Bill Clinton); if you have not heard them, that may be because (unlike many of my relatives) you do not live in Arkansas or Texas or other locales where the *New York Times* is not read. In these places, Kerry is widely spoken of as a scoundrel.

In the 2004 presidential election, over two-thirds of Kerry voters said they were motivated explicitly by the desire to defeat Bush. By early 2005, President Bush's approval rating, which stood at 94 percent among Republicans, was only 18 percent among Democrats—the largest such gap in the history of the Gallup Poll. These data, moreover, were said to reflect a mutual revulsion between whole geographical sections of the country, the so-called Red (Republican) states versus the so-called Blue (Democratic) states. As summed up by the distinguished social scientist who writes humor columns under the name of Dave Barry, residents of Red states are "ignorant racist fascist knuckle-dragging NASCAR-obsessed cousin-marrying road-kill-eating tobacco-juice-dribbling gun-fondling religious fanatic rednecks," while Blue-state residents are "godless unpatriotic pierced-nose Volvo-driving France-loving left-wing Communist latte-sucking tofu-chomping holistic-wacko neurotic vegan weenie perverts."

To be sure, other scholars differ with Dr. Barry. To them, polarization, although a real enough phenomenon, is almost entirely confined to a small number of political elites and members of Congress. In *Culture War?* (2004), which bears the subtitle "The Myth of a Polarized America," Morris Fiorina of Stanford argues that policy differences between voters in Red and Blue states are really quite small, and that most are in general agreement even on issues like abortion and homosexuality.

But the extent of polarization cannot properly be measured by the voting results in Red and Blue states. Many of these states are in fact deeply divided internally between liberal and conservative areas, and gave the nod to one candidate or the other by only a narrow margin. Inferring the views of individual citizens from the gross results of presidential balloting is a questionable procedure.

Nor does Fiorina's analysis capture the very real and very deep division over an issue like abortion. Between 1973, when *Roe v. Wade* was decided, and now, he writes, there has been no change in the degree to which people will or will not accept any one of six reasons to justify an abortion: (1) the woman's health is endangered; (2) she became pregnant because of a rape; (3) there is a strong chance of a fetal defect; (4) the family has a low income; (5) the woman is not married; (6) and the woman simply wants no more children. Fiorina may be right about that. Nevertheless, only about 40 percent of all Americans will support abortion for any of the last three reasons in his series, while over 80 percent will support it for one or another of the first three.

In other words, almost all Americans are for abortion in the case of maternal emergency, but fewer than half if it is simply a matter of the mother's preference. That split—a profoundly important one—has remained in place for over three decades, *and* it affects how people vote. In 2000 and again in 2004, 70 percent of those who thought abortion should always be legal voted for Al Gore or John Kerry, while over 70 percent of those who thought it should always be illegal voted for George Bush.

Division is just as great over other high-profile issues. Polarization over the war in Iraq, for example, is more pronounced than any war-related controversy in at least a half-century. In the fall of 2005, according to Gallup, 81 percent of Democrats but only 20 percent of Republicans thought the war in Iraq was a mistake. During the Vietnam war, by contrast, itself a famously contentious cause, there was more unanimity across party lines, whether for or against: in late 1968 and early 1969, about equal numbers of Democrats and Republicans thought the intervention there was a mistake. Pretty much the same was true of Korea: in early 1951, 44 percent of Democrats and 61 percent of Republicans thought the war was a mistake—a partisan split, but nowhere near as large as the one over our present campaign in Iraq.

Polarization, then, is real. But what explains its growth? And has it spread beyond the political elites to influence the opinions and attitudes of ordinary Americans?

The answer to the first question, I suspect, can be found in the changing politics of Congress, the new competitiveness of the mass media, and the rise of new interest groups.

That Congress is polarized seems beyond question. When, in 1998, the House deliberated whether to impeach President Clinton, all but four Republican members voted for at least one of the impeachment articles, while only five Democrats voted for even one. In the Senate, 91 percent of Republicans voted to convict on at least one article; every single Democrat voted for acquittal.

The impeachment issue was not an isolated case. In 1993, President Clinton's budget passed both the House and the Senate without a single Republican vote in favor. The same deep partisan split occurred over taxes and supplemental appropriations. Nor was this a blip: since 1950, there has been a steady increase in the percentage of votes in Congress pitting most Democrats against most Republicans.

In the midst of the struggle to pacify Iraq, Howard Dean, the chairman of the Democratic National Committee, said the war could not be won and Nancy Pelosi, the leader of the House Democrats, endorsed the view that American forces should be brought home as soon as possible. By contrast, although there was congressional grumbling (mostly by Republicans) about Korea and complaints (mostly by Democrats) about Vietnam, and although Senator George Aiken of Vermont famously proposed that we declare victory and withdraw, I cannot remember party leaders calling for unconditional surrender.

The reasons for the widening fissures in Congress are not far to seek. Each of the political parties was once a coalition of dissimilar forces: liberal Northern Democrats and conservative Southern Democrats, liberal coastal Republicans and conservative Midwestern Republicans. No longer; the realignments of the South (now overwhelmingly Republican) and of New England (now strongly Democratic) have all but eliminated legislators who deviate from the party's leadership. Conservative Democrats and liberal Republicans are endangered species now approaching extinction. At the same time, the ideological gap between the parties is growing: if there was once a large overlap between Democrats and Republicans—remember "Tweedledum and Tweedledee"?—today that congruence has almost disappeared. By the late 1990s, virtually every Democrat was more liberal than virtually every Republican.

The result has been not only intense partisanship but a sharp rise in congressional incivility. In 1995, a Republican-controlled Senate passed a budget that President Clinton proceeded to veto; in the loggerhead that followed, many federal agencies shut down (in a move that backfired on the Republicans). Congressional debates have seen an increase not only in heated exchanges but in the number of times a representative's words are either ruled out of order or "taken down" (that is, written by the clerk and then read aloud, with the offending member being asked if he or she wishes to withdraw them).

It has been suggested that congressional polarization is exacerbated by new districting arrangements that make each House seat safe for either a Democratic or a Republican incumbent. If only these seats were truly competitive, it is said, more centrist legislators would be elected. That seems plausible, but David C. King of Harvard has shown that it is wrong: in the House, the more competitive the district, the more extreme the views of the winner. This odd finding is apparently the consequence of a nomination process dominated by party activists. In primary races, where turnout is low (and seems to be getting lower), the ideologically motivated tend to exercise a preponderance of influence.

All this suggests a situation very unlike the half-century before the 1990s, if perhaps closer to certain periods in the 18th and 19th centuries. Then, too, incivility was common in Congress, with members not only passing the most scandalous remarks about each other but on occasion striking their rivals with canes or fists. Such partisan feeling ran highest when Congress was deeply divided over slavery before the Civil War and over Reconstruction after it. Today the issues are different, but the emotions are not dissimilar.

Next, the mass media. Not only are they themselves increasingly polarized, but consumers are well aware of it and act on that awareness. Fewer people now subscribe to newspapers or watch the network evening news. Although some of this decline may be explained by a preference for entertainment over news, some undoubtedly reflects the growing conviction that the mainstream press generally does not tell the truth, or at least not the whole truth.

In part, media bias feeds into, and off, an increase in business competition. In the 1950s, television news amounted to a brief 30-minute interlude in the day's programming, and not a very profitable one at that; for the rest of the time, the three networks supplied us with westerns and situation comedies. Today, television news is a vast, growing, and very profitable venture by the many broadcast and cable outlets that supply news twenty-four hours a day, seven days a week.

The news we get is not only more omnipresent, it is also more competitive and hence often more adversarial. When there were only three television networks, and radio stations were forbidden by the fairness doctrine from broadcasting controversial views, the media gravitated toward the middle of the ideological spectrum, where the large markets could be found. But now that technology has created cable news and the Internet, and now that the fairness doctrine has by and large been repealed, many media outlets find their markets at the ideological extremes.

Here is where the sharper antagonism among political leaders and their advisers and associates comes in. As one journalist has remarked about the change in his profession, "We don't deal in facts [any longer], but in attributed opinions." Or, these days, in unattributed opinions. And those opinions are more intensely rivalrous than was once the case.

The result is that, through commercial as well as ideological self-interest, the media contribute heavily to polarization. Broadcasters are eager for stories to fill their round-the-clock schedules, and at the same time reluctant to trust the government as a source for those stories. Many media outlets are clearly liberal in their orientation; with the arrival of Fox News and the growth of talk radio, many are now just as clearly conservative.

The evidence of liberal bias in the mainstream media is very strong. The Center for Media and Public Affairs (CMPA) has been systematically studying television broadcasts for a quarter-century. In the 2004 presidential campaign, John Kerry received more favorable mentions than any presidential candidate in CMPA's history, especially during the month before election day. This is not new: since 1980 (and setting aside the recent advent of Fox News), the Democratic candidate has received more favorable mentions than the Republican candidate in every race except the 1988 contest between Michael Dukakis and George H. W. Bush. A similarly clear orientation characterizes weekly newsmagazines like *Time* and *Newsweek*.

For its part, talk radio is listened to by about one-sixth of the adult public, and that one-sixth is made up mostly of conservatives. National Public Radio has an audience of about the same size; it is disproportionately liberal. The same breakdown affects cable-television news, where the rivalry is between CNN (and MSNBC) and Fox News. Those who watch CNN are more likely to be Democrats than Republicans; the reverse is emphatically true of Fox. As for news and opinion on the Internet, which has become an important source for college graduates in particular, it, too, is largely polarized along political and ideological lines, emphasized even more by the culture that has grown up around news blogs.

At one time, our culture was only weakly affected by the media because news organizations had only a few points of access to us and were largely moderate and audience-maximizing enterprises. Today the media have many lines of access, and reflect both the maximization of controversy and the cultivation of niche markets. Once the media talked to us; now they shout at us.

And then there are the interest groups. In the past, the major ones—the National Association of Manufacturers, the Chamber of Commerce, and labor organizations like the AFL-CIO—were concerned with their own material interests. They are still active, but the loudest messages today come from very different sources and have a very different cast to them. They are issued by groups concerned with social and cultural matters like civil rights, managing the environment, alternatives to the public schools, the role of women, access to firearms, and so forth, and they directly influence the way people view politics.

Interest groups preoccupied with material concerns can readily find ways to arrive at compromise solutions to their differences; interest groups divided by issues of rights or morality find compromise very difficult. The positions taken by many of these groups and their supporters, often operating within the two political parties, profoundly affect the selection of candidates for office. In brief, it is hard to imagine someone opposed to abortion receiving the Democratic nomination for President, or someone in favor of it receiving the Republican nomination.

Outside the realm of party politics, interest groups also file briefs in important court cases and can benefit from decisions that in turn help shape the political debate. Abortion became a hot controversy in the 1970s not because the American people were already polarized on the matter but because their (mainly centrist) views were not consulted; instead, national policy was determined by the Supreme Court in a decision, *Roe v. Wade*, that itself reflected a definition of "rights" vigorously promoted by certain well-defined interest groups.

Polarization not only is real and has increased, but it has also spread to rank-and-file voters through elite influence.

In *The Nature and Origins of Mass Opinion* (1992), John R. Zaller of UCLA listed a number of contemporary issues—homosexuality, a nuclear freeze, the war in Vietnam, busing for school integration, the 1990–91 war to expel Iraq from Kuwait—and measured the views held about them by politically aware citizens. (By "politically aware," Zaller meant people who did well answering neutral factual questions about politics.) His findings were illuminating.

Take the Persian Gulf war. Iraq had invaded Kuwait in August 1990. From that point through the congressional elections in November 1990, scarcely any elite voices were raised to warn against anything the United States might contemplate doing in response. Two days after the mid-term elections, however, President George H. W. Bush announced that he was sending many more troops to the Persian Gulf. This provoked strong criticism from some members of Congress, especially Democrats.

As it happens, a major public-opinion survey was under way just as these events were unfolding. Before criticism began to be voiced in Congress, both registered Democrats and registered Republicans had supported Bush's vaguely announced intention of coming to the aid of Kuwait; the more politically aware they were, the greater their support. *After* the onset of elite criticism, the support of Republican voters went up, but Democratic support flattened out. As Bush became more vigorous in enunciating his aims, politically aware voters began to differ sharply, with Democratic support declining and Republican support increasing further.

Much the same pattern can be seen in popular attitudes toward the other issues studied by Zaller. As political awareness increases, attitudes split apart, with, for example, highly aware liberals favoring busing and job guarantees and opposing the war in Vietnam, and highly aware conservatives opposing busing and job guarantees and supporting the war in Vietnam.

But why should this be surprising? To imagine that extremist politics has been confined to the chattering classes is to believe that Congress, the media, and American interest groups operate in an ideological vacuum. I find that assumption implausible.

As for the extent to which these extremist views have spread, that is probably best assessed by looking not at specific issues but at enduring political values and party preferences. In 2004, only 12 percent of Democrats approved of George Bush; at earlier periods, by contrast, three to four times as many Democrats approved of Ronald Reagan, Gerald Ford, Richard Nixon, and Dwight D. Eisenhower. Over the course of about two decades, in other words, party affiliation had come to exercise a critical influence over what people thought about a sitting president.

The same change can be seen in the public's view of military power. Since the late 1980s, Republicans have been more willing than Democrats to say that "the best way to ensure peace is through military strength." By the late 1990s and on into 2003, well over two-thirds of all Republicans agreed with this view, but far fewer than half of all Democrats did. In 2005, three-fourths of all

Democrats but fewer than a third of all Republicans told pollsters that good diplomacy was the best way to ensure peace. In the same survey, two-thirds of all Republicans but only one fourth of all Democrats said they would fight for this country "whether it is right or wrong."

Unlike in earlier years, the parties are no longer seen as Tweedledum and Tweedledee. To the contrary, as they sharpen their ideological differences, attentive voters have sharpened *their* ideological differences. They now like either the Democrats or the Republicans more than they once did, and are less apt to feel neutral toward either one.

How deep does this polarization reach? As measured by opinion polls, the gap between Democrats and Republicans was twice as great in 2004 as in 1972. In fact, rank-and-file Americans disagree more strongly today than did politically active Americans in 1972.

To be sure, this mass polarization involves only a minority of all voters, but the minority is sizable, and a significant part of it is made up of the college-educated. As Marc Hetherington of Vanderbilt puts it: "people with the greatest ability to assimilate new information, those with more formal education, are most affected by elite polarization." And that cohort has undeniably grown.

In 1900, only 10 percent of all young Americans went to high school. My father, in common with many men his age in the early 20th century, dropped out of school after the eighth grade. Even when I graduated from college, the first in my family to do so, fewer than one-tenth of all Americans over the age of twenty-five had gone that far. Today, 84 percent of adult Americans have graduated from high school and nearly 27 percent have graduated from college. This extraordinary growth in schooling has produced an ever larger audience for political agitation.

Ideologically, an even greater dividing line than undergraduate education is postgraduate education. People who have proceeded beyond college seem to be very different from those who stop with a high-school or college diploma. Thus, about a sixth of all voters describe themselves as liberals, but the figure for those with a postgraduate degree is well over a quarter. In mid-2004, about half of all voters trusted George Bush; less than a third of those with a postgraduate education did. In November of the same year, when over half of all college graduates voted for Bush, well over half of the smaller cohort who had done postgraduate work voted for Kerry. According to the Pew Center for Research on the People and the Press, more than half of all Democrats with a postgraduate education supported the antiwar candidacy of Howard Dean.

The effect of postgraduate education is reinforced by being in a profession. Between 1900 and 1960, write John B. Judis and Ruy Teixeira in *The Emerging Democratic Majority* (2002), professionals voted pretty much the same way as business managers; by 1988, the former began supporting Democrats while the latter supported Republicans. On the other hand, the effect of postgraduate education seems to outweigh the effect of affluence. For most voters, including college graduates, having higher incomes means becoming more conservative; not so for those with a postgraduate education, whose liberal predilections are immune to the wealth effect.

The results of this linkage between ideology, on the one hand, and congressional polarization, media influence, interest-group demands, and education on the other are easily read in the commentary surrounding the 2004 election. In their zeal to denigrate the president, liberals, pronounced one conservative pundit, had "gone quite around the twist." According to liberal spokesmen, conservatives with their "religious intolerance" and their determination to rewrite the Constitution had so befuddled their fellow Americans that a "great nation was felled by a poisonous nut."

If such wholesale slurs are not signs of polarization, then the word has no meaning. To a degree that we cannot precisely measure, and over issues that we cannot exactly list, polarization has seeped down into the public, where it has assumed the form of a culture war. The sociologist James Davison Hunter, who has written about this phenomenon in a mainly religious context, defines culture war as "political and social hostility rooted in different systems of moral understanding." Such conflicts, he writes, which can involve "fundamental ideas about who we are as Americans," are waged both across the religious/secular divide and within religions themselves, where those with an "orthodox" view of moral authority square off against those with a "progressive" view.

To some degree, this terminology is appropriate to today's political situation as well. We are indeed in a culture war in Hunter's sense, though I believe this war is itself but another component, or another symptom, of the larger ideological polarization that has us in its grip. Conservative thinking on political issues has religious roots, but it also has roots that are fully as secular as anything on the Left. By the same token, the liberal attack on conservatives derives in part from an explicitly "progressive" religious orientation—liberal Protestantism or Catholicism, or Reform Judaism—but in part from the same secular sources shared by many conservatives.

But what, one might ask, is wrong with having well-defined parties arguing vigorously about the issues that matter? Is it possible that polarized politics is a good thing, encouraging sharp debate and clear positions? Perhaps that is true on those issues where reasonable compromises can be devised. But there are two limits to such an arrangement.

First, many Americans believe that unbridgeable political differences have prevented leaders from addressing the problems they were elected to address. As a result, distrust of government mounts, leading to an alienation from politics altogether. The steep decline in popular approval of our national officials has many causes, but surely one of them is that ordinary voters agree among themselves more than political elites agree with each other—and the elites are far more numerous than they once were.

In the 1950s, a committee of the American Political Science Association (APSA) argued the case for a "responsible" two-party system. The model the APSA had in mind was the more ideological and therefore more "coherent" party system of Great Britain. At the time, scarcely anyone thought our parties could be transformed in such a supposedly salutary direction. Instead, as Governor George Wallace of Alabama put it in his failed third-party bid for the presidency, there was not a "dime's worth of difference" between Democrats and Republicans.

What Wallace forgot was that, however alike the parties were, the public liked them that way. A half-century ago, Tweedledum and Tweedledee enjoyed the support of the American people; the more different they have become, the greater has been the drop in popular confidence in both them and the federal government.

A final drawback of polarization is more profound. Sharpened debate is arguably helpful with respect to domestic issues, but not for the management of important foreign and military matters. The United States, an unrivaled superpower with unparalleled responsibilities for protecting the peace and defeating terrorists, is now forced to discharge those duties with its own political house in disarray.

We fought World War II as a united nation, even against two enemies (Germany and Italy) that had not attacked us. We began the wars in Korea and Vietnam with some degree of unity, too, although it was eventually whittled away. By the early 1990s, when we expelled Iraq from Kuwait, we had to do so over the objections of congressional critics; the first President Bush avoided putting the issue to Congress altogether. In 2003 we toppled Saddam Hussein in the face of catcalls from many domestic leaders and opinion-makers. Now, in stabilizing Iraq and helping that country create a new free government, we have proceeded despite intense and mounting criticism, much of it voiced by politicians who before the war agreed that Saddam Hussein was an evil menace in possession of weapons of mass destruction and that we had to remove him.

Denmark or Luxembourg can afford to exhibit domestic anguish and uncertainty over military policy; the United States cannot. A divided America encourages our enemies, disheartens our allies, and saps our resolve—potentially to fatal effect. What General Giap of North Vietnam once said of us is even truer today: America cannot be defeated on the battlefield, but it can be defeated at home. Polarization is a force that can defeat us.

Discussion Questions

1. Poll your friends or your class. How many in the group view themselves as "strongly liberal" or "strongly conservative"? How many classify themselves as "moderates"? Discuss what these terms mean. Using the survey results, would you classify your friends or your classmates as politically polarized?

2. Do you talk about politics with your friends? If you are a Democrat, do you have many friends who are Republican or vice versa? Do you think we tend to select friends who agree with us on issues and, if so, does this lead to more extreme points of view?

3. Is your neighborhood or your school predominantly of one political persuasion, or is it mixed? Does this make a difference in how people view each other politically?

4. Do you read publications or watch television programs that cover both sides of an issue or do you tend to consume partisan media?

5. Do you think the media focus too much on conflict and division, underplaying examples of agreement and cooperation?

6. What do you think of Rush Limbaugh or Michael Moore? Are they polarizing figures or do they represent healthy expressions of widely differing political perspectives?

7. Are most Americans uncomfortable with political conflict and, if so, why?

Suggested Readings and Internet Sources

Alan Wolfe's 1998 book, *One Nation, After All* (New York: Viking), studied eight communities in depth and concluded that Americans had become more tolerant, not less, on a range of cultural and political issues. In his much-debated book, *What's the Matter with Kansas?* (New York: Metropolitan Books, 2004), Thomas Frank argues that voters have been persuaded to vote against their economic interests by conservative political elites pushing hot-button cultural issues like abortion and gay rights. On the contrary, Patrick Buchanan argues in *The Death of the West* (New York: St. Martin's Press, 2002), politicians have ignored, at our peril, precisely the kinds of moral and culture issues Frank warns against. Jacob S. Hacker and Paul Pierson argue in *Off Center: The Republican Revolution & the Erosion of American Democracy* (New Haven, Conn.: Yale University Press, 2005) that polarization is mostly the result of Republican elites moving to the extreme right, not increasing polarization among ordinary voters. Two solid scholarly treatments of the polarization issue are Morris P. Fiorina (with Samuel J. Abrams and Jeremy C. Pope), *Culture War? The Myth of a Polarized America* (New York: Pearson Longman, 2006), and Pietro S. Nivola and David W. Brady, eds., *Red and Blue Nation? Characteristics and Causes of America's Polarized Politics* (Washington, D.C.: Brookings Institution Press, 2006).

The Gallup Organization
www.galluppoll.com
The Gallup Organization maintains a website that provides access to the Gallup Polls that have been conducted over the years, enabling scholars to track the changing views of Americans on political and social issues.

People for the American Way
www.pfaw.org
People for the American Way takes a liberal stance on moral and cultural issues and monitors what it views as extremist right-wing organizations.

Christian Coalition
www.cc.org
Founded by Pat Robertson, the Christian Coalition supports a more forceful role for Christian moral values in the political process.

Chapter 11

✳

Campaigns and Elections: Do Negative Ads Damage Democracy?

From the nineteenth century's smoke-filled conventions and torchlight parades to today's televised sound bites and attack ads, political campaigns have been a fixture of the American democratic landscape. Despite their hoopla and hype, electoral campaigns are serious business. Without them, voters would not have a choice, could not get organized, and would have to pick their representatives on Election Day in a state of isolation and ignorance.

However, few would argue that all is well with modern American campaigns and elections. Many critics complain that campaigns have become personality contests that trivialize the issues facing the American public. Candidates spend more time hurling accusations at one another than stating their own goals once in office. The media focus on blunders and misstatements, and devote more attention to which candidate is ahead in a "horse race" than to the contenders' leadership qualities or policy agendas. Meanwhile, voter participation is lower than in the distant past, even for the presidential contest, which draws the highest turnout.

Nonetheless, contemporary campaigns have their defenders. Most of those who choose to vote, these defenders observe, seem to have learned some things from campaigns by Election Day, and the more individuals participate in the campaign process, the higher the quality of the resulting democratic debate seems to be. Perhaps the critics expect too much from electoral democracy. Perhaps modern campaigns are simply one feature of our pervasive consumer culture, in which inflated claims by advertisers promise private satisfactions, and those who measure electoral democracy by ideal levels of participation and high-minded debate are employing standards that actual Americans will never meet.

Whatever one's judgment of the strengths and weaknesses of contemporary campaigns and elections in the United States, there is little dispute over who currently manages them. Whereas political parties, organized from the national level down to the local precinct, used to be the linchpin of campaigns and elections, today this realm is dominated by professional political consultants. Candidates for office, from the presidency down to local races, hire private firms with expertise in the expensive, high-tech arts of the modern electoral campaign. Some of these firms serve Republicans, others work only for Democrats, but their shared hallmark is the professionalization of campaign management.

The techniques used by political consultants have reshaped the nature of modern campaigning. The issues emphasized by candidates are based on polling and on focus groups. In the first of these, pollsters use the scientific techniques devised by public-opinion researchers to sample the views of large populations; in the second, small groups are convened by consultants to provide feedback on potential appeals and catchphrases that will win support for the candidate. On the basis of this information, consultants devise a media strategy, reaching voters through mail, phone, radio, and especially television and the Internet. Candidate webpages are now part of this communications blitz. Consultants, some of whom are now graduates of professional campaign management schools at major universities, can thus offer candidates an array of sophisticated and high-tech skills to mobilize enough voters on their behalf to win elections.

All of these skills, of course, come with a price. As modern campaigns have become more professionally managed and media-based, they have become vastly more expensive. In 2008, the combined expenditures of presidential candidates Barack Obama and John McCain topped one billion dollars. Paid advertising on television constitutes the largest single expense for a candidate for high office today. But everything about a modern campaign is costly—including the services of the consultants. To obtain such huge sums, candidates need to devote much of their time to raking in money long before an election. And they need to hire professional fundraisers—raising money costs money!

Occasionally, candidates pursue an alternative to the reign of the professional consultants: the *grass-roots campaign*. Whether grass-roots candidates are outsiders with little money or idealists who believe in popular democracy, they run their campaigns light on paid consultants and paid media, and heavy on activist volunteers. The grass-roots campaign draws ideas from candidates and their supporters rather than from polls and focus groups, raises funds from small donors rather than wealthy contributors, and approaches voters with volunteer workers knocking on their doors and calling them in their homes rather than through mass media advertising. With the advent of the Internet, grass-roots campaigns have been given a fresh boost, apparent in the newly minted word *netroots*, which links the older idea with the newer medium of communication. The Obama campaign of 2008 developed a creative blend of grass-roots and professional campaigning.

During the presidential campaign of 2008, campaign professionals devised some memorable negative advertising, including one McCain ad that mocked Obama as a shallow celebrity akin to Paris Hilton and Britney Spears. The impact of negative advertising on the American electorate has been widely discussed and debated by political scientists. Believing that survey research has failed to reveal the effects of negative ads on voters, political scientists Stephen Ansolabehere and Shanto Iyengar, authors of our first selection (drawn from their book *Going Negative*), use the technique of a controlled experiment to study the subject. Their research casts doubt on the prevailing view that negative ads are manipulative and misleading. However, it also suggests a disturbing effect of negative advertising on democracy: it shrinks and polarizes the electorate. Independent voters are turned off by high levels of negativity and become less likely to vote, while partisan voters are stimulated by hostile campaign charges to gravitate to more extreme positions at the poles of the political spectrum.

Political scientist John Geer challenges this account of negative advertising in our second selection (from his book *In Defense of Negativity*). Geer uses a different method than Ansolabehere and Iyengar to study negative ads: he samples televised ads from presidential campaigns, codes their contents, and assesses their value in informing the electorate. Geer argues that much of the criticism of negative advertising is misguided; negative ads, his findings suggest, actually contain more information on the issues and are better documented than are positive (usually personality-based) ads. Rather than bemoaning how negative our campaigns have become, he writes, we should recognize that negativity is a necessity for a democracy. Negative advertising is an essential component of a democratic election, a means of holding the powerful accountable for their actions and bringing into sharper relief for voters what difference it will make if they choose one candidate over the other.

Central to the debate between Ansolabehere and Iyengar on one side and Geer on the other is the question of how elections should be conducted in the United States. Do you agree with Ansolabehere and Iyengar that a reduction in negative ads in favor of a more positive dialogue between candidates would promote greater participation and mutual respect in American elections? Or do you agree with Geer that robust democracy has always required sharp-edged exchanges between candidates, with increases in negativity reflecting the fact that there are vital differences between them. How do you personally react when you view negative ads on television or on the Internet? Do these ads discourage you from voting or increase your interest in the campaign?

Negative Ads Shrink and Polarize the Electorate

STEPHEN ANSOLABEHERE AND SHANTO IYENGAR

Once upon a time, this country divided itself neatly along party lines. Most people voted; those who did not tended to be poorer, less well-educated, and more apathetic, but still party loyal. The line between participants and non-participants was a fault line of sorts, but it was not terribly worrisome. Civic duty ideally would involve everyone, but, even falling short of the ideal, we were at least expressing our national will in our elections. Television has changed all that. Now, we are split by a new division: between loyalists and apathetics. On the one hand, media propaganda can often shore up loyalists to vote for their traditional party; on the other hand, that same propaganda is increasingly peeling off a band of citizens who turn from independence to apathy, even antipathy, toward our political institutions.

Pollsters and political scientists first noticed this new fault line in 1964. The number of people who proclaimed themselves independent of traditional party labels rose sharply in the mid-1960s. At the same time, candidates embraced television as a new means of independent communication with the voters. Politicians no longer needed the legions of party workers to get their messages across; they could effectively establish personal connections with their constituents using television advertising. In addition, there arose a new class of campaign manager—the media consultant, who typically had worked on Madison Avenue and viewed selling politics much like selling any other product. By the end of the 1960s, media consultants had filled the shoes left vacant by the then-extinct ward healers and precinct captains. Within the political parties, chaos reigned. The old-style politicos in both the Democratic and Republican parties battled and lost to a new regime of populists and progressives, who opened up the parties' nominating process to all comers. By most accounts, these reforms did even greater harm to the parties, shamelessly opening schisms that in earlier years were smoothed over behind closed doors.

At the time many observers mistakenly saw in the combination of televised political advertising and the nonpartisan voter the advent of a new age in America. Television advertising was to have produced a new kind of independent politician, not beholden to special interests and not part of the problems that voters increasingly associated with Washington. That day has not dawned. To be sure, the ranks of Independent voters have swollen since 1964, and television advertising is now the mainstay of contemporary political campaigns. The political parties, however, remain ascendent in elections and in government. Despite an occasional Independent candidacy and the rise of the personal electoral followings of many candidates, electoral competition is still between Republicans and Democrats. What is more, government, especially Congress, has become even more polarized and partisan than ever. The parties in Congress represent two increasingly cohesive and extreme positions.

The electorate has reacted with frustration and anger. In recent years, the political pulsetakers have registered record lows in political participation, record highs in public cynicism and alienation, and record rates of disapproval of the House of Representatives, the institution designed to represent the public will.

The single biggest cause of the new, ugly regime is the proliferation of negative political advertising on TV. Our argument is that a new synthesis in American politics has failed to emerge precisely because of the ways that partisans and non-partisans react to televised political messages. Like product advertising, successful political advertising reflects people's beliefs, experiences, and preferences. One consequence of this simple axiom is that political campaigns reinforce the loyalties of partisans. Nonpartisans, by contrast, usually tune out political advertising. They find politicians, politics, and government distasteful; political advertising simply sounds like more of the same. Only negative messages resonate with such attitudes. As political campaigns have become more hostile over the last two decades, nonpartisans have heard plenty to reinforce their low opinions of politics. Unfortunately, negative campaigning only reinforces the nonpartisans' disillusionment and convinces them not to participate in a tainted process. As a result, nonpartisans have not become the electoral force that they might have. Instead, political advertising has produced a party renaissance, even though partisans are an increasingly unrepresentative segment of the public.

The evidence for this argument is drawn from a four-year study of how political advertisements affect the informedness, preferences, and participatory ethos of the electorate....

Our results are unexpected, in both big and small ways. They suggest that campaign advertising is not "a pack of lies." In fact, advertising on the issues informs voters about the candidates' positions and makes it more likely that voters will take their own preferences on the issues into account when choosing between the candidates. Our studies also suggest that the effects of advertisements on voters depend, among other things, upon the partisanship and gender of the sponsoring candidate, the issue being discussed, and the attentiveness of the audience. In these ways, perhaps our research might help political consultants choose the most effective tactic, but it provides no fodder for political reformers.

On the other hand, our most troubling finding is that negative or "attack" advertising actually suppresses voter turnout. Attack advertisements can be, and are, used strategically for this purpose. We would even go so far as to say that negative advertisements may pose a serious antidemocratic threat. In 1993, the Republican political consultant Ed Rollins boasted (apparently falsely) of paying black ministers in exchange for their abstaining from encouraging their congregations to vote. His claim caused an understandable firestorm of controversy. Our claim is in many ways more serious: we believe that candidates who might benefit from low turnout pay for negative advertising to discourage participation. The real concern for twenty-first century democracy is not manipulation of naïve voters by sophisticated "image makers," but the shrinking of the electorate by political strategists who are fully aware of the consequences of their actions.

What about the problem of distortion? Is the traditional argument valid? Clearly, the thirty-second commercial is a somewhat mindless form of communication. Candidates could surely develop their positions and arguments in greater detail were they, like Ross Perot, in a position to campaign on the basis of in-depth "infomercials." Our evidence indicates, however, that despite the typical advertisement's brevity and superficial format, voters can and do learn from advertising, even on matters of substance such as the candidates' positions on the issues. By permitting viewers to form impressions of the sponsoring candidates, advertising simplifies the task of voting. In some respects, the voters who are most likely to learn from campaign advertising are those who lack other sources of information. In terms of information, therefore, advertising works to level differences between the "haves" and "have-nots."

Our evidence also shows that political advertising is not manipulative. Instead, we find that exposure to advertising reinforces or "awakens" latent partisan predispositions. Voters who tend to prefer Democrats (such as African-Americans or blue-collar workers), for instance, are especially responsive to advertisements aired by Democratic candidates. Individuals for whom the potential for manipulation is presumably greatest—those lacking a sense of party affiliation—are, in fact, the least likely to be persuaded by campaign advertising. Overall, we find that exposure to advertising facilitates voters' "normal" or expected choice of candidates; voters exposed to campaign advertising are more likely to vote along partisan lines than those not exposed to advertising.

We found many interesting variations on the theme that advertising reinforces voters' partisanship. The persuasive effects of advertising are dependent upon several factors, including the tone of the advertising campaign, the party of the sponsoring candidate, and the particular issues under discussion. Republican candidates persuade their supporters more effectively with negative advertisements, while Democrats tend to be more persuasive with positive appeals. Moreover, whether voters react to advertising in keeping with their long-standing partisan loyalties itself depends on the issue on which the candidates advertise. Republican voters are especially drawn to "their" candidate when advertisements deal with issues on which the Republican party enjoys a favorable reputation, such as crime, illegal immigration, or national defense. Conversely, Democrats are more persuasive when they advertise on traditionally "Democratic" issues, such as unemployment or civil rights.

There's a catch to the good news findings of this book, however: advertising polarizes American elections. On the one hand, advertisements are informative and not manipulative, but they are dividing voters into more and more partisan camps. On the other hand, negative advertisements, which account for approximately half of all campaign messages, are shrinking the electorate, especially the nonpartisan electorate. As the independents in the middle stop voting, the partisans at the extremes come to dominate electoral politics. It is the voice of this increasingly small and increasingly polarized voting public that representatives hear....

In sum, advertising does pose a serious threat to democracy—but this threat is not one that is usually laid at its feet. Vote suppression is profoundly antidemocratic. It may not be the result of an explicit reaction to a particular message; voters simply grow to dislike negativity and withdraw accordingly. Nevertheless, it is a problem that cries out for consideration, if the free market approach to political speech is not to lead to a political implosion of apathy and withdrawal....

Forty years after the onset of large-scale campaign advertising, there is surprisingly little agreement over the effects of broadcast advertising on voters and elections. Obviously, the candidates and their political strategists impute considerable power to the thirty-second advertisement. Academic researchers, however, have been hard-pressed to identify any effects and have concluded that campaigns in general and campaign advertising in particular are relatively unimportant determinants of electoral outcomes. In fact, political scientists routinely forecast presidential and statewide elections using models that ignore campaign-related factors altogether. Presidential elections, for instance, are thought to hinge on the state of the country's economy and the popularity of the incumbent president, with the competing campaigns having negligible effects on the outcome.

For a multi-billion-dollar industry to leave no traces of influence on its targets is mysterious. And despite the claims of the academics, such an influence is hardly demonstrated. The primary impediment to a more sophisticated and thorough understanding of the effects of political advertising has been technical. Most of the "minimal effects" evidence uncovered by researchers in the political communication field rests on sample surveys or polls. Surveys are ill-equipped to detect the effects of campaign advertising....

Survey researchers who study the effects of campaigns rely on the logic of correlation. A representative sample of voters is contacted (generally over the phone) and asked various questions about their exposure to campaign messages. How often do they watch television news, listen to talk radio, read a newspaper, or converse about politics? Which prime-time programs do they watch? Do they remember watching any campaign advertisements? Which candidate do they prefer and why? And so on....

Individuals' memory for past events is notoriously frail, especially when the "event" in question concerns what they saw or did not see on television. Some survey respondents may have surmised that since it was election time, they must have seen a political advertisement. Among participants in our experimental studies who were exposed to *no* campaign advertisement, for example, 20 percent claimed to have seen one. Alternatively, many people who were unable to recall watching an advertisement may in fact have done so (repeatedly), only to then forget it. In our experiments, nearly half of all people who were exposed to a thirty-second advertisement could not recall that they had seen a political advertisement just one-half hour later. In short, survey measures of exposure to campaign communication are likely to be riddled with errors....

The alternative to the sample survey is the controlled experiment. It is no accident that experimentation is the methodological paradigm of choice in all scientific disciplines. Because the researcher himself manipulates the phenomenon under investigation, he knows that the experimental participants were either exposed or not exposed to it. In the case of advertising, an "experimental" group is shown a particular advertisement, and a "control" group is not shown the advertisement. Because participants are assigned to the two conditions on a purely random basis, the researcher can be confident that the conditions will be no different from each other in composition. These two basic features of the experiment—the ability to exercise physical control over the experimental stimulus and the use of comparison groups that are equivalent in all respects but the presence of the experimental stimulus—provide researchers with the all-important ability to attribute any observed difference between the experimental and control groups to the effects of the experimental stimulus.

If, for example, the experimental group proves to be more informed than the control group, the researcher knows that this difference was caused by exposure to political advertising, and nothing else.

Of course, experiments are not without their own liabilities. Most experiments are administered upon "captive" populations—college students who must serve as guinea pigs to gain course credit. As the eminent experimental psychologist Carl Hovland warned many years ago, college sophomores are not comparable to "real people." A further weakness of the typical experiment is the somewhat sterile, laboratory-like environment in which it is administered, an environment that bears little resemblance to the noise and confusion of election campaigns. Clearly, a considerable leap of faith is required to generalize experimental results to the real world.

Our own studies were designed to overcome the limited generalizability of the experimental method. The experimental participants represented a fair cross-section of the electorate, the experimental setting was casual and designed to emulate "real life," and our studies all took place during ongoing political campaigns characterized by extensive advertising....

Like party loyalty, political participation is a consequence of the electoral process. Political campaigns can instill the sense that voting is a duty, that an individual's vote matters, and that elected officials are responsive to the wishes of the electorate. Or, campaigns can breed cynicism and alienation.

In an earlier era, mobilization was the name of the game. The party machines of old lived and died by their ability to get their own voters to the polls. It was a labor-intensive enterprise that produced many electoral irregularities, such as the vote of the dead in Chicago and widespread vote buying. The practice of vote buying, in fact, was so widespread that one woman testified in court that she "thought it was the law to pay us for our votes." But for all its irregularities, fierce party competition pushed *up* voter turnout. A century ago, when party organizations were at the peak of their game, 70 to 80 percent of the eligible electorate voted.

Political parties still play a vital role in American elections, but campaigns are now run by and for individual candidates, who rely heavily on the techniques of mass marketing. Unfortunately, television advertising has divorced voter mobilization from the goal of winning elections. While it makes campaigns more efficient (and less corrupt), it leaves candidates little incentive to stimulate high levels of participation. Since broadcast advertisements reach friend and foe alike, candidates must focus on the techniques and strategies of persuasion. Increasingly, that means going on the attack and shrinking the size of the market. In the end, politicians are just as happy and some are even more likely to win with very low turnout as they are to win with very high turnout.

High levels of citizen involvement and political participation have thus become collective goods, and like all collective goods, they will be underproduced. Collective goods, such as common grazing lands and waterways, public parks and roads, and clean air, have two important features. First, everyone enjoys the benefits; second, no one experiences the direct consequence of his/her own actions or his/her own use of the good. The result, wrote Thomas Schelling, is that "people so impinge on each other in pursuing their own interests that collectively they might be better off if they could be restrained, but no one gains individually by self restraint."

Modern political campaigns present us with just such a tragedy of the political commons. We all benefit from a citizenry that feels a strong duty to vote and voice its preferences about government, but television advertising removes the incentives for candidates, journalists, and groups to foster public spiritedness. Candidates care only about their market shares, not about the total turnout. Reporters care only about getting their bylines, not about whether their stories foster faith in the political system. Interest groups care only about making an impact on government policy, not about whether that policy carries the public's blessing. Those who produce the main messages of political campaigns simply have no reason to make the people feel that the outcome of the elections is just.

This is not to say that television advertising cannot inspire participation and confidence in government. Candidates' positive campaign commercials bring people to the polls, just as attack ads turn them away. Many politicians do offer positive images of themselves and of government, and the candidates are not alone. Party committees and civic groups often take to the airwaves urging people to turn out and vote. Also, several recent lobbying campaigns have successfully used television advertising and other new technologies to rally people behind particular causes and encourage them to contact their representatives.

But against the trickle of ads urging people to vote rushes a flood of negative campaign commercials that erode the participatory ethos. Candidate after candidate has turned to negative advertising, and once the gates of negative campaigning are opened, they are difficult to close. The best way to answer an attack is with another attack, and journalists, who thrive on political conflict, echo the negativity of the campaigns in their own increasingly critical and cynical reporting.

Whatever its causes, negative politics generates disillusionment and distrust among the public. Attack advertisements resonate with the popular beliefs that government fails, that elected officials are out of touch and quite corrupt, and that voting is a hollow act. The end result: lower turnout and lower trust in government, regardless of which party rules.

The marginal voter—the Independent—feels the pinch of negative advertisements most sharply. Attack ads produce the highest drop in political efficacy and in intentions to participate among nonpartisans. Most of these people have shed their traditional party attachments not because they feel ambivalent about which of the two parties they should support, but because they dislike politics in general. The hostile tenor of campaign advertising further reinforces their contempt for candidates, parties, and government. As a result, negative campaigning divides the American electorate into a voting public of party loyalists and a nonvoting public of apathetics.

With each election this schism widens. Though their growth has been glacial, Independents are now the single largest of the "partisan" groups in the electorate—36 percent, according to the Gallup Poll. They tend not to vote, and regardless of which party is in the majority, they do not feel that the government represents their ideas and interests. Each succeeding election raises their frustration higher yet. Our evidence is that the political campaigns deserve much of the blame for the Independents' retreat from the polls. Positive campaign advertising generally fails to reach Independents. Nonpartisans do not find the typical political commercial compelling or persuasive, and they are only further angered, frustrated, and alienated by negative campaigning. The current climate of attack politics strengthens their resolve to remain Independents, but weakens their electoral voice.

As a consequence, electoral politics are becoming less representative. Elected officials respond mainly to the opinions of those who vote, which is increasingly a partisan and ideologically extreme crowd. Contemporary campaigning discourages nonpartisans from expressing their interests and frustrations at the polls; it thus obstructs politicians from hearing their anger.

Bad campaigns make for bad government. The shrillness and hostility of campaigns infect the day-to-day politics of legislatures. The making of sausage and of legislation, goes an old saw, are best left behind closed doors. Political advertising opens up those doors and shines the harshest of light on the proceedings. Politicians have always shied away from decisions that are difficult to explain to the folks back home, but fear of attack ads makes elected officials especially skittish about casting controversial votes....

The growing support for independent candidacies and the growing frustration with negative campaigning present both a threat and an opportunity for the parties. The threat is that if negative campaigning continues to alienate people, especially nonpartisans, then the parties will lose their legitimate claim to represent the majority will, and any policies that they enact while in government will be viewed as a minority's interests imposed on the majority. The seriousness of the threat, though, opens the doors for party renewal.... Facing the wrath of a frustrated and volatile electorate, the parties' leaders now have strong incentives to cooperate and reinvent the rules of political campaigning so as to foster more positive and responsible electoral behavior. Either that, or let negative candidate-centered campaigns drive one or both of the parties into extinction.

The Need for Negativity

JOHN G. GEER

There is a consensus among policy-makers and political elites that attack advertising in campaigns, like crack cocaine, is dangerous to the well-being of our society. Hardly a day goes by during an election season without some discussion of "negativity" and its adverse impact on our electoral process. We are, in effect, awash in a sea of negativity about negativity. David Broder, the dean of political journalists, claims that "trivial is too kind a word" for the content of today's campaigns, arguing that "the ads people are seeing are relentlessly negative: loaded words and nasty implications about the opposition candidates; often never a hint as to why a voter should support the person paying for the TV spot." Another observer, Victor Kamber, argues that negativity poisons the political debate by presenting arguments that are "ridiculous, irrelevant, and irresponsible," dragging down the discussion "to the level of tabloid scandal."

These types of concerns are commonplace. The title of Kathleen Jamieson's (1992) book represents the typical sentiment of pundits: *Dirty Politics: Deception, Distraction, and Democracy*. There is an unusually strong association between negativity and deception. Consider the fact that we rarely label negativity as "tough, competitive politics" or "heated exchanges" between combatants. Instead, it is almost always equaled with being "dirty"—something that is "not fair," "below the belt," and in need of a good "cleaning."

The public shares this distaste for negative advertising. As Larry Bartels notes, the "ordinary citizen's perception of the electoral process is marked by cynicism and dissatisfaction with the nature and tone of the contemporary campaign discourse." In poll after poll, data confirm Bartels's observation. In July 2000, nearly 60% of the public, according to a Gallup Poll, was dissatisfied with how candidates conduct their campaigns. A major part of the public's unhappiness with elections was tied to negativity. Only 19% of the public felt that negative advertisements even had "a place in campaigns." The vast majority of citizens do not even think you can learn anything of value from negative advertisements....

Scholars often join the fray, arguing that negativity has detrimental effects on the political process. Perhaps the most important of these concerns involves the so-called demobilization hypothesis. Stephen Ansolabehere and Shanto Iyengar contend that negative advertising disenfranchises voters by turning them off from the political process. Ansolabehere and Iyengar are sufficiently worried about the pernicious effects of negativity that they offer recommendations designed to decrease the use of attack ads in political campaigns....

In short, worries about negativity lie at the very center of concerns about the health of our electoral system and whether that system promotes a process that can be thought of as democratic. These are serious concerns that warrant serious attention. The problem is that we are all too quick to criticize the system and wring our hands over the ill-effects of negativity. We need to pause, reconsider starting assumptions, and marshal systematic data that will allow us to assess more fully these fears and concerns. For example, why are political commentators so troubled by negativity? Any deliberative process usually benefits from having criticism and debate. Why would attacks in campaigns be so problematic? Why do they not advance the debate? Politics is often rough and tumble; why isn't attack advertising thought of in those terms? Why are we so worried about "civility" in campaigns? If some aspect of a candidate's record is alarming, is it not important to raise that concern in an attention grabbing fashion? Shouldn't the public understand the seriousness of the problem?

Campaigns are not feel-good exercises; they are pitched battles for control of the government. The stakes are often high and the competition is usually fierce. The real issue should be whether or not candidates present the information in campaigns that is useful to voters. The tone of that information should be a secondary issue, at best....

Why Negativity Promotes Democracy

Whether one starts from the premise that negativity in politics is good, bad, or mixed, attacks have been a staple of political life for as long as there have been politics. Politics is about conflict, deciding who gets what share of limited resources. The result is disagreement about the distribution of those resources, which inevitably breeds negativity. At one level, everyone understands that conflict is part and parcel of politics. But at another level, there is a desire to sweep such disagreements under the rug and talk instead about "points of agreement." It may be more civil and understandable to downplay the core disagreements we all have. The problem with this approach, however, is that we often fail to appreciate the important role negativity can play in democratic government. Certainly the advocates of responsible party government understood the role of criticism and attack in a competitive party system. Their conception of democratic government rested heavily on having an effective and *vocal* opposition.

We rarely think of it in these terms, but this country was founded in large part through political attack. The Declaration of Independence—one of our most honored documents—was largely a set of negative appeals. The founders were unhappy with King George, and they expressed their unhappiness in this highly critical tract. In fact, by my count, about 70% of the statements in that famed document were criticisms of the British government. That is a high rate of negativity and it certainly outstrips modern presidential campaigns in the sheer frequency of attack. It was these criticisms that provided the basis for thinking about abuses of power and the centrality of certain basic human rights. Without such negativity, the argument for establishing a new nation that derived its "just powers from the consent of the government" would not have been possible.

The debate over the ratification of the Constitution is another example of negativity. William Riker demonstrated this fact clearly by documenting the nasty tone that characterized the struggle between the Federalists and Anti-Federalists as they debated the merits of the new Constitution. Nearly all of the arguments the Anti-Federalists offered were negative. The Federalists also frequently attacked the Anti-Federalists, although less often. This negativity not only provided the public and relevant elites a chance to evaluate the merits of a new Constitution, it led the founders to adopt the Bill of Rights—an invaluable set of reforms that assured important liberties.

As one flips the pages of American history, there are many other examples of negativity. A number of historians have called attention to the harsh partisan rhetoric of the 1790s and early 1800s. The Jackson–Adams election in 1828, for example, was exceptionally divisive. The former general was called, among other things, a murderer and a cannibal, while his wife was accused of being a whore. There are many examples of this highly caustic tone from the political battles of that era. Adams and Jefferson faced unheard-of attacks in their famous battle in 1800....

Despite the harshness of the rhetoric, our nation did not collapse. The experiment conducted by our founding fathers was far from a sure thing. No one knew if this republican form of government would endure. Yet even in its infancy, the nation survived the charges and countercharges hurled by the various combatants. Perhaps that should have been expected, since the rise of the nation was fueled in and of itself by criticism.

One might counter, however, that today's attacks are different and more destructive than those in the past. Some believe we have entered a new divisive era of politics that is more about tearing people down than passing legislation that will improve the lives of our citizens. Thomas Patterson, for example, acknowledges that

> Negative campaigns are as old as the Jefferson-Adams race of 1800, but today's version has no historical parallel. The volume is unlike anything that has gone before. "You can't compare a nasty quote about Thomas Jefferson," says former presidential speechwriter Richard Goodwin, "with the intensity and penetration [of today's attacks]."

Or as David Doak, Democratic political consultant, noted: "There were always negative things said on the stump, but not ... in your living room while you were eating popcorn." There appears to be genuine concern that the ability of the thirty-second attack ad to reach nearly all average voters represents a real threat to this nation's political system.

But these kinds of concerns seem at best premature and at worst, simply wrong. To begin with, we do not know enough about negativity in campaigns, current or past, to make any generalization with much confidence....

I cannot provide an answer to whether politics is more or less negative now than in the past. But this discussion highlights two important points. First, there is a tendency for political observers to leap to conclusions that the available data do not support. Second, real or not, there is a widespread belief that negativity is a problem in today's electoral process with little historical precedent, and that "reality" is leading the problem to draw more and more attention....

But I want to say more than just that democracy can survive negativity. I'm making a bolder claim: negativity can advance and improve the prospects for democracy. Without negativity, no nation can credibly think of itself as democratic. Just consider all the concern expressed during the 2004 Russian elections once the serious competition evaporated and Vladimir Putin was left effectively unchallenged. Observers viewed this as a bad development for the democratic process, because no one was around to criticize Putin and his record. Attacks may be painful to some, but they are essential for change to take place and for any nation to prosper. It is important to realize that the agents of change (e.g., candidates or parties) must first demonstrate the reasons why change is needed.

That is, they need to go negative before they can go positive. In short, attacks can enrich the quality of democratic life.

One of the hallmarks of a democracy is the chance for open and free expression. There has been a long-standing belief that for the best ideas and policies to surface, citizens and elites need an opportunity to criticize government and to debate the best course of action. In many ways, progress is the offspring of criticism, attacks, and negativity. Over 350 years ago, John Milton (1644–45) in *Areopagitica* argued that it was best to "let truth and falsehood grapple … in a free and open exchange." In this particular case, Milton was concerned about censorship by the British government, fearing that the curtailing of criticism would weaken society. John Stuart Mill (1859) some 200 years later went even further, contending that an opinion gains legitimacy and credibility if it faces criticism:

> If the (dissenting) opinion is right, they are deprived of the opportunity
> of exchanging error for truth: if wrong, they lose, what is almost as great
> a benefit, the clearer perception and livelier impression of the truth,
> produced by its collision with error (*On Liberty*)....

Negativity (and the threat of it) makes accountability possible. Without accountability, democracy falters. If an incumbent does a poor job in office, it is very unlikely that that person will be (publicly) self-critical. The opposition party, therefore, needs to serve "as a critic of the party in power, developing, defining, and presenting policy alternatives which are necessary for a true choice in reaching public decisions." Of course, challengers are likely to raise more problems than may actually exist. Hence, the incumbent needs to respond. The elected official needs not only to set the record straight, but also to point out potential weaknesses of the opposition. Negativity, therefore, creates a competitive dynamic that should yield a richer information environment than if candidates just talked about their own plans for government. In many ways, it is negativity that will draw candidates into the center of the ring.

These exchanges have additional benefits. Assume Candidate 1 has adopted positions on two issues, A and B, which the majority of voters support. Also assume Candidate 2 has offered views on two different issues, C and D, which the majority of voters support. With only positive campaigning, Candidate 1 would stress A and B, while Candidate 2 would talk about C and D. Voters would have noncomparable information about the two candidates—hardly an ideal way to choose between the two contenders. To make matter worse, there would not be any vetting of the two candidate's views on these issues. While Candidate 1 claims to hold a position on Issue A that the majority of the public backs, is it a fair representation of his or her true opinions? Has this candidate always held that position? What does the record indicate? The opposition, by attacking, could spur more discussion about the issue and raise doubts about Candidate 1's real position on Issue A. It is through negative appeals that voters can learn about the respective positions of candidates on all four issues. Candidates will be less able to duck issues and their stated views on other issues will be subjected to scrutiny. The end result should be an enriched information environment, leading to more rational decisions by the voting public....

Findings

[This study has] shown that there are two aspects of negative appeals that enrich the information environment available for voters. One, negative information is more issue oriented than positive appeals. Two, that attacks are more likely to be supported by evidence than self-promotional claims. These findings show some of the benefits of negativity for the information environment.

The fact that attacks need more documentation than positive appeals has important implications. For example, we should see attack ads sticking closely to the actual record of the opposition. We should not see things just made up about the other party's nominee. If this is true, we can expect negative information to be more *useful* than positive appeals in informing the public about the pressing concerns of the day....

The findings in this [study] offer a number of lessons about the role of personal attacks in presidential campaigns. First, personal attacks in presidential campaigns do not appear to be excessively harsh, nor are they particularly frequent. The concerns among political observers about personal attacks seem unwarranted in light of these data. Second, the rise of negativity over the last forty years is *not* tied to increasing personal attacks. This means by implication that issues most be the driving force behind the increase. Third, personal attacks have at least as much, if not more, credibility than positive trait appeals. We saw, for instance, that previous political experience of nominees compares reasonably well with how often competence and experience are mentioned in political ads. Moreover, the trait appeals raised in ads square with public opinion in general. There is a notable exception when it comes to attacks on integrity, but even those attacks appear to be part of the general dynamic behind negativity—the need for evidence....

[The findings] paint a far more favorable picture of attack politics than conventional wisdom suggests. The information environment of the public is enriched by attacks. These attacks are on important problems facing the country and these negative appeals change in response to real-world changes in the condition of the country. It would, in light of this evidence, be far harder to argue that attacks mislead and misinform. It would be even harder to argue that positive appeals provide more useful policy information than negative appeals. In addition, attacks are more specific in their presentation of an issue than are positive appeals. Campaign appeals are in general vague, but that is especially true for self-promotional issue appeals....

Since attacks tend to be tied to evidence, that dynamic encourages negativity to be about legitimate issues. Presidential candidates are not making up issues in an effort to distract. They are in some sense playing the hand they were dealt by the context of the election.

There are two additional lessons worthy of some comment. First, the public can learn more about real-world problems from negative appeals than from positive appeals. This story is very much different from what we normally hear about the ill effects of negativity.

A second implication of these findings is that the party government theorists were correct: the opposition does play an important role in forging accountability. Attacks by the opposition seem much more likely to be of value to voters as they make their choices. Most of the discussion of negativity has ignored this theoretical issue. If the public wants to have accountability, someone has to do the accounting and that accounting is not done through positive, feel-good appeals, but through harsh political attack where voters are made aware of the problems of the incumbent. Obviously, political campaigns of challengers offer much more than just advertising in their efforts to lure voters to their side. They have many ways of sending messages to voters. Nevertheless, at least in the presidential case, these messages seem to play a critical role in allowing elections to perform their democratic functions....

Explaining the Rise of Negativity

I have spent a great deal of time assessing negativity and developing ways to better understand attack politics in presidential campaigns. I have, however, ignored one question that merits attention, especially as this [essay] comes to a close. Why has negativity been on the rise in presidential elections?...

What structural features of American politics might account for this rise in negativity? To put it another way, what might explain the increasing rate of criticism between presidential candidates? One hypothesis involves the polarization of the parties over the recent past. Polarization means, among other things, a growing gap between the parties' views on issues and, therefore, more reasons to attack the other side. Polarization offers a theoretically compelling explanation for the rise of negativity. If the parties are close together on the issues, there are fewer disagreements and less incentive to attack. The reasoning is at least two-fold. First, parties off the median position are more open to criticism from each other. To criticize any action of the other side, there needs to be some difference in opinion. As the gap between the parties grows, so do the differences and, therefore, so do the opportunities for attack. Second, disagreements are more likely to be heated, because losing the election has more policy consequences in a polarized system than a nonpolarized one. If parties are battling over the "median" position, the loser will not see a big change in governmental policy. Each side wants to win, but the policy consequences simply are not as great. In short, the stakes of the election should increase along with polarization, providing more incentive to attack. Or as John McCain observed prior to the start of the 2004 campaign, this election will probably be "the nastiest we've ever seen from both sides because of the polarization that exists in politics today."

It is possible to draw the causal arrow in the other direction. Ansolabehere and Iyengar make exactly that case, contending that "negative advertising is ... fueling the polarization of American politics." They argue that negativity is driving the independent voter from the polls, generating a more partisan and hence more polarized electorate. That increasingly divided electorate, in turn, is giving rise to the polarization between the parties. While an interesting argument, there are at least three problems with it. First, they are assuming a model of party change that relies on a bottom up approach. That is, the changes in the electorate drive changes in the parties. That model is not widely supported in political science.... The second problem with this causal connection is that the literature ... shows little support for the demobilization hypothesis, which is so central to their argument. It is no longer credible to argue that negative advertising has this pernicious effect on the voting intentions of the electorate. The third problem is that this causal argument gives tremendous influence to the impact of advertising on the public. Spots do influence the public in many ways, but their impact is not so strong as to reshape the political landscape....

[A]s disagreement between the parties increases, so will attacks. When considered in this light, the rate of negativity Riker reports in the founding period makes even more sense. The stakes were extremely high and the disagreement fundamental, yielding lots of incentives to attack. The Anti-Federalists were waging a battle to stop a major change in the rules of the game that would move power from the states to the national government. It was more than disagreements about which policy to adopt; it was a disagreement about what institutions should exist to create policy.

If this basic argument is sound, we should also expect negativity to increase during times of realignment when disagreement between parties is at a peak and for it to decline once the party system stabilizes. Unfortunately, I do not have enough data about negativity in campaigns prior to 1960 to test for such possibilities....

The polarization of the country continues and shows little sign of ebbing. With the so-called blue and red states and the close partisan split in the electorate, there is little reason to think negativity will decline. Bush, who claimed to be a uniter not a divider, ran a very negative campaign [in 2004]. Over 50% of his spots were attacks on Kerry. He had real differences with Kerry on a number of issues and he made sure the public learned about those differences. Kerry too attacked Bush. He ran fewer negative ads than Bush (31%), turning more heavily to contrast ads (43%). There were a lot of differences and negativity was higher than at any time in the last five decades....

A Final Word ...

Negative advertising is usually not thought of as a process that helps shape and mold the course of government. Instead, we tend to think of it as simply misleading, frivolous, nasty, and counterproductive. The findings and arguments in these pages call into question those assumptions. It is important to realize that negativity, whether in the form of ads, speeches, or debates, can in fact inform the public. With a political system that seems to be increasingly prone to disagreement, we are not likely to see any decline in the attacks in political campaigns (or during the process of governing). Perhaps we can begin to think of negativity as an important part of democratic politics. Certainly, our founders understood its role. Thomas Jefferson once observed that

> in every free and deliberating society, there must from the nature of man be opposite parties, and violent dissensions and discords.... an association of men who will not quarrel with one another is a thing which never yet existed, from the greatest confederacy of nations down to a town meeting of vestry.

Disagreement goes hand in hand with democracy. We tend to lose sight of that fact, especially as observers seem to want to sweep our disagreements under the rug and avoid the conflicts between our political leaders.

Negativity provides a chance for those competing for power to make a case for why they should be given power and it gives those in power the chance to show the risks associated with the other side. This struggle may not be pretty and at times the rhetoric will cross the line of civility and even be insulting to our collective intelligence. We need, however, to make room for it in our politics and, moreover, we need to appreciate its contributions to the political process. Any effort to curtail negativity is far worse than enduring harsh rhetoric, since it means that the ability of the opposition to hold the other side accountable for their actions would be weakened. If negativity ever happened to disappear from our electoral battles, we can safely assume that so would our freedoms and any chance we have to lay claim to being a democratic nation.

Discussion Questions

1. Does the predominance of negative over positive ads reflect the win-at-all costs mentality of professional campaign managers in contemporary elections? Or were negative exchanges between candidates just as common in the past when parties ran their campaigns?

2. Do attack ads drive less-partisan citizens away from the voting booth, as Ansolabehere and Iyengar argue? What other reasons might there be that explain why rates of voting are so low in contemporary American elections?

3. Is negativity as important to democracy as Geer argues? Could candidates conduct campaigns in a more civil manner than at present without diminishing their democratic content?

4. What kind of campaign best fulfills your own conception of a democratic electoral process? What is the best balance of positive campaign ads and ads criticizing the other side? How much should a campaign rely on door-to-door canvassing by volunteers and how much on creative use of media at the national level?

Suggested Readings and Internet Resources

For texts that cover campaigns and elections in the United States, see Stephen K. Medvic, *Campaigns and Elections: Players and Processes* (Boston, Mass.: Wadsworth, 2010) and James A. Thurber and Candice J. Nelson, eds., *Campaigns and Elections American Style*, 3rd ed. (Boulder, Colo.: Westview Press, 2009). Darrell West presents a history of campaign advertising on television in *Air Wars: Televised Advertising in Election Campaigns: 1952–2008*, 5th ed. (Washington, D.C.: CQ Press, 2010). For a sophisticated portrait of the American electorate, see Karen M. Kaufmann, John R. Petrocik, and Daron R. Shaw, *Unconventional Wisdom: Facts and Myths About American Voters* (New York: Oxford University Press, 2008). Analyses of the remarkable 2008 elections can be found in Michael Nelson, ed., *The Elections of 2008* (Washington, D.C.: CQ Press, 2010) and James W. Ceaser, Andrew E. Busch, and John J. Pitney, Jr., *Epic Journey: The 2008 Elections and American Politics* (Lanham, Md.: Rowman and Littlefield, 2009).

Politics Magazine
www.politicsmagazine.com
An online magazine devoted to campaigns and elections.

Campaigns Wikia
www.campaigns.wikia.com
An interactive wikia site for those involved in electoral campaigning.

FiveThirtyEight
http://www.fivethirtyeight.com
Statistical guru Nate Silver provides powerful analyses of elections on his site, named for the total votes in the Electoral College, and political activists on the left and right flock to respond with their comments.

Chapter 12

✳

The Federal Budget: Is the Deficit a Threat to the Nation?

A big issue underlying the partisan divide in Washington (covered in Chapter 10) is the size of government. Simply put, Americans disagree about how big government, especially the federal government, should be. With the exception of the military, Republicans generally want to scale back the federal government and turn its functions over to state and local governments, the private sector, and nonprofits, including churches. Democrats generally defend a more vigorous role for the federal government, especially to protect the environment, children, workers, minorities, and the elderly. Underlying the nasty debate over health care reform in 2009–2010 was this philosophical difference about the size and role of government.

Debates over the size of government intensify when budget deficits soar. After a short period of federal budget surpluses (1998–2001), the federal government racked up the largest budget deficits in history under Presidents Bush and Obama. Bush passed massive tax cuts and just before he left office authorized the spending of $868 billion for bank bailouts and economic stimulus. The Congressional Budget Office estimates the Obama administration, in an effort to prop up a struggling financial system and stimulate an ailing economy, will have a record $1.5 trillion deficit for 2009. The Republicans have fiercely criticized Obama for expanding the deficit and the size of the federal government—with some calling it a socialist takeover. Obama defended the necessity of vigorous federal action, but in response to critics he promised to freeze expenditures on nonmilitary discretionary spending and he established a bipartisan deficit commission to recommend ways to get the federal government's fiscal house in order.

At the beginning of the twenty-first century, the democratic debate on deficits and the size of government has rarely been hotter.

It has not always been this way. At various points in history, Americans seemed to be approaching a consensus on the size of government. Driven by Franklin Roosevelt's New Deal and World War II, the size of the federal government grew tremendously during the 1930s and 1940s. Military spending declined rapidly right after World War II, but the Cold War with the Soviet Union caused it to shoot up again. When Republican Dwight Eisenhower won the presidency in 1952, he did not try to roll back the New Deal but accepted the broad contours of the welfare state. In the 1960s, Lyndon Johnson's Great Society expanded the size of federal government with new programs aimed both at the poor (Medicaid) and the elderly of all classes (Medicare). Despite his reputation as a conservative, Richard Nixon supported a large federal government, although he tried to reform many federal programs by giving more power over them to state and local governments.

The broad acceptance of a muscular federal government was supported by the belief that government could smooth out the business cycle and prevent depressions, like the one that crippled the U.S. economy in the 1930s. Known as Keynesian economics, this idea was developed by English economist John Maynard Keynes (1883–1946). Keynes argued that economic downturns are caused by inadequate consumer spending. As the economy begins to tumble into a recession, Keynes recommended that the government deliberately engineer deficits, spending more than it takes in from taxes. By pumping money into the economy, government spending, Keynes argued, would get the economy moving again toward full employment. By the 1960s, it was widely accepted that federal fiscal policy could prevent depressions and help keep unemployment low. Reflecting the consensus, Richard Nixon was quoted in a 1971 *Newsweek* cover story as saying, "We are all Keynesians now."

The election of Ronald Reagan in 1980 shattered the illusion that Americans agreed on the need for a large federal government. In his inaugural address, Reagan famously charged that "government is not the solution to our problems; government is the problem." In 1981, Reagan succeeded in enacting one of the largest tax cuts in American history.

Reagan's tax cuts were supported by an intellectual challenge to Keynesian economics known as supply-side economics. Supply-siders argue that economic stagnation is not caused by inadequate consumer spending but by problems on the supply (or production) side—basically, inadequate capital investment. High tax rates, they maintain, reduce the incentive to work and invest. (Ronald Reagan was fond of telling the story of how he quit making movies when the marginal tax rate hit 94 percent during World War II.)

Supply-siders go further, saying that reducing tax rates can actually lead to *greater* tax revenues by fueling economic growth. This idea is based on the Laffer curve, first proposed in 1974 by economist Arthur B. Laffer, a co-author of one of our selections. The Laffer curve plots how government revenues increase as tax rates go up. At higher rates the curve slopes downward, however, because higher tax rates discourage work and investment and therefore tax revenues go down even though rates are higher. When we are at this point on the Laffer curve, we can actually increase revenues by lowering tax rates because the lower rates will stimulate economic growth. (The debate is not about whether the Laffer curve exists but where we are on the curve. Critics maintain that we have not passed the point where increased tax rates actually decrease tax revenues.)

The Reagan administration was more successful at cutting taxes than at reducing the size of government. As a result, budget deficits soared in the 1980s. Debate continued on whether the tax cuts helped the economy. Following Reagan's lead, at the 1988 Republican convention George H. W. Bush made his famous "no new taxes" pledge—memorialized by the refrain "read my lips." As president, Bush came under tremendous pressure to deal with soaring deficits, and in 1990 he signed a budget bill that included modest tax increases. By agreeing to tax increases, Bush undermined his credibility, contributing to his defeat by Bill Clinton in 1992.

Early in his own presidency, Clinton narrowly passed a tax increase that fell almost entirely on the wealthy and he tried, but failed, to pass a major new expansion of the federal government to provide universal health insurance. In his 1995 State of the Union address Clinton seemed to embrace a new centrist view of a more modest role for the federal government when he declared, "The era of big government is over." Partly as a result of tax increases and restraints on spending, as well as vigorous economic growth in the 1990s, Clinton left office with large budget surpluses.

Record budget surpluses under Clinton turned to record budget deficits under his successor, George W. Bush. The causes of these deficits are subject to dispute, but everyone agrees that the economic recession played a role, as did the added expenses of the war on terrorism and the occupations of Afghanistan and Iraq. Also, during his first year in office, President Bush succeeded in passing a ten-year, $1.35 trillion tax cut that contributed significantly to the deficit. As we noted earlier, faced with an economic and financial crisis, budget deficits under Obama have soared far beyond those under Bush.

Our first selection is by Nobel prize-winning economist, Joseph Stiglitz, former Chair of the Council of Economic Advisers under President Clinton. Stiglitz argues that we should not be obsessed with deficit reduction, especially in times of economic recession. What matters, Stiglitz stresses, is not whether we engage in deficit spending but how those funds are invested: If we are going into debt to finance an ill-advised war or to give tax cuts to the wealthy, then deficit spending makes us worse off; but if we are going into debt to put people back to work and to invest in education and new technologies to address global warming, then deficit spending can make us stronger.

Arthur Laffer, an economic adviser under President Reagan, and Stephen Moore, president of the Club for Growth, an organization headquartered in Washington, D.C., which lobbies on behalf of smaller government, disagree with Stiglitz that government deficit spending can make us stronger. They argue that the government has "gone crazy" with deficit spending and transfer payments from the rich to the poor that are damaging the economy. Based on the "common sense" of supply-side economics, Laffer and Moore say that the truth is simple: "If government taxes people who work, and pays people who don't work, it should come as no surprise if a lot of people stop working." Putting government on a low-fat diet, they conclude, will lead to an outpouring of new investment and jobs.

The debate on deficits and the size of government often seems to hinge on technical issues, such as the disincentive effects of marginal tax rates. However, underlying the debate are value-laden questions. Supply-siders argue that cutting taxes on high incomes will stimulate more investment than will cutting taxes on working people. But are tax cuts for the wealthy fair—even if they do stimulate economic growth? Similarly, if you value negative freedom (see the introduction to this book), then you will want government to be as small as possible. But if you think that positive freedom requires an active government, you will see an enlarged federal government as a potential friend of liberty. The debate on the size of government and deficits resonates with many of the same value conflicts found in Chapter 3 on federalism and Chapter 5 on political economy.

The Federal Budget Deficit Is Not Necessarily a Threat to the Nation

JOSEPH STIGLITZ

Budget debates are a useful way of trying to focus attention on fundamental issues [of] the country's priorities. But they also reflect views of the economy, of economic behavior. I think it's understandable that there should be a lot of focus on the deficit at the current time [April 2007] given the absolute mismanagement of the budget macroeconomic policies over the last six years. The magnitude of the increase in the deficit in the last six years has been very large.

But as one recognizes that we've had six years of badly managed budgets and badly managed macroeconomics, we have to look at what the realities of our economy are today. And that includes addressing some of the important social and economic priorities. As we talk about deficits, we have to ask the following question about economic structure. If deficits lead to decreased growth, then a dollar spent on some activity has a cost that is in some sense greater than a dollar... [b]ecause we spend a dollar... [and] [w]e don't change taxes. The economy doesn't grow as well. On the other hand, if deficits lead to a stronger economy, then that means the net cost is less than a dollar. And to ascertain that, one has to make a judgment about where the economy is today.

There are four propositions I want to put forward.... The first is that we should never actually focus just on deficits, but on broader economic concepts. The deficit is only one of several accounting frameworks. And it's probably not the best way of assessing either the fiscal position of the economy or its economic position....

The second is deficits may or may not matter depending how the money is spent, how they arise and the state of the economy. The third is that the country has a large number of priorities, real priorities. I'll only talk about three of them, the challenge of globalization, the growing inequality, the health care crisis. But there are others such as our problems of energy and climate change. Meeting these, some of these, will require spending money that might create the larger deficit. And I'm going to try to argue that in fact if this money is spent well; it does make sense to do that, even if it led to a greater deficit.

And the fourth proposition is that the current state of the economy is such that deficit reduction, done the wrong way, could have a large macroeconomic cost. So that if you put it another way, if we spend money the right way, it could have two benefits, the direct benefit as well as the benefits that come from macroeconomic stimulation.

Maybe I should begin by giving what I think are two further points that are illustrative of these four points that I hope represent a consensus, not of everybody in Washington, but I think of all the right-thinking people in Washington.

The first is that we as a nation and world would be better off if we ended the war in Iraq and reduced defense expenditure. That not only the expenditures in Iraq, but Star Wars weapons, represent weapons that don't work against enemies that don't exist. And if you waste money, that's a bad thing. Keynes talked about digging holes and pump priming and argued that even that could be a benefit. But I think given the list of priorities that the country has, we have a lot better ways of spending money than this particular form of pump priming. And in fact, this particular form of pump priming doesn't prime the pump very much. Because, as I argued in my paper on the Iraq war costs, the feedbacks of the re-expenditures don't come back to America as strongly as other forms of expenditure.

The second proposition, illustrative of this general view, is that there are ways of changing our tax structure, raising taxes on upper-income individuals, lowering taxes on lower-income individuals, packages that could reduce the deficit and strengthen the macro economy. So, a redesign of our tax structure could accomplish several of the objectives that I have talked about earlier.

Now, behind what I'm saying right now is a view that the economy is potentially going through a difficult time. I think most people see the economy right now as being weak. The consensus forecasts are that growth in the United States will be slower this year than it was last year. And even conservative economists see a significant probability of a serious slowdown of the economy. Some people even see a recession. The mistakes in tax and monetary policy that we have made over the last six years are coming home to roost.

The mistaken tax policy, the tax cuts of 2001 and 2003, forced the burden of macroeconomic adjustment on monetary policy that led to low interest rates. Low interest rates did not lead to high levels of investments. The nation's balance sheet in a sense was such that people took on more debt. But they didn't spend that debt in productive real investments. In traditional monetary policy, lower interest rates lead to more investments.

So ... while there's more public debt, there's also an increase on the asset side. In this particular case, what happened was that people refinanced their mortgages, took out larger mortgages. And it was the real estate sector, both directly and indirectly through refinancing of housing that provided a major stimulus to the economy that helped us to get out of the recession of 2001. But that has left a legacy of indebtedness. And it's important in this not to look at average numbers, but the whole distribution.

And that we are now seeing real problems in the subprime sector. And it's now reflecting in some other sectors that are also risky sectors of the mortgage market. Forecasts continue to be that private housing prices will decline. It will be difficult to sustain the economy. In other words, in the last couple of years, consumption has been sustained by people taking money out of their houses. With house prices going down, that's going to be very difficult to continue, and let alone to increase in a way that would facilitate growth.

And that is one of the reasons that many people are pessimistic about the economy today. The problem is with that kind of weak economy, fiscal contraction—particularly poorly designed fiscal contraction—would exacerbate the problem and therefore risk the economy having a more significant slowdown than it otherwise would have had.

Now, that means we have to focus a great deal on managing aggregate demand and the difficult problem of rectifying the balances that we accumulated over the last six years. And there are ways of doing it.... We can redefine our tax structure in a way that would address the problem of the growing inequality in our society, stimulate the economy and reduce the deficit. But that will require careful modeling, careful analysis.

In 1993, at the beginning of the Clinton administration, we faced a problem of a very large deficit, much larger than today, and a weak economy. And we designed a package that had the effect of stimulating the economy. But we were very careful in designing the tax policies. We postponed the tax increases, most of the tax increases, until after the economy had recovered. And we focused what tax increases there were on upper-income individuals so the impact would be minimal.

As another example, I think stronger expenditures on social programs—strengthened safety nets, more provisions for unemployment insurance—could again enhance growth and stability and help the economy face the challenges of globalization.

Before talking about these challenges of globalization, I want ... to emphasize a little bit more ... what deficits mean and why we shouldn't focus on deficits themselves. What really matters is the country's balance sheet, its assets and its liabilities. Consider a company. You would never say, oh, this company is borrowing a lot and therefore, it is a bad company. You would always say what is it borrowing for? Is it for investment? You want to look at both its assets and its liabilities. You want to look at its balance sheet.

And you might also want to look at some of these cash accounts. But you would certainly want to look at its balance sheet. Well, when we talk about the deficit, we're talking about only one part of that balance sheet. We're talking about what's happening to the liabilities, what it owes, but not to what it's spending the money on.

And if you are borrowing money, which the United States has done, to finance a war in Iraq or to finance a tax cut for upper-income Americans, then the country is being left worse off. The balance sheet does look worse. You have a liability, but you don't have any asset on the other side. But if you are borrowing money to invest in education, technology, or, say, the safety net, then you may have a stronger economy. And this is particularly true when you're facing the kind of problem that our economy is facing today.

Yesterday, I was talking to the former Finance Minister of Sweden. And Sweden has been one of the countries that has been most successful in facing the challenges of globalization. It's a small economy, very open, with a significant manufacturing sector. In terms of some of the rhetoric that you hear in Washington and elsewhere, it should have been a disaster case. They have one of the highest tax rates. And it's not only true in Sweden: Finland and all the other Scandinavian also have very high tax rates. If you only looked at tax rates, you would say these countries would be a disaster. And we had a discussion in which the view was that their success was *in spite of*. No, it's not only in spite of, it was *because of* the high tax rates.

Why is that? It sounds counterintuitive. Well, the answer is it's how the money is spent. Again, looking at both sides of the balance sheet ... [i]t was spent in ways that led to a stronger economy, enabling the economy to face some of the challenges of globalization. The net result of this is that, for instance, Sweden and the other Scandinavian countries do much better than the United States on broader measures of success like human development indicators that look at not just GDP per capita, but also look at health and longevity in terms of labor force participation. They're doing very well. And they have a sense of social solidarity.

In a whole variety of indicators, they are doing not only well, but better than the United States. The United States has been, as I say, facing the big challenges of globalization and of inequality.... While U.S. GDP has been growing, median income in the United States has been stagnating, actually going down in the most recent years. And people at the bottom, salaries have also been stagnating, not just recently but for a number of years.

Globalization necessitates people responding to change or moving from job-to-job. And in the Swedish model, they responded by providing for active labor policies and systems of social insurance that facilitate people moving from job-to-job and provide them with security. One of the aspects of success in a modern economy is willingness to undertake risk. And they would argue that because they have greater security, people are more willing to take risk. They've managed their macro economy to have full employment. But not only full employment at low [inflation], but full employment at high wages.

And so they have addressed a lot of the problems of insecurity, not perfectly but far better I think than the United States. And the result is, at least in many of the countries of Scandinavia, a much greater willingness to embrace change, the kinds of change that one needs in a dynamic economy.

All of this takes money. It doesn't come free. How you finance that, whether you do it out of taxes or deficits, may be of second order importance.

In the long run, obviously, things have to be paid for. Resources have to be paid for. But as Keynes said, in the long run we're all dead. In the short run, we face a situation where we have the risk of a weak economy. And that short run context involves, a combination, I think, of a restructuring of our tax structure that would stimulate the economy more and provide greater equality to deal with the growing inequality that has faced the country over the last thirty years.

This would allow individuals to take more risk, invest more in education and technology, assisting active labor market policies that allow people to move from job-to-job. These kinds of comprehensive investment programs I think can provide the basis of a more dynamic economy that will in fact lead to, not only greater economic growth, but a more cohesive society.

Finally, let me just say a few words about a couple of the other issues that I think are areas that we need to spend more....

The first is that there has been a lot of misrepresentation of the nature of the problems that we face.... [There is] a problem with our health care system as a whole, both public and private. And there are a couple of things within our health care system that we can do that would potentially address again a very significant fraction of the problem.

For instance, we are facing skyrocketing drug costs. And a few reforms, like allowing the government to bargain for prices and creating a pharmacology list of drugs that are more effective like Australia does, would do wonders in using drugs more effectively. So what we need here is social science innovation—not even innovation, to compare with our innovation in our medical sciences—to figure out how to deliver the medicines in a way that is more efficient.

In general, the innovation system that we have for testing and making drugs is a very inefficient system based on monopoly and conflicts of interest, a variety of distortions, which lead to higher prices and I think less performance certainly per dollar spent.

A second observation is that practices, standard practices, on a large number of areas differ in various parts of the country. And in ways that are not really systematically related to outcome. And that at least suggests that if you switched from the most expensive to the least expensive practices that are consistent with equally good outcomes, there would be very large savings in costs that would help put the health care system on sound footing.

Now, the final challenge I wanted to just mention very briefly is climate change. I think the evidence that has come out this year has made it even more compelling than it was in the past. I was on the governmental panel of climate change in the 1995 review. And the evidence was overwhelming then. But we made a mistake. We did not expect, I think, it to play out as fast as it has. One of the aspects in which it's come out much faster is, for instance, we didn't anticipate the melting of the Arctic as rapidly....

[I]t is clear that the accumulation of greenhouse gases in the atmosphere represents a significant risk. If we had many planets, we'd conduct an experiment on this planet and if it comes out the way that almost all the scientists are agreed will happen, we go onto the next one and say, well, we made a mistake. Too bad. That would be one thing. But the fact is we can't go onto another planet. And if we make a mistake here, we have no alternative. And the consequences could be very severe....

Some of the things we can do to deal with global warming will actually save us money. Getting rid of the energy subsidies that we have, including the depletion allowances that we have for oil, would save us money. The ethanol subsidies are outrageous. It almost costs as much in oil to get a gallon of ethanol, so the net output of that system is almost negative. We have a 50-cent tax on sugar-based ethanol, for instance, from Brazil. And we give a 50-cent subsidy to American corn-based ethanol. So we have an enormously distorted system. And getting rid of some of these distortions in energy would actually save us money.

But there are other things we will need to spend money on. We will need to spend money on a whole variety of technological innovations to address the challenges proposed by global warming. Research expenditures in this area have actually gone down in the last twenty years. So these are examples of things where we will need to spend money.

In short ... don't just ever focus on the deficit. Look at the broader set of issues. Among the broader set of issues are where the economy is today? And the economy today, I think, has a certain degree of precariousness where unthoughtful deficit reduction could have adverse effects. I think there are ways of restructuring our tax structures that could stimulate the economy, address some of the most problems of growing and equality and reduce the deficit.

But more generally, there is a wide agenda facing our society, important priorities that need to be addressed that will require expenditures. And the value of spending has to be weighed against the cost of any deficit. I think there are lots of ways that we can cut expenditures, most importantly in the defense area. But if we fail to do that, it is still almost surely worthwhile spending money in these other areas even if it has some effect on the deficit.

The Federal Deficit Is a Threat to the Nation

ARTHUR B. LAFFER AND STEPHEN MOORE

I wouldn't have gone through the analysis of transfer payments and government spending in such detail if this administration's and Congress's stimulus package were small. But frankly, government stimulus spending over the past several years is not small, and worse, there's no sign that it's over yet. The Bush administration and the Obama administration, along with Congress, have gone crazy, and I mean crazy, on government spending and on transfer payments. Take a look at some of the numbers and their implications, as shown in Figure 12.1.

But the official federal government spending numbers in Figure 12.1 grossly understate the true amount of federal spending. The stimulus package in March 2008 was along the lines of $170 billion and is included in the spending number. But the equivalent of the spending bailout of AIG on a cumulative basis came out to a transfer payment of about $185 billion and is not in the spending numbers. And even before the bailout of AIG there were massive supplements to the housing and agricultural bills. Additionally, the Fed acquired a number of toxic assets from their asset swaps with Bear Stearns and other financial firms, and goodness only knows how much value those toxic assets have already lost. The loss in value wasn't trivial and is nowhere to be found in the published data.

Government guarantees of all the mortgage liabilities of Fannie Mae, Ginnie Mae, and Freddie Mac were also huge. Today Fannie Mae and Freddie Mac guarantee somewhere around $5.0 to $5.5 trillion worth of mortgages in the United States. The equivalent amount of transfers representing the unfunded liabilities from defaults of these guaranteed mortgages I put at about $550 billion. I obviously really can't be sure of that number, which I've estimated to be a little

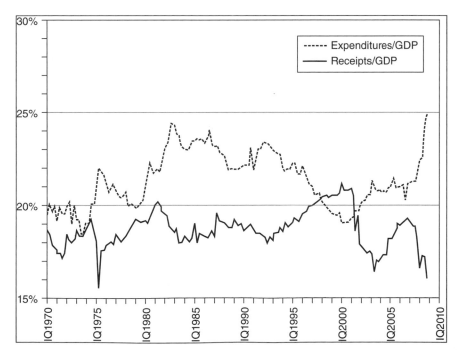

FIGURE 12.1   Federal Government Expenditures and Receipts as a % of GDP. (quarterly through IQ2009)

Source: Bureau of Economic Analysis, National Income and Product Accounts.

over 10 percent of the total guarantees in expected defaults. The unfunded liabilities number could be substantially larger than $550 billion.

After the Fannie Mae and Freddie Mac guarantees, along came the Paulson plan, the bailout plan, which was a $700 billion program on top of the earlier stimulus spending. The next stimulus package was $787 billion, which came in under President Barack Obama. In the meantime there were numerous bank bailouts, auto company takeovers, direct intervention in investment banks, taxpayer-funded acquisitions of insurance companies, guarantees of loans by banks via the FDIC, and a threatened total control of the health-care and health-insurance industries, not to mention more than thirty official policy czars tasked with micromanaging various sectors of the economy. These numbers, in the words of the incredible linguist Bill Safire of the *New York Times,* are MEGO numbers, which stands for "My Eyes Glaze Over!"

Altogether, including the projected federal budget deficit for fiscal year 2009 of about $1.8 trillion shown in Figure 12.2, I estimate the total amount of stimulus spending to be somewhere in the neighborhood of $3.6 trillion, net.

Back at the end of 2001, the federal net national debt was 35.3 percent of GDP. Today, that figure is reported to be 59.0 percent of GDP in 2009 and is estimated to be 69.3 percent in 2010. Over the past eight years there has been a huge increase in the net national debt as a share of GDP, as officially measured. But these numbers don't take into account the net losses or unfunded liabilities from the federal government's asset swaps. My guess, if you looked at the

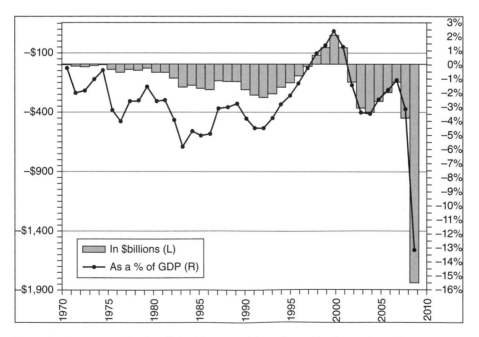

FIGURE 12.2   Federal Deficits (–)/Surplus (+), and as a % of GDP. (annual through 2009[e])

Source: Bureau of Economic Analysis, National Income and Product Accounts.

unfunded liabilities of Fannie Mae, Freddie Mac, AIG, and all these other government transfers, is that the grand total of federal net debt would be about 100 percent of GDP instead of 59.0 percent of GDP.

And the truly scary part is that President Obama does not want to change course. Martin Feldstein agrees with my assessment in a recent *Wall Street Journal* editorial:

> The deficits projected for the next decade and beyond are unprecedented.... The CBO's deficit, projections are based on the optimistic assumptions that the economy will grow at a healthy 3% pace with no recessions during the next decade; that there will be no new spending programs after this year's budget; and that the rising national debt will increase the rate of interest on government bonds by less than 1%. More realistic assumptions would imply a 2019 deficit of more than 8% of GDP and a government debt of more than 100% of GDP.

To get a flavor of what the 100 percent of GDP number by itself means, imagine a constant long-term government bond rate of interest of 4 percent. At the end of 2001, a national debt of 35 percent of GDP with a 4 percent rate of interest on that debt would mean that annual interest payments would be 1.4 percent of GDP.

Now in 2001, because we had such a strong economy and also because the tax codes are so highly progressive, federal tax receipts were 22 percent of GDP (please see Figure 12.1). Therefore, a little less than 6.5 percent of total tax receipts had to be dedicated to paying interest on the national debt. Today total debt is around 100 percent of GDP. With a 4 percent rate of interest on that debt, total annual interest payments will be 4 percent of GDP just to keep the official debt where it is.

Because of all these truly ill-conceived public policies under Presidents Bush and Obama, the economy is reaching new lows. Not only has GDP fallen dramatically, but also tax receipts as a share of GDP have fallen dramatically, again because of the very progressive nature of U.S. federal taxes (Figure 12.1). Today, federal tax receipts are 16 percent of GDP. To pay 4 percent of GDP in interest on the national debt, and yet collect only .16 percent of GDP in the form of taxes, means that 25 percent of total federal tax receipts has to go to pay annual interest on the national debt. Yikes!

In a mere eight years from 2001 to today, the United States has gone from a little under 6.5 percent of total tax receipts going to paying interest on the national debt to about 25 percent. This is a disastrous trend with no end in sight. Not only is it impossible for a poor person to spend himself into prosperity, it's also impossible for a country to borrow itself into prosperity.

The spending spree of 2008 and 2009 and the subsequent economic collapse has worsened an already insurmountable problem facing the United States—total unfunded liabilities of the U.S. federal government. Unfunded liabilities are promises for future payment that the federal government has made to individuals without having either the current resources or future taxes in place to pay for these promises. Unfunded liabilities include:

Unfunded Liability	Obligation ($ in trillions)
The actual federal debt as of 2009	7.6
Future Social Security payments	18.7
Future Medicare hospital insurance payments	14.5
Future Medicare Supplementary (Part B) payments	13.5
Future Medicare Prescription Drug Benefit payments	5.2
Disabled veterans' compensation	1.5
Pensions for military personnel	1.2
Pensions for other civilian government employees	1.5
Health benefits for military personnel	0.8
Health benefits for other civilian government employees	0.3
Railroad retirement fund	0.08
Expected Pension Benefit Guaranty Corporation costs	0.06
Expected costs to the FDIC	0.01
Other federal civilian employees benefits	0.05
Loan guarantees	0.07
Other military/veteran benefits	0.03
Other insurance	0.03
National flood insurance	0.005
TOTAL	65.135

These unfunded liabilities, when totaled, increased by $8.1 trillion in 2008 to $65.1 trillion. Put another way, every household in the United States today owes $557,745 due to the current federal unfunded liabilities! And these don't even include the potential unfunded liabilities that could arise due to the government's explicit backing of Fannie Mae's, Freddie Mac's, and Ginnie Mae's mortgage portfolios or the potential costs to the Federal Reserve's balance sheet due to all the risky assets they have purchased. Truly these numbers are astronomical.

When considered in the context of current U.S. GDP and federal tax receipts, the numbers surrounding unfunded liabilities are mind-numbing. At the end of 2008 total federal government unfunded liabilities were somewhere between four and five times U.S. annual GDP. The increase in these unfunded liabilities in 2008 alone was more than half of one year's GDP.

In terms of total federal tax revenues, total unfunded liabilities represent twenty-six-plus years of all taxes, including every tax now collected by the U.S. federal government. The increase in last year's unfunded liabilities represented more than three years' worth of federal tax receipts. These numbers swamp any official deficit numbers, and they don't even include the unfunded liabilities of state and local governments. The economy is like a train heading toward a granite wall at one hundred miles per hour. It will stop! The only question is how.

It astounds me how much damage a few people can cause when they take control of government. Their policies reflect a basic ignorance of Econ 1. If government taxes people who work, and pays people who don't work, it should come as no surprise if a lot of people stop working. It's just common sense.

If after all the tragedy that has befallen the U.S. economy since Secretary Paulson and Congress squealed like five-year-olds in a scary movie, you still believe that something should have been done, then I'll show you a far better way to solve the economy's problems. Imagine what would have happened if Presidents Bush or Obama had used the supply-side solution.

Total federal tax receipts are currently projected to be about $2.2 trillion on an annual basis. According to my estimates, the Bush and Obama administrations have used in total about $3.6 trillion in spending to stimulate the economy, which happens to be one and a half years' worth of total federal tax receipts. Imagine what the U.S. economy would look like today if instead of spending $3.6 trillion, we had instead had a federal tax holiday for a full one and one half years.

Total federal tax receipts today amount to $2.2 trillion. I'm not talking just about the income tax, either. The personal federal income tax is currently projected to raise almost $1 trillion in fiscal year 2009. The corporate income tax will raise $175 billion, and the federal payroll tax, both employer and employee contributions, should amount to $800 billion. And all federal excise taxes, including gas taxes, amount to about $66 billion. The inheritance tax will raise $26 billion. If you look at all federal taxes combined, you come up with a total number for all taxes of $2.2 trillion. Total federal taxes for a year and a half add up to $3.3 trillion, which is almost exactly what the Bush and Obama administrations spent to supposedly stimulate the economy.

Imagine what the unemployment rate would be today if President Obama had proposed a federal tax holiday for a year and a half. The unemployment rate today, instead of being about 10 percent, would be 3 percent. And people would not have dropped out of the labor force because there were no jobs. Average full-time hours would be way up, as would participation rates. High-paying jobs would be rapidly outpacing low-paying jobs and the number of part-time workers would be declining relative to full-time workers.

Not only would the unemployment rate have gone way down, but output, employment, and production would have soared, and the deficit consequences would have been no worse than they have been for all the misguided spending programs that President Obama, President Bush, and Congress have foisted on us.

That's what should have been done if anything should have been done at all. If only politicians understood Econ 1. If taxes on workers and producers are reduced there will be more workers and producers. Is that so hard to understand?

If more production and employment is what is wanted, then reduce taxes on employment and reduce taxes on production. That's how to create prosperity. Bingo.

Never again should our federal government be allowed to deliberately run a budget deficit larger than 5 percent of GDP including increases in unfunded liabilities of federal government programs. All federal programs, to the extent possible, should be based on defined-contribution characteristics, not defined-benefit characteristics.* Government accounting should be subjected to the same accounting standards private industry is currently required to adhere to, with similar penalties for malfeasance.

Put Government on a Low-Fat Diet   Addressing our long-term unfunded liabilities also requires addressing our current spending habits. The government is simply spending too much money. More troubling, much of this spending is being wasted on corporate bailouts and ineffective tax rebates that are worsening the unfunded-liabilities crisis.

To lessen the burden immediately, all stimulus and bailout funds that have not been spent should be impounded. Any ownership rights government has acquired in private companies via bailouts should be sold as quickly as is feasible, and the government should refrain from any exercise of control on those companies. Fannie Mae, Freddie Mac, and Ginnie Mae should stop buying and guaranteeing mortgages immediately and should develop a plan to sell their current inventory of mortgages they own in the private market. The Federal Reserve should be admonished not to acquire any major stakes in private firms save for very short-term stabilization reasons. These actions will have the effect of stopping the growth in our unfunded liabilities and will eventually begin to bring these liabilities down.

Longer-term, structural changes are required that will help prevent a recurrence of our current spending crisis. There are several simple reforms that will change the tax-and-spend incentives of Washington, D.C.

First, Congress and all government employees should be required to live by the letter of the law, and all the provisions that apply to other citizens for whom the laws apply. They should be required to retire on Social Security like everyone else and have no other retirement benefits provided separately by the government. They should be provided with health care and other perquisites commensurate with those given to other citizens. All laws should be applicable to all politicians.

Second, Congress should not be allowed to place earmarks on legislation and thereby circumvent the congressional vetting process. A bill in its final form should be allowed to be voted on only after two full weeks have elapsed to allow Congress to fully understand and assess the implications of all legislation.

Last, the president should be granted the authority for a line item veto that would require a two-thirds majority vote of Congress to override.

Discussion Questions

1.   Critics of large budget deficits argue that they benefit older Americans but push the costs forward to young people who will have to pay back the debt. Do you think young people are more concerned about deficits than older

---

* In defined-contribution plans, the employer's contribution to an employee's retirement plan is defined, but the future benefit is determined by contributions and investment returns. IRAs and 401(k) plans are common defined-contribution plans in the United States.

people? Do large deficits redistribute burdens from one generation to the next? How would Stiglitz respond to this charge?

2. Polls show that only a small percentage of voters are concerned about the record deficits. Why do you think this is? Are you concerned?

3. President Bush frequently criticized taxes because the government essentially takes "your money" from you. Do you agree? In what sense could it be argued that part of what we earn we "owe" to society? How do we know how much?

4. Some scholars argue that democracies have a built-in tendency toward deficits because politicians have incentives to spend more than they take in to get reelected. Do you think politicians pander to voters that way? Assuming deficits are a problem, do you think that voters will vote for someone who promises to raise taxes or cut spending in order to cut the deficit? Would you?

5. Do you think the present federal government is too big or too small? What programs would you like to see expanded? What programs would you like to see cut? Why?

Suggested Readings and Internet Resources

For a basic history of budget battles and the Republican Party's opposition to taxes, see Sheldon Pollack, *Refinancing America: The Republican Antitax Agenda* (Albany: State University of New York Press, 2003). Former Secretary of Commerce Peter G. Peterson criticizes both Republicans and Democrats for tolerating large deficits in *Running on Empty: How the Democratic and Republican Parties Are Bankrupting Our Future and What Americans Can Do About It* (New York: Picador, 2004). President Clinton's Treasury Secretary, Robert Rubin, tells how he worked to reduce deficits and deal with financial crises in a memoir (coauthored with Jacob Weisberg), *Uncertain World: Tough Choices from Wall Street to Washington* (New York: Random House, 2003). In *Locked in the Cabinet* (New York: Alfred A. Knopf, 1997), Robert Reich, Secretary of Labor under Clinton, gives a much more critical view of Rubin's deficit-reduction efforts, maintaining that the administration gave up on important domestic priorities in order to satisfy Wall Street.

Congressional Budget Office (CBO)
www.cbo.gov
The CBO is the staff arm of Congress on budgetary issues. To quote from its website: "CBO aims to provide the Congress with the objective, timely, nonpartisan analyses needed for economic and budgetary decisions and with the information and estimates required for the Congressional budget process."

OMB Watch
www.ombwatch.org
Located in Washington, D.C., OMB Watch was founded in 1983 to critically examine the information and analysis put out by the White House Office of

Management and Budget. A nonprofit research and advocacy organization dedicated to promoting government accountability and citizen participation, OMB Watch focuses on four main areas: the federal budget, regulatory policy, public access to government information, and policy participation by nonprofit organizations.

Club for Growth
www.clubforgrowth.org
This 9,000-member organization is guided by supply-side economics and campaigns and lobbies for tax cuts and smaller government. Its website provides analysis of budget issues from a conservative, free-market point of view, and its campaign contributions support candidates who pledge to reduce taxes.

Center on Budget and Policy Priorities
www.cbpp.org
This is a liberal policy think tank that analyzes budgets and spending programs at the federal and state levels. The site provides in-depth analysis of the federal budget, focusing on spending needs as well as deficit reduction.

Chapter 13

✳

Congress: Can Our Representatives Serve the Public Good?

O f the three branches of the federal government, Congress provides the most direct representation, and it is sometimes called "the people's branch." Yet the American people seldom seem pleased with the performance of "their" branch. Although constituents typically express a positive view of their own representatives or senators, Congress as a whole generally receives very low marks. In a Gallup Poll released in February 2010, for example, only 18 percent of those surveyed had a favorable view of Congress compared to 78 percent who evaluated the institution unfavorably. The public considers Congress to be ineffective at addressing national problems, captive to special interests, and even pockmarked with corrupt practices.

For the forty years between 1954 and 1994, Democrats were the majority party in the House and (with brief exceptions) in the Senate. Thus, they bore the brunt of mounting public disenchantment with Congress. Increasingly individualistic and lacking cohesion, congressional Democrats came to be portrayed, even by sympathetic observers, as running an inefficient and profligate legislature. Democratic rule in Congress was finally terminated in the 1994 elections, when the Republicans, led by master strategist and organizer Newt Gingrich, swept to power.

Gingrich proclaimed a revolution in the House of Representatives that promised to transform how the institution works. In place of a decentralized institution in which individual members catered to district or state interests, he sought to place the unifying forces of leadership and party in charge. Through new rules and bold assertions of leadership, Gingrich and his team consolidated power and kept the focus on the party's agenda. Gingrich made many enemies, and he fell from power in 1998, but his system, revised to bring even tighter control to the Republican leadership, continued under the sway of majority leader Tom DeLay.

Yet as the "Republican revolution" in Congress aged, it came to resemble the Democratic regime that it had overturned. Party leadership, which was supposed to meld individual members into a cohesive team, came to appear autocratic and power hungry. Individual members who had pledged to put principles above pork-barrel projects eagerly sought special benefits ("earmarks") for their districts. The taint of corruption from cozy and profitable ties with lobbyists brought down a number of prominent Republican legislators. Majority leader DeLay fell in 2006 after he was indicted by a grand jury in his home state of Texas.

In the elections of 2006, the Democrats returned to power in the House and the Senate. They significantly expanded their margin of control in both chambers in the 2008 elections. Even with bigger majorities than the Republicans had possessed, however, congressional Democrats were unable to force President Bush to alter his course in the war in Iraq and later struggled with mixed success to enact the top legislative priorities of President Obama. Critics charged that the Democrats were proving no better at running Congress than the Republicans had been. The voters, who had turned against congressional Republicans in recent elections, appeared poised, as the elections of 2010 approached, to take out their unhappiness on the Democrats this time around.

Is Congress today in as poor a shape as the critics allege and the voters believe? Two long-time observers of Congress, Thomas Mann and Norman Ornstein, say yes. In a book that we have excerpted for our first selection, Mann and Ornstein call Congress *The Broken Branch*. The two political scientists diagnose a rash of pathological features that render the current Congress dysfunctional: crude power tactics, nasty polarization, an explosion of earmarks, lax ethical standards, and above all a loss of the capacity for thoughtful deliberation on the problems of the nation. Mann and Ornstein conclude that the country will continue to suffer from these maladies of Congress unless its members adopt new rules and create new structures that will begin the institution's cure.

Another prominent political scientist who studies legislative politics, David Mayhew, replies to Mann and Ornstein with a defense of Congress. Congress only appears "broken," Mayhew contends, because we have an unrealistic standard for its performance. If congressional procedures are messy and policy disagreements are overheated, it is because the members of Congress represent the diverse and often contradictory desires of the constituencies that elected them. If congressional arguments lack the intellectual force of the expert pronouncements that issue from the executive and judicial branches, it is because Congress gives voice to what ordinary Americans think. Mayhew believes that Congress actually produces a steady stream of significant legislation, even when it is under the control of the party that does not occupy the White House. And if voters really become frustrated with its performance, they can—and periodically do—throw out the majority party and allow the former minority the chance to change the institution's direction.

The debate between Mann and Ornstein on one side and Mayhew on the other raises important questions about the role and current functioning of Congress in the American political system. After reading their analyses and arguments, do you think Congress deserves the very low marks that the public ordinarily gives it? Do the features of the contemporary Congress allow it to produce effective responses to the nation's problems? Would a Congress better suited for careful deliberation require that it downplay the popular concerns and grievances that legislators are supposed to represent? Is Congress today a problem for democracy—or a genuine reflection of democracy in action?

Congress Is the Broken Branch

THOMAS E. MANN AND NORMAN J. ORNSTEIN

The bill that brought House members to a fateful vote early on November 23, 2003, was not your average piece of legislation. It was the major social policy initiative of President George W. Bush and the top priority of his congressional leaders. Shortly before six o'clock in the morning on that Sunday, following a debate that began Saturday and a vote that began at 3 a.m., a House of Representatives described by the *New York Times* as "fiercely polarized" passed a bill to provide prescription drug benefits under Medicare. The 220 to 215 vote, begun under the normal procedure that routinely limits votes to fifteen minutes, took two hours and fifty-one minutes to complete; the *Times* piece said it took "an extraordinary bout of Republican arm-twisting to muster a majority."

. . . .

The Medicare prescription drug vote—three hours instead of fifteen minutes—was.... not a unique exception to standard practice, but the extension of a now-common tactic that ended up descending into one of the most breathtaking breaches of the legislative process in the modern history of the House. The way in which the issue played out, and the vote itself, are far more a pattern of the House in the new century—a pattern that more closely resembles the House of the nineteenth century than that of the twentieth....

The problems did not start with the Republican majority in 1995. Signs of institutional decline were much in evidence during the latter years of the longtime Democratic control of Congress. Under pressure from their increasingly ideologically unified members, Democratic leaders resorted to ad hoc arrangements that often circumvented the normal committee process, restrictive rules that limited debate and amendments on the House floor, and behemoth omnibus legislative packages that short-circuited the normal process, limited transparency, and rendered the majority less accountable. Sharp partisan differences on policy created an atmosphere in which the legislative ends could justify any procedural means. Tensions between the parties often reached a boiling point.

By the time the Republicans took control of both ends of Pennsylvania Avenue, it seemed almost natural for the House majority leadership to drive nearly every issue, controversial or not, in partisan ways .... The Democratic majority had in its final years begun to restrict debate and amendments on the House floor, but the practice accelerated sharply under Republican rule. Fewer bills were brought up under open rules, which allow members to offer amendments to the pending legislation. The Republican leadership resorted more frequently to totally closed rules on the House floor, shutting off all attempts at amendment. In the 103rd Congress, under the Democrats, 9 percent of bills came to the floor under closed rules. In both the 106th and 107th, under Republicans, the number went to 22 percent—and to 28 percent in the 108th, 2003–2004. Donald Wolfensberger, former Rules Committee staff director under Republican Chairman Gerald Solomon, has also noted the increased reliance by the GOP on "self-executing" rules, which alter bills automatically when they come to the floor, sometimes for technical corrections but often to accommodate the interests of majority members and leaders. Self-executing rules went from an average of 19 percent of all bills in the 101st–103rd Congresses to 29 percent in the 104th–107th. All of these practices, it should be noted, were roundly denounced by Republicans when they were in the minority....

The Senate managed in the 1990s to avoid much of the deeper division and acrimony that plagued the House, but it too has shown signs of institutional decline. The Senate evolved from a hierarchical institution that was shaped largely by the preferences of its senior conservative Democrats to one that spread the wealth to accommodate the interests—and whims—of every member. The parties in the Senate, just like the House, became more internally unified and ideologically polarized as voters realigned and turnover in the body accelerated. But Senate rules allowing unlimited debate and an open amendment process on the floor limited the degree of centralization and the power and resources given to party leaders.

The Senate became far more a bastion of individualism than the House. Its members more frequently were inclined to place "holds" on bills or nominations to extract concessions. The filibuster, which for decades had been limited to issues of great national significance, became a routine practice as leaders no longer brought the Senate to a halt for unlimited debate but simply raised the bar to two-thirds, and then sixty votes, not fifty, whenever a filibuster threat was raised. By the 1980s, it was used by the minority party as a core element of its legislative strategy on a wide range of bills.

Faced with a higher hurdle, Senate leaders began to make more expansive use of the budget reconciliation process, which operated under special procedures that barred filibusters and allowed a simple majority to act, and began to employ other forms of unorthodox lawmaking. In the past few years of heightened partisanship and shared party stakes between the president and Congress, the Senate has begun to consider more radical steps to move away from its roots and toward the House model. The willingness of Republican Senate leaders to consider seriously a unilateral act to block filibusters on judicial nominations—the so-called nuclear option—was a sign of a breakdown in comity that could easily fracture any remaining bipartisan cooperation in that body.

Of course, a time traveler from the nineteenth century would laugh at the idea that the Congress has careened out of control. Partisan acrimony? How about a senator caned to within an inch of his life on the Senate floor by a House member who disagreed with his abolitionist positions. Highhandedness by a Speaker? Penny-ante compared to the arbitrary exercise of power by Speakers Thomas Brackett Reed and Joseph Cannon in the era from 1890–1910. But the rough-and-tumble of the first hundred years of American democracy, before Congress became institutionalized to meet the needs of an industrial society, should not minimize the difficulties to the American system caused by a broken Congress in the post-industrial age of terrorism, in a society with a GDP of over $13 trillion and a federal budget approaching $3 trillion.

It would also be a mistake to suggest that the problems facing Congress are all the result of the actions or misjudgments of a handful of Republican leaders. As we have noted, many of the larger problems plaguing Congress, including partisan tensions, the demise of regular order, and growing incivility, began years ago, when Democrats were in the majority and Republicans in the minority. Their roots, and the reasons they have gotten demonstrably worse, are firmly implanted in larger political dynamics.

The Rise of Partisan Polarization

Members, and leaders, have choices. But the performance of Congress is shaped powerfully by the broader context in which it operates. Political developments in the South over the past fifty years, chronicled powerfully by Nelson Polsby in his book *How Congress Evolves,* profoundly changed the partisan dynamic in Congress and the ideological composition of the parties. The House of the 1930s through the 1970s had a Democratic majority populated by many Southern conservatives as well as Northern liberals. Conflicts on issues often crossed party lines, driven more by ideology and regional interests. The House lost virtually all of its Southern conservative Democrats, leaving a more homogeneous and left-of-center party. At the same time, the Republican Party, partly as a consequence of this secular realignment in the South, has become even more distinctively conservative, with an ambitious agenda revolving around tax cuts, an assertive national defense, and religious traditionalism.

This ideological sorting by party has now extended to voters, activists, and elected officials throughout the country, creating two rival teams whose internal unity and ideological polarization are deeply embedded in the body politic. Increasing geographical segregation of voters and successive waves of incumbent-friendly redistricting have contributed to this development by helping to reduce the number of competitive House seats to a few dozen. With the overwhelming majority of House seats safe for one party or the other, new and returning members are naturally most reflective of and responsive to their primary constituencies, the only realistic locus of potential opposition, which usually are dominated by those at the ideological extreme. This phenomenon has tended to move Democrats in the House left and Republicans, right.

Despite the fact that redistricting plays no role in the Senate, the same pattern of ideological polarization of the parties is present there, albeit shaped in part by politicians moving from service in the House to the Senate. Many senators brought with them to the chamber attitudes toward Congress that were shaped by the contentious combat in the House of the late 1980s and early 1990s.

In recent years a number of factors—the two parties at parity and ideologically polarized, a populist attack on Congress that has weakened its institutional self-defenses, a more partisan press and interest group alignment, and an electoral environment making legislative activity subordinate to the interests of the permanent campaign—have conspired to encourage a decline in congressional deliberation and a de facto delegation of authority and influence to the president.

The passage of the Medicare bill is a vivid illustration of an institution that has strayed far from its deliberative roots and a body that does not live up to the aspirations envisioned for it by the framers. This problem is not just stylistic, or something that offends academics and other analysts. Bad process leads to bad policy—and often can lead to bad behavior, including ethical lapses. Those consequences affect all of us....

The need for change, we believe, is compelling and urgent. In foreign policy, with an agonizing war in Iraq joining serious problems in the Middle East and elsewhere in the world, the need is clear for some broad consensus on America's role in the world, or at least for an understanding that these issues cannot be shoved aside in a kind of War of the Roses between the parties and the branches. In domestic affairs, unsustainable deficits looming in the next decade without a redirection of taxing and spending policies, along with unsolved problems in areas like pensions and health care, require a return to serious deliberation and measured bipartisanship. The country and its enduring constitutional pact should not, and cannot, endure a broken branch for long....

The Demise of Regular Order

The lack of interest in the admittedly arduous process of going through multiple levels and channels of discussion, debate, negotiation, and compromise that make up a robust deliberative process has been a symptom of the broader malady in the contemporary Congress—the belief, especially in the House, that deliberation, fairness, bipartisanship, and debate are impediments to the larger goal of achieving political and policy success. In other words, the credo that the ends justify the means.

The House, unlike the Senate, is a majoritarian institution. With its complete control of the Rules Committee, the majority leadership may write special rules to control debate and amendments on the House floor. As long as its party members support the Rules Committee, the leadership may waive any standing rule not specified in the Constitution, such as the requirement that conference committee reports lay over for three days before they are considered by the House. By controlling the position of presiding officer, in committee or on the floor, the majority may also adopt less formal means to advance its legislative agenda and weaken the position of the minority.

During the last decade of their forty-year control of the House, Democrats made increasing use of this power to deny the minority Republicans opportunity to participate in any meaningful fashion in the legislative process. Republicans chafed under the increasingly heavy hand of the majority. In 1993 ranking Rules Committee member David Dreier and his Republican committee colleagues issued a stinging report criticizing the tactics used by the majority to shut down "deliberative democracy." What was essential to the House but missing under the arbitrary rule of the Democrats, they argued, was a "full and free airing of conflicting opinions through hearings, debates, and amendments for the purpose of developing and improving legislation deserving of the respect and support of the people." Dreier acknowledged the majority's right to control the agenda and schedule and to structure legislation to advance its policy goals. But this can be accomplished, he asserted, without denying the minority an opportunity to be heard and have their ideas considered.

The 1994 election changed the majority party in the House but it did nothing to stem the decline of deliberative democracy. During more than a decade of Republican rule, the majority has tightened its grip on the House and the minority has been increasingly marginalized....

Committee deliberation on controversial legislation has become increasingly partisan and formalistic, with the serious work being done by the committee chair, party leadership, administration officials, and lobbyists. This pattern is repeated in conference committees, often without any pretence of a full committee mark-up with members of both political parties present. The Rules Committee routinely suspends its requirement of a 48-hour notice of meetings, invoking its authority to call an emergency meeting "at any time on any measure or matter which the Chair determines to be of an emergency nature." Those meetings, at which 60 percent of all rules during the 108th Congress were reported (a lot of emergencies), often were scheduled with little advance notice between 8 p.m. and 7 a.m. And their primary purpose was to dispense with regular order....

The Explosion of Earmarks

Another sign of the decline of the deliberative process is the startling rise of earmarking—legislating specific projects for specific districts or states instead of leaving the allocation of resources to professionals. Earmark fever has completely taken over the appropriations process as it earlier had consumed public works. The conservative watchdog group Citizens Against Government Waste commented in an open letter released in 2004, "Over the past ten years, pork-barrel spending has increased exponentially, from 1,430 projects totaling $10 billion in 1995 to 10,656 projects, totaling $22.9 billion, in 2004."

Scott Lilly, the longtime Democratic staff director of the House Appropriations Committee and a stellar career professional in the House, noted, "Earmarking has not simply grown in volume; the distribution of earmarks has also changed dramatically. In the 1980s, earmarks were largely rewards for Members who had persevered for years on the back benches and risen to positions of significant power on key committees. Today, earmarks are much more broadly distributed among the rank and file, and this most important advantage of incumbency affects election outcomes not just in a few districts of well-connected Members but in virtually all Congressional districts."

The most startling development on the earmark front has been in appropriations. In the definitive treatment of the appropriations committees, Richard F. Fenno's magisterial *The Power of the Purse* published in 1966, there is no reference to *earmark* in the index. That is because historically, appropriations bills have not explicitly targeted funds for particular programs in particular districts. They have shaped the direction of spending and often encouraged specific programs in report language. But appropriators avoided earmarks because they inevitably would lead to a kind of circus or bazaar, with rising pressure to add funds for each district or to use the earmark as a weapon to reward friends and punish enemies.

The House especially saw the danger in this process. The Senate was much happier to open the spigots and use the appropriations process to logroll and make each member happy. Earmarks took off in the Senate in the 1990s and have risen exponentially, with senators of both parties eager to take advantage. Only Senator John McCain (R-AZ) has stood up strongly against the practice. In the House, though, there were many voices opposing earmarks, including, particularly strongly, Republicans.

That is, until they took over the majority in the House. Now the House is at least as eager to use the earmarking process as the Senate, and the results are clear. In 1992, there were 892 specifically earmarked programs or projects, adding up to $2.6 billion in spending. The number more than doubled in six years (1998) to 2,000 earmarks, with spending jumping to $13.2 billion. By fiscal year 2002, the number of earmarks rose to 8,341, with spending up to $20 billion. By 2005, the number had escalated to 13,997 at a cost of $27.3 billion. The trends are obvious for almost every area of discretionary spending....

Of course, the use of projects or pork to protect incumbents or to logroll for votes is nothing new. But the sheer scope of their use in the past few years is a sharp break with tradition; that it occurred on the watch of self-proclaimed fiscal conservatives has left many real fiscal conservatives boiling....

Collapse of Ethical Standards

In early 2003, the *Washington Post* reported that the staff of House Financial Services Committee chair Mike Oxley, personal and committee, had pressured the Investment Company Institute to fire its chief lobbyist, Julie Domenick, and replace her with a Republican (Domenick was a Democrat...). According to the *Post,* committee staffer Sam Geduldig "told a group of lobbyists ... that Oxley's probe of the mutual fund industry was linked to Domenick's employment at the mutual fund group."

Following on DeLay's unethical effort to strong-arm the Electronics Industries Association, the effort to bludgeon the Investment Company Institute by threatening legislative retribution if its lobbyist were not canned made it clear that the K Street Project was more than merely another effort to extract money and jobs from interest groups.[1]

The difference was dramatized—perhaps typified—by lobbyist Jack Abramoff.... Abramoff rose dramatically to visibility, power, wealth, and notoriety as a lobbyist in Tom DeLay's Washington who used his connections to DeLay and other majority insiders to represent a range of clients, most notably Indian tribes

---

1. The K Street Project was initiated by Republican leaders to pressure the powerful lobbying firms lining Washington's K Street to fire Democrats and hire Republicans.

who were trying to get or keep gambling casinos—or stop other tribes from getting them—and the Northern Marianas Islands (Saipan), which was trying to keep preferential treatment for its sweatshop garment industry.

In just three years, Abramoff and his associates, including former DeLay key staffer Michael Scanlan, pulled in $82 million from the Indian tribes. This bonanza included taking fees from one tribe to prevent another from getting a casino and then taking fees from the second tribe to try to reverse the decision. Some of the money went to his law firm; but $66 million went to Scanlan's public affairs firm and to a series of nonprofits, including charities organized by Abramoff and the American International Center, a "think tank" Abramoff set up that was headquartered in the beach community of Rehoboth, Delaware, and run by a former lifeguard with no public policy experience. Some of the money was turned into fees for Grover Norquist and Ralph Reed, the former executive director of the Christian Coalition and former head of the Bush presidential campaign's Southern region, to help the Indian gambling effort by lobbying to block the licensing of rival casinos; other money was channeled to conservative organizations, including some affiliated with Norquist.[2]

Abramoff spread his largesse around widely, hosting lavish trips abroad for members of Congress and other officials, in some cases to golf resorts in St Andrews, Scotland, where he paid greens fees that approached $5,000 a day. DeLay and Ney were among the golfing junketeers.[3]

At the same time, Abramoff was pursuing other business ventures including the leasing and acquisition of federal properties and the purchase of gambling boats in Florida. In each case, he enlisted lawmakers and administration officials to help....

Conclusion

[T]he problems that make this Congress sharply different from past ones and clearly, in our view, a broken branch, are manifold. They include a loss of institutional identity, an abdication of institutional responsibility vis-à-vis the executive, the demise of regular order (in committee, on the floor, and in conference), and the consequent deterioration of the deliberative process—the signature comparative advantage of Congress as a legislative body.

Current members of Congress simply do not identify strongly as members of the first branch of government. Whether they place their ideology or partisan identity first, too many members of Congress now think little if at all about their primary role and responsibilities as members of the legislative branch. This is reflected in the Tuesday to Thursday schedule that prevents adequate time for sustained lawmaking and oversight; a tolerance of extraordinary measures, such as the nuclear option on judicial confirmations, that undermine institutional health for short-term political gains; and an unwillingness to meet their constitutional responsibility to police the conduct of members of Congress with a strong and independent ethics process.

---

2. Grover Norquist is a prominent Republican conservative strategist.

3. Robert Ney was a Republican congressman from Ohio caught up in the Abramoff scandal. Ney was compelled to resign his office and pled guilty to a charge of conspiracy.

The arrival of unified Republican government in 2001 transformed the aggressive and active GOP-led Congress of the Clinton years into a deferential and supine body, one extremely reluctant to demand information, scrub presidential proposals, or oversee the executive. The uncompromising assertion of executive authority by President Bush and Vice President Cheney was met with a whimper, not a principled fight, by the Republican Congress.

It is ironic that the methods used by the passive legislative branch to achieve the presidential goals were themselves super-aggressive, abrasive, and over-the-line. Regular order in a legislature—produced by an elaborate set of rules, precedents, and norms governing the conduct of business in committee, on the floor, and in conference—is designed to facilitate orderly and deliberate policy making, ensure fairness, and maintain the legitimacy of Congress and the constitutional system. Majorities are always tempted to dispense with regular order to advance their immediate policy and political objectives. Democrats were not reluctant to do so during their long rein in power, especially in the latter years. But Republicans have far exceeded Democratic abuses of power. Committees have been marginalized in myriad ways, from central party direction to ad hoc groups to omnibus bills. Floor debate and decision making is tightly controlled with restrictive rules and extended time for roll-call votes. Conferences to reconcile differences between the House and Senate are now the setting for breathtaking abuses: minority party members excluded from negotiations, entirely new provisions added in the stealth of night, and routine waivers of time for members to learn what is contained in the reports they must vote on.

These practices have produced a measurable decline in the quantity and quality of deliberation. The essence of lawmaking in Congress is deliberation. The dictionary defines *deliberate* as: 1. To think carefully and often slowly, as about a choice to be made; 2. To consult with another or others in a process of reaching a decision; 3. To consider (a matter) carefully and often slowly, as by weighing alternatives. Congress was designed to be deliberative, through its checks and balances, its decentralized decision making in committees and subcommittees, its large membership, its emphasis on debate and give-and-take, and its openness to individuals and organized groups in the society, all of which allow it to take time, consider alternatives, consult widely, discuss, negotiate, and compromise. Yet it is hard to look at the contemporary Congress and see deliberation as a core value in these terms....

We believe these developments have serious consequences for policy and governance. The absence of institutional regard among its leaders diminishes Congress in the constitutional scheme and encourages more unilateral and less responsible behavior in the executive. The failure of Congress to insist on more information from the executive translates into less effective congressional oversight of such crucially important matters as the war in Iraq and homeland security. The suspension of regular order in Congress creates greater opportunities for parochial, special interest provisions to be added to legislation out of public view and for poorly constructed laws to get enacted without being properly vetted and connected. The failure to discern and make explicit the true costs of important policy initiatives—from tax cuts to Medicare prescription drugs to the war in Iraq—make it impossible for a realistic cost-benefit analysis to enter the calculus before they are approved....

Manifestations of these maladies are littered throughout the record of the last several Congresses. We have described the absence of genuine deliberation, the shamefully deceptive cost accounting, and the special interest payoffs associated with the successful effort to add a prescription drug benefit to Medicare. The projected long-term costs of the law are staggering, dwarfing the projected shortfall in Social Security. The cost is not the only issue: as the law was implemented, liberal and conservative critics alike criticized its structure, complexity, and policy gaps....

The frontier atmosphere that characterized Congress through much of our early history occurred during a time when Congress convened almost part time and when the role of the federal government was much more limited. There was no mass mobilization, no mass media, no twenty-four-hour cable news. Now, Congress is much larger, more potent, and part of a federal government with remarkable scope and sweep. Each of its actions or inactions has more consequences. The decline in deliberation has resulted in shoddy and questionable policy—domestic and international. The unnecessarily partisan behavior of the House majority has poisoned the well enough to make any action to restrain the growth of entitlement programs and to restructure health care policy impossible and has badly strained the long tradition of bipartisanship on foreign policy at a particularly delicate time. The failure of both houses of Congress to do meaningful oversight contributed to the massive and unconscionable failures of the Department of Homeland Security and, after Hurricane Katrina, of its FEMA arm. The broken branch distresses us as longtime students of American democracy who believe Congress is the linchpin of our constitutional system. But the consequences go far beyond our sensibilities, resonating in ways that damage the country as a whole. Perhaps we can do little, as larger forces in society, driven by technological change, overwhelm any efforts to alter course. But we believe that individuals can make a difference, that every step must be taken and no stone unturned to try to mend the broken branch and restore the needed balance in our political system.

Is Congress "The Broken Branch"?
DAVID R. MAYHEW

Introduction

How should we think about Congress's role in the American system? Is the institution a "broken branch"? How might we decide whether it is broken? If it is broken, compared with what is it broken? What are the plausible counterfactuals? Is there a serious need for constitutional repair? Notwithstanding the none-too-attractive performance by Congress in recent times, I am skeptical about certain over-gloomy diagnoses and over-intrusive remedies. Below, I offer two arguments.

I. Congress, If Considered in Perspective, Is Not All That Bad

Congress is an unlovely institution, but it has always been unlovely. In a contest for the "most disparaged" branch of the United States national government during the course of American history, there is little doubt that Congress would emerge the winner hands-down. The tradition of disparagement as well as the congressional behavior, actual or alleged, that has brought it on is well-known. The themes go way back. For example, Tocqueville wrote: "When one enters the House of Representatives at Washington, one is struck by the vulgar demeanor of that great assembly." Mark Twain famously quipped: "[T]here is no distinctly native American criminal class except Congress"; and "[S]uppose you were an idiot. And suppose you were a member of Congress. But I repeat myself." As a final example, recall how Frank Capra depicted Congress in his 1939 film, *Mr. Smith Goes to Washington,* possibly Hollywood's leading statement on the institution: that fictional Congress was corrupt, pettifogging, self-centered, anti-democratic, and a procedural mess.

A census of the offending behaviors said to be rampant in Congress would include a number of familiar complaints. The members bicker and fight with each other incessantly. They blather too much—the Senator Claghorn image.[1] They let obstruction get in the way of action. They weave awkward compromises into law. They are prone to particularism—as in the growing custom of earmarks. They surrender to special-interest boondoggles—as in the agricultural subsidy bills. They are bought by campaign donors and pushed around by lobbyists. They do not do their homework. Perhaps as much as anything, they participate in arguments and decisions that all too often seem unintelligent: Why do they lean toward protectionism? Why did they intrude into the Terry Schiavo case the way they did?[2] Why can't they think and act right about global warming?

Indexing the disparagement, perhaps, is Congress's low rating in public opinion surveys. Recently in this realm, a Republican Congress scored a record low in 2006. But then a Democratic Congress scored even worse, below fifteen percent, in 2008.

In the face of an indictment like this, what could be the redeeming perspective? Perhaps the best argument is a familiar one: Congress is just one of the three governmental branches. It complements the others. Each sector of the government offers, or at least can offer, a distinctive menu of services. The presidency offers opinion leadership as well as, in its chief executive role, speed, coordination, and secrecy. The

1. Senator Claghorn was a fictional senator from the South whose distinctive character was a pompous speaking style.

2. When the husband of Terry Schiavo, a woman who had been in a vegetative state for many years, attempted with authorization from a court to terminate her life supports, Republican conservatives in Congress, aiming to appeal to religious voters, tried unsuccessfully to block his effort.

bureaucracy, also a component of the executive branch, offers technical expertise and hierarchical organization. The judiciary traffics in coherence, consistency, and justice.

Congress is the country's representative body. In this capacity, it offers certain services that often bring it into disagreement or conflict with the other branches as well as with the country's intelligentsia. The latter dissonance is relentless and important. In certain respects, Congress and the country's intelligentsia are natural enemies. This is not a new thing. At many junctures in American history, it would have been easy to assemble academics, journalists, and others into a conference to roast Congress.

One of those congressional services is the integration necessary for any action to occur. On Capitol Hill, the country's jangling tastes, as indexed in House and Senate constituencies, need to be woven into majority coalitions—in the Senate, often super-majority coalitions. This weaving is not easy—hence the frequent bickering, blathering, delay, and awkward compromises. Consider the recent $700 billion bailout of the financial industries, which entered Congress as a three-page blueprint yet exited as a 451-page enactment laden with expensive ornaments. The op-ed pieces assailing this kind of performance almost write themselves. Crisp, clear, decisive, theoretically elegant action is not ordinarily the congressional way.

Yet Congress's labored process is not entirely pointless. Matthew S. Shugart and John M. Carey have presented an interesting argument in a comparative study of presidential systems. In legislative terms, compared with chambers in other countries, the U.S. Congress is unusually powerful vis-à-vis its executive branch. Happily, such relative strength seems to correlate with the overall long-term legitimacy of a governmental system. This seems to be because elected assemblies, which are heterogeneous and multi-member, tend to be better than single-person presidencies at arranging compromises and accommodating a country's diversity. In this sense, the messiness and the other un-niceties associated with assemblies are functional. Assemblies may be untidy, but presidential systems that have strong ones seem to work better.

In a second kind of service, Congress exhibits a particular kind of popular democracy. It tends to incorporate popular ways of thinking—the tropes, the locutions, the moralisms, the assumptions, the causal stories and the rest that structure the meaning of political life in the mass public. Whether this is a service at all can be contested. But there it is. Generation after generation, Congress has juxtaposed popular styles of thinking to the thrusts of rationalization or high-mindedness often favored by the executive branch, the judiciary, or the intelligentsia. Congress offers an often-exasperating dose of average thinking. A couple of years ago, I remember seeing on television a panel of congressional pages where one of the youngsters remarked wide-eyed about Congress: "It's just like high school!"

In this vein, for example, presidents of both parties have ordinarily positioned themselves on the free-trade side of Congress. Congress has tended to be more protectionist. There are several reasons for this, but a better reach of the rationalizing logic of Economics 101 into the executive branch is probably one of them. In the area of agricultural policy, Democratic and Republican presidents of the last sixty years, working respectively from regulatory and free-market designs, have tried to impose rationalizing efficiency schemes. They have been met with indifferent success on Capitol Hill, where "let's help the farmers" seems to be a sufficient theme. In 1997, the Senate, unbowled over by the evolving science, voted ninety-five to zero to steer clear of the Kyoto Accord regarding global warming. Soon afterward, President Clinton signed on to the Accord in a symbolic gesture.

There are other examples of how Congress reflects ideas of popular democracy. The minimum wage, which has a simple accessible logic, is a congressional favorite notwithstanding its (at best) mixed reputation among economists. In the realm of crime control, including capital punishment, experts who advance rehabilitative theories encounter more of a bent for punitiveness on Capitol Hill. In general Congress, compared with the judiciary, seems to lean toward a common-sense utilitarianism as opposed to often newly minted rights theories. All this can cause handwringing and despair. Yet it is probably true that the battle between the popular and the high-minded needs to be fought out somewhere. In any society, common sense versus expertise is an opposition that will not go away. In the American system, it is up for grabs how much we are willing to trust scientific, bureaucratic, legal, or moral experts. Congress helps supply an assurance that their ideas need to be sold, not just proclaimed.

It is a paradox, to be sure, that Congress can at once purvey popular thinking and yet be unpopular itself. This is, however, by no means a new behavior. As far as I know, there has never existed an era when Congress rode particularly high in public opinion. A mid-1960s high in the congressional ratings statistics is often deployed as a baseline to highlight its dramatic subsequent decline. But that, however, was probably a local high, as no earlier golden age seems to exist. Mark Twain's old take on Congress is probably indicative.

Nonetheless, other evidence points to a more textured view of the institution. In a 2004 national survey conducted by the Annenberg Institutions of American Democracy Project, respondents strongly endorsed Congress's place in the system. The survey asked: "When it comes to making important policy decisions, do you think that decisions should be made by the Congress or by the president?" In response, 59.4% preferred Congress, 20.5% the President, and 13.9% desired joint decision-making. The respondents also emphatically endorsed the idea of checks and balances in answering the question: "Which view is closer to yours—legislative checks are good, or legislative checks cause gridlock and inaction?" In response, 69.9% chose "checks are good," with only 19.8% choosing "cause gridlock and inaction." Furthermore, a shrewd appreciation of the vagaries of the legislative process emerged. A question was posed: "Which one do you agree with most? (A) Conflict is a natural part of the legislative process, or (B) Members create conflict where there need not be any." Here, the (A) response handily beat out the (B) response, 62.7% to 31.5%.

These results do not necessarily conflict with the recurrent bad Gallup ratings on the question of whether Congress is doing a good job right now. Yet easily understandable comebacks to this latter question might be: Compared with what? What is the plausible counterfactual? What plausible alternative institutional setup would do better?

II. There is No Compelling Case for Revising the Constitution to Solve Any Problems

At square one, back in the late-eighteenth century, perhaps it would have been a good idea to institute a parliamentary system in the United States rather than a presidential one. That question can be argued endlessly, and it has been. But it does not seem a productive line of inquiry. We are stuck, or gifted, with a presidential system featuring separation of powers. As a theoretical matter, the Burke card is playable against any sweeping overhaul move.[3] As a practical matter, no significant desire seems to exist in the American public for any constitutional redesign of Congress. There is no modern analogue to the drive for popular elections of senators a century ago. At the level of constitutional design, nothing seems to be seriously wrong—or at least widely thought to be seriously wrong.

Undoubtedly, this quiescence has many causes. In this part of the Essay, I suggest certain reasons for it, all centering on the actual place or operation of Congress in the system. The three reasons are: (1) Congress can accomplish many goals even when there is divided control of government; (2) the Senate's malapportionment does not cause the problems it is purported to cause; and (3) elections act as the favored American avenue for change.

A. Divided Party Control is Not a Great Problem   First, the familiar "gridlock" case is flawed. Gridlock is the case that the American electoral system all too often produces divided party control of the national government, and so, little or nothing can get done (at least on the legislative front) in that circumstance. The case is weak. Granted, the laws enacted under divided party control are a heterogeneous lot, and they are often compromises rather than exhibits of pure ideology, but that is what one would expect. Yet substantial menus of laws are enacted. Consider the following list of legislation passed during the 2007–08 congressional term as a newly elected Democratic Congress faced the Bush presidency:

Legislation Passed in 2007:

- $70 billion in additional funding for the wars in Afghanistan and Iraq
- Minimum wage increase to $7.25 per hour
- Implementation of the security recommendations of the 9/11 Commission, including tightening security on air and sea cargo
- Ethics and lobbying reform
- Student-loan relief
- $23.2 billion for water projects (enacted over Bush veto)
- Free trade pact with Peru
- Increase in auto fuel-efficiency standards
- Overhaul of pharmaceutical regulations

---

3. Edmund Burke, an eighteenth-century British conservative writer, argued that political change should take place gradually, respecting the strengths of traditional institutions.

Legislation Passed in 2008:

- $168 billion economic stimulus package (February 13, 2008)
- $307 billion agricultural subsidy package (enacted over Bush veto)
- $162 billion in additional funding for the wars in Iraq and Afghanistan, and $63 billion for a new GI bill of rights
- Authorization of terrorism surveillance powers (the FISA fix)
- Up to $300 billion in mortgage relief (July 30, 2008)
- Overhaul of consumer-product-safety regulation
- Civil rights protection for the disabled
- Mental health parity mandate in health insurance
- Protection of the Great Lakes
- $700 billion financial rescue package
- Nuclear trade pact with India

Legislative politics during the 2007–08 term was certainly contentious, and many proposals from all sides were left on the cutting-room floor. But much legislating was done, sometimes by way of versatile coalitions. In the House, a minority rump of Democrats joined with the bulk of Republicans to approve the Bush Administration's war funding (twice) and Foreign Intelligence Surveillance Act ("FISA") fix. "I'm the Speaker of the House," reflected Nancy Pelosi as she presided over a "roll" of her own party in the Iraq funding controversy of 2007. "I have to take into consideration something broader than the majority of the majority in the Democratic Caucus." Yet there was a contrasting pattern. Also in the House, the costly mortgage bailout in July 2008, as well as the $700 billion financial rescue package in October 2008, both backed by the White House, drew the support of a majority of House Democrats yet only a minority of Republicans.

More angles could be explored here. Yet, in general, the American public does not seem to get upset about the idea or the circumstance of divided party control as such and probably for good reason.

B. The Senate's Malapportionment Is Not a Serious Problem   Second, the U.S. Senate, which could be causing serious outlier problems due to its composition, does not in fact seem to cause these problems. As is well known, the Senate is one of the most malapportioned legislative chambers in the world. In the 2000 Census, California registered sixty-nine times the population of Wyoming, but has equal representation in the Senate. This representational unfairness is obvious and unrelenting. But hardly anyone seems to care. In the United States, posters are plastered all over the place, all the time, promoting many causes, but I have not seen any attacking the Senate. Why is that?

Apparently, we have lucked out. In terms of Democratic and Republican partisanship, the propensities of the fifty states are nearly, albeit not perfectly, orthogonal to their population sizes. As a result the Senate, the House, and the presidency tend to move in a tight cluster in a Democratic or Republican direction all at once. One way to illustrate this propensity is with a cross-institution comparison for the presidential election years from 1948 through 2004. It involves the party share, say the Democratic share, of the major-party presidential vote—for example, the Kerry percentage of the Bush–Kerry vote in 2004. The comparison is between the Democratic share of the national popular presidential vote on the one hand, and the Democratic share of the presidential vote in the *median* House district (when the 435 districts are arrayed according to their presidential popular vote shares) and in the *median* Senate district (that is, state). Across the fifteen elections, in these calculations, the median House district placed an average of 1.1% to the Republican side of the Democratic national-level vote share. The median Senate district (that is, state) placed 1.3% to the Republican side. In short, a slight Republican bias, in this sense, has existed in both of Congress's electoral universes, but the House and Senate biases are virtually indistinguishable.

When we think of the malapportioned Senate, we tend to think of small-state Idaho, Wyoming, and Alaska. But we should also think of small-state Vermont, Rhode Island, and Delaware. In the face of these figures, there is no good reason to expect the Senate to behave as a distinct partisan or ideological outlier from the other elected institutions, and in fact, it does not. It has in the past. In the late-nineteenth century, for example, it leaned Republican. Two generations ago, a scholarship addressed the question: "Why is the Senate more liberal than the House?" A good bet for that latter time is that the answer lay in the political texture of the House before the districting revolution of the 1960s. But those days are past. In recent times, I have not seen any credible scholarship attributing any alleged policy, partisan, or ideological outlier status of the Senate to its curious Wyoming-through-California composition. Owing apparently to a fortuitous distribution of Democratic and Republican voters across the fifty states, we have lucked out.

Yes, there is also a distributive consideration. It is indeed true that the federal government, chiefly it seems at the behest of the Senate, tends to distribute more resources per capita, controlling for other relevant variables, to the small-population states than to the large-population states. But there is an emollient. The per capita cost to the residents of the large-population states seems to be rather small because it is spread over a large number of individuals. There are many donors, so to speak, in California, but far fewer recipients in Wyoming. In one careful estimate for the 1980s, Californians would have received roughly ten dollars more per capita a year from the government—that's all—if the sum of all federal discretionary and nondiscretionary benefits had been delivered on a national per capita basis absent any small-state skew. In another estimate for the 1970s and 1980s, people in the seventeen larger-population states underrepresented in the Senate forsook some thirty-five dollars per capita a year to subsidize people in the thirty-three smaller-population states overrepresented there. Burdens like these may be unfair, but they do not seem of a nature to spur reform action at the constitutional level. One analyst has reflected, after reciting a familiar litany of arithmetic downsides that *might in theory* accrue from the Senate's quite odd geographic base: "New Yorkers, Californians, et al. seem to just shrug." The shrugging is understandable.

C. Americans Look to Elections for Change   Third, there is the electoral universe. Generally speaking, Americans who hanker for change focus on the next election, not on a chance to revise the Constitution. Elections to the presidency, the Senate, and the House, backed up by party primaries that are more or less freely enterable, are a wondrous legitimizing device as well as a source of considerable flux in policies and personnel. Since World War II, the party holding the White House has held it eight times in presidential elections and lost it in eight. A closer match in results is not imaginable. Granted, party control in the congressional universe has been stickier. Most notably, Democrats held the House for a consecutive forty years between 1954 and 1994. A surge in the value of personal incumbency advantage in the mid-1960s, which favored chiefly Democrats, might have helped ensure that consecutiveness. Yet the House midterm sweeps of 1994 and 2006 have shown again how much of a force for change the electorate can be.

On the Senate side, the sizes of seat swings in elections, when a third of the chamber's seats are up each time, can be astonishing: thirteen in 1958, twelve in 1980, eight in 1986, and eight in 1994. Surprisingly, given its staggered terms, the Senate does not seem to lag behind the House in political texture. Since the Seventeenth Amendment was ratified in 1913, the Senate has switched party control every time the House has done so—and twice more, to boot, in 1980 and 1986. At the level of individual senators, the partisan flux is especially striking. Among the 100 senators serving in October 2008, fifty-five of them on initially taking their seats had succeeded members of the opposite party. Random draws would have yielded only fifty.

In this country, elections are the favored venue for political change. There is a lot of it. Consider the election of 2008. Ordinarily, revision of the Constitution does not rank high as a competing lever.

Conclusion

These are my two arguments. First, Congress is not all that defective an institution once its role is properly considered. To appraise it, we should appreciate the separation-of-powers complementarities of the American system, and we should consult real-world standards, not fanciful counterfactuals. Second, a compelling case does not exist for constitutional reform of Congress. Certainly, the American public is not worked up about any such need. Luckily, the odd and jangling aspects of the institutional universe that the presidency, the Senate, and the House add up to are not, in fact, causing the kinds of problems that they might.

Discussion Questions

1. Are Mann and Ornstein persuasive in their critique of Congress as "the broken branch"? Or does Mayhew make a persuasive case that Congress reflects what the American people demand from it?

2. Should Congress be structured to emphasize bipartisan deliberation or should it be structured to allow a majority party that won at the polls to enact its agenda?

3. Do you agree with Mayhew that elections, rather than internal reforms, are sufficient to change the direction of Congress? Do you agree with Mann and Ornstein that congressional maladies continue when one party replaces the other as the majority?

4. Considering the arguments presented by both sides in this debate, how well do you think Congress serves the public good?

Suggested Readings and Internet Resources

The central place of the electoral motive in congressional behavior is highlighted in David Mayhew, *Congress: The Electoral Connection* (New Haven, Conn.: Yale University Press, 1974), and Morris Fiorina, *Congress: Keystone of the Washington Establishment* (New Haven, Conn.: Yale University Press, 1989). For a rich descriptive account of the interactions of representatives and their constituents, see the classic work of Richard Fenno, *Home Style: House Members in Their Districts* (New York: Longman, 2002). A sophisticated historical analysis of how and why change occurs in Congress is Eric Schickler, *Disjointed Pluralism: Institutional Innovation and the Development of the U.S. Congress* (Princeton, N.J.: Princeton University Press, 2001). Heightened partisan conflict in Congress is the subject of Barbara Sinclair, *Party Wars: Polarization and the Politics of National Policy Making* (Norman: University of Oklahoma Press, 2006). See Lawrence C. Dodd and Bruce I. Oppenheimer, eds., *Congress Reconsidered*, 9th ed. (Washington, D.C.: CQ Press, 2009) for an anthology of articles by leading scholars in the field of congressional politics.

Free Congress Foundation
www.freecongress.org
This website, reflecting a conservative perspective on Congress, offers numerous publications and Internet links.

National Committee for an Effective Congress
www.ncec.org
This website, reflecting a liberal perspective on Congress, contains extensive coverage of liberal challengers to conservative incumbents.

Library of Congress
http://thomas.loc.gov
The Library of Congress website offers the Congressional Record and information on legislation and committee activity for current and recent Congresses.

Chapter 14

✳

The Presidency: How Much Difference Does the Individual Make?

The president of the United States is coming to your city. You may not like this president's personality, programs, or ideas, but you are likely to make an effort to see him (someday, her) in the flesh. Why? Because most Americans regard the president—any president—as the embodiment of the nation's history and greatness. The presidency is commonly seen as the personification of American democracy.

This equation of the presidency with democracy would have come as a surprise to the generation that established the American Republic. The men who drafted the U.S. Constitution believed that democracy had been carried too far in the revolutionary era. They conceived of the new president not as a democratic champion of the people but rather as a constitutional officer who would, by the length of his term and the loftiness of his stature, be insulated from the passions and pressures of ordinary citizens. Anti-Federalist critics of the Constitution, however, feared that the president would be too remote from the people and too reminiscent of the arbitrary executive that the Revolution had banished.

Neither Federalists nor Anti-Federalists viewed the executive as a democratic figure. In sharp contrast, modern presidents present themselves as the only elected representative of the whole people and the very embodiment of democracy itself. Other political actors—members of Congress, bureaucrats, political parties, interest groups—are taken to represent only partial and selfish interests. The president alone can claim to stand for the national interest and the public good.

The modern equation of the presidency with democracy began with Theodore Roosevelt and Woodrow Wilson and reached its zenith with Franklin Roosevelt. After Roosevelt, most journalists, political scientists, and historians came to believe that presidents were the principal agents of democratic purpose in the

American political system. Modern media, especially television, offered presidents a vehicle to bring their dramas of democratic leadership directly into people's homes.

Yet even as the bond between the presidency and democracy was celebrated, presidents were extending their powers in ways that threatened democratic values. With the Vietnam War, the Watergate scandal, and later the Iran-Contra affair, the undemocratic potential of executive power was revealed. A new and more skeptical view of the presidency began to emerge. At the same time, the perceived failures of most recent presidents left many Americans eager to see a reassertion of an effective presidency as a champion of democracy.

The role of presidents in American democracy depends on the relationship between an individual leader and an institutional system. For political scientist Fred Greenstein, the critical importance of each chief executive's individual qualities flows from "the highly personalized nature of the modern American presidency." He suggests that presidential performance will vary depending on how each president measures up on six personal dimensions: "effectiveness as a public communicator," "organizational capacity," "political skill," "vision," "cognitive style," and "emotional intelligence." Greenstein illustrates the impact of each of these six dimensions with material on modern presidents from Franklin D. Roosevelt to Barack Obama. No president, he suggests, is likely to be strong on all six dimensions, but the most effective presidents will possess several key skills and avoid the most crippling deficiencies, especially a flawed emotional nature.

Stephen Skowronek, another political scientist, criticizes the idea that individual attributes and skills are the important variables in presidential performance. For Skowronek, all of presidential history (and not just the "modern presidency") can be viewed in light of the rise and fall of political regimes. A regime marks an era in which one party is dominant in its electoral strength, coalition of interest groups, and ideas about the proper relationship between government and society (e.g., the liberal regime that began with Franklin D. Roosevelt and ended with Jimmy Carter). Skowronek suggests that presidents come into office confronting four types of political structures: (1) a "politics of reconstruction," in which the collapsing force of the previously dominant regime provides the opportunity for a president of the opposing coalition to launch a new regime and achieve greatness; (2) a "politics of disjunction," in which a president associated with a regime that is falling apart faces an "impossible leadership situation" and thereby appears incompetent; (3) a "politics of preemption," in which a president opposed to a still-vigorous regime tries to find success by blending the ideas of his own party with those of the dominant party; and (4) a "politics of articulation," in which a president associated with a still-vigorous regime tries to complete its unfinished agenda, at the risk of fostering divisions in the dominant coalition and evoking charges that he has betrayed the true faith set down by the reconstructive president who first formed the regime. In each of these cases, says Skowronek, what most matters about a president is not his character but his place in the changing structures of American politics.

The conflicting perspectives of Greenstein and Skowronek are illustrated by their very different interpretations of the unfolding presidency of Barack Obama.

From the perspective of Greenstein, American democracy has a great deal riding on the personal qualities of the individual elected every four years. From the perspective of Skowronek, the potential of each president is bound up with longer-term political structures that reflect dominant interests, institutions, and ideas. Are presidents, as Greenstein argues, likely to serve democracy well or poorly depending on the individual qualities they bring with them to their office? Or are presidents, as Skowronek argues, strengthened or weakened by the opportunity structures characteristic of the four types of leadership found throughout presidential history? How much of a difference can the individual in the White House make to the workings of democratic politics in the United States?

Lessons from the Modern Presidency

FRED I. GREENSTEIN

The executive branch of our government is like a chameleon. To a startling degree it reflects the character and personality of the President.
—CLARK M.CLIFFORD, 1972

The highly personalized nature of the modern American presidency makes the strengths and weaknesses of the White House incumbent of the utmost importance. It places a premium on the ability of chief executives to get the most out of their strong points and compensate for their limitations. It also places a great value on the ability of Americans to select presidents with attributes that serve well in the Oval Office....

The Qualities That Bear on Presidential Performance

Effectiveness as a Public Communicator   For an office that places so great a premium on the presidential pulpit, the modern presidency has been surprisingly lacking in effective public communicators. Most presidents have not addressed the public with anything approximating the professionalism of countless educators, members of the clergy, and radio and television broadcasters. Roosevelt, Kennedy, and Reagan—and Clinton at his best—are the shining exceptions.

Chief executives who find the most able of the presidential communicators daunting should be relieved to learn that their eloquence was in part the product of effort and experience. Roosevelt, Kennedy, and Reagan took part in drafting their speeches and rehearsed their presentations. In 1910, when Eleanor Roosevelt first heard her husband give a speech, she was taken aback by his long pauses and slow delivery. "I was worried for fear that he would never go on," she recalled. When Kennedy was a freshman congressman, he had a diffident, self-effacing public manner. And for all of Reagan's professionalism, he did not perfect the podium manner of his political years until the 1950s, when his film career drew to a close and he found employment on the speaking circuit.

One president who allowed himself to be fazed by an accomplished predecessor was George Bush [Senior], who seems to have concluded that since he could not compare with Reagan as a communicator, he should be his near antithesis. Bush used the White House briefing room for his public communications, only rarely addressing the nation from the Oval Office, and he instructed his speechwriters to temper his prose. Bush's initial three years of high public approval provide a reminder that formal addresses are not the only way for a president to remain in the good graces of the public. His defeat highlights the costs of a leadership style that gives short shrift to the teaching and preaching side of presidential leadership.

Organizational Capacity   A president's capacity as an organizer includes his ability to forge a team and get the most out of it, minimizing the tendency of subordinates to tell their boss what they sense he wants to hear. It also includes a quite different matter: his proficiency at creating effective institutional arrangements. There is an illuminating postpresidential indicator of a president's success as a team builder—the way that he is remembered by alumni of his administration. Veterans of the Truman, Eisenhower, Kennedy, Ford, and first Bush presidencies have nothing but praise for their erstwhile chiefs. In contrast, few Johnson, Carter, and Clinton lieutenants emerged from their White House service with unmixed views of the president they served. Most ambivalent are the former aides of Richard Nixon, a number of whom went to prison for their actions in his service.

Presidents also differ in their ability to avail themselves of a rich and varied fare of advice and information. FDR encouraged diversity in the recommendations that reached him by pitting his assistants against one another. Kennedy's method was to charge his brother Robert and his alter ego Theodore Sorensen with scrutinizing the proposals of his other advisors for flaws and pitfalls. The modern president with by far the greatest and most demanding organizational experience was Eisenhower, who had a highly developed view of the matter. "I know of only one way in which you can be sure you have done your best to make a wise decision," he declared in a 1967 interview:

> That is to get all of the [responsible policymakers] with their different viewpoints in front of you, and listen to them debate. I do not believe in bringing them in one at a time, and therefore being more impressed by the most recent one you hear than the earlier ones. You must get courageous men of strong views, and let them debate with each other.

Not all of the modern presidents have been open to vigorous give and take. Nixon and Reagan were uncomfortable in the presence of face-to-face disagreement. Johnson's Texas-sized personality had a chilling effect on some of his subordinates. His NSC staff member Chester Cooper recalled recurrent fantasies of facing down LBJ at NSC meetings when Johnson sought his concurrence on a matter relating to Vietnam by replying, "I most definitely do not agree."[1] But when LBJ turned to him and asked, "Mr. Cooper, do you agree?" Cooper found himself replying, "Yes, Mr. President, I agree."

The capacity to design effective institutional arrangements has been in even scarcer supply than effective public communication in the modern presidency. In this department, Eisenhower was in a class of his own. The most emulation-worthy of his departures was the set of arrangements that framed his administration's national security deliberations. Each week the top planners in the bodies represented in the NSC hammered out option papers stating the policy recommendations of their agencies. The disagreements were clearly delineated and set before the NSC, where they were the object of sharp, focused debate. The result was as important for preparing Eisenhower's foreign policy team to work together as it was for grounding it in the issues bearing on unfolding global contingencies.

Political Skill   The classic statement of the centrality of political skill to presidential performance is Richard E. Neustadt's *Presidential Power*, which has been described as the closest approximation to Machiavelli's writings in the literature of American politics. The question Neustadt addresses is how the chief executive can put his stamp on public policy in the readily stalemated American political system. Neustadt's prescription is for the president to use the powers of his office assertively, build and maintain public support, and establish a reputation among fellow policymakers as a skilled, determined political operator. If there ever was reason to doubt Neustadt's diagnosis, it was eliminated by the presidential experience of Jimmy Carter.

Lyndon Johnson seemed almost to have taken his methods from the pages of *Presidential Power*. Within hours after Kennedy's assassination, Johnson had begun to muster support for major domestic policy departures. He exhibited will as well as skill, cultivating his political reputation by keeping Congress in session until Christmas 1963 in order to prevail in one of his administration's first legislative contests. His actions won him strong public support, making it apparent to his opposite numbers on Capitol Hill that it would be politically costly to ignore his demands.

Vision   "Vision" is a term with a variety of connotations. One is the capacity to inspire. In this the rhetorically gifted presidents—Kennedy, Reagan, and above all FDR—excelled. In the narrower meaning employed here, "vision" refers to preoccupation with the content of policies, an ability to assess their feasibility, and the possession of a set of overarching goals. Here the standouts are Eisenhower, Nixon, and to a lesser extent Ronald Reagan, whose views were poorly grounded in

---

1. The letters NSC stand for National Security Council.

specifics. Vision also encompasses consistency of viewpoint. Presidents who stand firm are able to set the terms of policy discourse. In effect they serve as anchors for the rest of the political community. George H. W. Bush was not alone in his lack of "the vision thing." He falls in a class of presidential pragmatists that includes the great bulk of the modern chief executives. The costs of vision-free leadership include internally contradictory programs, policies that have unintended consequences, and sheer drift.

Cognitive Style   Presidents vary widely in their cognitive styles. Jimmy Carter had an engineer's proclivity to reduce issues to what he perceived to be their component parts. That style served him well in the 1978 Camp David negotiations, but it was ill suited for providing his administration with a sense of direction. Carter's cognitive qualities contrast with the kind of strategic intelligence that cuts to the heart of a problem, as Eisenhower did when he introduced his administration's deliberations on Dien Bien Phu with the incisive observation that the jungles of Indochina would "absorb our divisions by the dozens."

Another example of strategic intelligence is to be had from a chief executive who will never grace Mount Rushmore: Richard Nixon. Two years before entering the White House, Nixon laid down the goals of moving the United States beyond its military involvement in Vietnam, establishing a balance of power with the Soviet Union and an opening with China. By the final year of his first term, he had accomplished his purposes.

Nixon's first-term successes contrast with the paucity of major accomplishments in the two White House terms of the first presidential Rhodes scholar, Bill Clinton. Clinton possesses a formidable ability to absorb and process ideas and information, but his mind is more synthetic than analytic, and his political impulses sometimes lead him to substitute mere rationalization for reasoned analysis.

Two presidents who were marked by cognitive limitations were Harry Truman and Ronald Reagan. Truman's uncritical reading of works of popular history made him susceptible to false historical analogies. Reagan was notorious for his imperfect understanding of a number of his policy initiatives. That both presidents had major policy accomplishments shows that intelligence and information as measured by standardized tests is not the sole cause of presidential effectiveness.

Emotional Intelligence   Five of the modern presidents stand out as fundamentally free of distracting emotional perturbations: Eisenhower, Ford, the two Bushes, and Obama. Four others were marked by emotional undercurrents that did not significantly impair their leadership: Roosevelt, Truman, Kennedy, and Reagan. That leaves Johnson, Nixon, Carter, and Clinton, all of whom were emotionally handicapped. The vesuvian LBJ was subject to mood swings of clinical proportions. Jimmy Carter's rigidity was a significant impediment to his White House performance. The defective impulse control of Bill Clinton led him into actions that led to his impeachment.

Richard Nixon was the most emotionally flawed of the presidents considered here. His anger and suspiciousness were of Shakespearean proportions. He more than any other president summons up the classic notion of a tragic hero who is defeated by the very qualities that brought him success. It has been argued that the tortured psyche of a Nixon is a precondition of political creativity. This was the view of Elliot Richardson, who held that if Nixon's "rather petty flaws" had been taken away, "you would probably have removed that very inner core of insecurity that led to his rise." Richardson's claim is a variant of the proposition that the inner torment of a Van Gogh is the price of his creativity, but other great painters were free of Van Gogh's self-destructiveness, and the healthy-minded Eisenhower was as gifted as Nixon in the positive aspects of leadership. Great political ability does sometimes derive from troubled emotions, but the former does not justify the latter in the custodian of the most destructive military arsenal in human experience....

In the world of imagination it is possible to envisage a cognitively and emotionally intelligent chief executive, who happens also to be an inspiring public communicator, a capable White House organizer, and the possessor of exceptional political skill and vision. In the real world, human imperfection is inevitable, but some imperfections are more disabling than others. Many of the modern presidents have performed adequately without being brilliant orators. Only a few chief executives have been organizationally competent. A minimal level of political skill is a precondition of presidential effectiveness, but political skill is widely present in the handful of individuals who rise to the political summit. Vision is rarer than skill, but only Lyndon Johnson was disastrously deficient in the realm of policy.

Finally there are thought and emotion. The importance of cognitive strength in the presidency should be self-evident. Still, Presidents Johnson, Nixon, Carter, and Clinton had impressive intellects and defective temperaments. They reversed Justice Holmes's characterization of FDR.[2] Clinton's foibles made him an underachiever and national embarrassment. Carter's defective temperament contributed to making his time in office a period of lost opportunity. Johnson and Nixon presided over major policy breakthroughs, but also over two of the most unhappy episodes of the twentieth century. All four presidential experiences point to the following moral: Beware the presidential contender who lacks emotional intelligence. In its absence all else may turn to ashes....

Obama as President: Early Days

Obama's inaugural address included the inspirational rhetoric that is customary for such occasions, but much of it was devoted to an unemotional recitation of the nation's problems and his administration's plans to address them. Obama began making policy in his first week in office by issuing executive orders. He froze the pay of members of the White House staff earning more than $100,000 a year, ordered the closing of the controversial Guantanamo detention camp

---

2. Supreme Court Justice Oliver Wendell Holmes Jr. observed that Franklin D. Roosevelt had a "second-class intellect but a first-class temperament."

within the year (an order he was unable to act on), banned torture in the interrogation of terror suspects, and cancelled the previous administration's ban on funding groups that provide abortion services. In a later executive order, he reversed the Bush administration's policy of barring the use of federal funds for human embryonic stem cell research.

On January 29, the first piece of legislation reached the White House—an act that extends the period in which employees can file lawsuits alleging discrimination on the basis of sex, race, or age. On February 4, Obama signed a bill expanding the number of children receiving federally funded health insurance from 7 million to 11 million. On February 17, Congress passed the American Recovery and Reinvestment Act, a $787 billion administration measure designed to stimulate the economy. Included in it are tax cuts; unemployment benefits; and appropriations for education, health care, and infrastructure. By the final months of 2009, there was evidence that the stimulus program had contributed to an economic upturn. However, there continued to be high unemployment, and it was uncertain how robust the recovery would be.

The proposal in Obama's first-year legislative program that had the greatest potential for placing him on the short list of chief executives who preside over major policy breakthroughs relates to health insurance. As Obama pointed out in an address to Congress on health reform, the United States has long been the only wealthy nation that does not guarantee its citizens health care. In seeking to eliminate that discrepancy, Obama chose to state the goals he favored in general terms. These included a major expansion in the ranks of the insured, an end to the denial of health insurance to people with preexisting medical conditions, and a ban on lifetime limits on health insurance. Obama relied on Congress to supply the details of the measure. He did so to avoid the fate of President Clinton's health insurance bill, which was drafted by the White House with little congressional input and failed to be enacted.

By the final weeks of 2009, the House and the Senate had passed somewhat different bills, both of which were broadly consistent with Obama's guidelines. But before the two houses reached an agreement on a compromise bill, there was a political bombshell. In January 2010, Massachusetts elected a Republican to the Senate seat that had long been held by the late Edward Kennedy. No longer did the Democrats have the 60 votes needed to defeat a Senate filibuster. Moreover, there were growing signs that the public was uneasy about the proposed health insurance measure. Obama and the Democratic congressional leadership concluded that the way to proceed was for the House of Representatives to accept the Senate bill, which would make it unnecessary for the Senate to have another vote. Differences between the two chambers could then be resolved by a parliamentary procedure that requires only a majority vote.

The new strategy bore fruit on March 21, 2010, when the House of Representatives voted to accept the Senate bill. A number of anti-abortion House members had been balking at wording in the Senate measure they believed would permit governmental funding of abortions. Obama broke the impasse by promising to issue an executive order affirming that nothing in the new law would permit government funds to pay for the termination of pregnancies.

(As in the past, there would be an exception for pregnancies that were the result of rape or incest and in cases when the mother's life was in danger.) On March 23, Obama signed the Patient Protection and Affordable Care Act in the East Room of the White House. The importance of this addition to the social safety net available to Americans is comparable to that of the enactment of Medicare in 1965 and Social Security in 1935.

Obama's ambitious domestic program did not prevent him from being active in the foreign sphere. By the end of his first presidential year, he had exceeded all previous presidents in the number of early visits to other nations. In what was interpreted as a departure from the unilateralism of the Bush years, the Obama administration indicated that it would seek to improve relations with friendly nations and to win over those that are less than friendly. Obama placed a particular priority on improving relations with the Islamic world. He signaled this intention in a June 4 address at Cairo University, in which he called for "a new beginning between the United States and Muslims around the world ... based on mutual interest and mutual respect" and stated "the truth that America and Islam are not exclusive and need not be in competition."

Obama's response to the two wars he inherited differed. In the case of Iraq, he announced that the United States would not engage in combat after August 2010. In the case of Afghanistan, he presided over a policy review of unusual length and rigor that resulted in a two-stage policy. First, the United States was to increase its troop commitment with the goal of strengthening Afghanistan's military and political institutions. Then, in July 2011, it would begin to withdraw its troops. Neither Iraq nor Afghanistan was to be abandoned; the American aim was to leave each country to its own citizens to defend.

Obama's Leadership Qualities

Public Communication   In the use of the bully pulpit, Obama is in a league with the most gifted modern presidential public communicators: Franklin D. Roosevelt, John F. Kennedy, and Ronald Reagan. This proficiency was manifested in the 2004 Democratic convention address that put him on the national political map and continues to be evident in his presidency. His major presidential rhetorical efforts include his tribute to the late Senator Edward Kennedy, his addresses to Congress and the United Nations General Assembly, and his June 2009 address at Cairo University. Obama also met periodically with the press, gave numerous interviews, and even appeared on late-night comedy shows. In spite of this blizzard of communication, he cannot be said to have dominated political discourse. In part, it is because polarized addresses on domestic and foreign policy to joint sessions of Congress produce a steady flow of criticism or, as Obama might put it, "misrepresentation." But Obama has not consistently communicated his program in broadly accessible terms, perhaps because of his own immersion in its intricacies.

Organizational Capacity   It has been argued that senators make poor executives, because most of them lack the experience of presiding over large organizations.

The previous member of the Senate to win the presidency, John F. Kennedy, resembled Obama in his quick mind and the high qualifications of his associates, but that did not prevent him from signing off on the Bay of Pigs fiasco. Obama has indicated that he is aware of the danger of making decisions that have not been rigorously debated. It was no accident that he had chosen a team whose members had strong views, Obama remarked. He wanted to avoid a decision-making process "wrapped up in groupthink" in which "everybody agrees with everything and there's no discussion and there are no dissenting views."

Despite the strong personalities of Obama's cabinet and White House staff, his administration has been notably free of internal fissures. The most notable exception occurred in connection with the Obama administration's lengthy 2009 deliberation on Afghanistan, which was marked by the leak of a military proposal for a substantial troop increase. Obama's response was to rein in the leakers and continue the deliberation until the administration's policy was determined.

Political Skill   Obama's prepresidential record shows ample evidence of his political skill. His time in the Illinois legislature is particularly instructive because it is his most sustained governmental service … [H]e was quick to learn the tactics needed to become an influential player in the state capital, forming political alliances on the golf course and at the poker table, as well as in official settings. His political skill was also evident in the bonds he forged with legislators outside of Chicago and with the State Senate Democratic leader, which helped him position himself to run for the U.S. Senate. Obama's conciliatory leadership style is sometimes ill-suited to American politics in a period of polarization, however. This appears not to be lost on him, judging from his one-sided reliance on Democratic votes to pass the Patient Protection and Affordable Care Act.

Policy Vision   Obama's critics argue that his assertions about the need to transcend ideological divisions are belied by his own liberal policies. An instructive source of insight into his basic mindset is the reports of those who observed him when he was at Harvard Law School, a period during which his approach to politics appears to have taken shape. Obama was conspicuous at Harvard for his ability to work with students and faculty across the ideological spectrum. During that period, he worked closely with Professor Laurence Tribe, who describes him as a pragmatic problem-solver with little in the way of fixed ideology.

Cognitive Style   Obama was widely recognized for his intelligence and open-mindedness when he was at Harvard, where he was elected to preside over the nation's most prestigious law journal. His students at the University of Chicago were fascinated by his capacity to illuminate issues by arguing them from contrasting points of view. As these examples indicate, Obama's cognitive style is marked by analytic detachment and complex thinking. This helps explain his way of conducting policy deliberations, which is to open by posing the questions he wants answered, go on to elicit the views of the participants, and conclude by summarizing what he has taken from the meeting and how it might affect his actions.

Emotional Intelligence "I don't get too high when things are going well and I don't get too low when things are going tough," Obama has remarked. The *Washington Post*'s Joel Achenbach argues that Obama's even temperament contributed to the "uncanny knack for avoiding mistakes" he showed in his presidential campaign. "His opponents sneered that Obama has no experience," Achenbach continues, "but by the end of his campaign he didn't look green at all. He seemed fully in command of his own campaign and his own emotions."

That was not always the case. As a young man, Obama was unsettled in his racial identity and indulged in drugs and alcohol. Whatever the psychic alchemy, Obama eventually came to terms with his life experience and built on it to forge his leadership style. Barack Obama is a fascinating political specimen. Indeed, he appears to be the rare political leader who is marked by a first-rate temperament *and* a first-rate mind. His temperament is *so* even, however, that he risks failing to convey the passion needed to win support.

The Changing Political Structures of Presidential Leadership

STEPHEN SKOWRONEK

When a president succeeds, our natural inclination is to laud the special talents and skills he brought to the office; when things go wrong, we look for personal missteps and character flaws. There is something comforting in these judgments, for they sustain confidence in the office of the presidency no matter what the experience of the particular incumbent holding power at the moment. So long as performance is tied to the personal attributes of the man, success is always a possibility; it awaits only the right combination of character and skill. So long as the presidency is a true test of the man, its incumbents are free to become as great as they can be.

Much of what is written about the presidency reinforces these conceits. Typically, analysis begins by describing an office that all presidents have shared, a position defined by constitutional arrangements that have undergone remarkably little change since 1789. To this is added the trappings of modernity—new governing responsibilities imposed on the office in the wake of the Great Depression and World War II and new resources made available to it. These distinguish the leadership situation shared by all presidents after FDR from that of all their predecessors. Setting things up this way, the analysis holds the demands and capacities of the office constant over the latter half of the twentieth century and presents leadership as a problem of how best to apply the resources of the modern presidency to the responsibilities of the modern presidency. In effect, each modern incumbent becomes a new source of insight into what attributes of character and skill work best in the shared context, what strategies are most effective, what it takes to measure up.

In fact, however, the political demands on incumbents and the leadership capacities of the office of the presidency vary considerably from one administration to the next, and much of what we take to be evidence of personal flaws and leadership skills can be accounted for by closer attention to the particular relationships established between the presidency and the political system by each incumbent in turn. To see how, we first need access to these changing relationships, and that, in turn, entails thinking about presidential history itself a bit differently. Rather than set the modern presidents apart from the pre-moderns to treat them as a separate and coherent group, we will want to compare them individually with counterparts in earlier periods. By making better use of the whole history of presidential leadership, we can better assess the contextual conditions under which great leaders typically arise and identify the limitations on leadership possibilities imposed by less fortuitous circumstances.

The alternative history I have in mind charts change in American politics through the recurring establishment and disintegration of relatively durable political regimes. This regime-based structure of American political history has been widely observed by political scientists and historians alike. It demarcates the rise and decline of Federalist Nationalism between 1789 and 1800, of Jeffersonian Democracy between 1800 and 1828, of Jacksonian Democracy between 1828 and 1860, of Republican Nationalism between 1860 and 1932, and of New Deal Liberalism between 1932 and 1980. Each of these regimes can be identified with the empowerment of an insurgent political coalition whose reconstruction of basic governing arrangements endured through various subsequent configurations of party power. Just as America's fragmented constitutional system has made sweeping political change rare and difficult to achieve, it has worked similarly to perpetuate the ideological and programmatic commitments of the few insurgencies that have succeeded. To this extent at least, the regime structure of American political history may be considered a byproduct of the constitutional structure of American government. It is manifest today in the persistence of the conservative regime ushered in by Ronald Reagan in 1980.

Looking over the course of each of these regimes suggests a number of typically structured relationships between the presidency and the political system, and thinking about the modern presidents in these terms places each of them in a unique analytic relationship with the presidents of the past. I do not mean to suggest that regime formation and decay are processes external to presidential leadership; on the contrary, I mean to show that the active intervention of presidents at various stages in these processes has driven them forward. What I am suggesting is that we try to understand the political demands and challenges of presidential leadership as variables mediated by the generation and degeneration of these political orderings, that we reverse the standard analytic procedure by holding personality and skill constant and examining the typical political effects of presidential action in the differently structured political contexts characteristic of our constitutional system.

The Political Structures of Presidential Leadership

Each regime begins with the rise to power of a new political coalition out to construct and legitimize alternative governing arrangements, to recast relations between state and society in ways advantageous to its members. These coalitions will then attempt to extend their lease on power by elaborating and modifying their basic agenda in ways that are responsive to new political demands and changes in the nation at large. Once they are established, however, coalition interests can have an enervating effect on the governing capacities of these regimes. An immediate and constant problem is posed by conflicts of interest within the dominant coalition. The danger here is that attempts to elaborate the coalition's political agenda in ways responsive to new governing conditions will focus a sectarian struggle, weaken regime support through factional disaffection, and open new avenues to power for the political opposition. A longer-range, and ultimately more devastating, problem is posed by changes in the nation at large that throw into question the dominant coalition's most basic commitments of ideology and interest. The danger here, of course, is that the entire political regime will be called into question as an inadequate governing instrument and then repudiated wholesale in a nationwide crisis of political legitimacy.

Considering the history of the presidency in this light, two systemic relationships stand out as especially significant for an analysis of the politics of leadership. First is the president's affiliation with the political complex of interests, institutions, and ideas that dominated state/society relations prior to his coming to office. Second is the current standing of these governmental arrangements in the nation at large. These relationships are, of course, always highly nuanced, but the basic variations are easily discerned, and when it comes to explaining outcomes, they do a good deal of the work. For the sake of simplicity, we can conceptualize the leadership problem with reference to those institutions with which political regimes are invariably identified in America, namely the political parties. Using this shorthand, the leadership problem confronting each president can be framed by the answers to two simple questions: is the president affiliated with the political party that has defined the government's basic commitments of ideology and interest; are the governmental commitments of that party vulnerable to direct repudiation as failed and irrelevant responses to the problems of the day?

Answers to these questions specify four typical opportunity structures for the exercise of political leadership by a president. In the first, the basic governmental commitments of the previously dominant political party are

The Political Structures of Presidential Leadership

		Presidents' political identity	
		Opposed	*Affiliated*
Regime party commitments	Vulnerable	politics of reconstruction	politics of disjunction
	Resilient	politics of preemption	politics of articulation

vulnerable to direct repudiation, and the president is associated with the opposition to them. In the second, basic governmental commitments of the previously dominant political party are again on the line, but this time the president is politically affiliated with them. In the third, the governmental commitments of the previously dominant political party still appear timely and politically resilient, but the president is linked with the political opposition to them. In the fourth, the governmental commitments of the previously dominant political party again appear to hold out robust solutions to the problems of the day and the president is affiliated with them. These four opportunity structures are represented in [the table above], with the "previously dominant political party" designated as the "regime party" for easy reference.

Each of these structures defines a different institutional relationship between the presidency and the political system, each engages the president in a different type of politics, and each defines a different kind of leadership challenge. These differences are summarized in the four cells of the table. Before proceeding to a discussion of the table, two points of clarification are in order, both of which will come to bear on the discussion of President Obama's leadership later in the chapter. First, the table is a schematic presentation of pure types that are only more or less closely approximated in history. In the discussion that follows immediately, the presidents that best fit each type are grouped together. The objective is to highlight the distinctive problems and dynamics of political action that adhere to leadership in these situations and by implication to reconsider the problems and prospects faced by leaders in our own day. The procedure radically delimits the play of personality and skill in determining leadership outcomes, but in doing so, it may also allow a more precise determination of their significance. The second point is that this typology does not provide an independent explanation of the historical patterns on which it draws. There is no accounting here for whether a regime affiliate or a regime opponent will actually be elected (or otherwise come into office), nor for when in the course of the nation's development a regime's basic governmental commitments will be called into question. My purpose is to reorganize the analysis of the politics of leadership by cutting into political history at certain typical junctures. It is to suggest the rather blunt ways in which political structure has delimited the political capacities of the presidency and informed the impact of presidential action on the political system as a whole.

The *politics of reconstruction* has been most closely approximated in the administrations of Thomas Jefferson, Andrew Jackson, Abraham Lincoln, Franklin Roosevelt, and Ronald Reagan. Each led a political insurgency, and rose to power on the heels of an electoral upheaval in political control of the institutions of the federal government. More specifically, their victories were driven by a sustained crisis of political legitimacy and a rising tide of discontent with the established order of things. In the course of events, a long-established majority party was stigmatized as the very source of the nation's problems, its discipline and resolve were broken, and it was dislodged from its dominant position in Congress as well as the presidency. With political obligations to the past severed and old dividing lines disrupted, these presidents were thrust beyond the old regime into a political interregnum where they were directly engaged in a systemic recasting of the government's basic commitments of ideology and interest. It is in these circumstances, and apparently only in these circumstances, that presidents are free to do what all political leaders seek to do: they can redefine legitimate national government in their own terms.

These presidents are widely regarded as the most effective of all political leaders in presidential history; what is less well appreciated is that they shared the same basic relationship to the political system at large. They are all known as great communicators, but this seems to have less to do with any common training or shared skill than with the fact that they all had the same basic message to communicate. Each was able to repudiate received commitments of ideology and interest outright, to indict them forthrightly as failed and illegitimate responses to the problems of the day, and to identify his leadership with a new beginning, with the salvation of the nation from political bankruptcy. Safe to say, the political preeminence of the presidency is naturally pronounced when the old regime has been widely discredited, when old alliances have been thrown into disarray, and when new interests have been thrust afresh upon governmental institutions.

More important, however, is what the performance of leaders in this situation can tell us about the structured capacities of the presidency as a political institution. Order-shattering elections do not themselves shape the future, but they vastly expand the president's capacities to break prior governmental commitments and to orchestrate a political reordering of state/society relations. It is significant in this regard that none of the presidents who reconstructed the terms and conditions of legitimate national government had much success in actually resolving the tangible problems that gave rise to the nationwide crisis of political legitimacy in the first place. Jefferson's attempt to deal with the problems at issue in the international crisis of 1798 proved a total failure;[1] Jackson's attempt to deal with the long-festering problem of national banking precipitated an economic panic and ultimately exacerbated a devastating depression; Lincoln's proposed solution to the sectional conflict of the 1850s

---

1. The reference here is to President Jefferson's failed embargo policy in his second term.

plunged the nation into a civil war; and Roosevelt's New Deal failed to pull the nation out of the Depression. But what these presidents could do, that their predecessors could not, was to define for themselves the significance of the events they oversaw and to secure the legitimacy of the solutions they proposed. Released from the burden of upholding the integrity of the old regime, these presidents were not restricted in their leadership to mere problem solving. Situated just beyond the old regime, they reformulated the nation's political agenda as a direct response to the manifest failures of the immediate past, presented their solutions as the only alternative to national ruin, and galvanized political support for a government that eyed an entirely new set of possibilities.

The leadership opportunities afforded by this kind of political breakthrough are duly matched by its characteristic political challenges. Opposition leaders become "reconstructive" when they begin to reorder relations between state and society, and that entails securing a governmental infrastructure capable of perpetuating their new design. The shape of the new regime comes to depend on the way party lines are recast and on how institutional relationships within the government are reorganized. Accordingly, it will be observed that these were all great party-building presidencies, and that each president was engaged institutionally as a negative instrument, rooting out the residual institutional supports for the politics of the past. Court battles, Bank Wars, a real Civil War—great confrontations that dislodged entire frameworks of governing are the special province of the reconstructive leader, and they can be counted on to forge new forms of opposition as well as support.[2] The reconstructive leader passes to his successor a political system that is not only reconfigured in its basic commitments of ideology and interest but newly constricted in its potential for independent action.

The *politics of disjunction* has been most closely approximated in the administrations of John Adams, John Quincy Adams, Franklin Pierce, James Buchanan, Herbert Hoover, and Jimmy Carter. With due regard for the reputations of these men for political incompetence, it is evident in identifying them as a group that they shared what is quite simply an impossible leadership situation. Rather than orchestrating a political breakthrough in state-society relations, these presidents were compelled to cope with the breakdown of those relations. Their affiliation with the old regime at a time when its basic commitments of ideology and interest were being called into question severely limited their ability to control the meaning of their own actions, and this limitation ultimately turned their office into the focal point of a nationwide crisis of political legitimacy. This situation imparts to the president a consuming preoccupation with a political challenge that is really a prerequisite of leadership, that of simply establishing his own political credibility.

Each of the major historical episodes in the politics of disjunction has been foreshadowed by a long-festering identity crisis within the old majority party

---

2. Jefferson, Jackson, and Roosevelt tangled with the Supreme Court, while Jackson destroyed the Bank of the United States.

itself. But the distinctiveness of this juncture goes beyond these simmering tensions within the ranks; it lies in changes within the nation itself that obscure the regime's relevance as an instrument of governance and cloud its legitimacy as caretaker of the national interest. Affiliated leaders get elected in these circumstances by acknowledging serious problems within the old order and holding out the promise of rehabilitation and repair. The Adamses, Pierce, Hoover, and Carter are notable for their open recognition of the vulnerabilities of the establishments with which they were affiliated; each promised to solve national problems and restore the old order to vitality. But solving the nation's problems is a hard test for any president, and in this situation, where they have little else to offer, they find themselves in especially difficult straits. Actions that challenge established commitments in the name of rehabilitation and repair are likely to leave the president isolated from his most likely political allies; actions that reach out to allies and affirm established commitments will provide insurgents with proof positive that the president has nothing new to offer, that he really is nothing more than a symptom of the problems of the day.

Invariably these presidents drive forward the crisis of legitimacy they came into office to forestall. Unable to control the meaning of their own actions, they find their actions defined by others. Having acknowledged the vulnerabilities of the old order and having failed to deliver the promised rehabilitation, they become the leading symbols of systemic political failure and regime bankruptcy. Trying to force the old order to change its ways, they wreak havoc on discipline within the ranks. In this, they clear the ground for a reconstructive leader; in their hapless struggle for credibility they strengthen the case for forthright repudiation, offer the premise for a fundamental reordering, and provide new material for doing so. Certainly it is no accident that the presidents who have set the standard of political incompetence in American political history are succeeded by presidents who set the standards of political mastery. This recurrent coupling of dismal failure with towering success suggests that the contingent political relationship between the presidency and the political system is far more telling of leadership prospects than the contingencies of personality and skill.

The *politics of preemption* has engaged a large number of presidents, some of the more aggressive leaders among them being John Tyler, Andrew Johnson, Grover Cleveland, Woodrow Wilson, Richard Nixon, and Bill Clinton. The men in this grouping stand out as wild cards in American political history. As their experiences indicate, the politics of leadership in this situation are especially volatile, and perhaps least susceptible to generalization. Tyler was purged from the ranks of the party that elected him; Wilson took a disastrous plunge from the commanding heights of world leadership into the political abyss; Johnson and Nixon were crippled by impeachment proceedings. Of all the presidents that might be grouped in this situation, only Dwight Eisenhower finished a second term without suffering a precipitous reversal of political fortune, but this exception is itself suggestive, for Eisenhower alone kept whatever intentions he might have had for altering the shape of national politics well hidden.

As leader of the opposition to a regime that still claims formidable political, ideological, and institutional support, the president interrupts the working agenda of national politics and intrudes into the establishment as a threatening force. The opportunity for creative political leadership in this situation comes from the independence that the president enjoys by virtue of his opposition stance, but so long as the incumbent is unable to issue a forthright repudiation of established commitments as bankrupt and illegitimate solutions to the problems of the day, opposition leadership is limited in its reconstructive power. Short of authority to redefine legitimate national government, preemptive leaders are left to exploit their relative freedom from received political definitions. They disavow orthodoxies of all kinds. They offer hybrid political alternatives. Their attraction lies in their unabashedly mongrel appeal, their free mixing of different, seemingly contradictory political commitments.

As a practical matter, preempting the political discourse of an established regime means simultaneously carrying the support of its stalwart opponents, avoiding a frontal attack on the orthodoxy they oppose, and offering disaffected interests normally affiliated with the dominant coalition a modification of the regime's agenda that they will find more attractive. Floating free of established commitments, preemptive leaders look for and play upon latent interest cleavages and factional discontent within the ranks of the regime's traditional supporters. Though these opportunities are not hard to identify, the political terrain to be negotiated in exploiting them is treacherous. Testing both the tolerance of stalwart opponents and the resilience of establishment allies, preemptive leaders provoke the defenders of regime norms to assault the president's highly personalized, seemingly normless political manipulations.

Compared to presidents caught in a politics of disjunction, preemptive leaders have a much greater opportunity to establish and exploit their political independence; all preemptive leaders who were elected to office in the first instance were reelected to second terms. The danger here is not that the president will be paralyzed by his affiliations but that his independent stance will not provide an alternative clear enough to keep the opposition mobilized and abet a resurgence of regime support. Independence will open him to a relentless campaign of character assassination; his threat to received norms will reenergize their supporters; his standard will remain murky. Compared to a president engaged in the politics of reconstruction, these leaders do not cut into national politics deeply enough to rearrange its foundations and that makes personal political isolation an ever-present danger. Preemptive leadership is, in fact, historically unique in its propensity to provoke impeachment proceedings. Probing alternative lines of political cleavage, these presidents may well anticipate future party building strategies, but they are more effective at disrupting the established political regime than at replacing it.

The *politics of articulation* has engaged the largest number of presidents; in contemporary politics George H. W. Bush and George W. Bush both fit the bill. If no more "normal" a situation than any other, this situation does pinpoint the distinctive problems of political leadership that arise when relations between the incumbent and established regime commitments are most consonant. Here the presidency is the font of political orthodoxy and the president, the minister to the faithful. The leadership posture is wholly affirmative; the opportunity at hand is to service coalition interests, to deliver on outstanding political commitments on the regime's agenda, and to update these commitments to accord with the times. The corresponding challenge is to uphold definitions, to affirm established norms, to maintain a sense of regime coherence and integrity in changing times, to mitigate and manage the factional ruptures within the ranks of the regime's traditional supporters that inevitably accompany alterations in the status quo ante. These challenges have been met in various ways, and with varying degrees of skill, but a look at the record suggests that the political effects are pretty much the same.

Consider the most impressive of the bunch. In each of America's major political regimes, there has been one particular episode in orthodox innovation that stands out for its programmatic accomplishments. In the Jeffersonian era, it was the administration of James Monroe; in the Jacksonian era, the administration of James Polk; in the Republican era, the administration of Theodore Roosevelt; in the liberal era, the administration of Lyndon Johnson. These administrations were not only pivotal in the course of each regime's development but also emblematic of the problems this situation poses for presidential leadership. These men exercised power in what were, for all appearances, especially propitious circumstances for orthodox innovation. At the outset of each presidency, a long-established regime party was affirmed in its control of the entire national government, and the national posture was so strong at home and abroad that it left no excuses for not finally delivering on long-heralded regime promises. Each president thus set full sail at a time when it was possible to think about completing the unfinished business of national politics, about realizing the regime's vision of America and finally turning the party of orthodoxy into a consensual party of the nation. To that end, each pressed programmatic action at home and adopted an aggressive muscle-flexing posture toward the rest of the world.

But just as surely as a leadership project of culmination and completion suggests a great leap into the promised land, it accentuates the underlying problem of definition, of upholding fundamental commitments in some coherent fashion and having old allies see the new arrangements arrived at as the legitimate expression of their ideals. Each of America's great orthodox innovators found his administration mired in the dilemmas of reconciling old commitments with the expansive political possibilities at hand. Leading a regime at the apex of its projection of national power and purpose, each produced a regime vastly overextended in its governing commitments; pushing ahead with the received business while also embellishing regime commitments, each fomented deep schisms within his own ranks; effecting significant changes in the name of regime continuity, each undercut his ability to speak for the church. While most fully articulating his regime as a system of national government, these presidents were each charged with a betrayal of the faith, and each pulled the regime into an accelerated sectarian struggle over the true meaning of orthodoxy. These presidencies were not undermined by the assaults of their nominal political opponents but by the disaffection of their ostensible allies.

Articulation can look a lot like preemption. After all, leaders in both situations stretch established orthodoxies to accommodate new realities and purposes, broaching questions about their own legitimacy in the process. But the political dynamics are quite different. Whereas preemptive leaders openly seek to explode received definitions and established norms, orthodox innovators seek to maintain them. In the politics of preemption, political disaffection and factional divisions within the ranks of the dominant coalition provide opportunities that the leader has every incentive to exploit; in the politics of articulation they present risks that the leader is constrained to forestall. If the preemptive leader is a wild card openly disdainful of received conceptions of the alternatives, the orthodox innovator is a stalwart at pains to render change consistent with past commitments and to merge the new seamlessly into the old. Preemptive leaders probe for reconstructive possibilities; orthodox innovators seek to stave off the threat of a political disjunction.

Barack Obama: A Closer Look

So far we have described four political structures for presidential leadership, we have identified several cases of each type from across presidential history, and we have examined their characteristic politics. We have seen as well that these types are not randomly distributed across history. They have played out in fairly coherent sequences of political change spanning several decades of time: a durable reconstruction of commitments and priorities opens on to several interactive episodes of articulation and preemption before fomenting a politics of disjunction. All along the way, the role of personal attributes—character and skill—in determining the outcome of leadership efforts is closely circumscribed. There have been very few great political leaders in presidential history, but that is not because the necessary talents are in such short supply; it is because presidential leadership is rarely exercised in political circumstances conducive to sustaining its legitimacy.

There is more to this analysis, however, than fitting presidents into boxes. The typology does not sap individual efforts of significance; on the contrary, it identifies the prominent role presidential leadership plays in constructing these sequences and moving them along. Moreover, by illuminating the general contextual variables that have served, time and again, to distinguish one effort from the next, and by specifying the particular political dynamics that are likely to adhere to any given effort, the framework directs attention to the potential significance of elements in each that might otherwise be lost from view.

More specifically, calling attention to system-level variables invites us to look more closely at how individuals test opportunities and respond to constraints *as they are presented in the moment at hand*. When we control for basic types, we are likely to be less dismissive of the efforts of failed leaders and less enamored of the great success. Leadership is no longer about who has what it takes to make the system work but about how, and to what extent, individual efforts manipulate and alter these workings. Single out Jimmy Carter for special examination within this framework and we are immediately alerted to his relentless drive to challenge the constraint of his affiliation with a faltering establishment; single out Ronald Reagan and we are immediately alerted to his lack of success in actually dislodging institutions and programs vital to the regime he was repudiating. These subtle variations may not alter popular judgments of failure and success; absent the typology such distinctions might seem marginal. But presidents tend to play at the margins, they probe and stretch for new possibilities, and that is where analysis of their efforts should be directed. The typology is best read in this way, not as a static set of boxes but as a set of dynamic and interactive relationships that have operated over the full course of American political history and that continue to evolve with important implications for our political system as a whole.

This is certainly the most fruitful way to employ the framework in assessing the still-unfolding leadership of Barack Obama. Obama is the second opposition leader to come to power since the Reagan reconstruction and the establishment of the conservative regime. He follows in the immediate aftermath of a vigorous round of orthodox innovation under George W. Bush, a performance which, true to type, left the conservative cause seriously overextended and exposed in political commitments, foreign and domestic. Even before the collapse of the financial markets in the waning weeks of the Bush administration, issues swirling around the war in Iraq, the response to Hurricane Katrina, the drive to privatize Social Security, and middle-class insecurities had worked to foment discontent with Republican priorities and strengthened the hands of their opponents.

The typology speaks directly to these circumstances and clarifies the central leadership question they put in play. From the start of his campaign for the presidency, Obama's leadership has turned on the force and catalytic effect of his challenge to the conservative regime. Just how far would he push beyond the confines of preemptive politics toward a durable political reconstruction? History suggests that the commitments that comprise a political regime tend over time to lose their integrity and appeal, and that opposition leadership tends to become stronger as these regimes become more vulnerable. In short, an assault on the conservative regime more direct and explicit than Bill Clinton's was already in the cards. But historically, reconstruction has not followed simply as a matter of course; it has always required more than a keen ear for discontent and a strong critique. Richard Nixon's assault on the liberal establishment of the post–New Deal years was more forceful than Dwight Eisenhower's, and Woodrow Wilson's assault on the Republican establishment of the industrial era was more forceful than Grover Cleveland's. But neither of these opposition leaders altered the playing field sufficiently to secure a new standard of legitimate national government. In both cases, the immediate effect was that, once again, the old order surged back.

It is easy to identify contextual factors pushing Obama to play up the potential for something more than another preemption. First and foremost was the electoral imperative of distinguishing himself from the early front-runner for the Democratic nomination, Hillary Rodham Clinton. Clinton was a formidable candidate, well positioned to bring the Democrats back to power. Obama could not match her experience, nor did he have a significantly different policy agenda to offer. Moreover, it was uncertain at best whether the novelty of the first African American president would be more attractive to voters than the novelty of the first woman president. Denying Clinton the Democratic nomination was a long shot, and to do it, Obama had to make an issue of Clintonism itself, to play upon memories of its political limitations. He tapped the sense of the moment that conditions were ripe for something more than a mere restoration of Democratic control, that the time had come for something more definitive, something "transformational." The slogan "change we can believe in" was only one of many veiled references to the disappointments of the Clinton era. More direct was Obama's effort to bracket the Clinton years, to identify himself with a mission of greater import, and to anticipate a more potent form of leadership. Adopting the Reagan model, Obama sought at once to define the context for himself, to up the stakes of the contest at hand, and to make his bid for leadership seem less idiosyncratic: "I don't want to present myself as some sort of singular figure," Obama said. "I think part of what's different are the times. I do think that for example that 1980 was different. I think Ronald Reagan changed the trajectory of America in a way that Richard Nixon did not and in a way that Bill Clinton did not. He put us on a fundamentally different path because the country was ready for it."

Signaling of this sort makes perfect sense within our framework. The Obama campaign nosed past Clinton by filling the air with anticipation of a reconstructive moment. But our typology targets more than a set of aspirations. It invites us to examine the prospects for making good on them. By comparing Obama's circumstances and early actions with those of other reconstructive leaders, we are able to identify variations and scrutinize their likely impact on any bid to push opposition beyond preemption. Several novel elements in his rise to power immediately stand out for special attention in this regard.

First is the absence in this sequence of an affiliated president who had candidly acknowledged deep-seated problems within the older order and addressed his leadership to resolving them. George W. Bush may have left the conservative regime overextended and exposed, but his unbridled boosterism left open the possibility that these problems stemmed from his particular rendition of the old orthodoxy, not from the orthodoxy itself. There was no long drawn-out test of the prospects for rehabilitation and repair in the sequence leading up to Obama's victory, no clear demonstration that the nation was suffering from something more than "Bush fatigue." There is no mistaking the leader who might have done this. John McCain, the self-styled "maverick" of the Republican party, was about as clear an example of the insider critic of an established regime as American history affords. McCain's message in 2008 was that the Republican party had lost its way and that his leadership would put conservatism back on track. Like Obama, McCain appealed to Reagan, but he did not return to Reagan for a model of reconstructive leadership; he returned to Reagan to reaffirm the foundational commitments of contemporary conservatism and to guide a revitalization of the conservative regime. McCain's 2008 campaign was the perfect setup for a sustained politics of disjunction; a McCain victory would have ushered in a direct and sustained test of the conservatives' capacities to respond to manifest and accumulating problems without destroying themselves in the process. As it happened, the Obama reconstruction was left to ride on prospects for skipping this disjunctive phase or on hopes that Bush's second term might serve as a surrogate.

Disjunctive politics has traditionally operated in a dynamic relationship with reconstructive politics. It opens an extended struggle among supporters of the old regime over how to move forward, and in doing so it tends to deepen the conflict over the foundational principles of the regime. That has not yet happened to the conservatives, and until it does an opposition leader is likely to find it hard to rework coalitional alignments and institutional arrangements. Disjunctive politics abets reconstruction by so deepening the crisis of legitimacy and so weakening the commitments of regime supporters as to thrust the opposition leader beyond all semblance of order. Without a disjunctive episode, the line between preemptive politics and reconstructive politics becomes harder to cross.

The equivocal political effect (so far) of the financial collapse of the Fall of 2008 is especially telling in this regard. On the one hand, by indicting some of the founding principles of the conservative regime—its commitment to government deregulation and its faith in self-regulating markets—it significantly strengthened the prima facie case against it. From his earliest months in power, Obama has seized this opportunity to press a more expansive case for change. He has continually railed against "a legacy of misplaced priorities" and taken aim at systemic failures: "[This] crisis is neither the result of a normal turn in the business cycle nor an accident of history. We arrived at this point as a result of an era of profound irresponsibility that engulfed both private and public institutions from some of our companies' executive suites to the seats of power in Washington, D.C." On the other hand, the immediate fallout from this crisis and the burdens of crisis management did not fall on a conservative administration. Conservatives were not forced into a long drawn-out confrontation with their own fundamental principles. Instead, the Obama administration was, as a practical matter, immediately engaged in stabilizing the system it was repudiating. Notwithstanding its sweeping diagnosis of the problem, bold demonstrations of a new kind of politics took a back seat to bank bailouts and taxpayer support for corporations deemed "too big to fail." The absence of a disjunctive phase made it harder to act on the political premise that the financial collapse was a crisis of the old order, and the actions the administration did take to meet the emergency raised serious questions about its reconstructive credentials.

Prospects for skipping a disjunctive stage and moving directly to reconstruction have been clouded further by another conspicuous absence. Reconstructive leadership is associated historically with mass-based social movements, movements that have already ripened on discontent with the established order of things and that stand apart from the candidates and parties that promote their interests. The abolition movement was an independent force pushing Lincoln and the Republicans toward reconstructive politics; the labor movement was an independent force pushing FDR and the Democrats; the conservative movement an independent force pushing Ronald Reagan and the

Republicans. To the extent that Obama was a movement-based candidate, the movement was largely about Obama himself. It was based on his own personal charisma and his personal vision of a new kind of politics. Notwithstanding its organizational and technological innovations, this was not the sort of movement likely to have much leverage over the new president or over other Democrats in Congress.

In this regard, the size and scope of Obama's election victory may have been less significant than its shape. If the Obama movement attracted liberals and primary campaign voters with the promise of fundamental change, the new elements its leader brought to the Democratic column in November presented a more complicated picture. Obama's majority was built upon the addition of independent voters and on the incorporation of conservative-leaning states in the southeast and mountain west. It is unlikely that these voters were driven by interest in reconstructing the political system; more likely they were looking for some relief from rigidly ideological approaches to leadership and hoping for more effective responses to the immediate problems at hand. Accordingly, the early months of the administration have featured conspicuous displays of the difficulty of holding, and making use of, new support for the Democratic party without disillusioning its base, displays that seem to compromise the mobilizing appeals of reconstructive leadership and hold leadership more firmly on preemptive ground. One of the great ironies of the Obama administration as it has progressed thus far is that the populist critique of entrenched interests and unresponsive government that so often fuels reconstructive leadership has been turned against a leader who avows his commitment to fundamental change in government and politics. The only new social mobilization apparent in the nation at large is the Tea Party Nation, a movement that threatens to reenergize the conservative base and to radicalize conservative resistance to the president.

A final point of comparison is closely related to observations about the limited social mobilization pressing Obama's reconstruction forward. Anticipation of a reconstructive moment prompts close scrutiny of the transformative idea itself. Reconstructive leaders are politicians, not philosophers; nonetheless, they do tend to bring to power certain organizing principles that clearly make their mark on the reconstructive outcome. Even FDR, who shifted his tactics radically over the course of his presidency and who has a reputation among historians for inconsistency and pragmatism, gave a campaign address at the Commonwealth Club of San Francisco outlining the thrust of the New Deal and what would become the welfare state. Reagan, Lincoln, and Jefferson are even more closely identified with the promulgation of governing principles that were both substantively grounded and qualitatively new. By these standards, the Obama idea, at least as it has been promulgated thus far, is different. Where it is new, it is not particularly substantive, and where it is substantive, it is not particularly new.

First, there is the idea of Obama himself. He is a transformational figure by virtue of the racial barriers that fell with his election. It is hard to think of an idea that can compete with the political and cultural significance of an African American ascending to the presidency. Nonetheless, this event signals a particular kind of transformation, and how it comports with reconstructive leadership, as it has unfolded historically, is not self-evident. Indeed, in several important respects, Obama's rise to power was abetted by a set of ideas that seem to put him quite far afield of the traditional ground of reconstructive politics. When he envisions a different kind of politics, he tends to put process over substance. He speaks of a consensual approach aimed at finding common ground; he anticipates superseding differences and healing divisions. He evokes the promise of a "post-partisan" era of collective deliberation and reasoned discourse. Though that would certainly be something radically new, the contrast with the politics of reconstruction as practiced in America historically could not be more stark. Reconstructive leadership in America is associated with party *building*, with wrenching political assaults on the institutional supports of the old order, with a dogged will to repudiate forthrightly those who stand in the way of new priorities. If there is a personal factor of overriding importance in determining Obama's leadership, it may be this: that an African American president cannot yet risk the hard-edged and divisive confrontations that political reconstruction has, as a practical matter, always required.

The reconstructive thrust of Obama's leadership is clouded further on the substantive side, for it has joined the promise of a post-partisan politics with a promise to deliver on the liberals' traditional policy preferences. Obama has big policy ideas, but few of them are new ideas of the sort associated historically with political reconstructions. They are the same ideas that have been dividing liberals and conservatives for decades and, as such, they seem more likely to perpetuate current conflicts than to transcend them. It is hard enough to see how vigorous action on behalf of these ideas will reconfigure the political landscape, let alone how it will usher in a new era of bipartisan civility and common deliberation. The dissonance between the governmental vision and the governmental program would seem to impede decisive action on either front.

Skill in Context

If there is a conclusion to be drawn about Obama's leadership at this point in his presidency, it is that it takes more than individual talent, political skill, and personal appeal to "transform" American government and politics. There is no denying that Obama is a charismatic figure, no denying that he draws on a deep reservoir of personal resources, no denying that his election was in itself a momentous event. But thus far in his presidency, the systemic determinants of leadership outcomes seem to hold sway. Obama promised to do more than simply bring the Democratic opposition back to power. His campaign rhetoric discounted the preemptive leadership of Clinton and invoked reconstructive possibilities. In so doing, it has highlighted the line that distinguishes preemptive from reconstructive leadership and riveted attention on the factors that have made it difficult to cross over.

Historically, the reconstructive leader's greatest resource has been the authority to repudiate. In Obama's case, this authority has been compromised by several factors. The proximity of the economic collapse to his rise to power left him with full responsibility for stabilizing the very system he was rejecting rhetorically. There is no independent popular movement at the president's back agitating for a fundamental change, nothing to make a more radical rearrangement of interests and power an essential requisite to the restoration of order and stability. Finally, there is little that is new in the substantive agenda of reform that promises to alter the old terms of debate or recast the party divide. By the standards of prior episodes of reconstructive politics, these are formidable constraints, and it is hard to see how they can be overcome by personal effort alone.

Obama's historic victory in the monumental battle over comprehensive health care reform may be most telling of all in this regard. There is no denying the social significance of this accomplishment; its political significance, however, is less clear. What is striking is that this legislation overhauled the health care system and vastly expanded the social safety net in America without much change in the underlying distribution of political power. Indeed, it is hard to think of another reform on this scale that did so little to rearrange political power. The secret of Obama's success seems to be that he found a way to work a major reform *through* the interests in the health care industry rather than against them, keeping the power of all the major players largely intact. Even the private insurance companies, who bore the rhetorical burden of the reform drive, were never seriously threatened in their position as the cornerstone of the system. As in financial reform, the health care initiative seems to aim less at repudiating the system than at managing it more responsibly. To the extent that reconstruction has historically turned on dislodging or at least systematically disadvantaging interests and institutions of vital significance to the politics of the past, the Obama presidency has yet to make a decisive move.

This is not to judge Obama a failure. Quite the contrary, the point is to push the analysis of presidential leadership beyond crude judgments of that sort. As an opposition leader, Obama maintains considerable political independence and freedom to maneuver. He stands against a party and a regime that seem hard pressed to come up with constructive solutions of their own to the most pressing problems of the day. The situation is volatile. It is hardly inconceivable that a skillful exploitation of events will tip the balance in favor of more thoroughgoing rearrangements, and even if it doesn't, the Clintonians within the Obama administration are expert in exploiting the preemptive appeal of more moderate, hybrid alternatives. It should also be noted in this regard that reconstruction has historically played out over the full course of a presidency; it has never been firmly in hand after one year or even two years. Much depends on the incumbent's response to the push back against change and on his authority to repudiate those who stand in the way.

But the most profound question surrounding Obama's leadership may not be whether it will cross the line into reconstructive politics or merely agitate its cause in the preemptive mode. The history of reconstructive politics suggests that we may be witnessing the erosion of the authority of American presidents to transform things even in the most fortuitous of circumstances. For all the power the American presidency gained over the course of the twentieth century, the cleanest examples of reconstructive leadership in American history are the nineteenth-century examples. By the time we get to Franklin Roosevelt and the New Deal, we find the president going down to defeat on some of his most transformative initiatives, and by the time we get to Ronald Reagan and conservative "revolution," reconstruction appears more ideological and rhetorical than institutional. This suggests that prospects for actually dislodging established interests and institutions have been on the wane for some time, that interest networks are growing too strong and institutions too interdependent for any president to clear the ground for something categorically new. The first year of the Obama administration offered a vivid demonstration of the resilience of established networks of power and of the imperatives of working significant change through rather than against them. If that proves a permanent condition, if power arrangements are no longer susceptible to the presidential battering ram, the reconstructive mode of leadership may continue to weaken, and the characteristic method of renewing American politics through the presidency may prove to be a thing of the past.

Discussion Questions

1. Does Greenstein's emphasis on the individual or Skowronek's emphasis on the political structure provide the better understanding of presidential leadership?

2. How would Greenstein deal with the contention that even a president with strong character and skills would be unsuccessful in the face of unfavorable political circumstances?

3. How would Skowronek deal with the contention that even in the politics of reconstruction, the best opportunity structure a president can enjoy, the creation of a new regime requires vision and skill?

4. How do Greenstein and Skowronek differ in their analyses of Barack Obama? Whose interpretation of the Obama presidency do you find more persuasive?

Suggested Readings and Internet Resources

The classic study of how presidents can gain—or lose—power in the White House is Richard E. Neustadt, *Presidential Power and the Modern Presidents* (New York: Free Press, 1990). Stephen Skowronek demonstrates how presidential leadership is shaped by "political time" in *The Politics Presidents Make: Leadership from John Adams to Bill Clinton* (Cambridge, Mass.: Harvard University Press, 1997). For clashing perspectives on major topics in presidential politics, see Richard J. Ellis and Michael Nelson, eds., *Debating the Presidency*, 2nd ed.

(Washington, D.C.: Congressional Quarterly Press, 2010). Portraits of both elite democratic and popular democratic leadership are found in Bruce Miroff, *Icons of Democracy: American Leaders as Heroes, Aristocrats, Dissenters, and Democrats* (Lawrence: University Press of Kansas, 2000). For an intriguing argument that presidential rhetoric has been "dumbed down" at a significant cost for American democracy, see Elvin T. Lim, *The Anti-Intellectual Presidency: The Decline of Presidential Rhetoric from George Washington to George W. Bush* (New York: Oxford University Press, 2008).

The White House
www.whitehouse.gov
The president's website, containing speeches, documents, press briefings, and assorted information on the administration, also offers e-mail communication with the White House.

Center for the Study of the Presidency
www.cspresidency.org
This is the website of a nonpartisan organization that holds student conferences and publishes a scholarly journal. The site offers publications and provides links to research sites on the presidency.

Chapter 15

✳

The Judiciary: How Should It Interpret Our Constitution?

Americans like to think of the justices of the Supreme Court as grave and learned elders of the law, engaged in a search for justice that has little to do with the selfish interests and ambitions that we so often associate with politics. The justices themselves encourage this view, holding court in a marble temple (the Supreme Court Building), wearing black robes, shrouding their decision-making processes in secrecy. Yet an institution that makes authoritative decisions about many of the most troublesome issues of our times—abortion, affirmative action, the rights of the accused, the relationship between church and state—cannot be kept aloof from politics. Thus, the Supreme Court's role in the political system as the final arbiter of the Constitution has become one of the central issues in current debates about American democracy.

From one perspective, the Supreme Court is not really a democratic institution at all. The nine justices of the Supreme Court are not elected; they are nominated by the president and confirmed by the Senate. They serve during good behavior—that is, until they retire, die, or are impeached by the House and convicted by the Senate. Composed exclusively of practitioners of one profession, lawyers, the Court can use its power of judicial review to strike down laws passed by legislatures that have been elected by the majority.

From another perspective, however, the Supreme Court is an essential component of American democracy. Its most important role is as a guardian of the Constitution, which is the fundamental expression of the people's will. According to this view, the Court sometimes must oppose the wishes of a temporary majority in the name of the abiding principles and values contained in the Constitution.

During the past several decades, landmark decisions by the Supreme Court have often evoked democratic debates. Some decisions by the Court have been approved by a majority of Americans but have been fiercely resisted by intense minorities. Among these have been *Brown v. Board of Education* (1954), ordering school desegregation, and *Roe v. Wade* (1973), guaranteeing the right of a woman to choose to have an abortion. Other decisions have been opposed by a large majority. Among these have been *Engel v. Vitale* (1962), which forbade prayer in public schools, and *Miranda v. Arizona* (1966), which required police to inform criminal suspects of their rights before they could be interrogated.

Decisions such as these led critics to charge the Court with overstepping its proper role in the political system. The debate heated up during the presidency of Ronald Reagan. Reagan's attorney general, Edwin Meese III, accused the Court of substituting its own preferences and prejudices for the principles of the Constitution. Springing to the defense of the Court against Meese was Justice William Brennan Jr., who played an influential role in crafting many of the decisions that Meese was condemning. Since the 1980s, the debate has continued, as is evident in our selections written by two current members of the Supreme Court, Antonin Scalia and Stephen Breyer.

Antonin Scalia, the intellectual leader of the conservatives on the contemporary Court, is an advocate of "textualism." He argues that justices must read the text of the Constitution in light of its "original meaning" and not smuggle new meanings into its unchanging phrases. Any other method of constitutional interpretation, he warns, opens the door to a formless and standard-free subjectivity on the part of judges. Scalia is particularly critical of the idea of a "Living Constitution," which makes our fundamental law into a flexible instrument designed to change with the times. It is his view that this doctrine, favored by the liberals on the Court, allows justices to make the Constitution into whatever they—or the popular majority—prefer at the moment rather than what the framers originally set down in a text meant to endure.

Stephen Breyer, one of those whom Scalia criticizes, suggests that justices will inevitably interpret the Constitution with an eye to certain values that it contains. His proposal is that constitutional interpreters pay attention to "active liberty," the framers' commitment to the ancient ideal of a self-governing people, and consider how the consequences of the decisions they render serve this ideal. He believes that this approach does not turn the justices into freewheeling radicals, distorting the Constitution to mean whatever they want, but it does place the Supreme Court in the service of the higher objectives of the framers. Breyer is skeptical of Scalia's claim to honor the text and original meaning of the Constitution. In his argument, the "textualist" (sometimes called the "originalist") position is free of neither subjectivity nor choice, and it conceals the conservative goals of its proponents under the cloak of the constitutional framers.

Among the three branches of the national government, the judiciary is clearly the most elite in its selection process, composition, and form of deliberation. Yet in the debate between Scalia and Breyer, each tries to associate his view of the judiciary with the more democratic position. Which of the two has the superior argument? Should we be guided in interpreting the Constitution only by the "original meaning" of the words used by its framers, or must we read the Constitution in a more adaptive fashion consistent with our values and needs as a democratic people? Should our understanding of constitutional rights be squarely rooted in the text of the Constitution, or should we apply constitutional values to the protection of rights for individuals and groups that the framers never thought to protect? Must the Court, as an unelected branch of government, avoid undemocratic action by acting with deference toward the elected branches, or must it actively pursue the democratic aspirations of the Constitution even when this brings the judiciary into conflict with the elected branches?

Textualism and the Constitution

ANTONIN SCALIA

Textualism

The philosophy of interpretation I [describe] is known as textualism. In some sophisticated circles, it is considered simpleminded—"wooden," "unimaginative," "pedestrian." It is none of that. To be a textualist in good standing, one need not be too dull to perceive the broader social purposes that a statute is designed, or could be designed, to serve; or too hidebound to realize that new times require new laws. One need only hold the belief that judges have no authority to pursue those broader purposes or write those new laws.

Textualism should not be confused with so-called strict constructionism, a degraded form of textualism that brings the whole philosophy into disrepute. I am not a strict constructionist, and no one ought to be—though better that, I suppose, than a nontextualist. A text should not be construed strictly, and it should not be construed leniently; it should be construed reasonably, to contain all that it fairly means. The difference between textualism and strict constructionism can be seen in a case my Court decided [in 1993]. The statute at issue provided for an increased jail term if, "during and in relation to ... [a] drug trafficking crime," the defendant "uses ... a firearm." The defendant in this case had sought to purchase a quantity of cocaine; and what he had offered to give in exchange for the cocaine was an unloaded firearm, which he showed to the drug-seller. The Court held, I regret to say, that the defendant was subject to the increased penalty, because he had "used a firearm during and in relation to a drug trafficking crime." The vote was not even close (6–3). I dissented. Now I cannot say whether my colleagues in the majority voted the way they did because they are strict-construction textualists, or because they are not textualists at all. But a proper textualist, which is to say my kind of textualist, would surely have voted to acquit. The phrase "uses a gun" fairly connoted use of a gun for what guns are normally used for, that is, as a weapon. As I put the point in my dissent, when you ask someone, "Do you use a cane?" you are not inquiring whether he has hung his grandfather's antique cane as a decoration in the hallway.

But while the good textualist is not a literalist, neither is he a nihilist. Words do have a limited range of meaning, and no interpretation that goes beyond that range is permissible. My favorite example of a departure from text—and certainly the departure that has enabled judges to do more freewheeling lawmaking than any other—pertains to the Due Process Clause found in the Fifth and Fourteenth Amendments of the United States Constitution, which says that no person shall "be deprived of life, liberty, or property without due process of law." It has been interpreted to prevent the government from taking away certain liberties *beyond* those, such as freedom of speech and of religion, that are specifically named in the Constitution. (The first Supreme Court case to use the Due Process Clause in this fashion was, by the way, *Dred Scott*—not a desirable parentage.) Well, it may or may not be a good thing to guarantee additional liberties, but the Due Process Clause quite obviously does not bear that interpretation. By its inescapable terms, it guarantees only process. Property can be taken by the state; liberty can be taken; even life can be taken; but not without the *process* that our traditions require—notably, a validly enacted law and a fair trial. To say otherwise is to abandon textualism, and to render democratically adopted texts mere springboards for judicial lawmaking.

Of all the criticisms leveled against textualism, the most mindless is that it is "formalistic." The answer to that is, *of course it's formalistic!* The rule of law is *about* form. If, for example, a citizen performs an act—let us say the sale of certain technology to a foreign country—which is prohibited by a widely publicized bill proposed by the administration and passed by both houses of Congress, *but not yet signed by the President*, that sale is lawful. It is of no consequence that everyone knows both houses of Congress and the President wish to prevent that sale. Before the wish becomes a binding law, it must be embodied in a bill that passes both houses and is signed by the President. Is that not formalism? A murderer has been caught with blood on his hands, bending over the body of his victim; a neighbor with a video camera has filmed the crime; and the murderer has confessed in writing and on videotape. We nonetheless insist that before the state can punish this miscreant, it must conduct a full-dress criminal trial that results in a verdict of guilty. Is that not formalism? Long live formalism. It is what makes a government a government of laws and not of men....

Interpreting Constitutional Texts

... I wish to address a final subject: the distinctive problem of constitutional interpretation. The problem is distinctive, not because special principles of interpretation apply, but because the usual principles are being applied to an unusual text. Chief Justice Marshall put the point as well as it can be put in *McCulloch v. Maryland*:

> A constitution, to contain an accurate detail of all the subdivisions of which its great powers will admit, and of all the means by which they may be carried into execution, would partake of the prolixity of a legal code, and could scarcely be embraced by the human mind. It would probably never be understood by the public. Its nature, therefore, requires that only its great outlines should be marked, its important objects designated, and the minor ingredients which compose those objects be deduced from the nature of the objects themselves.

In textual interpretation, context is everything, and the context of the Constitution tells us not to expect nit-picking detail, and to give words and phrases an expansive rather than narrow interpretation—though not an interpretation that the language will not bear.

Take, for example, the provision of the First Amendment that forbids abridgment of "the freedom of speech, or of the press." That phrase does not list the full range of communicative expression. Handwritten letters, for example, are neither speech nor press. Yet surely there is no doubt they cannot be censored. In this constitutional context, speech and press, the two most common forms of communication, stand as a sort of synecdoche for the whole. That is not strict construction, but it is reasonable construction.

It is curious that most of those who insist that the drafter's intent gives meaning to a statute reject the drafter's intent as the criterion for interpretation of the Constitution. I reject it for both. I will consult the writings of some men who happened to be delegates to the Constitutional Convention—Hamilton's and Madison's writings in *The Federalist*, for example. I do so, however, not because they were Framers and therefore their intent is authoritative and must be the law; but rather because their writings, like those of other intelligent and informed people of the time, display how the text of the Constitution was originally understood. Thus I give equal weight to Jay's pieces in *The Federalist*, and to Jefferson's writings, even though neither of them was a Framer. What I look for in the Constitution is precisely what I look for in a statute: the original meaning of the text, not what the original draftsmen intended.

But the Great Divide with regard to constitutional interpretation is not that between Framers' intent and objective meaning, but rather that between *original* meaning (whether derived from Framers' intent or not) and *current* meaning. The ascendant school of constitutional interpretation affirms the existence of what is called The Living Constitution, a body of law that (unlike normal statutes) grows and changes from age to age, in order to meet the needs of a changing society. And it is the judges who determine those needs and "find" that changing law....

If you go into a constitutional law class, or study a constitutional law casebook, or read a brief filed in a constitutional law case, you will rarely find the discussion addressed to the text of the constitutional provision that is at issue, or to the question of what was the originally understood or even the originally intended meaning of that text. The starting point of the analysis will be Supreme Court cases, and the new issue will presumptively be decided according to the logic that those cases expressed, with no regard for how far that logic, thus extended, has distanced us from the original text and understanding. Worse still, however, it is known and understood that if that logic fails to produce what in the view of the current Supreme Court is the *desirable* result for the case at hand, then, like good common-law judges, the Court will distinguish its precedents, or narrow them, or if all else fails overrule them, in order that the Constitution might mean what it *ought* to mean. Should there be—to take one of the less controversial examples—a constitutional right to die? If so, there is. Should there be a constitutional right to reclaim a biological child put out for adoption by the other parent? Again, if so, there is. If it is good, it is so. Never mind the text that we are supposedly construing; we will smuggle these new rights in, if all else fails, under the Due Process Clause (which, as I have described, is textually incapable of containing them). Moreover, what the Constitution meant yesterday it does not necessarily mean today. As our opinions say in the context of our Eighth Amendment jurisprudence (the Cruel and Unusual Punishments Clause), its meaning changes to reflect "the evolving standards of decency that mark the progress of a maturing society." ...

One would suppose that the rule that a text does not change would apply a fortiori to a constitution. If courts felt too much bound by the democratic process to tinker with statutes, when their tinkering could be adjusted by the legislature, how much more should they feel bound not to tinker with a constitution, when their tinkering is virtually irreparable. It certainly cannot be said that a constitution naturally suggests changeability; to the contrary, its whole purpose is to prevent change—to embed certain rights in such a manner that future generations cannot readily take them away. A society that adopts a bill of rights is skeptical that "evolving standards of decency" always "mark progress," and that societies always "mature," as opposed to rot. Neither the text of such a document nor the intent of its framers (whichever you choose) can possibly lead to the conclusion that its only effect is to take the power of changing rights away from the legislature and give it to the courts.

Flexibility and Liberality of The Living Constitution

The argument most frequently made in favor of The Living Constitution is a pragmatic one: Such an evolutionary approach is necessary in order to provide the "flexibility" that a changing society requires; the Constitution would have snapped if it had not been permitted to bend and grow. This might be a persuasive argument if most of the "growing" that the proponents of this approach have brought upon us in the past, and are determined to bring upon us in the future, were the *elimination* of restrictions upon democratic government. But just the opposite is true. Historically, and particularly in the past thirty-five years, the "evolving" Constitution has imposed a vast array of new constraints—new inflexibilities—upon administrative, judicial, and legislative action. To mention only a few things that formerly could be done or not done, as the society desired, but now cannot be done:

- admitting in a state criminal trial evidence of guilt that was obtained by an unlawful search;

- permitting invocation of God at public-school graduations;

- electing one of the two houses of a state legislature the way the United States Senate is elected, i.e., on a basis that does not give all voters numerically equal representation;

- terminating welfare payments as soon as evidence of fraud is received, subject to restoration after hearing if the evidence is satisfactorily refuted;

- imposing property requirements as a condition of voting;

- prohibiting anonymous campaign literature;

- prohibiting pornography.

And the future agenda of constitutional evolutionists is mostly more of the same—the creation of *new* restrictions upon democratic government, rather than the elimination of old ones. *Less* flexibility in government, not *more*. As things now stand, the state and federal governments may either apply capital punishment or abolish it, permit suicide or forbid it—all as the changing times and the changing sentiments of society may demand. But when capital punishment is held to violate the Eighth Amendment, and suicide is held to be protected by the Fourteenth Amendment, all flexibility with regard to those matters will be gone. No, the reality of the matter is that, generally speaking, devotees of The Living Constitution do not seek to facilitate social change but to prevent it.

There are, I must admit, a few exceptions to that—a few instances in which, historically, greater flexibility has been the result of the process. But those exceptions serve only to refute another argument of the proponents of an evolving Constitution, that evolution will always be in the direction of greater personal liberty. (They consider that a great advantage, for reasons that I do not entirely understand. All government represents a balance between individual freedom and social order, and it is not true that every alteration of that balance in the direction of greater individual freedom is necessarily good.) But in any case, the record of history refutes the proposition that the evolving Constitution will invariably enlarge individual rights. The most obvious refutation is the modern Court's limitation of the constitutional protections afforded to property. The provision prohibiting impairment of the obligation of contracts, for example, has been gutted. I am sure that We the People agree with that development; we value property rights less than the Founders did. So also, we value the right to bear arms less than did the Founders (who thought the right of self-defense to be absolutely fundamental), and there will be few tears shed if and when the Second Amendment is held to guarantee nothing more than the state National Guard. But this just shows that the Founders were right when they feared that some (in their view misguided) future generation might wish to abandon liberties that they considered essential, and so sought to protect those liberties in a

Bill of Rights. We may *like* the abridgment of property rights and *like* the elimination of the right to bear arms; but let us not pretend that these are not *reductions* of *rights*.

Or if property rights are too cold to arouse enthusiasm, and the right to bear arms too dangerous, let me give another example: Several terms ago a case came before the Supreme Court involving a prosecution for sexual abuse of a young child. The trial court found that the child would be too frightened to testify in the presence of the (presumed) abuser, and so, pursuant to state law, she was permitted to testify with only the prosecutor and defense counsel present, with the defendant, the judge, and the jury watching over closed-circuit television. A reasonable enough procedure, and it was held to be constitutional by my Court. I dissented, because the Sixth Amendment provides that "[i]n *all* criminal prosecutions the accused shall enjoy the right ... to be confronted with the witnesses against him" (emphasis added). There is no doubt what confrontation meant—or indeed means today. It means face-to-face, not watching from another room. And there is no doubt what one of the major purposes of that provision was: to induce *precisely* that pressure upon the witness which the little girl found it difficult to endure. It is difficult to accuse someone to his face, particularly when you are lying. Now no extrinsic factors have changed since that provision was adopted in 1791. Sexual abuse existed then as it does now; little children were more easily upset than adults, then as now; a means of placing the defendant out of sight of the witness existed then as now (a screen could easily have been erected that would enable the defendant to see the witness, but not the witness the defendant). But the Sixth Amendment nonetheless gave *all* criminal defendants the right to *confront* the witnesses against them, because that was thought to be an important protection. The only significant things that *have* changed, I think, are the society's sensitivity to so-called psychic trauma (which is what we are told the child witness in such a situation suffers) and the society's assessment of where the proper balance ought to be struck between the two extremes of a procedure that assures convicting 100 percent of all child abusers, and a procedure that assures acquitting 100 percent of those falsely accused of child abuse. I have no doubt that the society is, as a whole, happy and pleased with what my Court decided. But we should not pretend that the decision did not *eliminate* a liberty that previously existed.

Lack of a Guiding Principle for Evolution

My pointing out that the American people may be satisfied with a reduction of their liberties should not be taken as a suggestion that the proponents of The Living Constitution *follow* the desires of the American people in determining how the Constitution should evolve. They follow nothing so precise; indeed, as a group they follow nothing at all. Perhaps the most glaring defect of Living Constitutionalism, next to its incompatibility with the whole antievolutionary purpose of a constitution, is that there is no agreement, and no chance of agreement, upon what is to be the guiding principle of the evolution.... What is it that the judge must consult to determine when, and in what direction, evolution has occurred? Is it the will of the majority, discerned from newspapers, radio talk shows, public opinion polls, and chats at the country club? Is it the philosophy of Hume, or of John Rawls, or of John Stuart Mill, or of Aristotle? As soon as the discussion goes beyond the issue of whether the Constitution is static, the evolutionists divide into as many camps as there are individual views of the good, the true, and the beautiful. I think that is inevitably so, which means that evolutionism is simply not a practicable constitutional philosophy.

I do not suggest, mind you, that originalists always agree upon their answer. There is plenty of room for disagreement as to what original meaning was, and even more as to how that original meaning applies to the situation before the court. But the originalist at least knows what he is looking for: the original meaning of the text. Often—indeed, I dare say usually—that is easy to discern and simple to apply. Sometimes (though not very often) there will be disagreement regarding the original meaning; and sometimes there will be disagreement as to how that original meaning applies to new and unforeseen phenomena. How, for example, does the First Amendment guarantee of "the freedom of speech" apply to new technologies that did not exist when the guarantee was created—to sound trucks, or to government-licensed over-the-air television? In such new fields the Court must follow the trajectory of the First Amendment, so to speak, to determine what it requires—and assuredly that enterprise is not entirely cut-and-dried but requires the exercise of judgment.

But the difficulties and uncertainties of determining original meaning and applying it to modern circumstances are negligible compared with the difficulties and uncertainties of the philosophy which says that the Constitution *changes*; that the very act which it once prohibited it now permits, and which it once permitted it now forbids; and that the key to that change is unknown and unknowable. The originalist, if he does not have all the answers, has many of them. The Confrontation Clause, for example, requires confrontation. For the evolutionist, on the other hand, every question is an open question, every day a new day. No fewer than three of the Justices with whom I have served have maintained that the death penalty is unconstitutional, *even though its use is explicitly contemplated in the Constitution*. The Due Process Clause of the Fifth and Fourteenth Amendments says that no person shall be deprived of life without due process of law; and the Grand Jury Clause of the Fifth Amendment says that no person shall be held to answer for a capital crime without grand jury indictment. No matter. Under The Living Constitution the death penalty may have *become* unconstitutional. And it is up to each Justice to decide for himself (under no standard I can discern) when that occurs.

In the last analysis, however, it probably does not matter what principle, among the innumerable possibilities, the evolutionist proposes to determine in what direction The Living Constitution will grow. Whatever he might propose, at the end of the day an evolving constitution will evolve the way the majority wishes. The people will be willing to leave interpretation of the Constitution to lawyers and law courts so long as the people believe that it is (like the interpretation of a statute) essentially lawyers' work—requiring a close examination of text, history of the text, traditional understanding of the text, judicial precedent, and so forth. But if the people come to believe that the Constitution is *not* a text like other texts; that it means, not what it says or what it was understood to mean, but what it *should* mean, in light of the "evolving standards of decency that mark the progress of a maturing society"—well, then, they will look for qualifications other than impartiality, judgment, and lawyerly acumen in those whom they select to interpret it. More specifically, they will look for judges who agree with *them* as to what the evolving standards have evolved to; who agree with *them* as to what the Constitution *ought* to be.

It seems to me that that is where we are heading, or perhaps even where we have arrived. Seventy-five years ago, we believed firmly enough in a rock-solid, unchanging Constitution that we felt it necessary to adopt the Nineteenth Amendment to give women the vote. The battle was not fought in the courts, and few thought that it could be, despite the constitutional guarantee of Equal Protection of the Laws; that provision did not, when it was adopted, and hence did not in 1920, guarantee equal access to the ballot but permitted distinctions on the basis not only of age but of property and of sex. Who can doubt that if the issue had been deferred until today, the Constitution would be (formally) unamended, and the courts would be the chosen instrumentality of change? The American people have been converted to belief in The Living Constitution, a "morphing" document that means, from age to age, what it ought to mean. And with that conversion has inevitably come the new phenomenon of selecting and confirming federal judges, at all levels, on the basis of their views regarding a whole series of proposals for constitutional evolution. If the courts are free to write the Constitution anew, they will, by God, write it the way the majority wants; the appointment and confirmation process will see to that. This, of course, is the end of the Bill of Rights, whose meaning will be committed to the very body it was meant to protect against: the majority. By trying to make the Constitution do everything that needs doing from age to age, we shall have caused it to do nothing at all.

Active Liberty and the Constitution

STEPHEN BREYER

The United States is a nation built upon principles of liberty. That liberty means not only freedom from government coercion but also the freedom to participate in the government itself. When Jefferson wrote, "I know no safe depository of the ultimate powers of the society but the people themselves," his concern was for abuse of government power. But when he spoke of the rights of the citizen as "a participator in the government of affairs," when Adams, his rival, added that all citizens have a "positive passion for the public good," and when the Founders referred to "public liberty," they had in mind more than freedom from a despotic government. They had invoked an idea of freedom as old as antiquity, the freedom of the individual citizen to participate in the government and thereby to share with others the right to make or to control the nation's public acts....

I focus primarily upon the active liberty of the ancients.... My thesis is that courts should take greater account of the Constitution's democratic nature when they interpret constitutional and statutory texts. That thesis encompasses well-known arguments for judicial modesty. The judge, compared to the legislator, lacks relevant expertise. The "people" must develop "the political experience" and they must obtain "the moral education and stimulus that come from ... correcting their own errors." Judges, too, must display that doubt, caution, and prudence, that not being "too sure" of oneself, that Judge Learned Hand[1] described as "the spirit of liberty."

But my thesis reaches beyond these classic arguments. It finds in the Constitution's democratic objective not simply restraint on judicial power or an ancient counterpart of more modern protection, but also a source of judicial authority and an interpretive aid to more effective protection of ancient and modern liberty alike. It finds a basic perspective that helps make sense of our Constitution's structure, illuminating aspects that otherwise seem less coherent. Through examples, my thesis illustrates how emphasizing this democratic objective can bring us closer to achieving the proper balance.... The examples suggest that increased emphasis upon that objective by judges when they interpret a legal text will yield better law—law that helps a community of individuals democratically find practical solutions to important contemporary social problems. They simultaneously illustrate the importance of a judge's considering practical consequences, that is, consequences valued in terms of constitutional purposes, when the interpretation of constitutional language is at issue.

In a word, my theme is democracy and the Constitution. I illustrate a democratic theme—"active liberty"—which resonates throughout the Constitution. In discussing its role, I hope to illustrate how this constitutional theme can affect a judge's interpretation of a constitutional text.

To illustrate a theme is not to present a general theory of constitutional interpretation. Nonetheless, themes play an important role in a judge's work. Learned Hand once compared the task of interpreting a statute to that of interpreting a musical score. No particular theory guarantees that the interpreter can fully capture the composer's intent. It makes sense to ask a musician to emphasize one theme more than another. And one can understand an interpretation that approaches a great symphony from a "romantic," as opposed to a "classical,"

---

1. Learned Hand was a famous and much-quoted judge on the U.S. Court of Appeals.

point of view. So might a judge pay greater attention to a document's democratic theme; and so might a judge view the Constitution through a more democratic lens. The matter is primarily one of approach, perspective, and emphasis. And approach, perspective, and emphasis, even if they are not theories, play a great role in law.

For one thing, emphasis matters when judges face difficult questions of statutory or constitutional interpretation. All judges use similar basic tools to help them accomplish the task. They read the text's language along with related language in other parts of the document. They take account of its history, including history that shows what the language likely meant to those who wrote it. They look to tradition indicating how the relevant language was, and is, used in the law. They examine precedents interpreting the phrase, holding or suggesting what the phrase means and how it has been applied. They try to understand the phrase's purposes or (in respect to many constitutional phrases) the values that it embodies, and they consider the likely consequences of the interpretive alternatives, valued in terms of the phrase's purposes. But the fact that most judges agree that these basic elements—language, history, tradition, precedent, purpose, and consequence—are useful does not mean they agree about just where and how to use them. Some judges emphasize the use of language, history, and tradition. Others emphasize purpose and consequence. These differences of emphasis matter....

For another thing, emphasis matters in respect to the specialized constitutional work of a Supreme Court Justice. In my view, that work, though appellate in nature, differs from the work of a lower appellate court in an important way. Because a Justice, unlike a judge on a trial or appellate court, faces a steady diet of constitutional cases, Supreme Court work leads the Justice to develop a view of the Constitution as a whole. My own view is likely similar to that of others insofar as I see the document as creating a coherent framework for a certain kind of government. Described generally, that government is democratic; it avoids concentration of too much power in too few hands; it protects personal liberty; it insists that the law respect each individual equally; and it acts only upon the basis of law itself. The document embodies these general objectives in discrete provisions. In respect to democratic government, for example, the Constitution insists that Congress meet at least once each year, that elections take place every two (or four or six) years, that representation be based upon a census that must take place every decade; and it has gradually extended the right to vote to all adult men and women of every race and religion. (It also guarantees the states a "republican form of government.")

But my view can differ from the views of various others in the way in which I understand the relation between the Constitution's democratic objective and its other general objectives. My view can differ in the comparative significance I attach to each general objective. And my view can differ in the way I understand how a particular objective should influence the interpretation of a broader provision, and not just those provisions that refer to it directly. These differences too are often a matter of degree, a matter of perspective, or emphasis, rather than a radical disagreement about the general nature of the Constitution or its basic objectives.

Finally, the fact that members of historically different Supreme Courts have emphasized different constitutional themes, objectives, or approaches over time allows us to characterize a Court during a period of its history and to speak meaningfully about changes in the Court's judicial "philosophy" over time. Thus, one can characterize the early nineteenth century as a period during which the Court, through its interpretations of the Constitution, helped to establish the authority of the federal government, including the federal judiciary. One can characterize the late nineteenth and early twentieth centuries as a period during which the Court overly emphasized the Constitution's protection of private property, as, for example, in *Lochner* v. *New York*, where (over the dissent of Justice Oliver Wendell Holmes) it held that state maximum hour laws violated "freedom of contract." At the same time, that Court wrongly underemphasized the basic objectives of the Civil War amendments. It tended to ignore that those amendments sought to draw all citizens, irrespective of race, into the community, and that those amendments, in guaranteeing that the law would equally respect all "persons," hoped to make the Constitution's opening phrase, "We the People," a political reality.

Later Courts—the New Deal Court and the Warren Court—emphasized ways in which the Constitution protected the citizen's "active liberty," i.e., the scope of the right to participate in government. The former dismantled various *Lochner*-era distinctions, thereby expanding the constitutional room available for citizens, through their elected representatives, to govern themselves. The latter interpreted the Civil War amendments in light of their basic purposes, thereby directly helping African Americans become full members of the nation's community of self-governing citizens—a community that the people had expanded through later amendments, for example, those extending the suffrage to women, and which the Court expanded further in its "one person, one vote" decisions. The Warren Court's emphasis (on the need to make the law's constitutional promises a legal reality) also led it to consider how the Civil War amendments (and later amendments) had changed the scope of pre-Civil War constitutional language, that is, by changing the assumptions, premises, or presuppositions upon which many earlier constitutional interpretations had rested. In doing so, it read the document as offering broader protection to "modern liberty" (protecting the citizen from government) as well. While I cannot easily characterize the current Court, I will suggest that it may have swung back too far, too often underemphasizing or overlooking the contemporary importance of active liberty....

★★★

I have urged attention to purpose and consequences. My discussion sees individual constitutional provisions as embodying certain basic purposes, often expressed in highly general terms. It sees the Constitution itself as a single document designed to further certain basic general purposes as a whole. It argues that an understanding of, and a focus upon, those general purposes will help a judge better to understand and to apply specific provisions. And it identifies consequences as an important yardstick to measure a given interpretation's faithfulness to these democratic purposes. In short, focus on purpose seeks to promote active liberty by insisting on interpretations, statutory as well as constitutional, that are consistent with the people's will. Focus on consequences, in turn, allows us to gauge whether and to what extent we have succeeded in facilitating workable outcomes which reflect that will.

Some lawyers, judges, and scholars, however, would caution strongly against the reliance upon purposes (particularly abstractly stated purposes) and assessment of consequences. They ask judges to focus primarily upon text, upon the Framers' original expectations, narrowly conceived, and upon historical tradition. They do not deny the occasional relevance of consequences or purposes (including such general purposes as democracy), but they believe that judges should use them sparingly in the interpretive endeavor. They ask judges who tend to find interpretive answers in those decision-making elements to rethink the problem to see whether language, history, tradition, and precedent by themselves will not yield an answer. They fear that, once judges become accustomed to justifying legal conclusions through appeal to real-world consequences, they will too often act subjectively and undemocratically, substituting an elite's views of good policy for sound law. They hope that language, history, tradition, and precedent will provide important safeguards against a judge's confusing his or her personal, un-democratic notion of what is good for that which the Constitution or statute demands. They tend also to emphasize the need for judicial opinions that set forth their legal conclusions in terms of rules that will guide other institutions, including lower courts.

This view, which I shall call "textualist" (in respect to statutes) or "originalist" (in respect to the Constitution) or "literalist" (shorthand for both), while logically consistent with emphasizing the Constitution's democratic objectives, is not hospitable to the kinds of arguments I have advanced. Nor is it easily reconciled with my illustrations. Why, then, does it not undercut my entire argument?

The answer, in my view, lies in the unsatisfactory nature of that interpretive approach. First, the more "originalist" judges cannot appeal to the Framers themselves in support of their interpretive views. The Framers did not say specifically what factors judges should take into account when they interpret statutes or the Constitution. This is obvious in the case of statutes. Why would the Framers have preferred (1) a system of interpretation that relies heavily on linguistic canons to (2) a system that seeks more directly to find the intent of the legislators who enacted the statute? It is close to obvious in respect to the Constitution. Why would the Framers, who disagreed even about the necessity of *including* a Bill of Rights in the Constitution, who disagreed about the *content* of that Bill of Rights, nonetheless have agreed about *what school of interpretive thought* should prove dominant in interpreting that Bill of Rights in the centuries to come?

In respect to content, the Constitution itself says that the "enumeration" in the Constitution of some rights "shall not be construed to deny or disparage others retained by the people." Professor [Bernard] Bailyn concludes that the Framers added this language to make clear that "rights, like law itself, should never be fixed, frozen, that new dangers and needs will emerge, and that to respond to these dangers and needs, rights must be newly specified to protect the individual's integrity and inherent dignity." Given the open-ended nature of *content*, why should one expect to find fixed views about the nature of interpretive practices?

If, however, justification for the literalist's interpretive practices cannot be found in the Framers' intentions, where can it be found—other than in an appeal to *consequences*, that is, in an appeal to the presumed beneficial consequences for the law or for the nation that will flow from adopting those practices? And that is just what we find argued. That is to say, literalist arguments often try to show that that approach will have favorable *results*, for example, that it will deter judges from substituting their own views about what is good for the public for those of Congress or for those embodied in the Constitution. They argue, in other words, that a more literal approach to interpretation will better control judicial subjectivity. Thus, while literalists eschew consideration of consequences case by case, their interpretive rationale is consequentialist in this important sense.

Second, I would ask whether it is true that judges who reject literalism necessarily open the door to subjectivity. They do not endorse subjectivity. And under their approach important safeguards of objectivity remain. For one thing, a judge who emphasizes consequences, no less than any other, is aware of the legal precedents, rules, standards, practices, and institutional understanding that a decision will affect. He or she also takes account of the way in which this system of legally related rules, institutions, and practices affects the world.

To be sure, a court focused on consequences may decide a case in a way that radically changes the law. But this is not always a bad thing. For example, after the late-nineteenth-century Court decided *Plessy v. Ferguson*, the case which permitted racial segregation that was, in principle, "separate but equal," it became apparent that segregation did not mean equality but meant disrespect for members of a minority race and led to a segregated society that was totally unequal, a consequence directly contrary to the purpose and demands of the Fourteenth Amendment. The Court, in *Brown v. Board of Education* and later decisions, overruled *Plessy*, and the law changed in a way that profoundly affected the lives of many.

In any event, to focus upon consequences does not automatically invite frequent dramatic legal change. Judges, including those who look to consequences, understand the human need to plan in reliance upon law, the need for predictability, the need for stability. And they understand that too radical, too frequent legal change has, as a consequence, a tendency to undercut those important law-related human needs. Similarly, each judge's individual need to be consistent over time constrains subjectivity. As Justice [Sandra Day] O'Connor has explained, a constitutional judge's initial decisions leave "footprints" that the judge, in later decisions, will almost inevitably follow.

Moreover, to consider consequences is not to consider simply whether the consequences of a proposed decision are good or bad, in a particular judge's opinion. Rather, to emphasize consequences is to emphasize consequences related to the particular textual provision at issue. The judge must examine the consequences through the lens of the relevant constitutional value or purpose.

The relevant values limit interpretive possibilities. If they are democratic values, they may well counsel modesty or restraint as well. And I believe that when a judge candidly acknowledges that, in addition to text, history, and precedent, consequences also guide his decision-making, he is more likely to be disciplined in emphasizing, for example, constitutionally relevant consequences rather than allowing his own subjectively held values to be outcome determinative. In all these ways, a focus on consequences will itself constrain subjectivity.

Here [is an example] of how these principles apply. The First Amendment says that "Congress shall make no law respecting an establishment of religion." I recently wrote (in dissent) that this clause prohibits government from providing vouchers to parents to help pay for the education of their children in parochial schools. The basic reason, in my view, is that the clause seeks to avoid among other things the "social conflict, potentially created when government becomes involved in religious education." Nineteenth- and twentieth-century immigration has produced a nation with fifty or more different religions. And that fact made the risk of "social conflict" far more serious after the Civil War and in twentieth-century America than the Framers, with their eighteenth-century experience, might have anticipated. The twentieth-century Supreme Court had held in applicable precedent that, given the changing nature of our society, in order to implement the basic value that the Framers wrote the clause to protect, it was necessary to interpret the clause more broadly than the Framers might have thought likely.

My opinion then turned to consequences. It said that voucher programs, if widely adopted, could provide billions of dollars to religious schools. At first blush, that may seem a fine idea. But will different religious groups become concerned about which groups are getting the money and how? What are the criteria? How are programs being implemented? Is a particular program biased against particular sects, say, because it forbids certain kinds of teaching? Are rival sects failing to live up to the relevant criteria, say, by teaching "civil disobedience" to "unjust laws"? How will claims for money, say, of one religious group against another, be adjudicated? In a society as religiously diverse as ours, I saw in the administration of huge grant programs for religious education the potential for religious strife. And that, it seemed to me, was the kind of problem the First Amendment's religion clauses seek to avoid....

Third, "subjectivity" is a two-edged criticism, which the literalist himself cannot escape. The literalist's tools—language and structure, history and tradition—often fail to provide objective guidance in those truly difficult cases about which I have spoken. Will canons of interpretation provide objective answers? One canon tells the court to choose an interpretation that gives every statutory word a meaning. Another permits the court to ignore a word, treating it as surplus, if otherwise the construction is repugnant to the statute's purpose. Shall the court read the statute narrowly as in keeping with the common law or broadly as remedial in purpose? Canons to the left of them, canons to the right of them, which canons shall the judges choose to follow?....

Fourth, I do not believe that textualist or originalist methods of interpretation are more likely to produce clear, workable legal rules. But even were they to do so, the advantages of legal rules can be overstated. Rules must be interpreted and applied. Every law student whose class grade is borderline knows that the benefits that rules produce for cases that fall within the heartland are often lost in cases that arise at the boundaries ...

For any or all of these reasons, I hope that those strongly committed to textualist or literalist views—those whom I am almost bound not to convince—are fairly small in number. I hope to have convinced some of the rest that active liberty has an important role to play in constitutional (and statutory) interpretation.

That role, I repeat, does not involve radical change in current professional interpretive methods nor does it involve ignoring the protection the Constitution grants fundamental (modern) liberties. It takes Thomas Jefferson's statement as a statement of goals that the Constitution now seeks to fulfill: "[A]ll men are created equal." They are endowed by their Creator with certain "unalienable Rights." "[T]o secure these Rights, Governments are instituted among Men, *deriving their just powers from the consent of the governed.*" It underscores, emphasizes, or reemphasizes the final democratic part of the famous phrase. That reemphasis, I believe, has practical value when judges seek to assure fidelity, in our modern society, to these ancient and unchanging ideals.

Discussion Questions

1. Should justices of the Supreme Court be guided by the "original meaning" of the words in the Constitution and the laws? What are the advantages of this approach to constitutional interpretation? What problems might justices face in trying to discover "original meaning"?

2. If "textualism" is not to be the standard approach to constitutional interpretation, what can the approach be? How might Breyer respond to Scalia's argument that if "original meaning" is rejected, the door is opened to justices arbitrarily pouring their own values and purposes into their decisions while claiming to base them on the Constitution?

3. Does the Constitution guarantee only those rights that are specified in its text? Can we derive such things as a right to privacy (the basis for Supreme Court decisions on contraception and abortion) from constitutional values even when the Constitution says nothing about such a right?

4. What is the place of the judiciary in American democracy? Does the Supreme Court's status as an unelected branch require that it play a limited and restrained role? Or does its claim to be the guardian of the Constitution warrant a more active role for the Court on behalf of democratic principles such as "active liberty"?

5. Is it possible to depoliticize the Supreme Court? Can the Supreme Court be removed from the central political controversies of American life?

Suggested Readings and Internet Resources

For a history of "originalism" as a method of constitutional interpretation, see Jonathan O'Neill, *Originalism in American Law and Politics: A Constitutional History* (Baltimore, Md.: Johns Hopkins University Press, 2005). Keith E. Whittington, a scholar of American political development, makes a distinctive case for "originalism" in *Constitutional Interpretation: Textual Meaning, Original Intent, and Judicial Review* (Lawrence: University Press of Kansas, 1999). For a criticism of Justice Scalia's originalist brand of jurisprudence by liberal legal scholars, see Laurence H. Tribe and Michael C. Dorf, *On Reading the Constitution* (Cambridge, Mass.: Harvard University Press, 2006). Mark Tushnet makes an argument for a populist constitutional law that would deny the judicial branch the exclusive authority to interpret the Constitution in *Taking the Constitution Away from the Courts* (Princeton, N.J.: Princeton University Press, 1999). For a popular democratic account of leading Supreme Court cases, see Peter Irons, *A People's History of the Supreme Court* (New York: Penguin Books, 2000). Jeffrey A. Segal and Harold J. Spaeth present the view that justices of all ideological stripes base their decisions primarily on their policy preferences in *The Supreme Court and the Attitudinal Model Revisited* (New York: Cambridge University Press, 2002).

Federalist Society
www.fed-soc.org
This website of a prominent organization of conservative lawyers offers perspectives on recent Supreme Court cases and other legal issues.

American Civil Liberties Union
www.aclu.org
This website discusses legal issues and court cases viewed from the perspective of the group who has argued many of the most prominent civil liberties issues before the U.S. Supreme Court.

University of Pittsburgh School of Law
www.jurist.law.pitt.edu
This site provides Supreme Court opinions and stories on constitutional law.

Supreme Court of the United States
www.supremecourtus.gov
The Supreme Court's website contains a searchable docket, the text of recent decisions in PDF format, and information on Court rules and procedures.

Chapter 16

✳

Economic Inequality: A Threat to Democracy?

The United States has the reputation as a land of opportunity. Unlike the class-divided societies of Europe, American society has always pride itself on being more fluid and open to individual ambition. In the United States you can rise from "rags to riches," as the saying goes. The "American Dream," which is defined in many different ways but almost always involves economic success, is supposedly within everyone's grasp. Millions of immigrants have been drawn to our shores by the lure of the American Dream. Not only is the United States a land of opportunity and upward mobility, but it is also generally believed that we lack the extremes of wealth and poverty that characterize other societies. The United States is basically a middle-class society.

Almost everyone agrees that equal opportunity and a strong middle class are essential to the healthy functioning of American society and its political system. Throughout our history, however, debates have periodically erupted about how to guarantee equal opportunity and how much economic inequality should be tolerated in a democracy before government should intervene. One of the first such debates was between two giants of American political history, Thomas Jefferson and Alexander Hamilton. Jefferson argued that the stability of American democracy rested on the backs of small farmers, who, because they made a living through their own efforts on their own land, were free to speak out and participate fully in politics without fear. Jefferson maintained that manufacturing and large cities created wide inequalities and dangerous dependencies that corrupted democracy. His opponent, Alexander Hamilton, was much less fearful of economic inequalities. In his *Report on Manufactures*, Hamilton argued that the government should encourage manufacturing as a way to tie the wealthy classes to government, thus providing a check against the turbulence of the masses.

In the long run, Hamilton's vision of industrial expansion prevailed over Jefferson's agricultural ideal. After the Civil War (1861–1865), industry began to take off in the United States. Entrepreneurs, such as Andrew Carnegie and

John D. Rockefeller, amassed huge fortunes, the likes of which had never been seen before in the New World. At the same time, millions of immigrants poured into U.S. cities to work in factories at low wages and for long hours. Many observers believed that events were proving Jefferson's fears correct. Mark Twain called this "Gilded Age" a time of money lust. Muckraking journalists exposed the ways that robber barons corrupted the political process, sometimes buying off whole state legislatures. The Populist movement of the late nineteenth century fought to protect the small farmer and limit the power of corporations. It proposed legislation to break up the large corporations, expand the money supply to ease the debt burden on small farmers, and impose a federal income tax to redistribute wealth.

The opponents of the Populists vigorously denied that industrialism was creating unfair inequalities that threatened American democracy. They did not deny that some people were very rich and others quite poor, but they argued that these inequalities were a natural result of economic competition that benefited the entire society. Social Darwinists applied Charles Darwin's theory of evolution to society, arguing that inequalities derived from economic competition resulted in the "survival of the fittest." The United States was a land of opportunity where self-made men could rise up out of the working class to great riches. The principles of Social Darwinism were spread to the broad public by a "success" literature that told vivid stories of poor boys rising up out of poverty through hard work and moral uprightness. A Unitarian minister by the name of Horatio Alger published 106 such rags-to-riches books from 1868 to 1904, many of which became bestsellers.

A century later the democratic debate about economic inequality is once again heating up, albeit in very different economic circumstances. From World War II until the 1970s, according to most observers, economic inequalities remained the same or even shrank somewhat. Sometime in the 1970s, however, wages began to stagnate and even fall for most workers. Many reasons have been offered for this, including global competition from low-wage countries and the shift from well-paying industrial jobs to lower-paying service-sector jobs. Partly driven by the spread of computers into practically every workplace, education and skills acquisition have become even more important to earning a good wage. The wages of those with a high school education or less have fallen, while people with postgraduate degrees have seen their salaries soar. You can no longer earn a decent wage by simply having a strong back and willingness to work hard.

As in the Gilded Age, at the same time that many workers are struggling to get by, huge fortunes are being amassed at the top. Personal computers, software, and the development of the Internet have created wealth more rapidly than at any time in American history. Bill Gates, the founder of Microsoft, which supplies the operating system for most personal computers, became the richest man in the world, worth well over $40 billion in 2009 (that's billion, not million!). His fortune, even after correcting for inflation, is many times that of John D. Rockefeller. Reminiscent of the government's effort to break up Rockefeller's Standard Oil Trust, the federal government has prosecuted Microsoft for antitrust violations.

As with the inequalities generated by nineteenth-century industrialism, the inequalities of the so-called postindustrial economy have prompted a spirited political and policy debate. The inequality debate was renewed in 2001 when President George W. Bush succeeded in passing a $1.35 trillion tax cut spread over ten years. Opponents charged that 38 percent of the benefits would go to the wealthiest 1 percent of taxpayers. Supporters responded that it was only fair that those who pay the most in taxes receive the most money back. In the 2008 presidential campaign, Obama called for action to address rising economic inequality and promised not to raise taxes on families making less than $250,000. The Obama administration subsequently came under attack, however, for allowing top executives of Wall Street firms that were bailed out by the federal government to accept huge bonuses.

The two selections that follow address the contemporary inequality debate in our rapidly changing economy. The first excerpt is from a 1999 book entitled *Myths of Rich and Poor* by W. Michael Cox, chief economist at the Federal Reserve Bank of Dallas, and Richard Alm. According to Cox and Alm, we should not concentrate on the gap between the top and the bottom but rather on whether those at the bottom are better or worse off. In the book from which this excerpt is taken, the authors make a convincing case that those at the bottom generally are better off in terms of *consumption*. Breakthroughs in technology mean that we have more conveniences than ever, such as DVD players, flat screen TVs, and iPods. In the section we have chosen, Cox and Alm also make the point that snapshots of inequality at one point in time do not capture the movement of people out of poverty over their lifetimes. It is still a land of opportunity, they argue.

In our other selection, Paul Krugman, a Nobel Prize–winning economist and iconoclastic editorial writer, argues that the widening gap between the rich and the poor threatens American democracy. The public, Krugman maintains, has little idea how swiftly the United States has moved from a middle-class society to one characterized by huge gaps between the haves and the have-nots. Inequalities are supposed to provide powerful incentives for work and investment, stimulating economic growth that benefits everyone. Instead, Krugman argues, the vast inequalities we have today harm economic growth by encouraging white-collar crime, and the benefits of economic growth are captured by the very rich, with little trickling down to benefit most Americans. Krugman concludes by holding out the possibility that economic inequalities will become self-reinforcing: As elites get richer, they will dominate the political process, passing laws that will make it easier for them to accumulate even more riches.

Before reading the two selections, you may want to look back at the discussion of inequality in the introduction to this book. Do the authors take a *process* orientation toward equality or a *results* orientation? Why do Cox and Alm think we should focus on what those at the bottom are able to consume, whereas Krugman says little about this and instead concentrates on the gap between the top and the bottom? Krugman clearly thinks that it is the political power of those at the top that is partly responsible for rising inequalities. What do Cox and Alm say is the cause of income differences?

Myths of Rich and Poor

W. MICHAEL COX AND RICHARD ALM

"L and of Opportunity." Anywhere in the world, those three words bring to mind just one place: the United States of America.

Opportunity defines our heritage. The American saga entails waves of immigrant farmers, shopkeepers, laborers, and entrepreneurs, all coming to the United States for the promise of a better life. Some amassed enormous fortunes—the Rockefellers, the Carnegies, the DuPonts, the Fords, the Vanderbilts, to name just a few. Even today, America's opportunity is always on display. Bill Gates in computer software, Ross Perot in data processing, Bill Cosby and Oprah Winfrey in entertainment, Warren Buffett in investing, Sam Walton in retailing, Michael Jordan in sports, and Mary Kay Ash in cosmetics could head a list of the many thousands who catapulted from society's lower or middle ranks to the top. Many millions more, descendants of those who arrived with little more than the clothes on their backs and a few bucks in their pockets, took advantage of an open economic system to improve their lot in life through talent and hard work.

Even pessimists acknowledge that the Gateses, Perots, Cosbys, Winfreys, Buffetts, Waltons, Jordans, and Ashes are getting filthy rich, along with Wall Street's wheeler-dealers, Hollywood moguls, and big-league ballplayers. At the nation's 350 largest companies, top executives' median total compensation in 1996 was $3.1 million, or 90 times what a typical factory hand earns. We often hear that ordinary Americans aren't keeping up, that success isn't as easy, or at least not as democratic, as it once was. At the close of the twentieth century, one disturbing vision portrays the United States as a society pulling apart at the seams, divided into separate and unequal camps, an enclave of fat cats gorging themselves on the fruits of others' labor surrounded by a working class left with ever more meager opportunities.

The most-cited evidence of ebbing opportunity is the *distribution of income*—the slicing up of the American pie. Examining the data, analysts seize on two points. First, there's a marked inequality in earnings between society's haves and have-nots. Second, and perhaps more ominous, the gap between the richest and poorest households has widened over the past two decades. The Census Bureau provides the statistical ballast for these claims. In 1997, the top 20 percent of American households received almost half of the nation's income. Average earnings among this group are $122,764 a year. The distribution of income to the four other groups of 20 percent was as follows: The second fifth had 23.2 percent, with average earnings of $57,582; the third fifth had 15.0 percent, with average earnings of $37,177; the fourth fifth had 8.9 percent, with average earnings of $22,098. The bottom 20 percent earned 3.6 percent of the economic pie, or an average of $8,872 a year.

The case for the existence of a growing rift between rich and poor rests on longer-term trends in the same Census Bureau data. Since 1975, only the top 20 percent of Americans managed to expand their allotment of the nation's income—from 43.2 percent to 49.4 percent. Over the same period, the distribution to the middle three groups slipped slightly. The share going to the lowest 20 percent of income earners fell from 4.4 percent to 3.6 percent. The shift of income toward the upper end of the distribution becomes even more striking when it's put in dollars. After adjusting for inflation, the income of households in the bottom 20 percent increased by only $207 from 1975 to 1997. The top tier, meanwhile, jumped by $37,633.

Once again, the pessimists have it wrong. The income distribution only reveals how one group is doing relative to others at a particular moment. That kind of you-vs.-me score keeping has little to do with whether any American can get ahead. By its very nature, opportunity is individual rather than collective. Even for an individual, the concept can't be divorced from its time element, an assessment of how well someone is doing today relative to yesterday, or how he can expect to do tomorrow compared to today. How many of us worked our way up? How quickly did we move from one rung to the next? How many of us fell? Studies of income inequality cannot say whether individuals are doing better or worse. They lump together Americans who differ in age, educational level, work effort, family and marital status, gender and race. The sample never stays the same from one year to another, and researchers haven't a clue about what happened to any individual in the income distribution.

Annual snapshots of the income distribution might deserve attention if we lived in a caste society, with rigid class lines determining who gets what share of the national income—but we don't live in a caste society. It takes a heroic leap to look at the disparity between rich and poor and conclude that any one individual's chances of getting ahead aren't what they used to be. Even the most sophisticated income-distribution statistics fail to tell us what we really want to know: Are the majority of Americans losing their birthright—a chance at upward mobility? Static portraits, moreover, don't tell us whether low-income households tend to remain at the bottom year after year. By definition, a fifth of society will always inhabit the lowest 20 percent of the income distribution. We don't know, however, whether individuals and families stay there over long periods. It's no great tragedy if the bottom rung is where many Americans start to climb the ladder of success. To argue that upward mobility is being lost, we would have to show that the poorest remain stuck where they are, with little hope of making themselves better off. Nothing could be further from the truth....

Making It from Bottom to Top

The Treasury Department affirms that most Americans still have a good shot at upward mobility. In a 1992 analysis covering nine years, researchers found that 86 percent of those in the lowest 20 percent of income earners in 1979 had moved to a higher grouping by 1988. Moreover, 66 percent reached the middle tier or above, with almost 15 percent making it all the way to the top fifth of income earners. Among Americans who started out above the bottom fifth in 1979, the Treasury found the same movement up the income ladder. Nearly 50 percent of those in the middle tier, for example, rose into the top two groupings, overwhelming whatever downward mobility that took place....

In addition to confirming that most Americans are still getting ahead in life, the Treasury study verifies that the quickest rise occurs among the young, an antidote to the prevailing ennui among the so-called Generation X. It also found that wage and salary income was primarily responsible for pushing people upward in the distribution, indicating that work, not luck, is the widest path to opportunity. Ours is not a *Wheel of Fortune* economy, where a few lucky individuals win big, leaving paltry gains to the great mass of people. Most of us get ahead because we strive to make ourselves and our families better off.

By carefully tracking individuals' incomes over many years ... the Treasury study show[s] that our economic system is biased toward success. These results should go a long way toward quelling fears of an America polarized between privileged rich and permanently poor. The rich may indeed be getting richer. We ought to have little problem with that. The poor are also getting richer. We ought to celebrate that. Indeed, what's so encouraging is the ability of those who start out in the lowest income brackets to jump into the middle and upper echelons. There's evidence that most Americans are making their way up the income distribution through education, experience, and hard work.

That's what the American Dream, a dream of opportunity, is all about....

The Common Thread: Lifetime Earnings

If so many Americans are rising through the income ranks, and if only a few of us stay stuck at the bottom, who makes up the lowest fifth of today's income earners? One group is the downwardly mobile, those who once took in enough money to be in a higher echelon. Descent can be voluntary, usually a result of retirement, or it can be involuntary, resulting from layoffs or other hard luck. Just changing jobs sometimes results in a dip in earnings. We've already seen, though, that downward mobility happens to only a small segment of the population. By far the largest number of low-income earners are new entrants into the world of work, mostly young people. Many of us begin our working lives as part of the bottom 20 percent, either as students with part-time jobs or as relatively unskilled entrants to the labor force. Many immigrants, whatever their age, start off with low incomes.

Although they usually start at the bottom, the young tend to rise through the income distribution as they become better educated, develop skills, and gain experience. In fact, income tends to follow a familiar pattern over a person's lifetime: It rises rapidly in the early years of working, peaks during middle age, then falls toward retirement. When the average earnings at each age are placed side by side, it creates a lifetime earnings profile, shaped like a pyramid.

The changes in lifetime earnings over the past four decades tell us quite a bit about the evolution of our economy. In 1951, workers reached their peak earning years in ages 35 to 44, when their average annual earnings were 1.6 times the income of those in the 20-to-24 age group. By 1973, the ratio had risen to 2.4

to 1. By 1993, the peak earning years had shifted to ages 45 to 54, and workers in this highly paid group earned almost 3.2 times more than the 20-to-24-year-olds....

A steeper lifetime earnings profile reflects greater opportunity. One way to see that is to imagine a perfectly flat pattern of lifetime income, with workers earning the same income every year. Paychecks for the middle years of life would match those for the early twenties. This would be a world devoid of upward mobility, offering workers no prospect of getting ahead during their lifetimes, no matter what their effort, no matter how much they improve their worth on the job.

What is behind the faster rise in Americans' lifetime earnings? Most likely, it's the by-product of broad changes in the way we work. When the economy was largely industrial, Americans worked with their hands and their backs. Today, more Americans than ever owe their paychecks to brainpower. The skills of the mind, unlike those of the body, are cumulative. Mental talents continue to sharpen long after muscles and dexterity begin to falter. These facts of physiology and economic development probably explain why the peak earning years have shifted to older age groups in the past two decades. As the United States retools itself for a more knowledge-intensive era, as the country moves from a blue-collar economy to a white-collar one, the rewards for education and experience are increasing.

The lifetime earnings profile is the thread that sews together recent trends in upward mobility and income inequality. As today's workers reap greater rewards for what they've learned on the job, earnings become sharply higher with experience. It's not that today's young workers are falling behind their counterparts of earlier generations. On the contrary, older workers are doing so much better than they used to. The result is an increase in the gap between youth and middle age. In the end, the steepening of lifetime earnings leads us to a surprising conclusion: Upward mobility may well be an important factor in the widening gap in income distribution.

All told, this isn't the harsh world seen by those who say the rich are getting richer and the poor are getting poorer. Both rich and poor are becoming better off. Are most of us going nowhere? Quite the contrary; the majority of Americans are busy climbing the income ladder. Greater returns to education and experience can skew income toward the upper end, but we would be foolhardy indeed to become so obsessed with the pecking order that we lose sight of what's really important—opportunity.

A steeper lifetime earnings profile also puts a different slant on the notion of a vanishing middle class. The center of the income distribution isn't a destination. It's just one step on the ladder of upward mobility. Forty years ago, with a flatter earnings profile, families spent most of their working lives in the middle income brackets. Today's more rapid rise in incomes means they move to the top faster, spending less time defined as "middle class." Worries about Generation X's future can be put to rest, too. Those entering the labor force in the 1900s may look at their parents' income and wonder how they will ever attain such heights. They should, however, find a steeper earnings profile encouraging. During their first two or three decades in the labor market, young workers are likely to see their incomes rise more quickly than their parents' did.

In the United States, getting ahead isn't a great mystery. The economy provides opportunity—more, in fact, than ever before—but it's up to each of us to grab it. Success isn't random. Luck and Daddy's money aren't the way most Americans get to the top. More often than not, the rewards go to education, experience, talent, ambition, vision, risk taking, readiness to change, and just plain hard work. Young people aren't guaranteed success any more than their parents were. Their chances will improve, though, if they make the right choices in life. Opportunity lies in the advice given by generations of parents and teachers: Study, work hard, and save. In short, the best advice for economic success is this: Listen to your elders....

Inequality Is Not Inequity

Judging from the public debate, at least some Americans would prefer a more equal distribution of income to a less equal one, perhaps on moral grounds, perhaps as a part of an ideal of civic virtue. There's no *economic* reason, however, to prefer one pattern of income distribution over another. In fact, the income statistics do little but confirm what's obvious: America isn't an egalitarian society. It wasn't designed to be. Socialism, a failed and receding system, sought to impose an artificial equality. Capitalism, a successful and expanding system, doesn't fight a fundamental fact of human nature—we vary greatly in capabilities, motivation, interests, and preferences. Some of us are driven to get ahead. Some of us are just plain lazy. Some of us are willing to work hard so we can afford a lifestyle rich in material goods. Some of us work just hard enough to provide a roof overhead, food, clothes, and a few amenities. It shouldn't come as a surprise that our incomes vary greatly.

Income inequality isn't an aberration. Quite the opposite, it's perfectly consistent with the laws that govern a free-enterprise system. In the early 1970s, three groups of unemployed Canadians, all in their twenties, all with at least 12 years of schooling, volunteered to participate in a stylized economy where the only employment was making woolen belts on small hand looms. They could work as much or as little as they liked, earning $2.50 for each belt. After 98 days, the results were anything but equal: 37.2 percent of the economy's income went to the 20 percent with the highest earnings. The bottom 20 percent received only 6.6 percent. This economic microcosm tells us one thing: Even among similar people with identical work options, some workers will earn more than others.

In a modern economy, incomes vary for plenty of reasons having little to do with fairness or equity. Education and experience, for example, usually yield higher pay. As industry becomes more sophisticated, the rewards to skilled labor tend to rise, adding to the number of high-income earners. Location matters. New Yorkers earn more than Mississippians. Lifestyle choices play a part, too. Simply by having an additional paycheck, two-income families make more money than those with a single breadwinner. Longer retirements, however, will add to the number of households with low income, even if many senior citizens live well from their savings. Demographic changes can twist the distribution of income. As the Baby Boom enters its peak earning years, the number of high-income households ought to rise. Economic forces create ripples in what we earn. The ebb and flow of industries can shift workers to both ends of the income distribution. Layoffs put some Americans into low-income groups, at least temporarily. Companies with new products and new technologies create jobs and, in most cases, share the bounty by offering workers higher pay. In technology industries, bonuses and stock options are becoming more common. Higher rates of return on investments—with, for example, a stock-market boom—will create a windfall for households with money riding on financial markets.

In and of itself, moreover, income distribution doesn't say much about the performance of an economy or the opportunities it offers. A widening gap isn't necessarily a sign of failure, nor does a narrowing one guarantee that an economy is functioning well. As a matter of fact, it's quite common to find a widening of income distribution in boom times, when almost everyone's earnings are rising rapidly. All it takes is for one segment of the workforce to become better off faster than others. However, the distribution can narrow in hard times, as companies facing declining demand cut back on jobs, hours, raises, and bonuses. In fact, we often see a compression of incomes in areas where people are sinking into poverty.

There's no denying that our system allows some Americans to become much richer than others. We must accept that, even celebrate it. Opportunity, not equality of income, is what made the U.S. economy grow and prosper. It's most important to provide equality of opportunity, not equality of results. There's ample evidence to refute any suggestion that the economy is no longer capable of providing opportunity for the vast majority of Americans. At the end of the twentieth century, upward mobility is alive and well. Even the lower-income households are sharing in the country's progress. What's more, data suggest that the populist view of America as a society torn between haves and have-nots, with rigid class lines, is just plain wrong. We are by no means a caste society.

For Richer

PAUL KRUGMAN

The Disappearing Middle

When I was a teenager growing up on Long Island, one of my favorite excursions was a trip to see the great Gilded Age mansions of the North Shore. Those mansions weren't just pieces of architectural history. They were monuments to a bygone social era, one in which the rich could afford the armies of servants needed to maintain a house the size of a European palace. By the time I saw them, of course, that era was long past. Almost none of the Long Island mansions were still private residences. Those that hadn't been turned into museums were occupied by nursing homes or private schools.

For the America I grew up in—the America of the 1950s and 1960s—was a middle-class society, both in reality and in feel. The vast income and wealth inequalities of the Gilded Age had disappeared. Yes, of course, there was the poverty of the underclass—but the conventional wisdom of the time viewed that as a social rather than an economic problem. Yes, of course, some wealthy businessmen and heirs to large fortunes lived far better than the average American. But they weren't rich the way the robber barons who built the mansions had been rich, and there weren't that many of them. The days when plutocrats were a force to be reckoned with in American society, economically or politically, seemed long past.

Daily experience confirmed the sense of a fairly equal society. The economic disparities you were conscious of were quite muted. Highly educated professionals—middle managers, college teachers, even lawyers—often claimed that they earned less than unionized blue-collar workers. Those considered very well off lived in split-levels, had a housecleaner come in once a week, and took summer vacations in Europe. But they sent their kids to public schools and drove themselves to work, just like everyone else.

But that was long ago. The middle-class America of my youth was another country.

We are now living in a new Gilded Age, as extravagant as the original. Mansions have made a comeback. The creations of Thierry Despont, the "eminence of excess," an architect who specializes in designing houses for the super-rich, typically range from 20,000 to 60,000 square feet; houses at the upper end of his range are not much smaller than the White House. Needless to say, the armies of servants are back, too. So are the yachts. Still, even J. P. Morgan didn't have a Gulfstream.

As the story about Despont suggests, it's not fair to say that the fact of widening inequality in America has gone unreported. Yet glimpses of the lifestyles of the rich and tasteless don't necessarily add up in people's minds to a clear picture of the tectonic shifts that have taken place in the distribution of income and wealth in this country. My sense is that few people are aware of just how much the gap between the very rich and the rest has widened over a relatively short period of time. In fact, even bringing up the subject exposes you to charges of "class warfare," the "politics of envy" and so on. And very few people indeed are willing to talk about the profound effects—economic, social and political—of that widening gap.

Yet you can't understand what's happening in America today without understanding the extent, causes, and consequences of the vast increase in inequality that has taken place over the last three decades, and in particular the astonishing concentration of income and wealth in just a few hands. To make sense of the current wave of corporate scandal, you need to understand how the man in the gray flannel suit has been replaced by the imperial C.E.O. The concentration of income at the top is a key reason that the United States, for all its economic achievements, has more poverty and lower life expectancy than any other major advanced nation. Above all, the growing concentration of wealth has reshaped our political system: it is at the root both of a general shift to the right and of an extreme polarization of our politics.

But before we get to all that, let's take a look at who gets what.

The New Gilded Age

The Securities and Exchange Commission hath no fury like a woman scorned. The messy divorce proceedings of Jack Welch, the legendary former C.E.O. of General Electric, have had one unintended benefit: they have given us a peek at the perks of the corporate elite, which are normally hidden from public view. For it turns out that when Welch retired, he was granted for life the use of a Manhattan apartment (including food, wine and laundry), access to corporate jets and a variety of other in-kind benefits, worth at least $2 million a year. The perks were revealing: they illustrated the extent to which corporate leaders now expect to be treated like ancien régime royalty. In monetary terms, how-ever, the perks must have meant little to Welch. In 2000, his last full year run-ning G.E., Welch was paid $123 million, mainly in stock and stock options.

Is it news that C.E.O.s of large American corporations make a lot of money? Actually, it is. They were always well paid compared with the average worker, but there is simply no comparison between what executives got a generation ago and what they are paid today.

Over the past 30 years most people have seen only modest salary increases: the average annual salary in America, expressed in 1998 dollars (that is, adjusted for inflation), rose from $32,522 in 1970 to $35,864 in 1999. That's about a 10 percent increase over 29 years—progress, but not much. Over the same period, however, according to *Fortune* magazine, the average real annual compensation of the top 100 C.E.O.s went from $1.3 million—39 times the pay of an average worker—to $37.5 million, more than 1,000 times the pay of ordinary workers.

The explosion in C.E.O. pay over the past 30 years is an amazing story in its own right, and an important one. But it is only the most spectacular indicator of a broader story, the reconcentration of income and wealth in the U.S. The rich have always been different from you and me, but they are far more different now than they were not long ago—indeed, they are as different now as they were when F. Scott Fitzgerald made his famous remark.

That's a controversial statement, though it shouldn't be. For at least the past 15 years it has been hard to deny the evidence for growing inequality in the United States. Census data clearly show a rising share of income going to the top 20 percent of families, and within that top 20 percent to the top 5 percent, with a declining share going to families in the middle. Nonetheless, denial of that evidence is a sizable, well-financed industry. Conservative think tanks have pro-duced scores of studies that try to discredit the data, the methodology and, not least, the motives of those who report the obvious. Studies that appear to refute claims of increasing inequality receive prominent endorsements on editorial pages and are eagerly cited by right-leaning government officials....

... In fact, the census data understate the case, because for technical reasons those data tend to undercount very high incomes—for example, it's unlikely that they reflect the explosion in C.E.O. compensation. And other evidence makes it clear not only that inequality is increasing but that the action gets bigger the closer you get to the top. That is, it's not simply that the top 20 percent of families have had bigger percentage gains than families near the middle: the top 5 percent have done better than the next 15, the top 1 percent better than the next 4, and so on up to Bill Gates.

Studies that try to do a better job of tracking high incomes have found startling results. For example, a recent study by the nonpartisan Congressional Budget Office used income tax data and other sources to improve on the census estimates. The C.B.O. study found that between 1979 and 1997, the after-tax incomes of the top 1 percent of families rose 157 percent, compared with only a 10 percent gain for families near the middle of the income distribution....

So claims that we've entered a second Gilded Age aren't exaggerated. In America's middle-class era, the mansion-building, yacht-owning classes had pretty much disappeared.... [I]n 1970 the top 0.01 percent of taxpayers had 0.7 percent of total income—that is, they earned "only" 70 times as much as the average, not enough to buy or maintain a mega-residence. But in 1998 the top 0.01 percent received more than 3 percent of all income. That meant that the 13,000 richest families in America had almost as much income as the 20 million poorest households; those 13,000 families had incomes 300 times that of average families.

And let me repeat: this transformation has happened very quickly, and it is still going on. You might think that 1987, the year Tom Wolfe published his novel *The Bonfire of the Vanities* and Oliver Stone released his movie *Wall Street*, marked the high tide of America's new money culture. But in 1987 the top 0.01 percent earned only about 40 percent of what they do today, and top executives less than a fifth as much. The America of *Wall Street* and *The Bonfire of the Vanities* was positively egalitarian compared with the country we live in today....

The Price of Inequality

It was one of those revealing moments. Responding to an e-mail message from a Canadian viewer, Robert Novak of "Crossfire" delivered a little speech: "Marg, like most Canadians, you're ill informed and wrong. The U.S. has the longest standard of living—longest life expectancy of any country in the world, including Canada. That's the truth."

But it was Novak who had his facts wrong. Canadians can expect to live about two years longer than Americans. In fact, life expectancy in the U.S. is well below that in Canada, Japan and every major nation in Western Europe. On average, we can expect lives a bit shorter than those of Greeks, a bit longer than those of Portuguese. Male life expectancy is lower in the U.S. than it is in Costa Rica.

Still, you can understand why Novak assumed that we were No. 1. After all, we really are the richest major nation, with real G.D.P. per capita about 20 percent higher than Canada's. And it has been an article of faith in this country that a rising tide lifts all boats. Doesn't our high and rising national wealth translate into a high standard of living—including good medical care—for all Americans?

Well, no. Although America has higher per capita income than other advanced countries, it turns out that that's mainly because our rich are much richer. And here's a radical thought: if the rich get more, that leaves less for everyone else.

That statement—which is simply a matter of arithmetic—is guaranteed to bring accusations of "class warfare." If the accuser gets more specific, he'll probably offer two reasons that it's foolish to make a fuss over the high incomes of a few people at the top of the income distribution. First, he'll tell you that what the elite get may look like a lot of money, but it's still a small share of the total—that is, when all is said and done the rich aren't getting that big a piece of the pie. Second, he'll tell you that trying to do anything to reduce incomes at the top will hurt, not help, people further down the distribution, because attempts to redistribute income damage incentives.

These arguments for lack of concern are plausible. And they were entirely correct, once upon a time—namely, back when we had a middle-class society. But there's a lot less truth to them now.

First, the share of the rich in total income is no longer trivial. These days 1 percent of families receive about 16 percent of total pretax income, and have about 14 percent of after-tax income. That share has roughly doubled over the past 30 years, and is now about as large as the share of the bottom 40 percent of the population. That's a big shift of income to the top; as a matter of pure arithmetic, it must mean that the incomes of less well off families grew considerably more slowly than average income. And they did. Adjusting for inflation, average family income—total income divided by the number of families—grew 28 percent from 1979 to 1997. But median family income—the income of a family in the middle of the distribution, a better indicator of how typical American families are doing—grew only 10 percent. And the incomes of the bottom fifth of families actually fell slightly.

Let me belabor this point for a bit. We pride ourselves, with considerable justification, on our record of economic growth. But over the last few decades it's remarkable how little of that growth has trickled down to ordinary families. Median family income has risen only about 0.5 percent per year—and as far as we can tell from somewhat unreliable data, just about all of that increase was due to wives working longer hours, with little or no gain in real wages. Furthermore, numbers about income don't reflect the growing riskiness of life for ordinary workers. In the days when General Motors was known in-house as Generous Motors, many workers felt that they had considerable job security—the company wouldn't fire them except in extremis. Many had contracts that guaranteed health insurance, even if they were laid off; they had pension benefits that did not depend on the stock market. Now mass firings from long-established companies are commonplace; losing your job means losing your insurance; and as millions of people have been learning, a 401(k) plan is no guarantee of a comfortable retirement.

Still, many people will say that while the U.S. economic system may generate a lot of inequality, it also generates much higher incomes than any alternative, so that everyone is better off.... But it's not true. Let me use the example of Sweden, that great conservative bête noire.

A few months ago the conservative cyberpundit Glenn Reynolds made a splash when he pointed out that Sweden's G.D.P. per capita is roughly comparable with that of Mississippi—see, those foolish believers in the welfare state have impoverished themselves! Presumably he assumed that this means that the typical Swede is as poor as the typical resident of Mississippi, and therefore much worse off than the typical American.

But life expectancy in Sweden is about three years higher than that of the U.S. Infant mortality is half the U.S. level, and less than a third the rate in Mississippi. Functional illiteracy is much less common than in the U.S.

How is this possible? One answer is that G.D.P. per capita is in some ways a misleading measure. Swedes take longer vacations than Americans, so they work fewer hours per year. That's a choice, not a failure of economic performance. Real G.D.P. per hour worked is 16 percent lower than in the United States, which makes Swedish productivity about the same as Canada's.

But the main point is that though Sweden may have lower average income than the United States, that's mainly because our rich are so much richer. The median Swedish family has a standard of living roughly comparable with that of the median U.S. family: wages are if anything higher in Sweden, and a higher tax burden is offset by public provision of health care and generally better public services. And as you move further down the income distribution, Swedish living standards are way ahead of those in the U.S. Swedish families with children that are at the 10th percentile—poorer than 90 percent of the population—have incomes 60 percent higher than their U.S. counterparts. And very few people in Sweden experience the deep poverty that is all too common in the United States. One measure: in 1994 only 6 percent of Swedes lived on less than $11 per day, compared with 14 percent in the U.S.

The moral of this comparison is that even if you think that America's high levels of inequality are the price of our high level of national income, it's not at all clear that this price is worth paying. The reason conservatives engage in bouts of Sweden-bashing is that they want to convince us that there is no trade-off between economic efficiency and equity—that if you try to take from the rich and give to the poor, you actually make everyone worse off. But the comparison between the U.S. and other advanced countries doesn't support this conclusion at all. Yes, we are the richest major nation. But because so much of our national income is concentrated in relatively few hands, large numbers of Americans are worse off economically than their counterparts in other advanced countries.

And we might even offer a challenge from the other side: inequality in the United States has arguably reached levels where it is counterproductive. That is, you can make a case that our society would be richer if its richest members didn't get quite so much.

I could make this argument on historical grounds. The most impressive economic growth in U.S. history coincided with the middle-class interregnum, the post–World War II generation, when incomes were most evenly distributed. But let's focus on a specific case, the extraordinary pay packages of today's top executives. Are these good for the economy?

Until recently it was almost unchallenged conventional wisdom that, whatever else you might say, the new imperial C.E.O.s had delivered results that dwarfed the expense of their compensation. But now that the stock bubble has burst, it has become increasingly clear that there was a price to those big pay packages, after all. In fact, the price paid by shareholders and society at large may have been many times larger than the amount actually paid to the executives.

It's easy to get boggled by the details of corporate scandal—insider loans, stock options, special-purpose entities, mark-to-market, round-tripping. But there's a simple reason that the details are so complicated. All of these schemes were designed to benefit corporate insiders—to inflate the pay of the C.E.O. and his inner circle. That is, they were all about the "chaos of competitive avarice" that, according to John Kenneth Galbraith, had been ruled out in the corporation of the 1960s. But while all restraint has vanished within the American corporation, the outside world—including stockholders—is still prudish, and open looting by executives is still not acceptable. So the looting has to be camouflaged, taking place through complicated schemes that can be rationalized to outsiders as clever corporate strategies.

Economists who study crime tell us that crime is inefficient—that is, the costs of crime to the economy are much larger than the amount stolen. Crime, and the fear of crime, divert resources away from productive uses: criminals spend their time stealing rather than producing, and potential victims spend time and money trying to protect their property. Also, the things people do to avoid becoming victims—like avoiding dangerous districts—have a cost even if they succeed in averting an actual crime.

The same holds true of corporate malfeasance, whether or not it actually involves breaking the law. Executives who devote their time to creating innovative ways to divert shareholder money into their own pockets probably aren't running the real business very well (think Enron, WorldCom, Tyco, Global Crossing, Adelphia ...). Investments chosen because they create the illusion of profitability while insiders cash in their stock options are a waste of scarce resources. And if the supply of funds from lenders and shareholders dries up because of a lack of trust, the economy as a whole suffers. Just ask Indonesia.

The argument for a system in which some people get very rich has always been that the lure of wealth provides powerful incentives. But the question is, incentives to do what? As we learn more about what has actually been going on in corporate America, it's becoming less and less clear whether those incentives have actually made executives work on behalf of the rest of us.

Inequality and Politics

In September [2002] the Senate debated a proposed measure that would impose a one-time capital gains tax on Americans who renounce their citizenship in order to avoid paying U.S. taxes. Senator Phil Gramm was not pleased, declaring that the proposal was "right out of Nazi Germany." Pretty strong language, but no stronger than the metaphor Daniel Mitchell of the Heritage Foundation used, in an op-ed article in the *Washington Times*, to describe a bill designed to prevent corporations from rechartering abroad for tax purposes: Mitchell described this legislation as the "Dred Scott tax bill," referring to the infamous 1857 Supreme Court ruling that required free states to return escaped slaves.

Twenty years ago, would a prominent senator have likened those who want wealthy people to pay taxes to Nazis? Would a member of a think tank with close ties to the administration have drawn a parallel between corporate taxation and slavery? I don't think so. The remarks by Gramm and Mitchell, while stronger than usual, were indicators of two huge changes in American politics. One is the growing polarization of our politics—our politicians are less and less inclined to offer even the appearance of moderation. The other is the growing tendency of policy and policy makers to cater to the interests of the wealthy. And I mean the wealthy, not the merely well-off: only someone with a net worth of at least several million dollars is likely to find it worthwhile to become a tax exile.

You don't need a political scientist to tell you that modern American politics is bitterly polarized. But wasn't it always thus? No, it wasn't. From World War II until the 1970s—the same era during which income inequality was historically low—political partisanship was much more muted than it is today. That's not just a subjective assessment. My Princeton political science colleagues Nolan McCarty and Howard Rosenthal, together with Keith Poole at the University of Houston, have done a statistical analysis showing that the voting behavior of a congressman is much better predicted by his party affiliation today than it was 25 years ago. In fact, the division between the parties is sharper now than it has been since the 1920s.

What are the parties divided about? The answer is simple: economics. McCarty, Rosenthal, and Poole write that "voting in Congress is highly ideological—one-dimensional left/right, liberal versus conservative." It may sound simplistic to describe Democrats as the party that wants to tax the rich and help the poor, and Republicans as the party that wants to keep taxes and social spending as low as possible. And during the era of middle-class America that would indeed have been simplistic: politics wasn't defined by economic issues. But that was a different country; as McCarty, Rosenthal, and Poole put it, "If income and wealth are distributed in a fairly equitable way, little is to be gained for politicians to organize politics around nonexistent conflicts." Now the conflicts are real, and our politics is organized around them. In other words, the growing inequality of our incomes probably lies behind the growing divisiveness of our politics.

But the politics of rich and poor hasn't played out the way you might think. Since the incomes of America's wealthy have soared while ordinary families have seen at best small gains, you might have expected politicians to seek votes by proposing to soak the rich. In fact, however, the polarization of politics has occurred because the Republicans have moved to the right, not because the Democrats have moved to the left. And actual economic policy has moved steadily in favor of the wealthy. The major tax cuts of the past 25 years, the Reagan cuts in the 1980s and the recent Bush cuts, were both heavily tilted toward the very well off. (Despite obfuscations, it remains true that more than half the Bush tax cut will eventually go to the top 1 percent of families.) The major tax increase over that period, the increase in payroll taxes in the 1980s, fell most heavily on working-class families.

The most remarkable example of how politics has shifted in favor of the wealthy—an example that helps us understand why economic policy has reinforced, not countered, the movement toward greater inequality—is the drive to repeal the estate tax. The estate tax is, overwhelmingly, a tax on the wealthy. In 1999, only the top 2 percent of estates paid any tax at all, and half the estate tax was paid by only 3,300 estates, 0.16 percent of the total, with a minimum value of $5 million and an average value of $17 million. A quarter of the tax was paid by just 467 estates worth more than $20 million. Tales of family farms and businesses broken up to pay the estate tax are basically rural legends; hardly any real examples have been found, despite diligent searching.

You might have thought that a tax that falls on so few people yet yields a significant amount of revenue would be politically popular; you certainly wouldn't expect widespread opposition. Moreover, there has long been an argument that the estate tax promotes democratic values, precisely because it limits the ability of the wealthy to form dynasties. So why has there been a powerful political drive to repeal the estate tax, and why was such a repeal a centerpiece of the Bush tax cut?

There is an economic argument for repealing the estate tax, but it's hard to believe that many people take it seriously. More significant for members of Congress, surely, is the question of who would benefit from repeal: while those who will actually benefit from estate tax repeal are few in number, they have a lot of money and control even more (corporate C.E.O.s can now count on leaving taxable estates behind). That is, they are the sort of people who command the attention of politicians in search of campaign funds.

But it's not just about campaign contributions: much of the general public has been convinced that the estate tax is a bad thing. If you try talking about the tax to a group of moderately prosperous retirees, you get some interesting reactions. They refer to it as the "death tax"; many of them believe that their estates will face punitive taxation, even though most of them will pay little or nothing; they are convinced that small businesses and family farms bear the brunt of the tax.

These misconceptions don't arise by accident. They have, instead, been deliberately promoted. For example, a Heritage Foundation document titled "Time to Repeal Federal Death Taxes: The Nightmare of the American Dream" emphasizes stories that rarely, if ever, happen in real life: "Small-business owners, particularly minority owners, suffer anxious moments wondering whether the businesses they hope to hand down to their children will be destroyed by the death tax bill, ... Women whose children are grown struggle to find ways to re-enter the work force without upsetting the family's estate tax avoidance plan." And who finances the Heritage Foundation? Why, foundations created by wealthy families, of course.

The point is that it is no accident that strongly conservative views, views that militate against taxes on the rich, have spread even as the rich get richer compared with the rest of us: in addition to directly buying influence, money can be used to shape public perceptions. The liberal group People for the American Way's report on how conservative foundations have deployed vast sums to support think tanks, friendly media and other institutions that promote right-wing causes is titled "Buying a Movement."

Not to put too fine a point on it: as the rich get richer, they can buy a lot of things besides goods and services. Money buys political influence; used cleverly, it also buys intellectual influence. A result is that growing income disparities in the United States, far from leading to demands to soak the rich, have been accompanied by a growing movement to let them keep more of their earnings and to pass their wealth on to their children.

This obviously raises the possibility of a self-reinforcing process. As the gap between the rich and the rest of the population grows, economic policy increasingly caters to the interests of the elite, while public services for the population at large—above all, public education—are starved of resources. As policy increasingly favors the interests of the rich and neglects the interests of the general population, income disparities grow even wider....

Discussion Questions

1. Poll your class. Do most members of your class think they will be economically better off or worse off than their parents? Define *better off* and *worse off*.

2. Women (especially single mothers) and minorities are disproportionately poor. Part of the debate on inequality concerns whether existing inequalities reflect people's talents and work effort or whether there is still significant racial and gender discrimination in job markets. What do you think, and how does your conclusion affect your attitude toward present inequalities?

3. No one favors a complete leveling of income and wealth, nor does anybody want all wealth to be concentrated in a few hands. But where do we draw the line? What level of inequality should be tolerated in our democracy before government is required to take action?

4. Do you think the present level of economic inequality is corrupting our political processes? Will campaign finance laws protect the system from the unaccountable power of money, or do we need to reduce economic inequality itself?

5. In their book, Cox and Alm suggest that, because of technological advances, the average American is better off today than a millionaire was in the 1890s. Agree or disagree.

Suggested Readings and Internet Resources

For further elaboration of Cox and Alm's argument that nearly everyone is benefiting from our dynamic economy, see their *Myths of Rich and Poor: Why We're Better Off Than We Think* (New York: Basic Books, 1999), from which our excerpt was taken. The best compilation of data on the changing distribution of income and wealth (which can be viewed as a rejoinder to Cox and Alm) is *The State of Working America 2008–2009* (Ithaca, N.Y.: Cornell University Press, 2009) by Lawrence Mishel, Jared Bernstein, and Heidi Shierholz. In a highly controversial book, *The Bell Curve: Intelligence and Class Structure in American Life* (New York: Free Press, 1994), Richard J. Herrnstein and Charles Murray argue that economic inequalities in our technological society fairly reflect differences in people's intelligence, or IQ. Paul Krugman elaborates his critique of economic inequality in *The Conscience of a Liberal* (New York: W. W. Norton, 2009). For a scholarly analysis of public attitudes on economic inequality, see Benjamin I. Page and Lawrence R. Jacobs, *Class War? What Americans Really Think About Economic Inequality* (Chicago: University of Chicago Press, 2009). Larry Bartels examines the political causes and consequences of economic inequality in *Unequal Democracy: The Political Economy of the New Gilded Age* (New York: Russell Sage Foundation, 2008).

United for a Fair Economy
www.faireconomy.org
This website spotlights the dangers of growing income and wealth inequality in the United States and supports actions to reduce the gap.

Economic Policy Institute
www.epinet.org
The Economic Policy Institute is a nonprofit, labor-supported think tank that seeks to broaden the public debate about strategies to achieve a strong economy. Their website stresses real-world analysis and a concern for the living standards of working people.

Heritage Foundation
www.heritage.org
The Heritage Foundation website stresses the principles of free enterprise, limited government, individual freedom, traditional American values, and a strong national defense.

Cato Institute
www.cato.org
The Cato Institute seeks to broaden the parameters of public policy debate to allow consideration of more options that are consistent with the traditional American principle of limited government. This website reflects the libertarian values of the Cato Institute and its commitment to limited government.

Chapter 17

✸

Foreign Policy: Has the United States Become an Imperial Power?

The terrorist attacks of September 11, 2001, stunned and horrified an America that had largely lost interest in global politics after the end of the Cold War a decade earlier. The vast majority of Americans rallied behind the Bush administration in its military campaign against the al Qaeda organization that had carried out the terror strike and the Taliban regime in Afghanistan that had harbored al Qaeda. After ousting the Taliban regime from power, President George W. Bush swiftly moved on to a larger campaign, condemning an "axis of evil" that included Iraq, Iran, and North Korea, and calling for the largest American defense buildup in two decades. Claiming that Iraq, under Saddam Hussein, threatened America with weapons of mass destruction and had ties to the al Qaeda terror network, Bush defied many of America's traditional allies and, along with Great Britain, waged a war that toppled Hussein's regime in the spring of 2003.

Although Americans have been united since September 11 on the need to combat terrorism, the war in Iraq produced new divisions at home. As U.S. forces suffered mounting casualties at the hands of an Iraqi insurgency, a majority of Americans came to oppose the war that Bush had initiated. Barack Obama made his national reputation largely on the basis of his early opposition to Bush's war and pledged a thorough makeover of foreign policy as president. While many Republicans were unhappy with Bush for the failures of his strategy in Iraq, they continued to share his basic assumptions and assailed Obama's approach to the world as weak. During the Obama presidency as well as during the Bush presidency, therefore, the debate over U.S. foreign policy has become one of the most important facing the American people.

A provocative question in this debate is whether the United States has become an imperial power. From the time of the American founding to the late nineteenth century, the keynote of American foreign policy was isolationism, coupled with an expansionism that drove the European powers off the North American continent and extended American power into Latin America. At the beginning of the twentieth century, however, American leaders such as Theodore Roosevelt and Woodrow Wilson pioneered a global role for the United States.

This global role took on far greater dimensions through American involvement in World War II and the Cold War that soon followed it. The United States was now the self-proclaimed leader of the "Free World," and the newly strengthened presidency, military, and intelligence services projected American power on every continent and every ocean. During the Cold War, the United States was in competition with another "superpower," the Soviet Union, which was seen as the source of challenges to the Free World around the globe. Once the Soviet Union collapsed unexpectedly at the end of the 1980s, the United States stood alone at the pinnacle of international power.

After a decade in which the challenges to American power appeared small-scale and scattered, the new threat of terror attacks from Islamic fundamentalists has evoked conflicting views on U.S. global strategy. The Bush administration favored a unilateral response in the "war on terror," as the United States charted a course that relied heavily on its military superiority and rebuffed the more cautious views of traditional allies. The Obama administration has come to power pledging a more multilateral strategy that emphasizes cooperation with allies and a preference for diplomacy over military action. Yet even as Obama was awarded the Nobel Prize for Peace in 2009 for his shift from Bush's foreign policy, he was announcing that an expanded American military involvement was indispensable in Afghanistan.

From the initial American response to September 11, to the escalation of armed conflict in Afghanistan, the United States has been at war for nearly a decade. Is this "long war," with no current end in sight, simply a defensive response to attacks on the American homeland? Or does it reflect the arrogance of an imperial power harboring the illusion that it can bend developments in faraway nations to its own needs? International relations scholar Andrew J. Bacevich, a West Point graduate and army officer who served in Vietnam, believes that the latter position is correct. Bacevich recognizes that the United States faces hostile foes, yet he believes that the driving force for American foreign policy comes from within. Americans cherish their freedom, which is now primarily defined in materialistic terms, and they want the rest of the world to underwrite it. Unlike earlier generations, however, most do not want the responsibilities—serving in the armed forces or paying the taxes—that are required for global dominance. As a result, Bacevich argues, America is following the same disastrous path that led to the destruction of earlier empires, piling up debt and stretching its professional military beyond its capacity. He is sharply critical of President George W. Bush, yet he fears that President Barack Obama is prone to the same kind of illusions about American imperial power as his predecessor.

International relations scholar Michael Mandelbaum agrees with Bacevich that the vast American role in the world today is rooted in self-interest rather than altruism. Unlike Bacevich, however, he suggests that the consequences of the nation's unrivaled standing in the first decade of the twenty-first century are largely beneficial for both the United States and other nations. Denying that the United States actually is an empire, Mandelbaum portrays it as a benign Goliath, whose exercise of strength is the basis for security and prosperity around the globe. He acknowledges that American power can be misapplied: thus, President Bush's doctrine of "preventive war," put into practice in Iraq, reveals more about the limits than it does about the effectiveness of military might. Nonetheless, he cautions against the significant retreat from international involvements for which Bacevich calls. From Mandelbaum's perspective, a world lacking the power of the American Goliath would also lack military, political, and economic stability.

The essays by Bacevich and Mandelbaum raise central issues for the democratic debate over U.S. foreign policy. Is the United States correctly described as an empire, with the negative connotations that this term implies? Are Americans prone to an arrogant belief that we can manage world affairs to our satisfaction and our benefit? Or is the United States predominantly a force for stability and progress when it exercises its unparalleled power abroad? Is the American Goliath a benefactor to the world—or a threat?

The Limits of American Power

ANDREW J. BACEVICH

For the United States, the passing of the Cold War yielded neither a "peace dividend" nor anything remotely resembling peace.[1] Instead, what was hailed as a historic victory gave way almost immediately to renewed unrest and conflict. By the time the East–West standoff that some historians had termed the "Long Peace" ended in 1991, the United States had already embarked upon a decade of unprecedented interventionism. In the years that followed, Americans became inured to reports of U.S. forces going into action—fighting in Panama and the Persian Gulf, occupying Bosnia and Haiti, lambasting Kosovo, Afghanistan, and Sudan from the air. Yet all of these turned out to be mere preliminaries. In 2001 came the main event, an open-ended global war on terror, soon known in some quarters as the "Long War."

---

1. Many analysts expected the United States to enjoy a peace dividend—large savings from a reduced defense budget—with the end of the Cold War.

Viewed in retrospect, indications that the Long Peace began almost immediately to give way to conditions antithetical to peace seem blindingly obvious. Prior to 9/11, however, the implications of developments like the 1993 bombing of the World Trade Center or the failure of the U.S. military mission to Somalia that same year were difficult to discern. After all, these small events left unaltered what many took to be the defining reality of the contemporary era: the preeminence of the United States, which seemed beyond challenge.

During the 1990s, at the urging of politicians and pundits, Americans became accustomed to thinking of their country as "the indispensable nation." Indispensability carried with it both responsibilities and prerogatives.

The chief responsibility was to preside over a grand project of political-economic convergence and integration commonly referred to as globalization. In point of fact, however, globalization served as a euphemism for soft, or informal, empire. The collapse of the Soviet Union appeared to offer an opportunity to expand and perpetuate that empire, creating something akin to a global Pax Americana.

The indispensable nation's chief prerogative, self-assigned, was to establish and enforce the norms governing the post–Cold War international order. Even in the best of circumstances, imperial policing is a demanding task, requiring not only considerable acumen but also an abundance of determination. The preferred American approach was to rely, whenever possible, on suasion. Yet if pressed, Washington did not hesitate to use force, as its numerous military adventures during the 1990s demonstrated.

Whatever means were employed, the management of empire assumed the existence of bountiful reserves of power—economic, political, cultural, but above all military. In the immediate aftermath of the Cold War, few questioned that assumption. The status of the United States as "sole superpower" appeared unassailable. Its dominance was unquestioned and unambiguous. This was not hypernationalistic chest-thumping; it was the conventional wisdom.

Recalling how Washington saw the post–Cold War world and America's place in (or atop) it helps us understand why policy makers failed to anticipate, deter, or deflect the terrorist attacks of September 11, 2001. A political elite preoccupied with the governance of empire paid little attention to protecting the United States itself. In practical terms, prior to 9/11 the mission of homeland defense was unassigned.

The institution nominally referred to as the Department of Defense didn't actually do defense; it specialized in power projection. In 2001, the Pentagon was prepared for any number of contingencies in the Balkans or Northeast Asia or the Persian Gulf. It was just not prepared to address threats to the nation's eastern seaboard. Well-trained and equipped U.S. forces stood ready to defend Seoul or Riyadh; Manhattan was left to fend for itself.

Odd as they may seem, these priorities reflected a core principle of national security policy: When it came to defending vital American interests, asserting control over the imperial periphery took precedence over guarding the nation's own perimeter.

After 9/11, the Bush administration affirmed this core principle. Although it cobbled together a new agency to attend to "homeland security," the administration also redoubled its efforts to shore up the Pax Americana and charged the Department of Defense with focusing on this task. This meant using any means necessary—suasion where possible, force as required—to bring the Islamic world into conformity with prescribed American norms. Rather than soft and consensual, the approach to imperial governance became harder and more coercive.

So, for the United States after 9/11, war became a seemingly permanent condition. President George W. Bush and members of his administration outlined a campaign against terror that they suggested might last decades, if not longer. On the national political scene, few questioned that prospect. In the Pentagon, senior military officers spoke in terms of "generational war," lasting up to a century. Just two weeks after 9/11, Secretary of Defense Donald Rumsfeld was already instructing Americans to "forget about 'exit strategies'; we're looking at a sustained engagement that carries no deadlines."

By and large, Americans were slow to grasp the implications of a global war with no exits and no deadlines. To earlier generations, place names like Iraq and Afghanistan had been synonymous with European rashness—the sort of obscure and unwelcoming jurisdictions to which overly ambitious kings and slightly mad adventurers might repair to squabble. For the present generation, it has already become part of the natural order of things that GIs should be exerting themselves at great cost to pacify such far-off domains. For the average American tuning in to the nightly news, reports of U.S. casualties incurred in distant lands now seem hardly more out of the ordinary than reports of partisan shenanigans on Capitol Hill or brush fires raging out of control in Southern California.

How exactly did the end of the Long Peace so quickly yield the Long War? Seeing themselves as a peaceful people, Americans remain wedded to the conviction that the conflicts in which they find themselves embroiled are not of their own making. The global war on terror is no exception. Certain of our own benign intentions, we reflexively assign responsibility for war to others, typically malignant Hitler-like figures inexplicably bent on denying us the peace that is our fondest wish.

This [essay] challenges that supposition. It argues that the actions of Saddam Hussein and Osama bin Laden, however malevolent, cannot explain why the United States today finds itself enmeshed in seemingly never-ending conflict. Although critics of U.S. foreign policy, and especially of the Iraq War, have already advanced a variety of alternative explanations—variously fingering President Bush, members of his inner circle, jingoistic neoconservatives, greedy oil executives, or even the Israel lobby—it also finds those explanations inadequate. Certainly, the president and his advisers, along with neocons always looking for opportunities to flex American military muscle, bear considerable culpability for our current predicament. Yet to charge them with primary responsibility is to credit them with undeserved historical significance. It's the equivalent of blaming Herbert Hoover for the Great

Depression or of attributing McCarthyism entirely to the antics of Senator Joseph McCarthy.

The impulses that have landed us in a war of no exits and no deadlines come from within. Foreign policy has, for decades, provided an outward manifestation of American domestic ambitions, urges, and fears. In our own time, it has increasingly become an expression of domestic dysfunction—an attempt to manage or defer coming to terms with contradictions besetting the American way of life. Those contradictions have found their ultimate expression in the perpetual state of war afflicting the United States today.

Gauging their implications requires that we acknowledge their source: They reflect the accumulated detritus of freedom, the by-products of our frantic pursuit of life, liberty, and happiness.

Freedom is the altar at which Americans worship, whatever their nominal religious persuasion. "No one sings odes to liberty as the final end of life with greater fervor than Americans," the theologian Reinhold Niebuhr once observed. Yet even as they celebrate freedom, Americans exempt the object of their veneration from critical examination. In our public discourse, freedom is not so much a word or even a value as an incantation, its very mention enough to stifle doubt and terminate all debate....

[T]his heedless worship of freedom has been a mixed blessing. In our pursuit of freedom, we have accrued obligations and piled up debts that we are increasingly hard-pressed to meet. Especially since the 1960s, freedom itself has undercut the nation's ability to fulfill its commitments. We teeter on the edge of insolvency, desperately trying to balance accounts by relying on our presumably invincible armed forces. Yet there, too, having exaggerated our military might, we court bankruptcy.

The United States today finds itself threatened by three interlocking crises. The first of these crises is economic and cultural, the second political, and the third military. All three share this characteristic: They are of our own making. In assessing the predicament that results from these crises, [this essay] employs what might be called a Niebuhrean perspective. Writing decades ago, Reinhold Niebuhr anticipated that predicament with uncanny accuracy and astonishing prescience. As such, perhaps more than any other figure in our recent history, he may help us discern a way out.

As pastor, teacher, activist, theologian, and prolific author, Niebuhr was a towering presence in American intellectual life from the 1930s through the 1960s. Even today, he deserves recognition as the most clear-eyed of American prophets. Niebuhr speaks to us from the past, offering truths of enormous relevance to the present. As prophet, he warned that what he called "our dreams of managing history"—born of a peculiar combination of arrogance and narcissism—posed a potentially mortal threat to the United States. Today, we ignore that warning at our peril.

Niebuhr entertained few illusions about the nature of man, the possibilities of politics, or the pliability of history. Global economic crisis, total war, genocide, totalitarianism, and nuclear arsenals capable of destroying civilization itself—he viewed all of these with an unblinking eye that allowed no room for hypocrisy, hokum, or self-deception. Realism and humility formed the core of his world-view, each infused with a deeply felt Christian sensibility.

Realism in this sense implies an obligation to see the world as it actually is, not as we might like it to be. The enemy of realism is hubris, which in Niebuhr's day, and in our own, finds expression in an outsized confidence in the efficacy of American power as an instrument to reshape the global order.

Humility imposes an obligation of a different sort. It summons Americans to see themselves without blinders. The enemy of humility is sanctimony, which gives rise to the conviction that American values and beliefs are universal and that the nation itself serves providentially assigned purposes. This conviction finds expression in a determination to remake the world in what we imagine to be America's image.

In our own day, realism and humility have proven in short supply. What Niebuhr wrote after World War II proved truer still in the immediate aftermath of the Cold War: Good fortune and a position of apparent preeminence placed the United States "under the most grievous temptations to self-adulation." Americans have given themselves over to those temptations. Hubris and sanctimony have become the paramount expressions of American statecraft. After 9/11, they combined to produce the Bush administration's war of no exits and no deadlines.

President Bush has likened today's war against what he calls "Islamofascism" to America's war with Nazi Germany—a great struggle waged on behalf of liberty. That President Bush is waging his global war on terror to preserve American freedom is no doubt the case. Yet that commitment, however well intentioned, begs several larger questions: As actually expressed and experienced, what is freedom today? What is its content? What costs does the exercise of freedom impose? Who pays?

These are fundamental questions, which cannot be dismissed with a rhetorical wave of the hand. Great wartime presidents of the past—one thinks especially of Abraham Lincoln speaking at Gettysburg—have not hesitated to confront such questions directly. That President Bush seems oblivious to their very existence offers one measure of his shortcomings as a statesman.

Freedom is not static, nor is it necessarily benign. In practice, freedom constantly evolves and in doing so generates new requirements and abolishes old constraints. The common understanding of freedom that prevailed in December 1941 when the United States entered the war against Imperial Japan and Nazi Germany has long since become obsolete. In some respects, this must be cause for celebration. In others, it might be cause for regret.

The changes have been both qualitative and quantitative. In many respects, Americans are freer today than ever before, with more citizens than ever before enjoying unencumbered access to the promise of American life. Yet especially since the 1960s, the reinterpretation of freedom has had a transformative impact on our society and culture. That transformation has produced a paradoxical legacy. As individuals, our appetites and expectations have grown exponentially. Niebuhr once wrote disapprovingly of Americans, their "culture soft and vulgar, equating joy with happiness and happiness with comfort." Were he alive today, Niebuhr might amend that judgment, with Americans increasingly equating comfort with self-indulgence.

The collective capacity of our domestic political economy to satisfy those appetites has not kept pace with demand. As a result, sustaining our pursuit of life, liberty, and happiness at home requires increasingly that Americans look beyond our borders. Whether the issue at hand is oil, credit, or the availability of cheap consumer goods, we expect the world to accommodate the American way of life.

The resulting sense of entitlement has great implications for foreign policy. Simply put, as the American appetite for freedom has grown, so too has our penchant for empire. The connection between these two tendencies is a causal one. In an earlier age, Americans saw empire as the antithesis of freedom. Today, as illustrated above all by the Bush administration's efforts to dominate the energy-rich Persian Gulf, empire has seemingly become a prerequisite of freedom.

There is a further paradox: The actual exercise of American freedom is no longer conducive to generating the power required to establish and maintain an imperial order. If anything, the reverse is true: Centered on consumption and individual autonomy, the exercise of freedom is contributing to the gradual erosion of our national power. At precisely the moment when the ability to wield power—especially military power—has become the sine qua non for preserving American freedom, our reserves of power are being depleted.

One sees this, for example, in the way that heightened claims of individual autonomy have eviscerated the concept of citizenship. Yesterday's civic obligations have become today's civic options. What once rated as duties—rallying to the country's defense at times of great emergency, for example—are now matters of choice. As individuals, Americans never cease to expect more. As members of a community, especially as members of a national community, they choose to contribute less.

Meanwhile, American political leaders—especially at the national level—have proven unable (or unwilling) to address the disparity between how much we want and what we can afford to pay. Successive administrations, abetted by Congress, have deepened a looming crisis of debt and dependency through unbridled spending. As Vice President Dick Cheney, a self-described conservative, announced when told that cutting taxes might be at odds with invading Iraq, "Deficits don't matter." Politicians of both parties certainly act as if they don't.

Expectations that the world beyond our borders should accommodate the American way of life are hardly new. Since 9/11, however, our demands have become more insistent. In that regard, the neoconservative writer Robert Kagan is surely correct in observing that "America did not change on September 11. It only became more itself." In the aftermath of the attacks on the World Trade Center and the Pentagon, Washington's resolve that nothing interfere with the individual American's pursuit of life, liberty, and happiness only hardened. That resolve found expression in the Bush administration's with-us-or-against-us rhetoric, in its disdain for the United Nations and traditional American allies, in its contempt for international law, and above all in its embrace of preventive war.

When President Bush declared in his second inaugural that the "survival of liberty in our land increasingly depends on the success of liberty in other lands," he was in effect claiming for the United States as freedom's chief agent the prerogative of waging war when and where it sees fit, those wars by definition being fought on freedom's behalf. In this sense, the Long War genuinely qualifies as a war to preserve the American way of life (centered on a specific conception of liberty) and simultaneously as a war to extend the American imperium (centered on dreams of a world remade in America's image), the former widely assumed to require the latter.

Yet, as events have made plain, the United States is ill-prepared to wage a global war of no exits and no deadlines. The sole superpower lacks the resources—economic, political, and military—to support a large-scale, protracted conflict without, at the very least, inflicting severe economic and political damage on itself. American power has limits and is inadequate to the ambitions to which hubris and sanctimony have given rise.

Here is the central paradox of our time: While the defense of American freedom seems to demand that U.S. troops fight in places like Iraq and Afghanistan, the exercise of that freedom at home undermines the nation's capacity to fight. A grand bazaar provides an inadequate basis upon which to erect a vast empire.

Meanwhile, a stubborn insistence on staying the course militarily ends up jeopardizing freedom at home. With Americans, even in wartime, refusing to curb their appetites, the Long War aggravates the economic contradictions that continue to produce debt and dependency. Moreover, a state of perpetual national security emergency aggravates the disorders afflicting our political system, allowing the executive branch to accrue ever more authority at the expense of the Congress and disfiguring the Constitution. In this sense, the Long War is both self-defeating and irrational.

Niebuhr once wrote, "One of the most pathetic aspects of human history is that every civilization expresses itself most pretentiously, compounds its partial and universal values most convincingly and claims immortality for its finite existence at the very moment when the decay which leads to death has already begun." Future generations of historians may well cite Niebuhr's dictum as a concise explanation of the folly that propelled the United States into its Long War.

In an immediate sense, it is the soldier who bears the burden of such folly. U.S. troops in battle dress and body armor, whom Americans profess to admire and support, pay the price for the nation's collective refusal to confront our domestic dysfunction. In many ways, the condition of the military today offers the most urgent expression of that dysfunction. Seven years into its confrontation with radical Islam, the United States finds itself with too much war for too few warriors—and with no prospect of producing the additional soldiers needed to close the gap. In effect, Americans now confront a looming military crisis to go along with the economic and political crises that they have labored so earnestly to ignore.

The Iraq War deserves our attention as the clearest manifestation of these three crises, demonstrating the extent to which they are inextricably linked and mutually reinforcing. That war was always unnecessary. Except in the eyes of the deluded and the disingenuous, it has long since become a fool's errand. Of perhaps even greater significance, it is both counterproductive and unsustainable.

Yet ironically Iraq may yet prove to be the source of our salvation. For the United States, the ongoing war makes plain the imperative of putting America's house in order. Iraq has revealed the futility of counting on military power to sustain our habits of profligacy. The day of reckoning approaches. Expending the lives of more American soldiers in hopes of deferring that day is profoundly wrong. History will not judge kindly a people who find nothing amiss in the prospect of endless armed conflict so long as they themselves are spared the effects. Nor will it view with favor an electorate that delivers political power into the hands of leaders unable to envision any alternative to perpetual war.

Rather than insisting that the world accommodate the United States, Americans need to reassert control over their own destiny, ending their condition of dependency and abandoning their imperial delusions. Of perhaps even greater difficulty, the combination of economic, political, and military crisis summons Americans to reexamine exactly what freedom entails. Soldiers cannot accomplish these tasks, nor should we expect politicians to do so. The onus of responsibility falls squarely on citizens....

No single factor can explain the extraordinary excitement generated by Barack Obama's successful run for the White House. The candidate's intelligence, vigor, eloquence, cool persona, and compelling personal story all figured in important ways. Self-discipline, impressive organizational skills, and a pronounced knack for raising money certainly helped. Yet the key to Obama's victory lay in his oft-repeated promise to "change the way Washington works." Obama's very election expressed a popular desire, as deep-seated as it was widespread, to repudiate all that Washington had come to represent in the era of George W. Bush.

Satisfying this yearning for change, however, implies something more than tacking from starboard to port. On November 4, 2008, the millions who watched Obama claim his victory in Chicago's Grant Park—"Because of what we did, on this day change has come to America"—were counting on the nation's new captain to set the United States on an entirely different azimuth, headed toward a new and better destination.

Yet substantive change will remain little more than a slogan absent a willingness to consider this proposition: When it comes to national security, the standard navigational charts used to guide the ship of state are obsolete. The assumptions, doctrines, habits, and routines falling under the rubric of "national security policy" have outlived their usefulness. The antidote to the disappointments and failures of the Bush years, illustrated most vividly in the never-ending wars in Iraq and Afghanistan, is not to try harder, but to think differently. Only then will it become possible to avoid the patently self-destructive behavior that today finds Americans facing the prospect of perpetual conflict that neither our army nor our economy can sustain.

That President Obama will find a way out of this predicament—that he will make good on his promise of change—must be the fervent hope of all persons of good will. Doing so will require not only ideas but the people and the wherewithal to implement those ideas.

To fill his cabinet and to staff the White House, Obama has recruited an impressive array of talent. Yet whether his chief lieutenants will serve as agents of real change—or whether they will settle, as is so often the case in Washington, for some modest updating—remains to be seen.

Consider Obama's national security team, headed by Secretary of State Hillary Clinton, Secretary of Defense Robert Gates, General James Jones as national security adviser, and Admiral Dennis Blair as director of national intelligence. Each and every one is a seasoned professional: competent, well-informed, pragmatic, and wise in the ways of Washington. Yet however imposing their résumés, they are establishment figures, utterly conventional in their outlook. That a career intelligence official like Gates or a retired Marine four-star like Jones will question the core assumptions informing standard national security practices is by no means an impossibility. It's just not especially likely. One might as well look to the CEOs of Detroit's Big Three to promote mass transit as a preferred alternative to the automobile....

Candidate Obama differed with Bush (and with the man who ran against him, Senator John McCain) not on fundamental principles but on operational priorities. Obama never directly questioned the wisdom of perpetuating the global war that Bush had conceived; he merely conveyed the sense that he would fight that war more effectively.

Should President Obama's actions in office affirm open-ended armed conflict as his preferred antidote to violent Islamic radicalism, Bush himself and his dwindling band of supporters will no doubt rejoice. In that event, however, Obama will run the risk of seeing his presidency hijacked. Just as, forty years ago, Richard Nixon quickly discovered that Lyndon Johnson's war became his, so too Obama will face the prospect of Bush's wars, especially in Afghanistan, becoming his own. And the likelihood of his making good on his promise of change will diminish accordingly.

In Grant Park on November 4, Obama declared that the time had come for Americans "to put their hands on the arc of history and bend it once more toward the hope of a better day." That our history has a discernible arc and that Americans possess the capacity to bend it to their will are propositions to which any number of earlier presidents—Obama's immediate predecessor not least among them—have fervently subscribed.

Perhaps this solemn genuflection before the altar of American exceptionalism amounted to little more than a rhetorical flourish meant to punctuate a night of exuberant celebration. We must hope so. This much we can say with certainty: If Obama's vision of change really does center on the expectation of somehow taming history, then he and his supporters are headed for disappointment....

The Case for Goliath

MICHAEL MANDELBAUM

When the Cold War ended, a question arose: What would succeed that great political, military, economic, and ideological conflict as the central issue in international relations? By the middle of the first decade of the twenty-first century, the question had been answered. The enormous power and pervasive influence of the United States was universally acknowledged to be the defining feature of world affairs.

In the eyes of many, American supremacy counted as a great misfortune. The foreign policy of the world's strongest country, in this account, resembled the conduct of a school yard bully who randomly assaults others, steals the lunch money of weaker students, and generally makes life unpleasant wherever he goes. The United States was seen as the world's Goliath.

In some ways the United States in the early years of the twenty-first century does resemble the Philistine giant whom David, the son of Jesse, felled with a sling and a stone according to the Bible and thereby saved Israel. Like Goliath, the United States surpasses all others in military might. And just as Goliath was, by virtue of his size and power, the logical candidate to represent his tribe in its confrontation with the people of Israel, so the United States has undertaken broad responsibilities that redound to the benefit of others.

Although the United States looks like Goliath, however, in important ways the world's strongest power does not act like him. If America is a Goliath, it is a benign one. Unlike the case of Goliath, moreover, no David, or group of Davids, has stepped forward to confront the United States. This [essay] explains other countries' acceptance of the American role in the world by painting a different and more benign picture of that role than the one implied by the comparison with Western civilization's archetypal bully. As portrayed in the pages that follow, it has something in common with the sun's relationship to the rest of the solar system. Both confer benefits on the entities with which they are in regular contact. The sun keeps the planets in their orbits by the force of gravity and radiates the heat and light that make life possible on one of them. Similarly, the United States furnishes services to other countries, the same services, as it happens, that governments provide within sovereign states to the people they govern. The United States therefore functions as the world's government. The origins, the details, and the implications of this twenty-first-century American international role are the subjects [that] present the case for Goliath....

[This essay] describes the ways in which the United States performs, within the international system, the first duty of all governments: providing security. One of the principal American policies during the Cold War—deterrence—was transformed, in the wake of the conflict, into a related but distinct mission: reassurance. Another Cold War policy, preventing the spread of nuclear weapons, gained in importance in the post–Cold War period. The United States has introduced two new purposes for the use of force: preventive war and humanitarian intervention. Both led to yet another governmental undertaking, popularly called nation-building.

[Other] American foreign policies ... correspond to the economic tasks that governments perform within sovereign states. One is the enforcement of contracts and the protection of property in their jurisdictions. America's international military deployments have these effects on transactions across borders. Governments also supply the power and water without which industrial economies cannot function. Similarly, the United States helps to assure global access to the economically indispensable mineral, oil. Governments supply the money used in economic transactions: The American dollar serves as the world's money. At the outset of the post–World War II period and thereafter, the United States fostered the conditions in which yet another major economic activity—trade—flourished and expanded. Finally, just as, in the twentieth century, governments took it upon themselves to sustain the level of consumption within their societies in order to support a high level of production and thus of employment, so the huge American appetite for consumer products has helped to sustain economic activity the world over, especially in East Asia....

Empire

At the beginning of the twenty-first century, a term came into use to refer to the American role in the world that conjured up images of Roman legions with helmets, metal breastplates, and sharp lances keeping order in the ancient world, bearded Habsburg grandees riding on horseback along cobblestone streets in Central Europe, and British colonial officials in pith helmets presiding over tropical kingdoms. The term was "empire." Many books and articles appeared advancing and exploring the proposition that the United States had become, without officially acknowledging it, what the largest and most powerful political units of the past had proudly proclaimed themselves to be.

Applied to the United States, the term "empire" had a jarring effect. For empire had seemed, as the twenty-first century began, the dinosaur of international history, having dominated the planet for much of recorded history but then become extinct, its place taken everywhere by the more cohesive and legitimate nation-state. The ideas that had underpinned the empires of the past—the glory of war and conquest, the commercial advantages of political monopolies, the natural hierarchy of the human race that made some people fit to govern others—had all fallen decisively out of favor.

The United States seemed a particularly unlikely candidate for an imperial role. Although America had once had an empire, it had been acquired later, had been given up earlier, and even at its zenith had been considerably smaller than the empires of the British, the French, the Austrian Habsburgs, the Russian Romanovs, or the Ottoman Turks. Moreover, the United States had been founded in revolt against empire, and even when it *was* an imperial power had harbored powerful anti-imperial sentiment. Its first and most expansive exercise in imperial conquest, the Spanish–American War of 1898 and the direct possession of the Philippines and indirect control of Cuba that resulted from its victory in that war, aroused considerable opposition in the United States Congress and among such eminent private citizens as Mark Twain and Andrew Carnegie.

What accounts for the revival of a seemingly obsolete and, in the case of the United States, inappropriate term? Behind the use of the word "empire" to describe American relations with other countries lay two motives—one descriptive, the other derisive.

The global status of the United States at the outset of the twenty-first century seemed to require a new term because the American presence in the world had changed. It was an unprecedentedly powerful one. The range of the military, economic, and cultural influence that the United States could bring to bear was impressively wide. Even more impressive was the margin of power that separated America from every other country. The American economy produced 30 percent of the world's output; no other country was responsible for even half that much. The American defense budget exceeded, in dollars expended, the military spending of the next fifteen countries combined, and the United States had some military assets—its highly accurate missiles, for example—that no other country possessed.

As a term to describe this latter-day colossus, "empire" did have some advantages. America's global role did bear some resemblance to the empires of the past. Its military forces were deployed in many countries—upward of 150 by one count. As with the great empires of the past, the language most frequently employed in international discussions was the one Americans spoke: English. The American government itself noticed the similarity: The Department of Defense commissioned a study of the great empires of the past, with particular emphasis on how they had maintained their dominant positions—or failed to do so.

Moreover, if the word "empire" seemed, in some ways, to capture the reality of the twenty-first century American global presence, more familiar and recent terms did not. The United States had surely become more than a great power, which is what the major European countries (many of them, to be sure, also empires) had been called in the nineteenth century and at the beginning of the twentieth. It had outgrown the status that, along with the Soviet Union, it had enjoyed during the Cold War, when both were called nuclear "superpowers." The great powers and even the superpowers of the past had, after all, had international peers: The twenty-first century United States had none.

Because it suggested a greater, grander status than either of the other two terms, it was empire that came to seem to many the most appropriate way to describe America's international status.

If one reason for using this term was to describe America's role in the world, another was to denounce it. By the twenty-first century, the word "empire" had ceased, in all but the most academic discourse, to be purely descriptive. It carried a negative connotation. Like slavery, dictatorship, and discrimination, it was widely understood to refer to a political practice that, while once common and acceptable, had come to be seen as an odious exercise in wrongful subordination. Two of the most powerful ideologies of the twentieth century, nationalism and Marxism, defined their respective historical missions as prominently including the defeat and abolition of imperialism. To call the American role in the world imperial was, for many who did so, a way of asserting that the United States was misusing its power beyond its borders and, in so doing, subverting its founding political principles within them.

The use of the term "empire" to describe the American role in the world in the twenty-first century, whatever its advantages, has one major shortcoming: It is inaccurate. Many criticisms may plausibly be leveled at the United States for the way it conducts its foreign policy, but the charge that that policy is essentially an imperial one is not among them....

Like the creation and maintenance of empires throughout history, the provision of international public goods by the United States is not an act of altruism. Self-interest motivates the world's strongest power to undertake its twenty-first-century global tasks, just as self-interest lay behind the expansion of Roman, Habsburg, and British imperial power. But in other ways the American global role differs dramatically from—indeed is the opposite of—imperial rule.

Empire stands condemned in the twenty-first century because it has always rested on an imbalance of power between the ruling and the ruled societies. Inequality of any kind, once considered a normal, natural part of human existence, came to be seen in the course of the twentieth century as increasingly illegitimate. For the provision of international public goods, however, inequality is desirable. Indeed, it is essential. The advantage over all other countries in wealth and power that the United States enjoys, and that those who term it a latter-day empire decry by their use of the term, is the necessary condition for the American role as the world's government.

That role also reverses the distribution of benefits commonly attributed to empire. Traditionally, the imperial power has been seen as a predator, drawing economic profit and political gain from its control of the imperial possession, while the members of the society it controls suffer; or, if they do benefit from the relationship, the ruled gain far less than their imperial masters. In its role as the provider of international public goods, by contrast, it is the United States that pays and the rest of the world that benefits without having to pay. The biblical Goliath served the Philistines but not the people of Israel. The twenty-first-century United States does both. It is not the lion of the international system, terrorizing and preying on smaller, weaker animals in order to survive itself. It is, rather, the elephant, which supports a wide variety of other creatures—smaller mammals, birds, and insects—by generating nourishment for them as it goes about the business of feeding itself.

To understand the United States as the world's government rather than as an empire, finally, suggests a different future for the American international role.

Empires vanished because they became too expensive. The cost of imperial rule rose sharply in the twentieth century because the societies that imperial powers governed mobilized to oppose their rule. Internal resistance by the governed raised the cost of controlling them beyond what the metropolitan societies could or would pay.

Whether, and for how long, the United States will remain the world's government is an open question, the answer to which will depend on the willingness of the American public, the ultimate arbiter of American foreign policy, to sustain the costs of this role. Because the rest of the world benefits from the services that the United States provides, however, the world's other major countries are unlikely to act deliberately, as societies under imperial rule did, to raise those costs.

Why has the United States assumed the role of the world's government? America has sufficient power, as no other country does, for this purpose. But the role arises from demand as well as from supply. The world has a greater need for governance in the twenty-first century than ever before....

The War in Iraq

The lesson that the responsible officials drew from the events of September 11 was ... that in dealing with aggressive terrorist groups or rogue states, the better part of valor is not discretion but rather boldness. The safety of the United States and the well-being of the world, they concluded, might well require attacking these ill-intentioned and dangerous forces *before* they could strike. "The gravest danger our Nation faces," according to the National Security Strategy of the United States, a document issued over the name of President George W. Bush on September 17, 2002,

> lies at the crossroads of radicalism and technology. Our enemies have openly declared that they are seeking weapons of mass destruction, and evidence indicates that they are doing so with determination. The United States will not allow these efforts to succeed.... And, as a matter of common sense and self-defense, America will act against such emerging threats before they are fully formed. We cannot defend America and our friends by hoping for the best.... History will judge harshly those who saw this coming danger but failed to act. In the new world we have entered, the only path to peace and security is the path of action.

The new doctrine was sometimes wrongly called one of "preemptive war." Preemption, however, involves attacking when the enemy is just about to attack: that is, when an assault is imminent and certain. With its new security doctrine the United States was embracing something different: *preventive* war, which involves attacking *before* an attack is imminent. "I will not wait on events, while dangers gather," the president said in his 2002 State of the Union address. "I will not stand by as peril draws closer and closer. The United States of America will not permit the world's most dangerous regimes to threaten us with the world's most destructive weapons." The United States, the new doctrine asserted, would act to eliminate some threats before they became imminent:

> The United States has long maintained the option of preemptive actions to counter a sufficient threat to our national security. The greater the threat, the greater is the risk of inaction—and the more compelling the case for taking anticipatory action to defend ourselves, even if uncertainty remains as to the time and place of the enemy's attack.

The country to which this new doctrine seemed, in the eyes of President Bush and his colleagues, most aptly and urgently to apply was Iraq. That country's conduct in the 1990s had confirmed its standing as an American adversary, an international outlaw, and a regional and perhaps global menace. Under the brutal dictatorship of Saddam Hussein, Iraq had initiated and waged a war against neighboring Iran from 1979 to 1988 and then, in August 1990, had attacked, occupied, and plundered the tiny sheikhdom of Kuwait on its southern border. The United States assembled and led a multinational coalition that evicted the occupying troops in February 1991. Much of the country rose up against Saddam's rule in the aftermath of his defeat, but his security forces and army crushed the rebellions and he remained in power.

By the terms of the 1991 agreement that ended the war, the Iraqi government was obliged to declare and destroy all the nuclear, chemical, and biological materials that it had accumulated. The United Nations was authorized to conduct inspections to verify compliance with these terms. Saddam's regime, however, gave the inspection teams limited and grudging cooperation, concealed materials and programs it was supposed to declare and abandon, and finally, in 1998, evicted the inspectors altogether.

For this reason, in the aftermath of the attacks of September 11, it was impossible to know just what weapons Iraq had. The regime was widely believed to have retained stores of toxic chemicals; and after the 1991 war it had been discovered to have come much closer to fabricating a nuclear weapon than Western intelligence agencies and nonproliferation organizations had estimated. Historically, moreover, nuclear weapons programs around the world had progressed farther, faster, than those charged with tracking their progress had believed....

In the fall of 2002, the American government therefore demanded full Iraqi compliance with the series of United Nations resolutions on its weapons programs that Saddam Hussein had flouted. When he failed to comply fully, the United States, joined by Great Britain, attacked Iraq and by mid-April 2003 had vanquished the regime and occupied the country.

From a strictly military standpoint, the Iraq war was a resounding success. The American and British military forces achieved their objective in only three weeks, with minimal casualties. Unlike the Cold War doctrines of containment and deterrence, however, which the events of 1945 to 1950—the Marshall Plan, the Truman Doctrine, the Berlin blockade, and the Korean War—had confirmed as the central features of American foreign policy, the war in Iraq, despite its initial success, did not augur a comparable twenty-first-century status for preventive war. Indeed, the American experience in Iraq demonstrated just how limited the scope for putting this doctrine into practice was likely to be.

The two other members of the axis of evil did not lend themselves to the kind of treatment that Iraq received. North Korea had armed itself so heavily that even without nuclear weapons it was able to deter an American attack. Although the Communist regime was certain to lose a war fought against the United States, it had the military capacity to inflict vast damage on prosperous, democratic South Korea before being conquered. Thus, South Korea was anxious to avoid a shooting war, as were Japan and China, neighboring countries with an interest in events on the Korean peninsula whose views the United States had to respect.

Larger and more populous than Iraq, Iran presented a more formidable military challenge. The clerical regime in power in Tehran was also far less politically isolated than Saddam Hussein's had been.

Although a sponsor of terrorism, it had not waged two wars of aggression, it was not subject to United Nations sanctions, and it was not defying a series of UN resolutions, as Iraq was in 2003. In Iran, discontent with the rule of the mullahs was widespread and visible, leading to the hope that, unlike in Iraq, the Islamic republic might ultimately be overthrown from within, without any assistance from outside the country.

Furthermore, public support for the application of the doctrine of preventive war to Iraq was less than wholehearted in the United States and even thinner in Great Britain, for several reasons. For one thing, the conflict in Iraq qualified, for the United States, as a war of choice. Saddam Hussein had not attacked the United States, or any other country, as he did to provoke the 1991 war. The 2003 conflict could not, therefore, be justified on the grounds of self-defense, which is the rationale that most strongly disposes democracies to fight and provokes Western democracies to overcome their powerful twenty-first-century bias against war.

Moreover, a preventive war has a self-canceling quality to it. If it is successful it removes the threat that, were it to grow to menacing proportions, would clearly justify military action. It removes, in effect, the evidence that would convince people of the wisdom of waging war....

A World without America

If public pressure within the United States were to compel the American government to withdraw most or all of the military forces stationed beyond North America and to do far less than it had become accustomed to doing to discourage the spread of nuclear weapons, to cope with the consequences of fiscal crises outside its borders, and to help keep global markets open to trade, what impact would this have on the rest of the world?

The last occasion on which the United States placed itself on the periphery rather than at the center of international affairs, the period between the two world wars, was not a happy one. Indeed, the antecedents of the American twenty-first-century role as the world's government lie in the fear, after World War II, that in the absence of an expansive American international presence the world would experience repetitions of the two global disasters of the 1930s and the 1940s—the Great Depression and World War II. It was to prevent a recurrence of these economic and political calamities that the United States assumed the responsibilities it bore during the Cold War, which, modified and extended, comprise its post–Cold War role as the world's government. Although the history of the interwar era will not precisely repeat itself even if the United States takes a far less active part in international affairs, a substantial contraction of the American global role would risk making the world a less secure and less prosperous place....

The overall American role in the world since World War II therefore has something in common with the theme of the Frank Capra film *It's a Wonderful Life*, in which the angel Clarence, played by Henry Travers, shows James Stewart, playing the bank clerk George Bailey, who believes his existence to have been worthless, how life in his small town of Bedford Falls would have unfolded had he never been born. George Bailey learns that people he knows and loves turn out to be far worse off without him. So it is with the United States and its role as the world's government....

The abdication by the United States of some or all of the responsibilities for international security that it had come to bear in the first decade of the twenty-first century would deprive the international system of one of its principal safety features, which keeps countries from smashing into each other, as they are historically prone to do. In this sense, a world without America would be the equivalent of a freeway full of cars without brakes. Similarly, should the American government abandon some or all of the ways in which it had, at the dawn of the new century, come to support global economic activity, the world economy would function less effectively and might even suffer a severe and costly breakdown. A world without the United States would in this way resemble a fleet of cars without gasoline.

Their awareness, sometimes dim and almost never explicitly spelled out, of the political, military, and economic dangers that would come with the retreat of American power causes other countries to refrain from combining to try to displace the United States from its place at the center of the international system. Virtually all of them harbor some grievance or other against the twenty-first-century international order, but none would welcome the absence of any order at all, which is what the collapse of American power might well bring. Grudgingly, tacitly, silently, other countries support the American role as the world's government out of the well-grounded fear that while the conduct of the United States may be clumsy, overbearing, and even occasionally insufferable, the alternative would be even worse, perhaps much worse....

Discussion Questions

1. Do you agree with Bacevich that the United States has become an imperial power? Or do you agree with Mandelbaum that the United States is a benign Goliath in international affairs rather than an empire?

2. To what extent is U.S. foreign policy shaped by our reactions to developments in other countries? To what extent is it a projection onto the world of our ideas, values, and needs?

3. What are the most effective tools in combating the threat of terrorists? Is military power still the best weapon for the U.S. or should it play a more restricted role as compared to diplomatic and law enforcement approaches?

4. Has President Obama broken sharply from the foreign policy of President Bush? Or has his administration increasingly turned, especially in the case of Afghanistan, to the same kind of strategies that Obama criticized while Bush was in office?

Suggested Readings and Internet Resources

The interplay among rival American traditions in foreign policy is the subject of Walter Russell Mead, *Special Providence: American Foreign Policy and How It Reshaped the World* (New York: Alfred A. Knopf, 2001). An important new version of realist thinking in international relations is John J. Mearsheimer, *The Tragedy of Great Power Politics* (New York: W. W. Norton, 2001). For an argument that the United States must be unapologetic in asserting global leadership in the post–September 11 world, see Robert J. Lieber, *The American Era: Power and Strategy for the 21st Century* (New York: Cambridge University Press, 2005). The ideas of the most famous left-wing critic of American foreign policy, Noam Chomsky, can be found in *The Essential Chomsky* (New York: New Press, 2008). David Sanger, a *New York Times* journalist, depicts the messy international situation bequeathed to President Obama by President Bush in *The Inheritance: The World Obama Confronts and the Challenges to American Power* (New York: Three Rivers Press, 2010).

Council on Foreign Relations
www.cfr.org
The website for the premier mainstream organization of U.S. foreign policy offers information on numerous dimensions of international relations.

Center for Defense Information
www.cdi.org
This site offers detailed information and analyses on foreign policy issues and includes a frequently updated "terrorism program."

Federation of American Scientists
www.fas.org
This site offers extensive coverage of global security issues.

Credits

ALLEN, BROOKE: "Our Godless Constitution." Reprinted with permission from the February 21, 2005, issue of *The Nation*. For subscription information, call 1-800-333-8536. Portions of each week's Nation magazine can be accessed at http://www.thenation.com.

ANSOLABEHERE, STEPHEN, AND SHANTO IYENGAR: From *Going Negative: How Political Advertisements Shrink and Polarize the Electorate* by Stephen Ansolabehere and Shanto Iyengar. Copyright © 1995 by Stephen Ansolabehere and Shanto Iyengar. Reprinted with the permission of The Free Press, a Division of Simon & Schuster, Inc.

BACEVICH, ANDREW J.: "Introduction: War Without Exits" and Afterword from *The Limits of Power: The End of American Exceptionalism* by Andrew J. Bacevich. Copyright © 2008 by Andrew J. Bacevich. Reprinted by arrangement with Henry Holt and Company, LLC.

BENNETT, W. LANCE, ed.: From *Civic Life Online: Learning How Digital Media Can Engage Youth,* pp. 1–24. Copyright © 2008. By permission of The MIT Press.

BOWLES, SAMUEL, FRANK ROOSEVELT, AND RICHARD EDWARDS: From *Corporate Capitalism Hurts American Democracy* by Samuel Bowles, Frank Roosevelt, and Richard Edwards. Copyright © 2004. By permission of Oxford University Press.

COX, W. MICHAEL, AND RICHARD ALM: From *Myths of Rich and Poor* by W. Michael W. Cox and Richard Alm. Copyright © 1999 by W. Michael Cox and Richard Alm. Reprinted by permission of Basic Books, a member of the Perseus Books Group.

DONAHUE, JOHN. From *Disunited States* by John Donahue. Copyright © 1997 by John Donahue. Reprinted by permission of Basic Books, a member of the Perseus Books Group.

EGGERS, WILLIAM D., AND JOHN O'LEARY: From *Revolution at the Roots: Making Our Government Smaller, Better, and Closer to Home* by William D. Eggers and John O'Leary. Copyright © 1995 by William D. Eggers and John O'Leary. Reprinted with the permission of The Free Press, a Division of Simon & Schuster, Inc,

FRIEDMAN, MILTON: From *Capitalism and Freedom* by Milton Friedman. Reprinted by permission of the publisher, the University of Chicago Press.

GEER, JOHN G.: From *In Defense of Negativity: Attack Ads in Presidential Campaigns* by John G. Geer. Copyright © 2006. Reprinted by permission of University of Chicago Press.

GERSTMANN, EVAN: From *Same-Sex Marriage and the Constitution.* Copyright © 2003, 2008 by Evan Gerstmann. Reprinted by permission of Cambridge University Press.